Inflation, Unemployment and Monetary Control

Collected Papers from the 1973 - 1976 Konstanz Seminars

Beihefte zu Kredit und Kapital

Heft 5

Inflation, Unemployment and Monetary Control

Collected papers from the 1973 - 1976 Konstanz Seminars

Edited by

Karl Brunner
University of Rochester and University of Bern

Manfred J. M. Neumann
Freie Universität Berlin

DUNCKER & HUMBLOT · BERLIN

This volume was published with the support of the
Center for Research in Government Policy and
Business at the University of Rochester.

Gedruckt 1979 bei fotokop wilhelm weihert, Darmstadt
Printed in Germany

ISBN 3 428 04314 6

CONTENTS

CONTRIBUTORS

Robert J. Barro, University of Rochester

Rudiger Dornbusch, Massachusetts Institute of Technology

Jacob A. Frenkel, University of Chicago

Benjamin M. Friedman, Harvard University

Michael J. Hamburger, Federal Reserve Bank of New York

Pentii J. K. Kouri, Yale University

Richard M. Levich, New York University

Allan H. Meltzer, Carnegie-Mellon University

Manfred J. M. Neumann, Freie Universität Berlin

Michael Parkin, University of Western Ontario

Robert H. Rasche, Michigan State University

Kurt Schiltknecht, Schweizerische Nationalbank

Helmut Schlesinger, Deutsche Bundesbank

Larry A. Sjaastad, University of Chicago

PREFACE

Since 1970 the Konstanz Seminar has offered a European forum for discussion in the field of monetary theory and monetary policy. Scholars from Europe or America and staff members from central banks assemble annually on the (virtual) island of Reichenau near the city of Konstanz in the lake named after the city. For three days every year, the seminar attends to recent developments in monetary theory and important issues of monetary policy.

The current volume is the second publication resulting from the Konstanz Seminar. The first volume contained the papers discussed at the First Konstanz Seminar in 1970. The second volume collects papers from the 1973 - 76 Konstanz Seminars. Most of the papers included here have been published in professional journals. They have been assembled in order to document the range of discussion at this international seminar on the Reichenau.

The volume opens with three papers by Rudiger Dornbusch and Larry Sjaastad. They offer to the reader some excellent illustrations of the monetary approach to the balance-of-payments problem. Dornbusch analyzes in the first paper the impact and the long-run effects of open-market operations, devaluation, and taxation for a small open economy. He uses for this purpose a portfolio-balance model with nontradeable real capital and tradeable financial assets consisting of money and debt. Dornbusch's second paper concentrates on a partial-equilibrium model of financial asset markets with tradeable and non-tradeable securities. He demonstrates that the choice of assets in open-market operations determines the nature of the consequences resulting from these operations. Sjaastad examines, on the other hand, the dependence of short-run fluctuations in the balance of payments on changes in the rate of domestic credit expansion under fixed and floating exchange rates. He concludes that the balance of payments will be more volatile in the short run under a system of floating rates.

The next group of three papers by Pentti Kouri, Michael Hamburger, and Manfred Neumann examines aspects of the German monetary processes during the period of fixed exchange rates. Kouri investigates the extent to which monetary policy is offset by short-term capital flows, concluding that monetary policy was substantially but not completely offset. Hamburger considers the properties of the demand function for the narrowly defined money stock in open economies. His results suggest that domestic and foreign securities are relatively close substitutes in the German context. Neumann weighs the role of the anticipated rate of inflation as one among other determinants of the nominal rate of interest. Estimates of a reduced form indicate that in the shorter run the Fisher effect is closer to one-half than to unity.

Jacob Frenkel and Richard Levich examine the effects of transaction costs on the efficacy of covered interest arbitrage between various currency areas. Their study separates several episodes: the periods of the "tranquil" and the "turbulent" peg and the period of floating exchange rates. They find uniformly — for all periods and all currencies — that profit opportunities are systematically exploited by economic agents once transaction costs are properly accounted for.

The papers by Robert Barro and Allan H. Meltzer deal with the comparative effects of unanticipated and anticipated changes in the money stock on economic activity and the price level. Barro tests and finds supported the hypothesis that only unanticipated changes in the money stock affect unemployment. Meltzer assesses Milton Friedman's proposition that inflation is always a monetary phenomenon by separating a maintained rate of price-level change from once-and-for-all price-level changes. The maintained average rate of monetary expansion determines the anticipated rate of inflation in this analysis. He finds that current and past monetary growth are the principal determinants of the current rate of price-level change.

Various theoretical and empirical issues of monetary policy are taken up in a group of four papers by Benjamin Friedman, Robert Rasche, Helmut Schlesinger, and Kurt Schiltknecht. Friedman analyzes the target-and-instruments structure of the monetary control problem in a stochastic world with full information and a Keynesian structure and concludes that central banks should rely on a targets-instruments planning rather than on an intermediate target-and-indicator conception of policymaking. Rasche concentrates more narrowly on the design of an optimal control rule for the short run when the authorities are confronted with deviations of the intermediate target variable from the desired path. Schlesinger reviews the control experience of the Deutsche Bundesbank since the transition to floating exchange rates in 1973 and explains the Bundesbank's rationale for adopting annual growth targets for "central bank money" rather than for a money stock or the monetary base. Schiltknecht discusses the recent policy experiences of the

Schweizerische Nationalbank and documents the bank's procedure of setting a money-stock target and of controlling it by suitable adjustments of the monetary base.

The final paper by Michael Parkin deals with the indexation problem. A comparative analysis of an indexed and a nonindexed economy establishes that there is no justification for the popular view that indexation introduces a destabilizing mechanism.

We use the opportunity offered by this publication to acknowledge gratefully the continued financial support for the Konstanz Seminars by the Gesellschaft zur Förderung der wissenschaftlichen Forschung über das Spar- und Girowesen.

Karl Brunner
University of Rochester
and University of Bern

Manfred J. M. Neumann
Freie Universität Berlin

A PORTFOLIO-BALANCE MODEL OF THE OPEN ECONOMY*

Rudiger Dornbusch**
Massachusetts Institute of Technology

This paper develops a framework in which to investigate the effects of macroeconomic policies. The key building blocks are those of Metzler (1968, 1973) in the form of a wealth-saving relation and the emphasis on portfolio considerations; the model in its dynamic aspects is extended in a manner suggested in the work of Foley and Sidrauski (1971) and Mussa (1973), where the asset accumulation implied by short-run equilibrium is pursued over time.

A large body of literature on the implications of asset mobility for macroeconomic policy has accumulated during the last decade. Following the work of Mundell (1968) on capital mobility and the policy mix, that literature has primarily taken a perspective of stabilization policy and has therefore espoused a short-run view of the economy in describing it in terms of the IS-LM model—more or less appropriately modified to accommodate the openness of the economy and the mobility of assets.[1] Alternative routes with a longer time perspective, though still maintaining the assumption of a perfectly elastic supply of output at current prices, have been offered by McKinnon (1969), Tower (1972), and Branson (1972).

---

* Reprinted, with some changes, by permission of the author and North-Holland Publishing Co. from the JOURNAL OF MONETARY ECONOMICS 1 (1975): 3-20. An earlier version of the paper was presented at the 1973 Konstanz Seminar.

** In preparing this paper I had the benefit of extensive suggestions from Michael Mussa, whose approach has helped me formulate some of the issues discussed here. I wish to acknowledge, too, Jacob Frenkel's suggestions for revision.

1. For a recent survey, see Von Neumann-Whitman (1970). Earlier literature includes Jones (1968), McKinnon and Oates (1966), Roper (1969), and Swoboda (1972).

The approach taken here assumes flexibility of relative prices, full employment, and continuous market clearing, thereby assuming away a host of interesting short-run problems and substituting a set of issues that center on the time path of the economy, the endogeneity of asset supplies, and the long-run effects of policies.[2]

In sections 1 and 2 of this paper the basic model and its equilibrium properties are developed. Three applications of the model are considered in section 3, and in section 4 some observations on possible extensions and limitations of the model are offered.

1. THE MODEL

The home country produces two commodities, consumption goods and investment goods, and technology is described by the standard neoclassical two-sector model with capital goods labor-intensive.[3] The labor force is assumed constant, and capital depreciates at a constant exponential rate. With this specification, the flow (supply) of physical net investment, $\dot{K}$, is a function of the relative price of capital in terms of consumption goods, q, and the stock of real capital, K. Furthermore, by the Stolper-Samuelson theorem the relative price of capital is inversely related to the yield on real capital, r, so that we can write the rate of investment as a function of the yield on capital and the stock of capital,[4]

$$\dot{K} = \dot{K}(r, K), \quad \text{with} \quad \dot{K}_r < 0, \quad \dot{K}_K < 0. \tag{1}$$

---

2. For work along these lines, see, for example, Allen (1972), Boyer (1971), Frenkel (1970), Lee (1972), and Mussa (1971*b*).

3. The structure of the two-sector model is readily available in various places and hence is dealt with briefly here. See, for example, Foley and Sidrauski (1971).

4. We assume that capital accumulation is exclusively financed by the issue of equity—one share per unit of physical capital.

To each rate of interest there exists a corresponding stock of capital, $\bar{K}$, such that net investment is zero ($\dot{K} = 0$):

$$\bar{K} = \bar{K}(r), \quad \text{with} \quad \bar{K}_r < 0. \tag{2}$$

The value of investment, I, and the capital stock, k, measured in terms of consumption goods are defined in (3) and (4).

$$I \equiv q\dot{K} = I(r, K), \quad \text{with} \quad I_r < 0, \quad I_K < 0. \tag{3}$$

$$k \equiv qK = k(r, K), \quad \text{with} \quad k_r < 0, \quad k_K < 0. \tag{4}$$

Substituting (2) in (3) defines the steady-state value of the capital stock, $\bar{k}$, as a reduced-form function of the yield on real capital:[5]

$$\bar{k} = \bar{k}(r), \quad \text{with} \quad \bar{k}_r < 0. \tag{5}$$

On the demand side, we will assume a saving function of the stock-adjustment variety according to which the planned level of saving is proportional to the excess of desired (target) wealth, $\bar{w}$, over actual wealth, w, both measured in terms of consumption goods.[6]

$$S = \phi(\bar{w} - w), \tag{6}$$

where the desired level of wealth is, in turn, a function of the yield on real capital, r, and the yield on debt, i:

$$\bar{w} = \bar{w}(r, i), \quad \text{with} \quad \bar{w}_r > 0, \quad \bar{w}_i > 0. \tag{7}$$

We assume that there are three assets: money, real capital or equity, and debt. Accordingly, actual wealth is defined as the sum of real balances, m, real capital holdings, k, and real debt holdings, b, all measured in terms of consumption goods:

5. Throughout this paper, a bar over a variable denotes its steady-state value.

6. This type of saving behavior was assumed in Metzler's classical article (1973) and subsequently in Jones (1969). The particular functional form of (6) would be implied by a savings function that is linear in asset yield and wealth.

$$w \equiv m + b + k. \tag{8}$$

Asset preferences of the private sector are characterized by equations (9) to (11), which state that the demands for the three assets are proportional to actual wealth and where the shares, by the budget constraint on asset holdings, add up to unity.[7]

$$m^d = \alpha(r, i)w. \tag{9}$$

$$b^d = \gamma(r, i)w. \tag{10}$$

$$k^d = \beta(r, i)w. \tag{11}$$

We assume that debt is short-term and indexed in terms of consumption goods, so that the capital value is essentially independent of the interest rate and the real value is independent of the price level.[8] For subsequent references it will be useful to define the sum of real money and debt holdings, ν, hereafter referred to as "financial assets":

$$\nu \equiv m + b. \tag{12}$$

The government spends at the rate G on consumption goods and levies an amount T in lump-sum taxes. The budget is balanced so that

$$T = G + iB, \tag{13}$$

where B is the stock of government debt outstanding.

Finally, we recall from the definitions of the balance-of-payments accounts that the current account surplus equals the excess of saving over investment. The trade balance surplus equals the current account surplus less interest earnings on the excess of private debt holdings over domestic debt issue:[9]

$$(S - I) - i(b - B). \tag{14}$$

---

7. The appropriate formulation of asset-demand functions is clearly developed in Metzler (1973). See, too, Friedman (1969), Tobin (1969), Mussa (1973), and Foley and Sidrauski (1971).

8. Bond holdings as specified by (19) may be negative for high values of r and low values of i, though we proceed in the text on the assumption that they are positive. Eq. (10) may be viewed as the private sector's *excess* demand for debt.

9. The definition of income anticipates our subsequent assumption that claims to income from capital are nontradeable. The assumption that

For the main part of this paper we will assume that the home country is "small" in the sense that it can buy and sell consumption goods at a fixed foreign currency price and can borrow or lend in the form of debt at a fixed interest rate, i^*. An important additional assumption is that neither physical capital nor claims to income from physical capital (equity) are internationally tradeable; physical capital and the claims to the income they generate are treated as nontraded goods, and accordingly their relative price, q, and the rate of return on physical capital, r, remain endogenously determined.[10]

Lastly, we assume that the home country is on fixed exchange rates, so that the domestic currency price of consumption goods is given, and in the absence of domestic credit creation the balance of payments equals the rate of change of the domestic nominal quantity of money.

2. EQUILIBRIUM

In this section we discuss the equilibrium of the system. The first subsection describes the short-run equilibrium, the second investigates the dynamics of the system, and in the third examines the properties of long-run equilibrium.

2.1 Short-run Equilibrium

At any point in time, the physical stock of capital and the value of "financial assets," ν, are given by past accumulation; the public can vary the composition of ν at the given interest rate on debt, i^*, in order to attain the desired portfolio composition in terms of money and bonds, but it cannot affect the total.

---

taxes are lump-sum is required in order to leave realized asset yields and hence portfolio composition independent of income taxes.

10. If physical capital were tradeable, an investment function would not be defined, nor would the stock of capital located in the home country be determinate in the nonspecialized region. If claims on capital were tradeable, but machines remained nontradeable, both the stock of capital and wealth would adjust according to a stock-adjustment process defined by (2) and (8). See Dornbusch (1971*b*) and Frenkel and Fischer (1972).

The stock constraint relevant to asset choices implies that the excess demand for equity is equal to the excess supply of assets other than equity. Furthermore, since claims to income from capital are not internationally tradeable, the market for equity will only be in equilibrium when the yield on capital, or the relative price of capital, is such that the existing stock is willingly held.[11] This equilibrium condition is stated as

$$k(r, K^o) = \beta(r, i)\,[v^o + k(r, K^o)] \tag{15}$$

and is shown in figure 1*b* as the market equilibrium schedule *kk*.[12] The schedule is negatively sloped, since, given the physical stock of capital, an increase in the yield on capital creates an excess demand for equities and hence requires a reduction in the nonequity component of wealth to reduce demand and maintain market equilibrium. Given the initial level of real balances and real debt, v^o, the equilibrium yield on capital is $\tilde{r}$. At that yield, wealth and the desired composition of assets are such that the existing stock of capital is willingly held. Corresponding to that equilibrium yield on capital is an equilibrium composition of the financial components of wealth, money and debt; given the fixed interest rate on debt in the world market and the fixed exchange rate, that equilibrium composition can be instantaneously attained by trading money for debt in the world market.

At the level of flows, the equilibrium yield on capital and the implied value of real wealth determine the rate of saving, $\tilde{S}$, while the yield on capital together with the current stock of physical capital determine the rate of net investment, $\tilde{I}$.

---

11. Throughout this paper it will be assumed that equilibrium exists, is unique, and occurs in the nonspecialized region.

12. Fig. 1 will be recognized as essentially Metzler's (1968, 1973) representation of short-run equilibrium in the open economy.

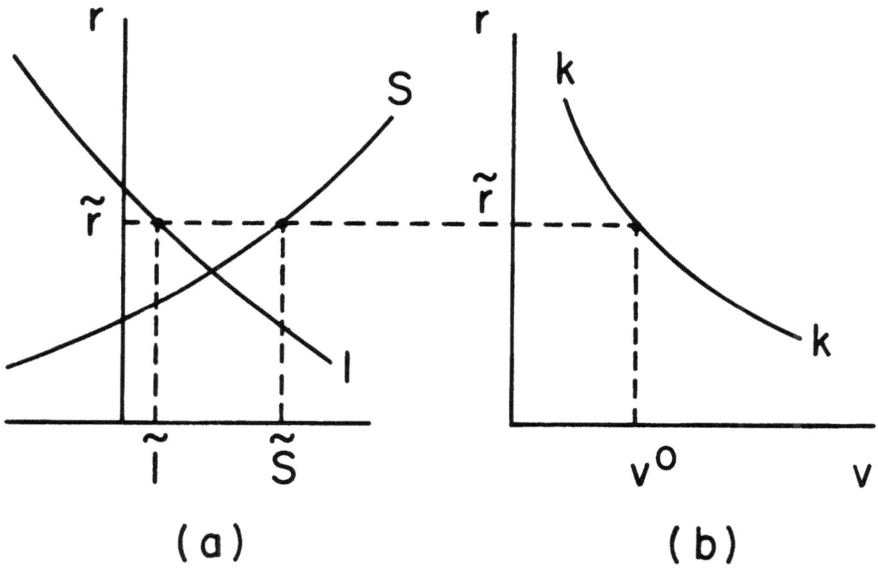

Figure 1

Saving and investment schedules are shown in figure 1 *a*. The saving schedule is drawn for a given stock of financial assets, v^o, and a given physical stock of capital; it is drawn as an increasing function of the yield on capital, since an increase in that rate lowers the value of the stock of capital and hence actual real wealth while at the same time raising desired wealth, so that by (6), saving increases.

The investment function is drawn for a given physical stock of capital; it is drawn as a decreasing function of the yield on capital, since an increase in that rate lowers the relative price of capital and hence reduces the flow supply.

The short-run equilibrium shown in figure 1 implies accumulation of physical capital, since net investment is positive; and at the same time accumulation of financial assets, money, and debt, since saving exceeds investment and accordingly the current account is in surplus.

2.2 Dynamics

The additions to the stock of physical capital and the stock of financial assets, implied by the short-run equilibrium described in figure 1, will over time affect the equilibrium position of the economy. The manner in which the system moves over time is defined by the equilibrium rates of physical capital formation, investment, and saving.

To determine that path, we solve (15) for the equilibrium yield on capital, $\tilde{r}$, as a function of the physical stock of capital and financial assets:

$$\tilde{r} = \tilde{r}(\nu, K). \tag{16}$$

This yield, in turn, can be substituted in (1) to obtain a reduced-form expression for the *equilibrium* rate of capital formation:

$$\dot{K} = \dot{K}(\tilde{r}, K) \equiv \phi(K, \nu). \tag{17}$$

The *equilibrium* rate of investment, by (3), is

$$I = I(\tilde{r}, K) \equiv \tilde{I}(\nu, K), \tag{18}$$

and the *equilibrium* rate of saving, using (6), (7), and (8), is

$$S = \phi\,[\overline{w}(\tilde{r}, i) - \nu - k(\tilde{r}, K)] \equiv \tilde{S}(\nu, K). \tag{19}$$

From the definition of the balance-of-payments accounts, the equilibrium rate of increase in financial assets, $\dot{\nu}$, is equal to the excess of saving over investment, or the current account surplus:

$$\dot{\nu} = \tilde{S}(\nu, K) - \tilde{I}(\nu, K) \equiv \pi(\nu, K). \tag{20}$$

It will be recalled that short-run equilibrium was defined by the existing stock of physical capital and the stock of financial assets; correspondingly, the reduced forms for their equilibrium rates of increase, stated in (17) and (20), describe the behavior of the system over time.

To understand the dynamics of the system, it is convenient to consider the effects of discrete changes in the stock of physical capital and the stock of financial assets on the equilibrium rates of change of capital and financial assets. Consider first an increase in financial assets. This corresponds to a movement along the *kk* schedule in figure 1*a* and an upward shift of the saving schedule in figure 1*b*. It follows that the equilibrium interest rate unambiguously falls; the equilibrium rate of saving decreases, since actual wealth increases while desired wealth declines. The equilibrium rate of capital accumulation, both in physical and value terms, increases. Accordingly,

$$\pi_V < 0, \qquad \sigma_V > 0. \tag{21}$$

An increase in the physical stock of capital is slightly more complicated to handle. In figure 1*a* the *kk* schedule shifts upward, since the increase in the physical stock of capital at the initial yield on capital and stock of financial assets creates an excess supply for equity; accordingly, the yield on capital has to increase in order to induce the public to hold a larger stock of capital. In figure 1*b* the investment schedule shifts to the left due to the Jones-Rybczynski effect, while the wealth effect on saving shifts the saving schedule to the left. Corresponding to the higher interest rate and capital stock, there is an unambiguously lower rate of capital accumulation. The effect on the accumulation of financial assets is ambiguous; since we have both a movement along and a shift of the saving schedule, the equilibrium rate of saving may rise or fall. Accordingly,

$$\sigma_K < 0, \qquad \pi_K \gtrless 0. \tag{22}$$

For the local stability of long-run equilibrium we require that the following restrictions obtain on the linearized system:

$$\sigma_K + \pi_V < 0, \qquad \sigma_K \pi_V - \sigma_V \pi_K > 0.$$

The phase diagram for a stable configuration of the system of equations defined by (17) and (20) is shown in figure 2. Steady-state equilibrium will obtain at a stock of financial assets $\bar{v}$ and a stock of physical capital $\bar{K}$. The approach to equilibrium for the case shown in figure 2 will be asymptotic.

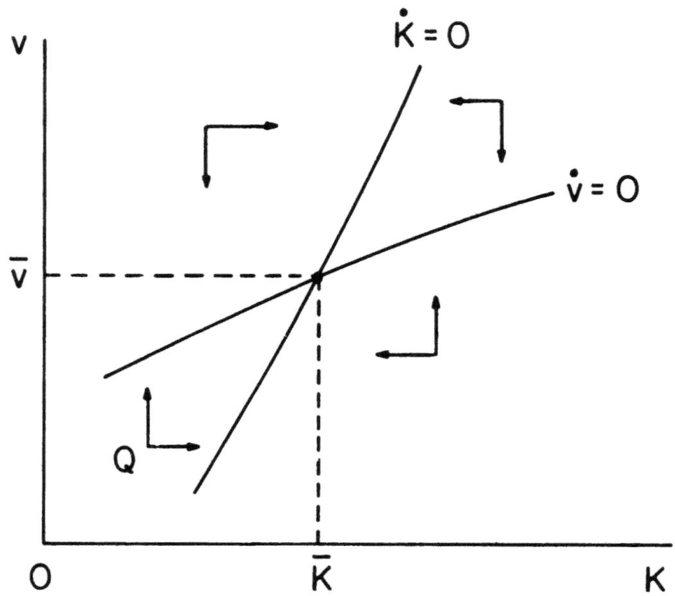

Figure 2

2.3 Long-run Equilibrium

In this section we develop a description of the properties of long-run equilibrium in terms of the composition of assets and the structure of the balance of payments.

Given that there is in this model no exogenous element of growth such as productivity change or population change, all the private-sector stock and flow variables are constant in the steady state; in particular, the private sector is in balance-of-payments equilibrium, and net additions to the stock of capital, money, and debt holdings are zero.

Furthermore, the current account surplus will be zero, so that the trade balance deficit is financed by the net interest earnings on the excess of private-sector holdings of debt over public debt issue:

$$i[\,\gamma(\bar{r},\, i)\bar{w}(\bar{r}) - B\,],$$

where $\bar{r}$ is the steady-state yield on capital. To the extent that the steady-state yield on capital is sufficiently high for domestic residents to be net issuers of debt, the service account may be in deficit for any given issue of government debt. Next we observe that there is no reason to constrain the government to be a net debtor; in particular, if the government chose to take the counterpart of the private sector's position, the service account would be zero, as would the trade balance.

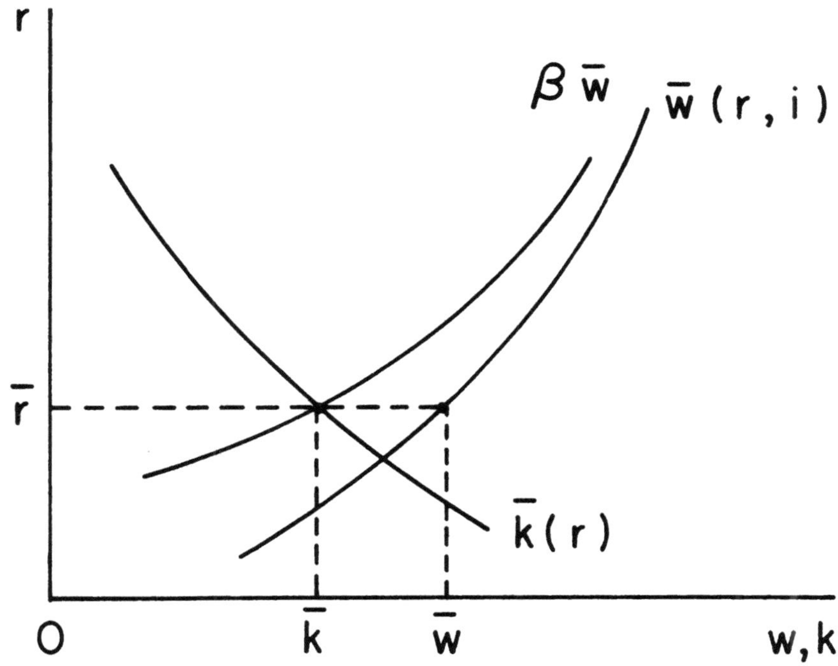

Figure 3

The long-run equilibrium is shown in figure 3. In the steady state, actual equals desired assets, and the market for equities clears. The downward-sloping schedule, $\bar{k}(r)$, shows the steady-state value of the capital stock—combinations of physical capital and interest rates such that net investment is zero. The schedule $\bar{w}(r, i)$ shows desired wealth such that saving is zero, and the schedule $\beta\bar{w}$ shows the part of assets the public desires to hold in the form of equities. Long-run equilibrium obtains at an interest rate $\bar{r}$ where saving is zero and the demand for equities equals the steady-state supply of equities. Figure 3 shows, too, the composition of wealth between equities and other assets; the case shown is one where steady-state wealth exceeds the value of the capital stock, so that net holdings of the remaining assets are positive and equal to

$$\bar{v} \equiv \bar{w}(\bar{r}) - \bar{k}(\bar{r}).$$

The distribution of $\bar{v}$ between money and debt, given the interest rate on debt, is determined by the equilibrium yield on capital.

The strong assumptions about the formal structure of the model are clearly reflected in figure 3. Technology together with the capital intensity assumption account for a negatively sloped long-run supply of capital, while the target wealth assumption makes the long-run equilibrium independent of disposable income and hence taxation. The assumption of capital mobility for debt makes the long-run equilibrium independent of the issue of public debt, while the fixed exchange rate determines the price level exogenously.

3. SOME IMPLICATIONS OF THE MODEL

In this section we develop some of the properties of the model by inquiring into the time path of variables under the influence of specific government policies. Prior to that analysis, it may be useful to inquire into the behavior of the system in the absence of any specific intervention other than the pegging of exchange rates. Under this assumption, as the discusison in section 2 above reveals, the time path of wealth, its composition, and the balance of payments will depend both on the initial condition and on whether adjustment is asymptotic or cyclical. A particular path of adjustment that may be associated with the "monetary approach" to the balance of payments in its more extreme variant can be seen in figure 2 for an initial stock of real capital and financial assets below their steady-state level, a point Q. Adjustment would proceed via the accumulation of physical capital and financial assets, with a falling rate of interest. To the extent that the government fails to monetize and capitalize the growth process, the adjustment implies a balance-of-payments surplus and a capital account deficit as the community over time increases its stock of real balances and holdings of debt.[13]

More generally, the balance of payments will be in surplus if the planned rate of addition to cash balances by the private sector exceeds the rate of domestic credit creation, and the capital account will be in deficit if the rate of public debt issue falls short of the planned rate of addition to debt holdings by the private sector.

In the remainder of this part we will study the impact and long-run effects of particular government policies. The *impact* effect is defined as the effect of a policy as of a given physical stock of capital and stock of financial assets, while the *long-run* effects allow both of these quantities to come to their stationary levels.[14] We will begin with a discussion of open-market operations, discuss next the effects of a devaluation, and consider last the effects of taxation.

3.1 Open-Market Operations

We may consider two alternative ways in which the government can conduct open-market operations: purchases of debt and equity. Consider first the case where the government purchases debt and sells money. Given the assumption that the exchange rate is fixed and the home country can

---

13. On growth and the balance of payments, see Mundell (1968, 1971), Komiya (1969), Frenkel (1971), Boyer (1971), Purvis (1972), Johnson (1972), Dornbusch (1971*a*), Mussa (1971*b*), and Allen (1972).

14. This particular conceptualization of the effects of a policy on the time path of variables is extensively employed in Mussa (1973) and is an effective substitute for the study of the entire path of variables.

borrow and lend in the form of debt in the world market at a given interest rate, such a policy will have no effect whatsoever on the private sector. Indeed, the private sector will instantaneously resell its increased debt holdings in the world market, and the central bank will incur an equivalent loss of foreign exchange reserves. This is an extreme form of the endogeneity of the domestic quantity of money, which has been strongly emphasized in the work of Mundell (1968, 1971). The only long-run effect of this policy is that the central bank has substituted interest-earning assets for reserves in its portfolio.

The previous example suggests that monetary policy has no repercussion effects on the private sector only on the assumption that the government intervenes in the market for internationally tradeable assets—money and debt--and that these assets are in perfectly elastic supply in the world market under fixed exchange rates and perfect capital (debt) mobility. These extreme results will not obtain when one of the assets is not internationally tradeable.

Consider now the case where the government purchases real capital (equity) with domestic money. Since claims to real capital are not internationally tradeable, the private sector cannot reverse the operation by recourse to the world market; accordingly, we expect real effects on the private-sector equilibrium. The impact effect of this open-market operation is to create an excess demand for equities and an excess supply of financial assets at the initial yield on capital, thereby causing the relative price of capital to rise and its yield to decline. Associated with that lower yield on capital we have a decline in the rate of saving and an increase in the rate of investment and thus a current account deficit. These short-run real effects depend crucially on two assumptions: that equity is not tradeable and that it is an imperfect substitute in portfolios for money and/or debt.

The long-run effects of this open-market operation are shown in figure 4. They derive from the fact that the steady-state supply of equity to the private sector, at each level of the yield on capital, is reduced by the government's holdings of equity, thereby shifting the schedule $\bar{k}(r)$ to the left to $\bar{k}'(r)$. Neither the desired stock of wealth, $\bar{w}(r)$, nor the long-run demand for equity, $\beta\bar{w}(r)$, are affected by the policy change. The new long-run equilibrium implies a lower equilibrium yield on capital, $\bar{r}'$, and corresponding to that lower yield, a higher stock of real capital, $\bar{k}''$. The private sector's equilibrium level of wealth declines, and so does the privately held stock of equity.

While the *share* of financial assets in wealth increases, net holdings of financial assets may decline. To derive definite results about the change in financial assets and the composition of financial assets in long-run equilibrium, we require further restrictions on the demand function in equations (9) to (11). In particular, we might assume that a decline in the steady-state rate of interest implies an increase in financial asset holdings and that the composition of financial assets between money and debt is independent of the yield on capital. Under these circumstances the open-market purchase of capital would lead in the steady state to increased holdings of financial assets, a cumulative foreign exchange reserve gain on the part of the central bank and an increased net creditor position on the part of the private sector and, correspondingly, an increased trade balance deficit in the steady state.

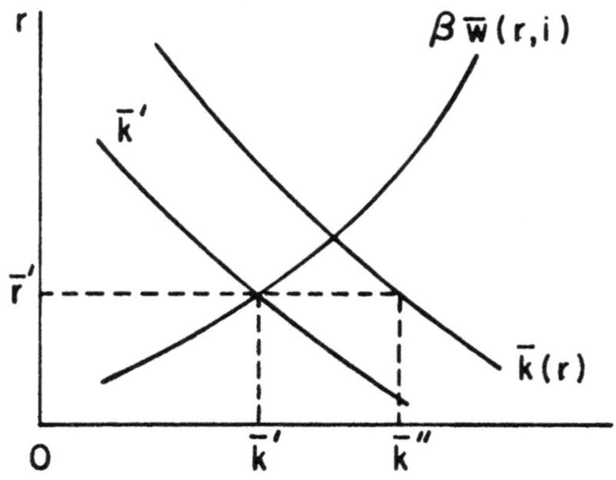

Figure 4

So far we have not discussed the manner in which the government disposes of the income on its portion of the capital stock. One manner of disposition is to rebate the proceeds via transfers to the public. Alternatively, the government might spend them directly or reduce taxes without affecting the aggregate results. If instead the government used the proceeds to reduce the public debt or the nominal quantity of money, private-sector equilibrium would continue to be described by figure 4, while the balance-of-payments accounts would reflect the government's activities; absorption inclusive of the government would fall short of aggregate disposable income, thereby financing debt or reserve acquisition by the government.

3.2 The Effects of a Devaluation

In this section we investigate the time path of the system following an unanticipated currency depreciation. The effect of a devaluation on the part of the home country is to reduce the real value of the domestic nominal quantity of money and thus the real value of financial assets and wealth at the initial level of the yield on capital. The decline in the real value of money causes an excess demand for real balances and an excess supply of debt and equity. Domestic residents will instantaneously sell off (issue) debt to recover part of their real money holdings, while at the same time attempting to sell off equity. Since in the aggregate the physical stock of capital has to be held, the aggregate attempt to sell off equity will cause its relative price to decline and its yield to increase to the point where the community is willing to hold the existing stock of capital; accordingly, the excess demand for financial assets—in particular, money—is zero.

Corresponding to this higher yield on real capital and the lower real value of wealth, there is a higher rate of saving and a lower rate of investment or a decline in absorption and an improvement in the current account. It follows that the impact effect of a devaluation is to cause both an instantaneous balance-of-payments surplus due to the exchange of debt for money and an equilibrium rate of accumulation of financial assets at a rate equal to the excess of saving over investment.[15]

The time path of financial assets and the physical stock of capital can be seen in figure 5 on the assumption that adjustment is asymptotic.[16] The devaluation lowers instantaneously the real value of financial assets from their initial steady-state level to point Q. At point Q the current account is in surplus, so that net accumulation of financial assets takes place while negative levels of net investment, due to the increase in the interest rate, cause the physical stock of capital to decline. Over time the accumulation of financial assets causes interest rates to start falling back toward their initial level, thereby causing the disinvestment process in physical capital to be reversed. At the same time, the community starts recovering its initial level of wealth, which, together with the declining interest rates, causes saving to decline over time, thereby lowering the rate at which financial assets are acquired. The adjustment path is asymptotic in the sense that financial assets, after their initial decline, keep increasing without overshooting, while the physical stock of capital initially declines in order then to recover its initial steady-state level.

As in any homogeneous system, a devaluation will have only transitory real effects and will not influence in any manner the long-run real equilibrium of the system. Furthermore, it operates exclusively via the effect of a reduction in the real value of money on equilibrium interest rates and wealth and thereby on portfolio composition and the desired levels of saving and investment.

---

15. A similar line of argument is developed in Salop (1973). In earlier work (Dornbusch 1973), I have found it useful to analyze the effects of devaluation in a world where money is the only marketable asset and where a devaluation operates via a direct effect of the reduction in the real value of money on absorption. I owe the emphasis on the asset-market effects of a devaluation to Mussa (1971*a*, *b*).

16. See above, sec. 2.2.

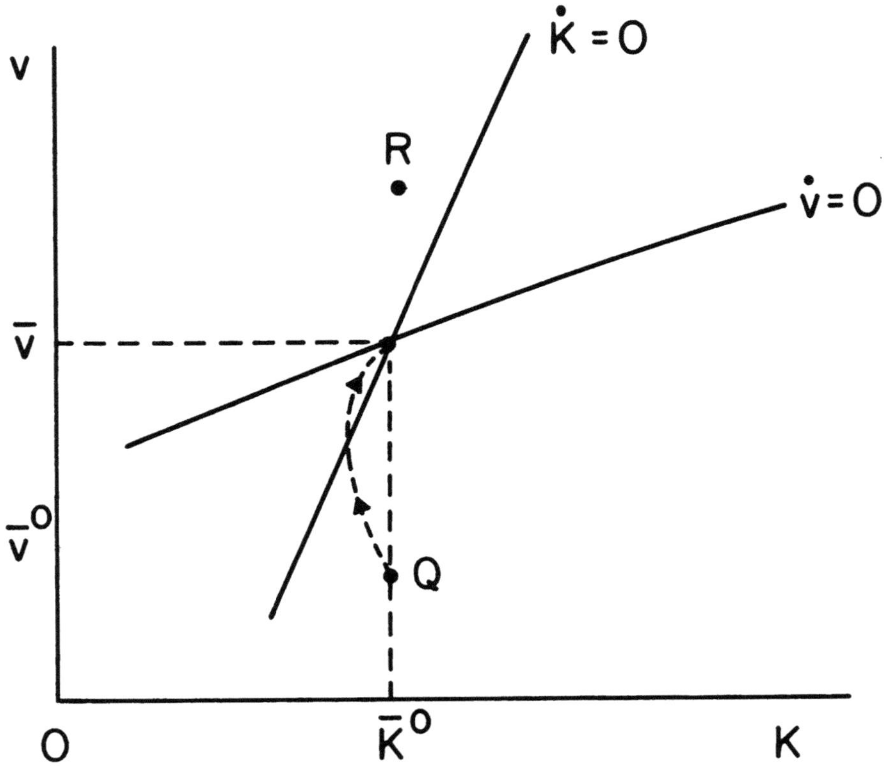

Figure 5

So far we have considered a devaluation from an initial position of long-run equilibrium, an unlikely setting for circumstances giving rise to a devaluation. Consider, alternatively, an initial position of short-run equilibrium at point *R* in figure 5. Here we have a balance-of-payments deficit and net decumulation of assets together with accumulation of capital. An appropriately chosen rate of devaluation can bring the system instantaneously back to full equilibrium rather than allowing it to pursue the path of disequilibrium and a cycle in the stock of capital.

3.3 Taxation

In this section we investigate the effects of a particular form of taxation on the equilibrium position of the system. The analysis is confined to a tax on lending abroad. The purpose of the analysis is to highlight the fact that taxation affects asset choices and thereby the equilibrium position of the economy as well as the balance of payments and its composition.

A tax on lending and borrowing in the world market introduces a spread between domestic borrowing and lending rates and the world interest rate on debt. Assuming that after the imposition of the tax the home country remains a net creditor, the tax will reduce the realized return on debt holdings and thereby induces a shift in portfolios from debt to money and equity.[17] This latter is the impact effect of the policy. The shift toward equities creates an excess demand that will cause their yield to decline, while the shift out of debt into money generates an instantaneous jump in the central bank's holdings of foreign exchange. The tax policy causes, too, a current account deficit, since it raises investment by lowering the yield on capital, while reducing the rate of saving in response to the decline in asset yields and the increase in actual real wealth.

The long-run effects of the policy change are ambiguous; the decline in the yield on debt would, other things equal, raise the share of money and equity in wealth and lower that of debt holdings. The long-run yield on capital, however, is endogenous and may reverse these conclusions. To derive a definite set of results we may impose further structure on the *long-run* asset-demand functions:

$$\bar{m}^d \equiv \alpha(r, i)\bar{w}(r, i) = \bar{m}^d(r, i), \qquad \bar{m}^d_r < 0, \quad \bar{m}^d_i < 0; \tag{23}$$

---

17. The assumption that the home country remains a net lender, or for that purpose a net borrower, is required to maintain a relationship with the world interest rate, since the possibility of a segmentation of the capital market arises from the spread between the return to lending abroad, $i^*(1 - t)$, and the cost of borrowing abroad, $i^*(1 + t)$, a spread that may be sufficient to leave the domestic capital market in autarky.

$$\bar{b}^d \equiv \gamma(r, i)\bar{w}(r, i) = \bar{b}^d(r, i), \qquad \bar{b}^d_r < 0, \quad \bar{b}^d_i > 0; \tag{24}$$

$$\bar{k}^d \equiv \beta(r, i)\bar{w}(r, i) = \bar{k}^d(r, i), \qquad \bar{k}^d_r > 0, \quad \bar{k}^d_i < 0. \tag{25}$$

With this additional structure, the decline in the return on debt increases the long-run demand for equity at each level of the yield on capital and hence raises the equilibrium long-run stock of capital and value of equity while lowering the equilibrium long-run level of wealth. The reduction in the yield on alternative assets lowers the opportunity cost of holding money and invites substitution toward money sufficiently so that long-run holdings of money increase despite the decline in wealth. The long-run holdings of debt, finally, decline in absolute terms.

The cumulative balance-of-payments effect of the policy is to generate a net increase in foreign exchange reserves on the part of the central bank, assuming no domestic credit creation, and a deterioration in the net creditor position together with an improvement in the long-run balance of trade.

4. FURTHER OBSERVATIONS

In this part we propose to sketch the implications of alternative assumptions or extensions of the model as well as draw attention to the limitations of our approach.

Consider first some possible extensions. We might wish to consider the case where neither debt nor capital is internationally mobile and inquire into the long-run effects of an open-market sale of debt. The effects of such a policy, assuming the long-run gross substitutability of assets described in equations (23) to (25), are to raise the yield on both capital and debt and to reduce the stock of both capital and real balances, thus implying a cumulative balance-of-payments deficit.

An alternative set of questions would relate to the exchange rate regime, and we might wish to investigate the effects of policy changes under flexible-exchange-rate changes. To suggest an example, consider the effects of an open-market purchase of debt under flexible exchange rates

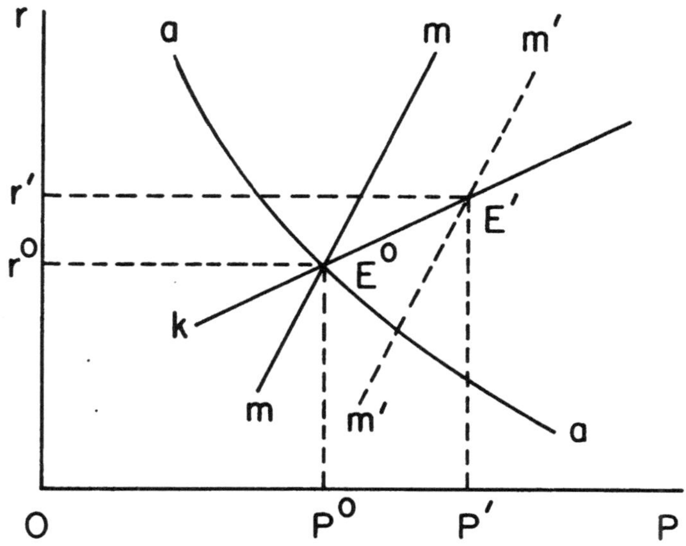

Figure 6

and perfect debt mobility, as shown in figure 6. The schedule *mm* shows combinations of the domestic price level and the yield on real capital such that the given nominal quantity of money is willingly held. Similarly, the *kk* schedule corresponds to equilibrium in the equity market. The *mm* schedule is positively sloped, since an increase in the price level creates an excess demand for real balances and has to be accompanied by an increase in the opportunity cost of holding money in order to maintain monetary equilibrium. The *kk* schedule is positively sloped, since an increase in the price level lowers real wealth and thus the demand for equities and hence calls for an increase in the yield on capital in order to induce the public to hold the existing stock. Along the schedule *aa*, saving is equal to investment. The schedule is negatively sloped, since an increase in the price level lowers real wealth and hence raises saving and therefore requires a decline in the yield on capital—which reduces saving and raises investment, thus restoring the equality of saving and investment or, equivalently, current account equilibrium. (All three schedules are drawn for a given nominal quantity of money and a given stock of debt holdings.)

At the initial long-run price level (exchange rate) and yield on capital at E^0, the exchange of assets leaves private wealth unchanged and creates an excess demand for debt and an equal excess supply of money; the equity market remains in equilibrium at E^0, and saving at that point remains equal to investment; the excess supply of money, however, shifts the money-market equilibrium schedule from mm to $m'm'$, since now a higher price level and/or lower yield on equity is required to induce the public to hold a larger nominal quantity of money. The short-run equilibrium condition in the flexible-exchange-rate model is that the market for both money and equity clear; perfect debt mobility notwithstanding, the community cannot trade stocks of debt for stocks of money in the world market, since money is no longer an internationally traded asset as it would be under fixed rates. The attempt by the private sector to sell money for debt in the world market causes the exchange rate and hence the price level to increase, thereby reducing real wealth and causing an excess supply of equity, which gives rise to a decline in the relative price of equity to the point where the community is satisfied to hold the existing stock of debt and physical capital as well as the nominal quantity of money. In figure 6 this short-run asset-market equilibrium obtains at point E'. Corresponding to the higher price level and yield on capital at E', we have a reduction in investment and an increase in saving and hence a current account surplus that serves to finance the acquisition of debt over time by the private sector in the world market.

The endogeneity of the private sector's holdings of debt in the long run implies that an open-market operation will have no long-run real effects and that the long-run price level will increase in the same proportion as the nominal quantity of money. Two points of this analysis are important to recognize. One is the crucial role of asset-market equilibrium conditions in determining exchange rate changes; this is an independent (and ad hoc) flow-of-capital function. The second point is the role played by the condition that capital and equity are not traded, which implied that an open-market operation has short-run real effects on the yield on capital.

Rather than pursue further applications of the model, it is time now to reconsider some of the building blocks of the formulation offered here. The approach essentially amounts to assuming a convenient set of consistent reduced-form behavioral equations and to explore the implications of those assumed properties. On the convenience side, one would primarily point to the assumptions about technology and hence the investment function and the implied steady-state equity-supply function, $\bar{k}(r)$; the Metzleric saving function and the implied steady-state wealth, $\bar{w}(r, i)$; and the stock-demand function for capital, βw, that jointly define the steady state of the system and thus close the time path of the model in an unambiguous manner. Convenience notwithstanding, these assumptions impose an extraordinary amount of structure on the model and, by implication, on the propositions that can be derived from it. Given their vital role in this respect, it stands to reason that one might wish to establish these (reduced-form) behavioral assumptions from more primitive considerations about intertemporal maximization by households and firms and the circumstances that give rise to the portfolio diversification implied by the asset-demand functions. Three further strong assumptions are made. One is that wage payments, transfers, and taxes are not capitalizable and negotiable; changes in relative prices and the financing of government activities have effects that are implied specifically by that assumption. The next assumption, of import particularly with respect to the time path of the system, is that of static expectations, though this assumption may be somewhat less objectionable. Finally, the strong differentiation between equity and debt that is assumed in this model runs counter to the substantial evidence on institutional intermediation and again would require support in terms of more basic considerations of risk or borrowing constraints on intermediaries.

Among the more rewarding features of this formulation, one might wish to list the emphasis on the time path of variables under the influence of a policy rather than the impact effect. There is, too, the emphasis on the endogeneity of asset supplies, with the obvious and possibly trivial implication that policy goals may be served in the short run by varying the relative supplies of assets, while in the long run what has to be affected is the attractiveness of holding or reproducing alternative assets. Next we wish to draw attention to the role played by the assumption that equity is not traded and is an imperfect substitute for debt in portfolios. While this formalization may be excessive for most practical purposes, it does suggest nevertheless that the aggregation in the theoretical literature may be misleading in its description of the transmission mechanism of monetary changes in the open economy; nontraded assets unquestionably loom large in any economy, and the choice of asset in which the central bank intervenes is bound to be of consequence.[18]

---

18. The point raised here closely parallels the discussion in Cagan (1958) and Tobin (1961). Also, it relies on the role of nontraded goods, as opposed to assets, in the transmission mechanism of monetary changes, a point forcefully made by Hawtrey (1928) and recently revived.

REFERENCES

Allen, P. R. 1972. "Money and Growth in Open Economies." REVIEW OF ECONOMIC STUDIES 39: 213-19.

Boyer, R. 1971. "The Dynamics of an Open, Monetary Economy: Growth and the Balance of Payments." Ph.D. diss., University of Chicago.

Branson, W. 1972. "Macroeconomic Equilibrium with Portfolio Balance in Open Economies." Unpublished. Stockholm: Institute for International Economic Studies.

Cagan, P. 1958. "Why Do We Use Money in Open Market Operations?" JOURNAL OF POLITICAL ECONOMY, Feb.

Dornbusch, R. 1971*a*. "Notes on Growth and the Balance of Payments." CANADIAN JOURNAL OF ECONOMICS, Aug.

_____. 1971*b*. NOTES ON TWO-SECTOR SMALL COUNTRY GROWTH. Center for Mathematical Studies in Business and Economics Report 7154. Chicago: University of Chicago.

_____. 1973. "Money, Devaluation and Nontraded Goods." AMERICAN ECONOMIC REVIEW.

Foley, D., and Sidrauski, M. 1971. MONETARY AND FISCAL POLICY IN A GROWING ECONOMY. New York: Macmillan.

Frenkel, J. A. 1970. "Money, Wealth and the Balance of Payments in a Model of Accumulation." Ph.D. diss., University of Chicago.

_____. 1971. "A Theory of Money, Trade and the Balance of Payments." JOURNAL OF INTERNATIONAL ECONOMICS, May.

Frenkel, J. A., and Fischer, S. 1972. "International Capital Movements along Balanced Growth Paths: Comments and Extensions." ECONOMIC RECORD, June.

Friedman, M. 1969. THE OPTIMUM QUANTITY OF MONEY AND OTHER ESSAYS, chap. 2. Chicago: Aldine.

Hawtrey, R. G. 1928. "The Gold Standard and the Balance of Payments." ECONOMIC JOURNAL.

Johnson, H. G. 1972. "The Monetary Approach to Balance of Payments Theory." JOURNAL OF FINANCIAL AND QUANTITATIVE ANALYSIS, Mar.

Jones, R. W. 1968. "Monetary and Fiscal Policy for an Economy with Fixed Exchange Rates." JOURNAL OF POLITICAL ECONOMY, July/Aug.

_____. 1969. "Portfolio Balance and International Payments Adjustment." In MONETARY PROBLEMS OF THE INTERNATIONAL ECONOMY, edited by R. A. Mundell and A. Swoboda. Chicago: University of Chicago Press.

Komiya, R. 1969. "Economic Growth and the Balance of Payments." JOURNAL OF POLITICAL ECONOMY, Jan./Feb.

Lee, J. 1972. "Money, Trade and Capital Movement for a Growing Small Economy." Unpublished. Rochester: University of Rochester.

McKinnon, R. 1969. "Portfolio Balance and International Payments Adjustment." in MONETARY PROBLEMS OF THE INTERNATIONAL ECONOMY, edited by R. A. Mundell and A. Swoboda. Chicago: University of Chicago Press.

McKinnon, R., and Oates, W. 1966. THE IMPLICATIONS OF INTERNATIONAL ECONOMIC INTEGRATION FOR MONETARY, FISCAL AND EXCHANGE RATE POLICY. Studies in International Finance, no. 16. Princeton: Princeton University, International Finance Section.

Metzler, L. 1968. "The Process of International Adjustment under Conditions of Full Employment: A Keynesian View." In READINGS IN INTERNATIONAL ECONOMICS, edited by H. Johnson and R. Caves. Homewood, Ill.: Irwin.

_____. 1973. "Wealth, Saving and the Rate of Interest." In his COLLECTED PAPERS. Cambridge, Mass.: Harvard University Press.

Mundell, R. A. 1968. INTERNATIONAL ECONOMICS. New York: Macmillan.

_____. 1971. MONETARY THEORY. Pacific Palisades, Calif.: Goodyear.

Mussa, M. 1971*a*. "Twice the Transfer Problem plus David Hume." Unpublished. Chicago: University of Chicago.

_____. 1971*b*. "A Simple General Equilibrium Model of Trade and the Balance of Payments." Unpublished. Chicago: University of Chicago.

_____. 1973. "A Study in Macroeconomic Dynamics: A Metzleric Approach." Unpublished. Rochester: University of Rochester.

Purvis, D. 1972. "More on Growth and the Balance of Payments: The Adjustment Process." CANADIAN JOURNAL OF ECONOMICS, Nov.

Roper, D. 1969. "Macroeconomic Policies and the Distribution of the World Money Supply." QUARTERLY JOURNAL OF ECONOMICS, May.

Salop, J. 1973. "The Exchange Rate and the Terms of Trade." Unpublished. Washington, D.C.: Board of Governors of the Federal Reserve System.

Swoboda, A. 1972. "Equilibrium, Quasi-Equilibrium and Macroeconomic Policies under Fixed Exchange Rates." QUARTERLY JOURNAL OF ECONOMICS, Feb.

Tobin, J. 1961. "Money, Capital and Other Stores of Value." AMERICAN ECONOMIC REVIEW, May.

_____. 1969. "A General Equilibrium Approach to Monetary Theory." JOURNAL OF MONEY, CREDIT AND BANKING, Feb.

Tower, E. 1972. "Monetary and Fiscal Policy under Fixed and Flexible Exchange Rates in the Inter-Run." JOURNAL OF MONEY, CREDIT AND BANKING, Nov.

Von Neumann-Whitman, M. 1970. POLICIES FOR INTERNAL AND EXTERNAL BALANCE. Special Papers in International Economics, no. 9. Princeton: Princeton University, International Finance Section.

CAPITAL MOBILITY AND PORTFOLIO BALANCE*

Rudiger Dornbusch**
Massachusetts Institute of Technology

In his work on monetary and fiscal policy in the open economy under fixed exchange rates, Mundell (1968) has demonstrated the role of capital mobility.[1] Perfect capital mobility was shown to imply endogeneity of the world distribution of money and the ineffectiveness of monetary policy in a small country. The implications of capital mobility for macroeconomic questions were sufficiently forceful at a highly aggregative level for a detailed formulation of the implied portfolio-balance relations to seem redundant. Attempts at monetary policy in individual countries reflect, too, the recognition of a high degree of capital mobility, and it is for this reason that policies have primarily taken the form of regulation of the financial industry, taxation of ownership, or attempts at changing the relative yields of relatively nontradeable securities, over which domestic authorities may exert more leverage than over their tradeable counterparts.

The present paper develops a formal framework in which such asset-market policies can be analyzed. The framework is a partial-equilibrium model of the asset markets that takes the real side of the economy as given. Conceptually, it is therefore similar to studies of the money supply process (Burger 1971; Brunner 1973) or portfolio-balance models (Tobin 1969). The conclusions that emerge from such a formulation are not so much new

---

* Reprinted, with some changes, by permission of the author and the Graduate School of Business, the University of Chicago, from THE POLITICAL ECONOMY OF MONETARY REFORM, ed. R. Aliber (London: Macmillan, 1977), pp. 106-25. An earlier version of the paper was presented at the 1974 Konstanz Seminar.

** In preparing this paper, I have drawn on helpful discussions with Karl Brunner and Dale Henderson. I have benefited, too, from reading an unpublished paper by Girton and Henderson (1973).

1. For a recent review and extensive references to the literature, see Myrhman (1975).

insights about the operation of an open economy; rather, they pertain to the exact detail of the effects of policies, and they provide a description of the relevant parameters that determine the magnitude and direction of these effects. The model differs in two respects from the standard macroeconomic treatment of these issues. First, there is an explicit development of the banking sector, and second, a nontraded asset is introduced in order to highlight the implications of capital mobility.[2]

In section 1 the portfolio-balance model under perfect capital mobility is restated, and it is shown that the individual central bank, in order to be effective, has to change the world interest rate and that it will do so at a reserve loss inversely proportional to its effective size. In section 2 a banking system is added, and it is concluded that the analysis remains essentially unchanged except that now the authorities command more instruments.

In sections 3 and 4 nontraded assets are introduced. In section 3 the small-country case is analyzed, and the determination of the "domestic" interest rate and the equilibrium stock of reserves is developed. In section 4 that analysis is extended to the two-country model, and comparisons are made between open-market operations in traded and nontraded debt. It is concluded that interventions in nontraded debt yield a lower reserve loss and are more effective in changing the domestic rate of interest.

In section 5 a model of the simultaneous determination of the yield on "domestic" securities and the premium on forward exchange is developed. The model emphasizes that these rates are determined by the conditions of portfolio equilibrium and permits the demonstration of the equivalence of open-market operations and interventions in the forward market.

---

2. The concept of nontraded assets is used, too, in Branson (1972, 1977), Boyer (1975), and Dornbusch (1975). I am indebted to Walter Salant for pointing out that "nontransferable assets" play a key role in Scitovsky (1969).

1. CAPITAL MOBILITY AND PORTFOLIO BALANCE

The purpose of this section is to review the concept of capital mobility as it has been developed by Mundell. Perfect capital mobility is understood as an integrated *world* market for the existing stocks of assets and, accordingly, equalization of yields on identical assets, independent of location. The counterpart of the integration of markets or the "law of one price" is the endogeneity of both the quantity of money and the distribution of central-bank reserves.

This concept of capital mobility can readily be formulated by adopting a partial-equilibrium approach and restricting the analysis to asset markets.[3] We assume there is one kind of debt instrument in the world and two monies. The demand for money in each country is a function of the opportunity cost of holding money, r, income, Y, and wealth, W:

$$L = L(r, Y_o, W_o), \qquad (1)$$
$$L^* = L^*(r, Y_o^*, W_o^*),$$

where an asterisk denotes the foreign country and income and wealth are treated as parametrically given. In the absence of a banking system, the money supply is equal to the central bank's holdings of reserves, R, and domestic credit, D:

$$M = R + D, \qquad (2)$$
$$M^* = R^* + D^*. \qquad (3)$$

Finally, we assume that the world stock of reserves, $\bar{R}$, is given, so that

$$\bar{R}_o = R + R^*. \qquad (4)$$

---

3. The following formalization is a one-bond variant of the model developed in Girton and Henderson (1976), who consider a world with perfect capital mobility and two imperfectly substitutable bonds. It is, too, the asset-market description of the model developed in Mundell (1968) and tested in Kouri and Porter (1974).

Given income, wealth, and world reserves, the variables that are to be determined are the equilibrium interest rate, the distribution of reserves, and the national money supplies and debt holdings. To determine these variables we study the equilibrium conditions in the money markets:

$$R + D_o = L(r, Y_o, W_o), \tag{5}$$

$$\bar{R}_o - R + D_o^* = L^*(r, Y_o^*, W_o^*). \tag{6}$$

In figure 1 we show equation 5 as the LM schedule and equation (6) as the L^*M^* schedule. The home country's money-market equilibrium schedule is negatively sloped, since an increase in reserves raises the money supply and thus requires a reduction in the interest rate to encourage the public to hold the increased quantity of money. The foreign money-market equilibrium schedule is positively sloped, since by (4) and (3) an increase in domestic reserves implies a reduction in the foreign money supply, therefore requiring an increase in the interest rate to maintain foreign monetary equilibrium. The equilibrium interest rate and distribution of reserves, r_o and R_o, obtains when both money markets clear. That equilibrium is contingent on the income, wealth, and domestic credit parameters.

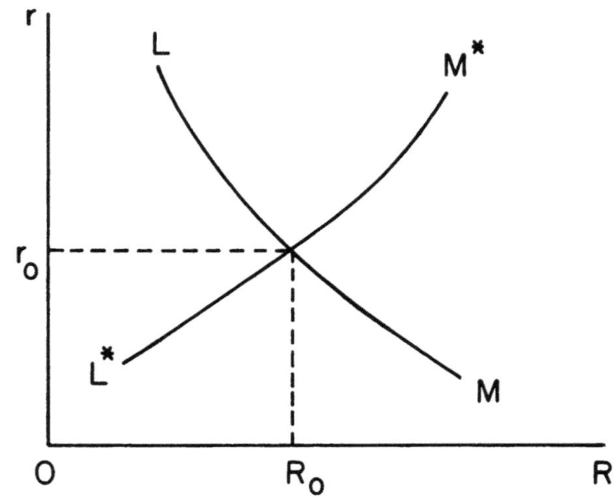

Figure 1

An increase in domestic credit in the home country, as shown in figure 2, shifts the home country's money-market equilibrium schedule to the left by the increase in domestic credit, thereby creating an excess supply of money and an excess demand for debt. The equilibrium interest rate will decline to r' and the domestic stock of reserves will decrease to R'. The decline in reserves, however, is smaller than the increase in domestic credit and depends on the relative *effective size* of the two countries. Effective size is here defined as the product of the interest elasticity of the demand for money and a country's share in the world money supply and will be denoted by β and β^*, respectively. Using these definitions and differentiating equations (5) and (6), we obtain the effect of credit expansion on reserves:

$$dR = -\frac{\beta^*}{\beta + \beta^*}\, dD + \frac{\beta}{\beta + \beta^*}\, dD^*. \tag{7}$$

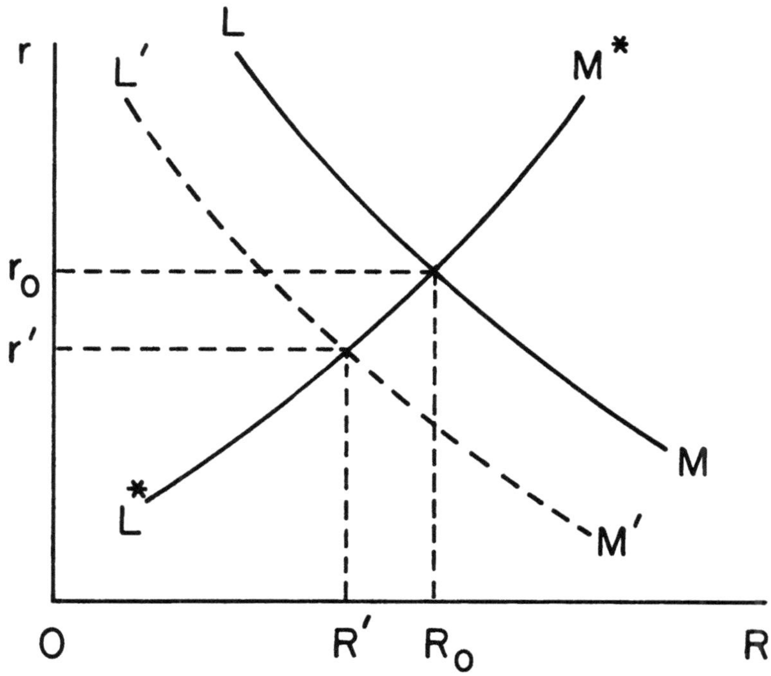

Figure 2

It is important to note that this framework does not suggest that a small country cannot modify the world interest rate or its quantity of money. What it does say is that the cost of doing so in terms of reserve losses (or gains) is inversely proportional to its effective size. Thus as a limiting case in (7), domestic credit expansion is met by an equal loss of reserves—the small-country case to which Mundell has drawn attention.

The change in the domestic quantity of money due to credit creation is independent of the origin of that credit creation:

$$dM = dR + dD = \frac{\beta}{\beta + \beta^*} (dD + dD^*). \tag{8}$$

According to (8), the increase in the domestic quantity of money is a fraction of the *world* credit creation, where the fraction, in turn, is determined by relative effective size.

The analysis so far has been conducted in terms of the money markets. It is revealing, however, to use the budget constraint and translate the analysis into the world market for debt. In each country the excess supply of money is equal to the excess demand for debt, so that, using (1) to (4), the world excess demand for debt, $\bar{B}$, is obtained.

$$\bar{B} = \bar{R} + D + D^* - L - L^* . \tag{9}$$

The world excess demand for debt is independent of the distribution of reserves and domestic credit and, given the parameters D, D^*, Y, Y^*, W, W^*, will only be a function of the rate of interest. Accordingly, the world debt-market equilibrium schedule will be a horizontal line in figures 1 and 2 and will pass through the intersection of the money-market equilibrium schedules. It follows that we can use equation (9) to determine the equilibrium interest rate and either (5) or (6) to determine the equilibrium distribution of reserves. With this formulation, the equilibrium can be described as follows: the interest rate is such that the world stock of debt is willingly held, and the distribution of reserves is such that the supply of money equals the demand for money in each country.

2. FINANCIAL INTERMEDIATION

In this section we introduce financial intermediation in the form of a commercial banking system. This modifies the foregoing analysis in two respects. The money supply will now be determined by the monetary base and commercial bank reserve preferences. At the same time, commercial banks appear as suppliers of loans or demanders of debt.

With these modifications we can write the money-market equilibrium conditions of the previous section as follows:

$$m(r, \nu)(R + D) = L(r, \ldots), \tag{5'}$$

$$m^*(r, \nu^*)(\bar{R} - R + D^*) = L^*(r, \ldots), \tag{6'}$$

where m and m^* are the money multipliers.[4] They are functions of the yield on debt and central-bank controls summarized in the parameters ν and ν^*.

The characteristics of the model developed in the previous section are not essentially altered by the introduction of a banking system except in two respects. A source of disturbance arises now from portfolio shifts on the part of the banking system between bank reserves and securities. The central bank, on the other hand, gains a further instrument in its ability to influence or regulate the banking system's reserve ratio and balance sheet.

Consider now the effect of increased reserve requirements in the home country. At the initial equilibrium interest rate, commercial banks will relinquish earning assets for high-powered money in the world market, thereby creating an excess supply of debt. The equilibrium interest rate will increase and so will the domestic stock of reserves, while the money supply declines in both countries. The private sectors' holdings of debt rise in both countries. In both countries, the size of the banking system contracts; in the home country, earning assets decline relative to deposits, while they increase abroad.

The effects of restrictive monetary policy remain essentially unaltered by the existence of financial intermediation; the instruments of monetary policy become larger in number, but it continues to be true that a central bank, in order to be effective, has to change the world interest rates. To change this feature of the model we introduce in the next section "domestic assets."

---

4. For a convenient discussion of money and credit multipliers, see Burger (1971).

3. DOMESTIC ASSETS AND THE SMALL-COUNTRY MODEL

The preceding analysis is modified in this section to allow for the existence of "domestic" or "nontraded" debt. We will specifically assume that it is held by the commercial banking system and the central bank and is supplied by the domestic private sector. Both commercial banks and the central bank hold, along with domestic debt, internationally tradeable debt; the commercial banks may, however, hold negative amounts of internationally tradeable debt to the extent that they borrow in the world market in order to finance local loans. The private sector holds money and internationally tradeable debt and is a net supplier of nontradeable debt. The analysis will proceed first to determine the equilibrium in a "small" economy that faces a given rate of interest in the world market, $\bar{r}$.

Given the rate of interest in the world market, $\bar{r}$, we need to determine for the small country the equilibrium interest rate on nontradeable debt, i, and the equilibrium stock of foreign exchange reserves. Given these variables and the central bank's policy variables, we will have determined the money supply and commercial bank credit and holdings of securities.

The interest rate on domestic assets and the stock of foreign exchange reserves are jointly determined by the equilibrium in the markets for domestic money and debt. The domestic money supply is proportional to high-powered money:

$$M = m(r, i, \nu)(R + D + N), \tag{10}$$

where the multiplier now reflects the yields on both types of assets commercial banks will hold, and where N is the central bank's holdings of domestic debt. The demand for money, similarly, reflects the alternative costs of holding money:

$$L = L(r, i, Y, W). \tag{11}$$

The supply of domestic loans by the commercial banking system, K, is proportional to the base and is an increasing function of the yield on domestic loans and a decreasing function of the yield on internationally tradeable debt:

$$K = \phi(r, i, \nu)(R + D + N). \tag{12}$$

The private sector's excess demand for loans, V, will be a function of the same arguments as the demand for money and increases with the world interest rate and decreases with the cost of domestic loans.

$$V = V(r, i, Y, W). \tag{13}$$

The equilibrium yield on domestic loans and the equilibrium stock of reserves are determined by the equilibrium conditions in (14) and (15), given the parameters v^o, Y^o, W^o, N^o, D^o.

$$m(r, i, v)(R + D + N) = L(r, i, Y, W). \tag{14}$$

$$\phi(r, i, v)(R + D + N) = V(r, i, Y, W) - N. \tag{15}$$

The determination of the equilibrium is graphically shown in figure 3, where the *KV* schedule corresponds to the equilibrium in the domestic credit market shown in (15), while the *LM* schedule reflects monetary equilibrium as shown by (14). Both schedules are negatively sloped, since an increase in the interest rate yields an excess supply and thus has to be accompanied by a reduction in the base in order to maintain market equilibrium. The relative slopes assume that the credit market is more responsive to the yield on debt than is the money market.[5]

Point A^o shows the equilibrium yield on domestic debt and the equilibrium stock of reserves such that the money and domestic loan markets simultaneously clear. That equilibrium is contingent on the values of the parameters, and we can now turn to the comparative static effects of altering those parameters.

---

5. In addition to the restrictions on the signs of the partial derivative of the behavioral equations in (10) to (14), we impose the restriction implicit in the relative slopes of the *LM* and *KV* curves in figure 3:

$$-\phi/(\phi_i H - V_i) > -m/(m_i H - L_i), \quad H \equiv R + D + N.$$

Defining the elasticity of excess supply of money and credit respectively, as

$$\varepsilon \equiv (m_i H - L_i)(i/M),$$

$$\lambda \equiv (\phi_i H - V_i)(i/K),$$

we can write this restriction as $\lambda > \varepsilon$, so that we are assuming that the elasticity of excess supply of credit exceeds that of money.

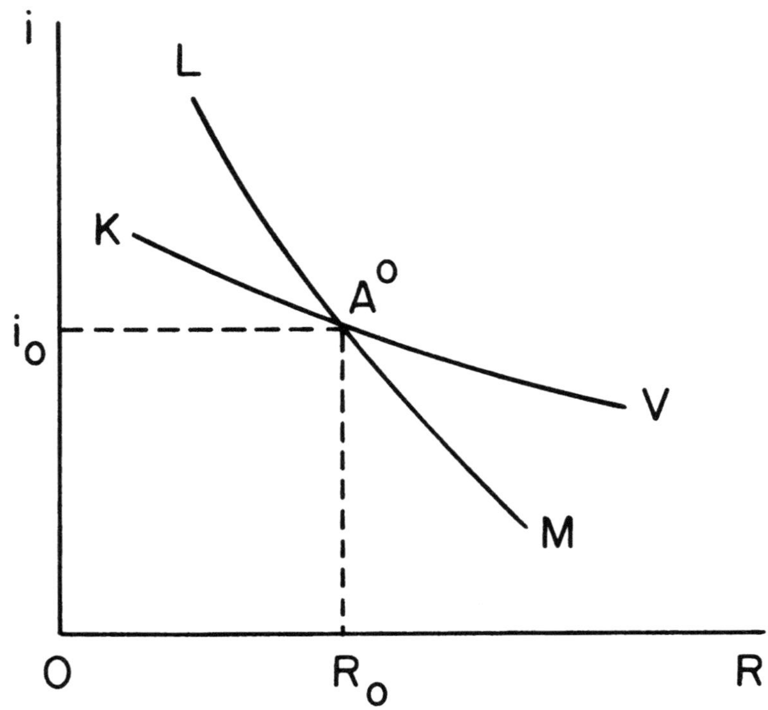

Figure 3

To study the working of the model, consider the effect of an open-market purchase of domestic debt by the central bank, or in terms of the notation of (14) and (15), an increase in N. At point A^o in figure 4, there is now an excess supply of both money and domestic credit, so that both market equilibrium schedules shift to the left, the VK schedule shifting relatively more than the LM schedule.[6] The new equilibrium at point A' is one of a lower interest rate and a decrease in the stock of reserves. The change in reserves will depend on the elasticities of excess demand with respect to the interest rate and the domestic loan multiplier. Calculating from (14) and (15) the effect on reserves of an increase in N we have

$$\frac{dR}{dN} = - \left[1 - \frac{\varepsilon}{\phi(\lambda - \varepsilon)}\right] \equiv -\gamma, \qquad -0 \leq \gamma \leq 1.$$

6. The LM schedule shifts by $dR = -dN$, and the VK schedule by $dR = -(1 + 1/\phi)dN$.

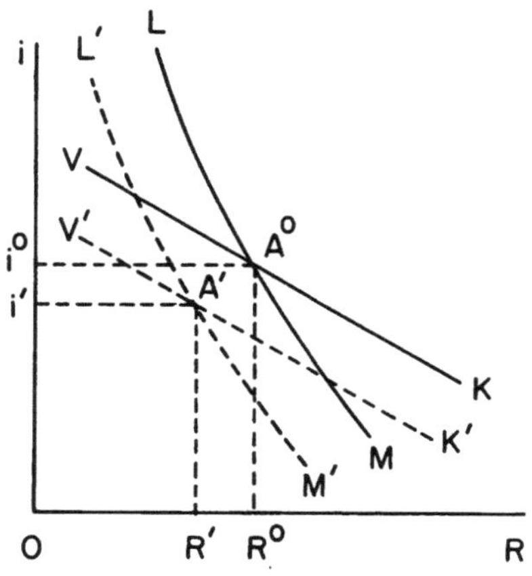

Figure 4

Several features of (16) are worth noting. First, if domestic and foreign assets are highly substitutable, we revert to the one-asset model where an open-market operation is matched by an equal reserve loss. In general, the reserve loss will be a fraction of the open-market operation, so that we have less than a full offset. With imperfect substitutability between domestic and international assets, the yield on domestic assets will decline, and in response to that decline the public will wish to hold larger stocks of both money and foreign assets. The increased money holding is financed directly by the open-market operation. The reserve loss is the counterpart of increased holdings of foreign assets, since in the aggregate, the only way the country can acquire external assets is by relinquishing reserves. Of a given open-market purchase of domestic assets, therefore, a fraction γ is substituted into foreign assets and a fraction $1 - \gamma$ is held in the form of additional money balances. The relative size of the additional holdings of money and foreign assets will depend on the excess-supply elasticities of domestic assets and money, which between themselves imply an elasticity of demand for foreign assets. Given the excess-supply elasticity of money, a larger excess-supply elasticity of domestic assets implies a larger reserve loss or, equivalently, a relatively large addition to foreign assets and a relatively small addition to money holdings.

Table 1 summarizes the effects of alternative changes in parameters on the endogenous variables. In particular, we consider an increase in reserve requirements or reserve preferences, ν, open-market purchases of D and N, as well as increases in the world interest rate, $\bar{r}$, and domestic income. The relevant endogenous variables are domestic loans of the commercial banking system, reserves, the money supply, and the domestic interest rate.[7]

Table 1

	ν	D	N	$\bar{r}$	Y
K	-	o	+	-	+
R	+	-	-	-	+
M	-	o	+	-	+
i	+	o	-	+	+

The basic features of the model can be further emphasized by considering policies that are specific to the banking system or to the distinction between tradeable and nontradeable assets. While that distinction is already emphasized by a comparison of the effects of open-market operations in tradeable and nontradeable debt, it is further enhanced by considering tax, subsidy, and regulatory devices. As a particular example, consider a policy of taxing resident holdings of international debt or subsidizing bank holdings of tradeable debt. These policies, at a given world interest rate, will change the desired portfolio composition of both the private sector and banks and thereby affect the equilibrium yield on domestic debt, the quantity of money, and the stock of reserves.

7. In deriving these results we have imposed additional structure on the supply of domestic loans in assuming that $\phi(r, i, \nu) = \alpha(r, i)(m - 1)$, so that the allocation of earning assets between domestic and international loans is independent of ν. We further assume that $L_y = Y_y$. The reader will recognize that these restrictions have a ready interpretation in terms of the relative shifts of the LM and VK schedules. See, too, the Appendix.

Consider next the regulation of the commercial banking system's earning assets and assume that the authorities reduce the banking system's holdings of tradeable debt in favor of nontradeable debt. Such a policy will affect the domestic credit market as shown in figure 5. At the initial interest rate there will be an excess supply of domestic loans, so that the *VK* curve shifts to *V'K'* and the equilibrium interest rate declines to *i'*.[8] Along with the decline in the yield on domestic loans, we have an increase in the demand for money and the stock of reserves. Such a policy is of obvious interest to a country that wishes to lower domestic interest rates without impairing its reserve position.

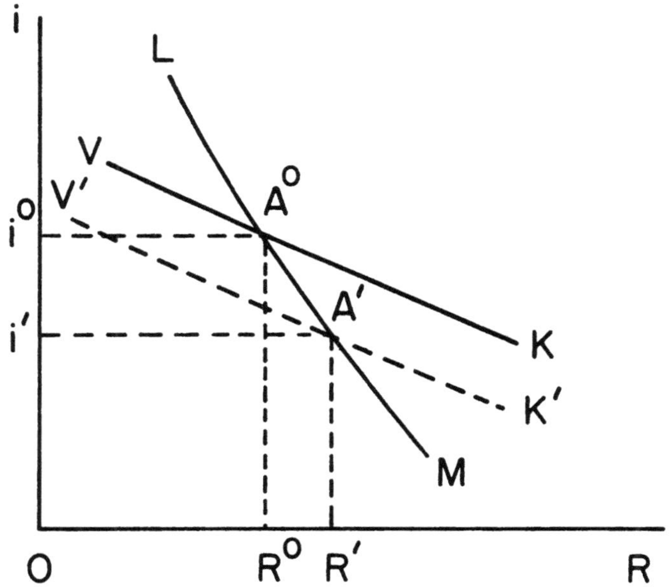

Figure 5

8. The analysis assumes that the money mulitplier *m* is unaffected by the regulation. See footnote 7.

The reserve changes that are induced by the policies we have considered require financing, and it is important to recognize that for the consolidated home country we only have a change in the composition of assets between reserves and tradeable debt. For the policy described in figure 5, the financing of reserve acquisitions is primarily via the commercial banks' liquidation of their holdings of tradeable debt. For other changes in parameters such as an increase in income, the reserve acquisition may be financed predominantly by private liquidation of international debt and commercial bank borrowing in the world market.

The possibility of commercial bank borrowing in the world market for the purpose of financing domestic loans proves to be a serious impediment to the effectiveness of monetary policies. In terms of figure 3, it amounts to a high substitutability between domestic loans and tradeable assets and thus generates a rather flat VK schedule. The leverage that the central bank can gain by operating in the market for domestic loans may thus be offset by a high substitutability between domestic and international assets in intermediaries' portfolios. To regain that leverage, one policy that has been used is the imposition of ceilings on domestic loans by the commercial banking system. Such a policy should prove successful, the ingenuity of the market notwithstanding, if commercial banks play a substantial role in the retail credit market.

We conclude this section by a summary of its main message. In a small country the leverage of monetary policy is likely to come from the existence of nontradeable assets. To the extent that these assets are, however, close substitutes for tradeable assets in the portfolios of financial intermediaries, and particularly commercial banks, that leverage may be easily lost; then more specific policies—in particular, regulation or taxation—are required to implement policies, and the banking system offers a suitable body on which to perpetrate these interventions.

4. DOMESTIC ASSETS AND THE WORLD MODEL

The analysis of the preceding section assumed that the world rate of interest was parametrically given and independent of the home country's actions. We alter that assumption now by considering a two-country model similar to that in section 2 but with the addition that we allow for one tradeable asset and one nontraded asset in each country.

The equilibrium conditions in this model will be that the money market clears in each country and that the market for nontradeable debt clears in each country. The budget constraint implies that when these conditions are satisfied the world market for tradeable debt will clear identically. These equilibrium conditions are given in equations (17) to (20).

$$m(r, i, \nu)(R + D + N) = L(r, i, Y, W). \tag{17}$$

$$m^*(r, i^*, \nu^*)(\bar{R} - R + D^* + N^*) = L^*(r, i^*, Y^*, W^*). \tag{18}$$

$$\phi(r, i, \nu)(R + D + N) = V(r, i, Y, W) - N. \tag{19}$$

$$\phi^*(r, i^*, \nu^*)(\bar{R} - R + D^* + N^*) = V^*(r, i^*, Y^*, W^*) - N^*. \tag{20}$$

To develop the analogy with sections 1 and 2 we draw on the results in the previous section to express the equilibrium interest rate on domestic debt as a function of the parameters ν, N, Y, r:

$$i = i(\nu, N, Y, r), \tag{21}$$

$$i^* = i^*(\nu^*, N^*, Y^*, r). \tag{22}$$

Substituting these reduced-form expressions for the domestic interest rates in (17) and (18) allows us to discard the domestic loan-market equations (19) and (20), the equilibrium of which is implicit in the expressions for the domestic interest rates. Performing this substitution leaves us then with a system formally identical to equations (5) and (6) but with the particular interpretation that in the background the markets for nontradeable debt clear.

We can proceed to ask in what manner the introduction of nontradeable assets alters the conclusions of sections 1 and 2 and in what manner the world model differs from the small-country case. For that purpose, it is instructive to compare the reserve loss arising from open-market purchases of domestic and tradeable debt, respectively (see Appendix):

$$\frac{dR}{dN} = -\gamma \frac{\delta^* m}{\delta^* m + \delta m^*}, \quad 1 > \gamma > 0 \tag{23}$$

$$\frac{dR}{dD} = - \frac{\delta^* m}{\delta^* m + \delta m^*} .$$

We note that open-market interventions in domestic debt will produce a smaller reserve drain than those in tradeable debt and that for both cases the reserve loss, barring the small-country case, is less than proportionate to the open-market operation. Relative to the small-country case, we note that the reserve losses will be smaller in the present model, as can be seen by a comparison of (16) and (23). This is so because an open-market operation in either form of debt will lower the world interest rate and thus further increase the demand for money and hence the derived demand for high-powered money.

The counterpart of the observation that interventions in domestic debt minimize the reserve loss associated with open-market operations is the fact that they are more effective, too, in lowering the domestic interest rate. It can be shown that, per dollar, an intervention in domestic debt lowers the domestic interest rate by more than a purchase of tradeable debt. Conversely, international debt is the more effective asset with respect to the yield on tradeable debt. Some further comparative static results of this model are summarized in table 2 and are derived in detail in the Appendix.

We summarize the main conclusions of this section noting that non-traded assets and a banking system can readily be added to the more conventional models of perfect capital mobility and that such an addition is useful because it emphasizes the differential impact central banks will achieve depending on whom they regulate or what asset they intervene in. While the differential impact is emphasized, it is true at the same time that the basic message of Mundell regarding capital mobility and the endogeneity of the quantity of money continues to hold.

Table 2

	ν	D	N	Y
R	+	-	-	+
r	+	-	-	+
i	+	-	-	+
M	-	+	+	+
i^*	+	-	-	+

5. FORWARD-MARKET AND ASSET-MARKET EQUILIBRIUM

The models of the previous section can readily be extended to incorporate a forward market for foreign exchange and the effects of uncertainty about future spot rates on the allocation between alternative assets. To develop this extension we simplify the preceding models by omitting the banking system and introduce a "domestic" security that is denominated in terms of domestic currency and is an imperfect substitute for foreign assets. This domestic security is held by domestic and possibly foreign residents as well as by the domestic central bank. We further assume a fixed current spot rate and an interest rate on foreign assets that is, for the small country under consideration, exogenously given.

The excess demand for domestic securities by domestic and foreign residents will depend on the yield on domestic securities, i, and the given yield on foreign assets, r, as well as on the premium on forward exchange, the expected future spot rate, and in addition, the parametrically given income and wealth variables. In equilibrium, the domestic and foreign excess supply of domestic securities will equal the central bank's holdings of that asset:

$$\bar{B} = B(i, r, p, \bar{p}, \ldots) + B^*(i, r, p, \bar{p}, \ldots), \tag{24}$$

where B and B^* denote the domestic and foreign excess supply of domestic securities and $\bar{B}$ denotes the central bank's holdings. The premium on forward foreign exchange is denoted by p, and the expected future spot rate expressed as a fraction of the current spot rate is $\bar{p}$.[9]

We will assume that an increase in the yield on domestic assets creates an excess demand for these securities, while an increase in the premium on forward foreign exchange will create an excess supply, since it lowers the covered return on domestic securities and raises the covered return on foreign securities. An increase in the expected future spot rate shifts people out of domestic securities in anticipation of the capital loss on securities denominated in domestic currency.

---

9. The expected future spot rate is treated as an exogenous variable along with other parameters of the distribution that are implicitly suppressed into the functional form of (24).

The excess demand for forward foreign exchange on the part of the domestic and foreign private sector will be an increasing function of the yield on domestic securities and a decreasing function of the premium on forward exchange. An increase in the expected future rate will in turn raise the excess demand for forward cover. In equilibrium, the private excess demand for forward cover will equal the central bank's stock supply of forward contracts:

$$\bar{F} = F(i, r, p, \bar{p}, \ldots), \tag{25}$$

where F denotes the private excess demand for forward exchange, and $\bar{F}$ the stock supply of forward foreign exchange contracts issued by the central bank.

The determination of the equilibrium yield on domestic securities and the forward premium is shown in figure 6 for a given expected future rate, $\bar{p}^o$, and given stocks of central bank holdings of domestic debts, $\bar{B}^o$, and forward contracts, $\bar{F}^o$. Along the schedule FF the forward market is in equilibrium, while along BB the domestic security market clears.

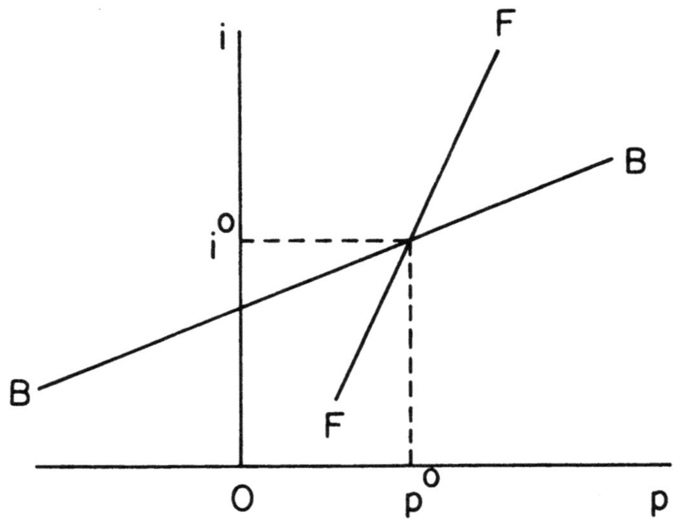

Figure 6

This framework of analysis is an extension of the Fleming-Mundell (1964) model in that it shows the simultaneous determination of interest rates and forward rates. It shares with that model, however, an emphasis on the determination of forward rates in the asset markets or the markets for *stocks* of debt and forward contracts. The model is useful for the analysis of the asset-market effects of changes in asset supplies, and it represents, too, a framework in which to investigate the effects of speculation.

Consider first the effects of open-market and forward-market operations on the part of the central bank. An increase in the central bank's holdings of domestic securities will create an excess demand for these assets and will therefore lower the equilibrium yield at each level of the premium. In terms of figure 6 this corresponds to a shift in the *BB* schedule down and to the right and, accordingly, to a decline in the equilibrium yield and the premium. A sale of forward exchange will similarly cause the domestic interest rate and the premium to decline, since it shifts the *FF* schedule up and to the left. We note, therefore, that forward- and open-market operations are equivalent in their effects on interest rates and forward rates. This conclusion is well in the tradition of the Keynes-Jasay-Spraos advocacy of active "managed forward markets."

Consider next the implications for reserves of interventions in the domestic debt or forward markets. Here the effects are asymmetrical in that an open-market purchase of debt causes, in general, a reserve loss, while a forward-market operation causes a reserve gain. The reason for this asymmetry is that both policies, by lowering the premium and the domestic interest rate, will raise the demand for money; but, whereas a forward intervention leaves the domestic base unaffected, the purchase of debt will directly increase the money supply. These points can be seen from the equation for the equilibrium stock of reserves, which in this model is determined by the demand for money and the domestic source component of the base:

$$R = L(i, p, \bar{p}, r, \ldots) - \bar{B} \qquad (26)$$

Differentiating (26) we obtain the effect on reserves of interventions by the central bank:

$$\frac{dR}{d\bar{B}} = \frac{dL}{d\bar{B}} - 1 , \tag{27}$$

$$\frac{dR}{d\bar{F}} = \frac{dL}{d\bar{F}} > 0 , \tag{28}$$

where the terms $dL/d\bar{B}$ and $dL/d\bar{F}$ will depend on the parameters of the demand for money and the comparative statics of (24) and (25). We will assume that an increase in either the yield on domestic securities or the premium will reduce the demand for money. With these restrictions, we know from (28) that a forward-market sale will raise reserves. To obtain the result that an open-market purchase of securities will lower reserves in (27), we require more restrictions on the system so as to make $dL/d\bar{B}$ smaller than unity.

Consider next the effects of a "speculative attack," represented here by an increase in the expected future spot rate, $\bar{p}$. The anticipation of depreciation will shift the public out of domestic securities and will increase the excess demand for forward exchange. It will therefore, in figure 6, shift the *FF* schedule down and to the right and the *BB* schedule up and to the left, so that the equilibrium interest rate and forward premium both increase. The effect of expected depreciation on interest rates and forward rates is akin to the "Fisher effect" of expected inflation on nominal interest and arises for exactly the same reason, namely, the anticipated depreciation of assets fixed in terms of domestic currency.

The expected depreciation will cause a shift out of money, too, and to that extent will, by (26), cause a loss in reserves. That decline in the demand for money is due both to the direct effect of a change in $\bar{p}$ on the demand for money as well as to the induced changes in the demand for money that arise from the increase in interest rates and the premium. It is important to note that the loss in reserves is not directly due to a shift out of domestic into foreign securities, since the domestic stock of securities will have to be held; rather, it operates through a change in the demand for money, which, however, is not independent of the change in the equilibrium asset yields. This point is important, for it shows that a policy that aims at maintaining reserves in the face of a loss of confidence in the domestic parity will have to aim at the demand and will have to operate via a reduction in domestic interest rates and/or the premium. The ideal policy, then, will be sales of forward exchange on a scale sufficient to *lower* the premium enough to compensate for the effect of expected depreciation on the demand for money. Provided $dL/d\bar{B}$ is smaller than unity, such a policy can be supplemented by open-market sales of securities. This is obviously the standard policy package, at least in Britain, when the currency comes under attack.

CONCLUSION

This paper has developed a formal framework for the study of asset markets that are linked through an integrated world capital market and financial intermediation. The conclusions that emerge from this formulation uphold the Mundellian principle that "the open economy leaks." The disaggregation in asset markets that is proposed here shows further, however, that a distinction between domestic assets and tradeable securities is of interest, since it permits the formulation of the differential effect of open-market operations depending on the type of security the central bank intervenes in or the manner in which it regulates the banking system.

In linking the discussion to the forward market, we show the simultaneous determination of domestic interest rates and the forward premium, and we show, too, the equivalence between open-market operations and forward-market interventions.

APPENDIX

This appendix derives the comparative static results discussed in section 3 of the paper. To derive these results we use the equilibrium conditions for the domestic money and loan markets, repeated here for convenience:

$$m(r, i, v)(R + D + N) = L(r, i, Y, W), \tag{A-1}$$

$$\alpha(r, i)(m(r, i, v) - 1)(R + D + N) = V(r, i, Y, W) - N. \tag{A-2}$$

We further use the following notation, definitions, and restrictions:

$$\phi = \alpha(m - 1), \quad H \equiv R + D + N, \quad K \equiv \phi H;$$

$$\lambda \equiv (\phi_i H - V)i/K > 0;$$

$$\varepsilon \equiv (m_i H - L_i)i/M > 0;$$

$$\eta \equiv (m_r H - L_r)r/M > 0;$$

$$\rho \equiv -(\phi_r H - V_r)r/K > 0;$$

$$m_\nu < 0, \quad L_\nu = V_\nu > 0, \; \phi - m < 0, \; \lambda - \varepsilon > 0.$$

Differentiating the equilibrium conditions in (A-1) and (A-2) and solving for the change in the equilibrium interest rate on domestic debt yields:

$$\frac{di/i}{dN} = -\frac{1}{\phi H(\lambda - \varepsilon)} < 0; \tag{A-3}$$

$$\frac{di/i}{dY} = \frac{m - \phi}{m\phi H(\lambda - \varepsilon)} L_y > 0;$$

$$\frac{di/i}{d\nu} = -\frac{m_\nu}{m\phi(\lambda - \varepsilon)} > 0;$$

$$\frac{di/i}{dr/r} = \frac{\eta + \rho}{\lambda - \varepsilon} > 0.$$

The change in the equilibrium stock of reserves is:

$$\frac{dR}{dN} = -\gamma < 0; \tag{A-4}$$

$$\frac{dR}{d\nu} = \frac{m_\nu H(\alpha\varepsilon - \lambda)}{\phi(\lambda - \varepsilon)} > 0;$$

$$\frac{dR}{dY} = \frac{L_y(\phi\lambda - m\varepsilon)}{m\phi(\lambda - \varepsilon)} > 0;$$

$$\frac{dR}{dr/r} = -\frac{H(\varepsilon\rho + \lambda\eta)}{\lambda - \varepsilon} < 0,$$

where we assume that

$$\gamma \equiv 1 - \frac{\varepsilon}{\phi(\lambda - \varepsilon)} > 0;$$

$$\phi\lambda - m\varepsilon > 0.$$

For the discussion of section 4 it is convenient to define some reduced-form expressions. We are interested in the change in the excess supply of money allowing the market for nontradeable debt to clear. The effect of a change in the rate of interest on tradeable debt on the excess supply of money is

$$\left[r(m_r H - L_r) + i(m_i H - L_i) \frac{di/i}{dr/r} \right] dr/r, \tag{A-5}$$

which reduces after substitution from (A-3) to

$$\left[M \frac{\eta\lambda + \varepsilon\rho}{\lambda - \varepsilon} \right] dr/r \equiv \delta(dr/r).$$

Proceeding in a similar manner we derive the following expressions for the remaining parametric changes:

$$\left[i(m_i H - L_i) \frac{di/i}{dN} + m \right] dN = m\gamma(dN), \tag{A-6}$$

$$\left[i(m_i H - L_i) \frac{di/i}{dv} + m_v H \right] dv = m_v \gamma H(dv), \tag{A-7}$$

$$\left[i(m_i H - L_i) \frac{di/i}{dY} - L_y \right] dY = \frac{\varepsilon m - \phi\lambda}{\phi(\lambda - \varepsilon)} L_y(dY) \equiv \Phi(dY). \tag{A-8}$$

We can now proceed to determine the effects of policy and parameter changes in the two-country model in a manner similar to section 1. The equilibrium conditions we shall use are those for the two money markets:

$$m(r, i, \nu)(R + D + N) = L(r, i, Y, W), \tag{A-9}$$

$$m^*(r, i^*, \nu^*)(\bar{R} - R + D^* + N^*) = L^*(r, i^*, Y^*, W^*). \tag{A-10}$$

To ensure that the comparative static results derived from (A-9) and (A-10) satisfy the equilibrium conditions in the respective markets for nontradeable debt, we will use (A-5) to (A-8). Differentiating the above equilibrium conditions and substituting from (A-5) to (A-8), we obtain the following results:

$$\frac{dr/r}{dN} = - mm^* \gamma/\Delta < 0, \quad \frac{dr/r}{d\nu} = - m^* m_\nu \gamma H/\Delta > 0; \tag{A-11}$$

$$\frac{dr/r}{dD} = - mm^*/\Delta < 0, \quad \frac{dr/r}{dY} = - m^* \Phi/\Delta > 0;$$

$$\frac{dR}{dN} = - \delta^* m \gamma/\Delta < 0, \quad \frac{dR}{d\nu} = - \delta^* m_\nu \gamma H/\Delta > 0;$$

$$\frac{dR}{dD} = - \delta^* m/\Delta < 0, \quad \frac{dR}{dY} = - \delta^* \Phi/\Delta > 0,$$

where $\Delta \equiv \delta^* m + \delta m^* > 0$.

REFERENCES

Boyer, R. 1975. "Commodity Markets and Bond Markets in a Small Fixed Exchange Rate Economy." CANADIAN JOURNAL OF ECONOMICS, Feb.

Branson, W. 1972. "Macroeconomic Equilibrium with Portfolio Balance in Open Economies." Unpublished. Stockholm: Institute for International Economic Studies.

_____. 1977. "International Transmission of Inflation: A Keynesian Approach." In WORLD INFLATION: THEORY AND RECENT EXPERIENCE, edited by L. Krause. Washington, D.C.: Brookings Institution.

Brunner, K. 1973. "Money Supply Processes and Monetary Policy in an Open Economy." In INTERNATIONAL TRADE AND MONEY, edited by M. Connolly and A. Swoboda. London: Allen & Unwin.

Burger, A. 1971. THE MONEY SUPPLY PROCESS. Belmont, Calif.: Wadsworth.

Dornbusch, R. 1975. "A Portfolio-Balance Model of the Open Economy." JOURNAL OF MONETARY ECONOMICS, Jan. Reprinted in this volume.

Fleming, M., and Mundell, R. A. 1964. "Official Intervention on the Forward Foreign Exchange Market." I.M.F. STAFF PAPERS, Mar.

Girton, L., and Henderson, D. 1976. "Financial Capital Movements and Central Bank Behavior in a Class of Two Country, Short Run Portfolio Balance Models." JOURNAL OF MONETARY ECONOMICS, Jan.

Kouri, P., and Porter, M. 1974. "International Capital Flows and Portfolio Equilibrium." JOURNAL OF POLITICAL ECONOMY, May/June.

Mundell, R. A. 1968. INTERNATIONAL ECONOMICS. New York: Macmillan.

Myrhman, J. 1975. "Monetary Policy in Open Economies." Unpublished. Stockholm: Institute for International Economic Studies.

Scitovsky, T. 1969. MONEY AND THE BALANCE OF PAYMENTS. London: Allen & Unwin.

Tobin, J. 1969. "A General Equilibrium Approach to Monetary Theory." JOURNAL OF MONEY, CREDIT AND BANKING, Feb.

ON THE MONETARY THEORY OF THE BALANCE OF PAYMENTS: AN EXTENSION*

Larry A. Sjaastad
University of Chicago

One of the main implications of the monetary approach to the balance of payments is that, under fixed exchange rates, the central bank of a country can choose the composition but not the quantity of (nominal) assets of the banking system, since the principal liability of that system—the nominal money supply—is demand-determined. In its long-run version, that approach usually assumes equilibrium between the supply of and demand for cash balances and derives the behavior of foreign exchange reserves that is required to maintain that equilibrium. In the short run, disequilibrium in the balance of payments is usually attributed to an imbalance between the demand for and supply of money, with demand and supply referring to stocks rather than flows. This paper examines the nature of very short-run fluctuations in the balance of payments and concludes that neither a stock nor a flow disequilibrium is essential to generate movements of reserves. The emphasis of this aspect of the paper is on credit policy and on the distinction between ex ante and ex post flow supplies of money.

The second contribution of the paper concerns exchange rates. The monetary approach grew up in the context of fixed rates, whereas currently, the major currencies of the world are floating. The proposed extension of the monetary approach to floating rates is relatively straightforward, requiring a change in emphasis rather than in the substance of the existing approach. Some interesting results are obtained with respect to the magnitude of capital flows under floating rates.

---

* An earlier version of the paper was presented at the 1975 Konstanz Seminar.

The remainder of this paper is divided into four parts. The first section specifies the assumptions to be employed in the subsequent analysis. The second section develops the analysis for the case of fixed exchange rates; the next, for floating rates. A final section summarizes the conclusions.

ASSUMPTIONS

As our concern is with the short-run relationship between monetary policy and the balance of payments, we assume there is no systematic growth of real output; a minor inconsistency arises later in the paper when we assume that saving and investment is taking place, but this need not cause a problem, since the expected value of both saving and investment could be zero. Moreover, we focus only on the very short run, during which changes in real output in response to both policy-induced and other shocks can be ignored. This does not mean that these shocks may not affect real output, but rather that they affect it only over time; as we confine our analysis to the *impact* effects of changes in monetary policy on the balance of payments (in the case of fixed exchange rates) and the exchange rate (when rates are floating), we will see that subsequent changes in real output can be safely ignored.

Since it is not our intention to investigate the effects of fiscal policy per se, it is convenient to devise a model such that pure fiscal policy does not matter. To fully neutralize pure fiscal policy, we assume that tax collections and bond sales to the public are equivalent in their effects on private-sector spending and that government expenditure, be it for transfer payments or for provision of real output, is not only realized as income by the private sector but also valued by the recipients in an amount equal to the cost to the government of providing that output. These assumptions are admittedly heroic and do not reflect any a priori judgments about the effectiveness of fiscal policy; they are made for analytical convenience only. It is to be stressed, therefore, that no implications concerning pure fiscal policy are to be drawn from the analysis contained in this paper.

It is further assumed that only the private sector has a demand for cash balances, said demand depending upon the nominal rate of interest and the level of real output. Private-sector expenditure is taken to depend upon the real rate of interest and upon a concept of disposable income to be explicitly developed below. Imports and exports of goods and services are assumed to be *excess* demand and supply functions, respectively, and hence the current account balance responds directly to aggregate demand in a straightforward Keynesian fashion. The model is not Keynesian, however, in its conception of the role of the exchange rate in the system. While the exchange rate, defined as the price of foreign currency, clearly allocates existing domestic demand between traded and nontraded goods and services, it cannot by itself affect the level of absorption independently of the level of output. The reason for this is that if, for example, a change in the exchange rate were to induce an increase in real absorption over real output (plus the "normal" capital inflow to be dealt with below), there must be an equal increase in real income over real output; and as the latter is not automatically forthcoming, changes in the exchange rate can affect absorption relative to output only to the extent that something else fortuitously and simultaneously changes income relative to output. In the model developed below, these latter changes are effected through monetary policy in such a way as to stabilize the demand for domestic output in the face of potential changes in absorption.

Our final assumption concerns the international capital market. We identify two distinct types of capital flows even though in practice it may well be impossible to distinguish between them. These two types take the form of portfolio adjustments, on the one hand, and foreign investment, on the other.

Portfolio adjustments are assumed to create arbitrarily large capital flows for arbitrarily short periods of time, thus, under a system of truly fixed exchange rates, maintaining equality of nominal interest rates in all markets at all times.[1] Capital movements arising from these portfolio adjustments take the form of "spikes," and their effect on the balance of payments is, therefore, ignored.

The other type of capital flow, and the one that will concern us, arises from differentials in the *real* rates of interest that would prevail if the various economies in the system were closed. Differences in tastes, investment opportunities, etc., will cause some countries to be foreign investors while others act as hosts for that investment; hence, despite continuous equality of nominal interest rates in all markets, there will exist systematic capital flows that, given the nominal rates of interest, respond to changes in real rates. For example, a (temporary) increase in the rate of inflation in one country, the inflation rate of her trading partners being constant, would lower the real rate in that country, thus increasing the willingness of domestic investors to borrow while simultaneously decreasing the supply of funds forthcoming from domestic savers, thereby increasing the rate of foreign investment in the country.

THE CASE OF FIXED EXCHANGE RATES

It is central to the monetary approach to the balance of payments that, apart from the central reserve country, fixed exchange rates cause the nominal quantity of money to be endogenous, with the consequence that long-run rates of inflation in all countries tend to a common level. Fixed rates do not by themselves cause that common level to be zero; rather, that level will be determined perhaps by general agreement concerning the rate and means of creation of reserves for the system or, as with the Bretton Woods system, by the behavior of the monetary authorities in the central reserve country. Thus, with fixed rates there is no compelling reason to

---

1. This assumption is stronger than necessary; all that is required is that the arbitrageurs do not permit change in the differentials in nominal interest rates in the various markets, whatever may be the underlying explanation for the differentials themselves.

postulate price stability in the long run, and perhaps more important, there is also no reason to postulate equal rates of inflation in all countries in the short run. The most that fixed rates can accomplish in the short run is equality of nominal rates of interest in all markets, which in turn implies that real rates, at any given moment in time and in any given country, are under the influence of monetary policy or, more correctly, domestic credit policy. As it is widely accepted that real expenditure (consumption and investment) depends upon real rather than nominal rates of interest, it follows immediately that monetary (domestic credit) policy can have a direct impact on domestic spending, and hence absorption, in the short run. It is important to note that this effect is not dependent upon the existence of excess stock supply or demand for money.

This effect of monetary policy is not, however, the most interesting from the point of view of the balance of payments, the reason being that any increase in absorption brought about by temporarily driving down the real rate of interest through an increase in the rate of domestic inflation is self-financing through compensating flows responding to changes in the real rate of interest. Any changes in reserves will therefore be of a minor order of magnitude in comparison with the monetary disturbance itself. The conclusion one is drawn to in this context is that, while short-run monetary disturbances might play a role in short-run movements in exports and imports by affecting consumption and investment via the real rate of interest, their effect on the balance of payments must come about by some other route.

That other route is not difficult to trace out; to do so it is necessary only to integrate two observations. First, it is becoming increasingly apparent that changes in the rate of change in the *nominal* money supply cause the rate of change of the *real* money supply to move in the same direction in the short run, whereas in the long run those changes are in opposite directions owing to balance-of-payments effects in an open economy and to changes in the rate of inflation and hence the nominal rate of interest in a closed economy. The second observation is that, apart from changes in reserves, an increase in the rate of monetary expansion is necessarily a consequence of and thus accompanied by an increase in the rate of expansion of either (or both) private or public-sector credit, and this credit expansion either augments total spending or competes with and hence diminishes the normal capital inflow.[2] Suppose, for example, that the rate of central-bank lending to the public sector is expanded to finance an increase in government expenditure or a tax reduction; in either case, private-sector income and hence consumption plus investment are increased, leading directly to a worsening of the balance of payments.[3] If public-sector spending and taxes are unaffected by the increased credit, then it follows that the credit will be used either to forgo planned bond sales to engage in debt retirement; the effect of either of these outcomes is to directly reduce the normal capital inflow, and thus, again, the balance of payments deteriorates.

An increase in the rate of credit creation for the private sector has effects similar to those described above, except that there is no presumption that private-sector spending will increase simply because the commercial banking system is willing to lend more (on the same terms). What occurs in this case is that the excess demand for funds, which is met by the capital inflow, is reduced; hence that capital inflow itself is reduced, directly worsening the balance of payments. Thus, the direction of the effects on the balance of payments is independent of whether the additional credit is allocated to the public or the private sector and, if the former, is independent of the use made of it.

---

2. It is important to note that the capital inflow of the sort we are concerned with is a residual equal to the excess of domestic demand for funds and domestic supply, with both demand and supply being in flow terms.

3. *Privately financed* consumption and investment need not increase in the case of a rise in government expenditure; all that is needed in order for total expenditure to rise is that there be no reduction in privately financed expenditure.

The above line of argument holds, of course, only to the extent that an increase in the rate of expansion of nominal credit also increases the rate of expansion of real credit; that this will be the case in the short run is ensured by the strong presumption that real credit will increase at a rate at least as large as the rate of increase in the real money supply. The real money supply will in fact increase at a positive rate either until the rate of domestic inflation catches up with the rate of monetary expansion or until the latter is reduced to the rate of domestic inflation by a progressive worsening of the balance of payments. It is the main point of the analysis, of course, to demonstrate that the balance of payments will in fact worsen when the rate of expansion of domestic credit is increased, and vice versa.

It is important to note that the above analysis predicts that the effect on the balance of payments of a change in the rate of expansion of domestic credit *will be virtually instantaneous.* That is, there is no need for stock disequilibrium to exist in order for monetary policy to affect the balance of payments; hence the effects of monetary policy on the balance of payments need not be delayed in order for the stock disequilibrium to develop. It is precisely this need for stock disequilibrium that has been the most perplexing aspect of short-run versions of the monetary approach as previously expounded.

It is equally important to recognize that none of the effects described above are dependent upon flow disequilibrium insofar as the demand for and supply of money are concerned. Implicit in the analysis is the idea that any implied growth or decline in the stock of real money is willingly held in the very short run; this idea is consistent with the position that one of the key roles of money in an economic system is that of a shock absorber. We do not require, of course, that the growth in the stock of money be willingly held; indeed, the effects on the balance of payments would be even stronger if individuals attempted to spend the flow supply of money as well as the credit that created it.

The above analysis is based upon two rather simple ideas: first, increases in the stock of nominal money will not be immediately dissipated by increases in the rate of inflation; and second, the stock of money can increase, in the absence of a balance-of-payments surplus, only if the stock of domestic credit also increases. These ideas readily lend themselves to quantification in the form of a simple model that produces rather precise results. As with all models, this precision is deceptive in that it is obtained at the expense of enormous simplification of the problem at hand. With this caveat in mind, we turn to the model itself.

To simplify the analysis, we assume that government obtains credit only from the central bank, and because central-bank profits are taxed at a 100 percent rate, it essentially obtains that credit on an interest-free basis.[4] The budget constraint for the government is:

$$g = t + b + \frac{\dot{C}_g}{P} \,, \tag{1}$$

where g is real government expenditure on goods and services,

t is real tax revenue minus real transfers (including interest on debt),

b is real revenue from net bond sales,

$\dot{C}_g$ is the time rate of change of central-bank advances to government, and

P is the domestic price level.

Government operations enter directly into the private sector's concept of its disposable income, q:

$$q = y + g - t - b = y + \frac{\dot{C}_g}{P} \,, \tag{2}$$

---

4. This is the condition for additions to the money supply arising from government borrowing to be considered outside money.

where y is real output on the economy (net of international factor payments). Equation (2) reflects our earlier assumption that people are indifferent between taxes and bond sales to the public, an idea that has recurred periodically in public finance and with less frequency in the macroeconomic literature. As was pointed out earlier, we employ this extreme assumption only to simplify the analysis and do so at little cost, since we abstain from analysis of the effects of pure fiscal policy on the balance of payments.

The definition of private-sector disposable income also reflects the assumption that government output is valued at its cost of production; as is well known, this is the condition for neutrality of the budget (balanced-budget multiplier of zero). That this assumption is less controversial than the one with respect to bond versus tax finance is readily appreciated by making simple international comparisons of the (relative) size of public sectors. One may wonder, however, why government bond sales are excluded from disposable income whereas credit extended to the public sector by the central bank is not. The explanation is straightforward. Whenever the government borrows from the central bank and spends the proceeds, the supply of outside money is increased; and outside money carries with it no future stream of interest payments to maintain it. On the other hand, government borrowing from the commercial banking system is equivalent to issuing bonds to the private sector, as future tax liabilities are increased by the amount of interest to be paid on the new borrowing.[5]

Thus the private sector is justified in treating government expenditure of any form financed via the central bank as a net addition to its income. Put another way, the government is in effect issuing money rather than bonds, and while the public may associate future tax obligations with new issues of government bonds, it can logically fail to do so with respect to money, there being no interest payments nor any presumption that the money stock will ever be retired.

---

5. Note that we can ignore the asset position of the consolidated banking system because if, as is conventional in this type of analysis, we neglect the capital of that system, its net assets are always zero.

As government expenditure is already incorporated into private-sector decision, we can write the real expenditure function as:

$$y^e = f(q, r), \qquad f_1 > 0, \quad f_2 < 0;$$

where r is the real rate of interest,

f_1 is the marginal propensity to spend for the economy, and

f_2 is the response of consumption and investment to the real interest rate.

Expenditure on real goods and services, however, is given by

$$y^e - \frac{(\dot{M})^d}{P},$$

where $(\dot{M})^d$ is the rate at which the private sector wishes to accumulate nominal cash balances. That is, y^e is expenditure on goods, services, *and* money, whereas only expenditure on goods and services is to be compared with real output, y.

Equilibrium in the goods market is established by:

$$f(q, r) - \frac{(\dot{M})^d}{P} = y + \frac{D}{P}, \tag{3}$$

where D is the deficit on current account (excess of imports over exports) measured in nominal terms and in domestic currency. As the nominal rate of interest is determined externally, we assume that the flow demand for nominal cash balances, $(\dot{M})^d$, is for replacement purposes only and that we depart from a position of stock equilibrium, i.e., $M = M^d$. Denoting the rate of domestic inflation by π, the replacement demand is exactly πM, permitting us to rewrite equation (3) as

$$f(q, r) - \pi m = y + \frac{D}{P}, \tag{3'}$$

where $m = M/P$. Equation (3') has the usual interpretation that, in the absence of domestic inflation, expenditure is equal to output plus the deficit on current account. Inflation tends to reduce expenditure on goods and services by requiring the private sector to divert part of its real income to the maintenance of its real cash balances.

We next investigate the impact effects of stepwise changes in the rate of domestic credit expansion, said changes being represented by the differencing operator, Δ. We assume throughout that $\Delta y = \Delta M = \Delta P = 0$; there can be no instantaneous changes in real output, nominal money, or the price level. Applying the differencing operator to equation (3') under these assumptions yields

$$\frac{f_1 \Delta \dot{C}_g}{P} + f_2 \Delta r - m\, \Delta \pi = \frac{\Delta D}{P} . \tag{4}$$

As was pointed out earlier, the nominal rate of interest, i, is unaffected by changes in real expenditure or money creation, and hence $\Delta r = - \Delta \pi$. But as was also pointed out, any effect on the current account induced by changes in the real rate of interest is compensated by equal changes in the capital inflow; thus there is no point in concerning ourselves with the term $f_2 \Delta r$ at this stage.

The third term of equation (4) will be simplified as follows. The rate of change of prices of traded goods is assumed to be externally determined, so that the response of the domestic rate of inflation to monetary policy is determined solely by the nontraded-goods sector. There is a growing body of empirical evidence, largely from Latin America, that lends support to an inflation equation of the following form:

$$\pi = a\lambda + (1 - a)\pi^* + \delta(m - m^d) - \frac{\beta \dot{y}}{y} + \dots ,$$

where λ is the rate of monetary expansion, $\dot{M}/M$,

m^d is the desired stock of real cash balances, and

π^* is the expected rate of inflation.

While one can raise a number of questions concerning the specification of this inflation equation, as well as concerning the manner in which it has been estimated, the evidence very strongly indicates that the coefficient a is less than unity—a stepwise increase in the rate of monetary expansion results in an *initial* increase in the rate of inflation that is smaller than the increase in monetary expansion. This finding is also highly consistent with casual observation; we do not observe slavish obedience of the rate of inflation to the rate of monetary expansion in the short run. This is the basis for the above argument that real and nominal cash balances tend to move together in the short run. Thus we assume:

$$\Delta \pi = a \Delta \lambda, \qquad 0 < a < 1. \tag{5}$$

We next develop the relationship between money, reserves, and credit. If we neglect the capital account and nondeposit liabilities of the consolidated banking system and assume that the exchange rate has never been altered, it is readily established that

$$M = C + ER, \tag{6}$$

where C is domestic plus nonreserve foreign assets of the banking system,
E is the price of foreign exchange, and
R is the volume of reserve assets.

Differentiating (6) with respect to time, we have

$$\lambda m = \frac{C}{P} \lambda_c + \frac{E}{P} \dot{R},$$

or alternatively,

$$(\Delta \lambda) m = \frac{C}{P} \Delta \lambda_c + \frac{E}{P} \Delta \dot{R}, \tag{7}$$

where λ_c is the rate of increase in aggregate domestic credit, $\dot{C}/C$. Combining equations (4), (5), and (7), we obtain an equation for the current account deficit as a function of rates of domestic credit creation, changes in reserves, and the change in the real rate of interest:

$$\frac{\Delta D}{P} = \frac{f_1 \Delta \dot{C}_g}{P} + f_2 \Delta r - a \left(\frac{\Delta \dot{C}}{P} + \frac{E}{P} \Delta \dot{R} \right). \tag{8}$$

The system is closed by the identity relating the capital account, the current account, and changes in reserves:

$$E\dot{R} \equiv K - D, \tag{9}$$

where K is the normal capital inflow denominated in domestic currency. This identity states merely that any current account deficit not covered by the capital inflow must be met by a change in reserves. The capital inflow is determined by the excess demand for funds, which from a national-income-accounting point of view can be viewed as the excess of domestic investment over domestic saving plus credit creation for the private sector, $\dot{C}_P$, all of which is assumed to originate in commercial banks. By once again invoking the small-country assumption and recognizing that spending on consumption and investment is a function of the real rate of interest, we can write the following equation for K:

$$K = K(r) - \dot{C}_P, \qquad K' = Pf_2;$$

and therefore

$$\Delta K = Pf_2 \Delta r - \Delta \dot{C}_P. \tag{10}$$

In view of our assumed private-sector indifference between tax and bond finance, the validity of equation (10) is independent of the option chosen by the government for disposition of that increment to public sector credit, $\Delta \dot{C}_g$. Obviously the allocation of that increment between spending on goods or tax reduction has no effect on the domestic capital market, but one might argue that debt retirement will discourage the capital inflow, as the government is intervening in the capital market on the side of savers. But this is not the case because bond retirement adds directly to the wealth of the private sector; hence, such an intervention will reduce private saving by precisely the amount of the intervention, leaving unchanged the excess demand for capital to be filled by foreign investment.

A second equation for $(\Delta D)/P$ is obtained by combining equation (10) with the differenced form of (9).

$$\frac{\Delta D}{P} = f_2 \Delta r - \frac{\Delta \dot{C}_P}{P} - \frac{E}{P} \Delta \dot{R}. \tag{11}$$

Solving out ΔD by combining equations (8) and (11), we arrive at the impact effect on the balance of payments of a change in domestic credit expansion.

$$E(\Delta \dot{R}) = - \frac{(\Delta \dot{C})[(1-\gamma) + f_1 - a]}{1-a} , \tag{12}$$

where the coefficient γ is the fraction of the increased credit expansion that is captured by the public sector (and extended by the central bank):

$$\Delta \dot{C}_g = \gamma(\Delta \dot{C}), \qquad 0 \leq \gamma \leq 1.$$

Clearly the source (and allocation) of the credit makes a difference.[6] If all new credit comes from the central bank and goes to the public sector, equation (12) becomes:

$$E(\Delta \dot{R}) = - \frac{(\Delta \dot{C})(f_1 - a)}{1-a} , \tag{13}$$

which is negative and less than unity on the condition that f_1, the marginal propensity to spend, is less than unity but greater than a.[7] Alternatively, if all new credit originated in commercial banks and were captured by the private sector, equation (12) becomes:

$$E(\Delta \dot{R}) = - \Delta \dot{C}. \tag{14}$$

---

6. Both the source and the allocation of the credit are relevant. Only central bank credit increases outside money, and only if that credit goes to the public sector is there clearly an immediate increase in spending.

7. We expect that f_1 is greater than a for the following reason. Ignoring changes in the real rate of interest, the change in expenditure on goods associated with a change in monetary expansion is:

$$f_1 dq - m(d\pi) = f_1(d\lambda)m - ma(d\lambda) = m(d\lambda)(f_1 - a).$$

As we expect an increase in the rate of monetary expansion to increase total expenditure on goods, it follows that f_1 exceeds a. While this argument holds strictly only in a closed economy ($M = \dot{C}$), we expect that a will be even smaller in an open economy, where prices for traded goods are fixed externally.

The interpretation of (14) is simple; if commercial banks find themselves able to lend more to the private sector but do so under the same terms (the nominal rate of interest is unchanged), that lending simply displaces funds that were previously coming from abroad. Total borrowing is unaffected, and hence total spending is unchanged. Reserves decline in response to the reduced capital inflow so as to maintain the rate of change of the money supply at its previous level. We see a worsening of the balance of payments but no other effects.

The three terms in the bracketed portion of equation (12) reflect three distinct effects on the balance of payments associated with a change in the rate of domestic credit expansion. The first term, $1-\gamma$, is the substitution, or displacement, effect described in the immediately preceding paragraph: to the extent that part of the credit expansion is from commercial banks and is destined for the private sector, the capital inflow is directly reduced and reserves fall accordingly. The second term, γf_1, is an income-expenditure effect; as the coefficient γ indicates the increase in private-sector income per dollar of change in the rate of credit expansion, and f_1 tells us the response of the expenditure to that change in income. The increased expenditure, of course, worsens the balance of payments through the current account. The final term, $-a$, is the inflation effect. Increased expenditure increases the rate of domestic inflation, which in turn erodes the very increase in income that provoked the increase in expenditure. Equation (12) clearly indicates that the magnitude of the net effect of credit creation depends upon both *sources* and *uses* of new credit; this is an important point not previously recognized in the monetary approach to the balance of payments.

Equations similar to (12) can be obtained for the other endogenous variables in the system; in the interest of brevity, we present only the one for the money supply:

$$\Delta \dot{M} = (\Delta \dot{C})\gamma\left(\frac{1-f_1}{1-a}\right).$$

This equation suggests a distinction between ex ante and ex post changes in the money supply; the term $\Delta\dot{M}$ is obviously the ex post change, and $\Delta\dot{C}$ is the ex ante change in the rate of change of the money supply. Only by accident will these two changes be identical; so trying to estimate the effect of credit policy on the balance of payments by using the quantity of money (or the rate of change therein) as the exogenous variable will clearly lead to a result that is highly biased. This can be seen by combining the above result with equation (12).

$$E(\Delta\dot{R}) = -(\Delta\dot{M})\left(\frac{1 - a}{\gamma(1 - f_1)} - 1\right). \tag{12'}$$

Comparing equations (12) and (12') reveals that the coefficient of money is likely to be several orders of magnitudes larger (in absolute value) than that of credit in a balance-of-payments equation.[8]

THE CASE OF FLOATING RATES

The major modifications on the preceding model required to handle the case of floating exchange rates are twofold: first, changes in the money supply are now governed by changes in credit alone; and second, we can no longer assume that the nominal rates of interest are equal in all markets, but rather they will differ systematically by the rate of change of exchange rates. While the central bank may continue to hold reserves as partial backing for the money supply, those reserves will not change in response to balance-of-payments disequilibrium, as the central bank is no longer committed to maintaining a fixed exchange rate. The private sector now assumes the function of the speculator, and changes in reserves attributed to the balance of payments will affect private rather than official holdings of foreign currency. Balance-of-payments disequilibria can exist under floating as well as fixed exchange rates, but in the former case the private sector rather than the central bank provides and absorbs the liquidity.

---

8. One monetary effect has been ignored in the preceding analysis. Although it seems reasonable to assume that monetary and credit policy cannot produce stepwise change in the *level* of real output, those policies presumably can introduce such changes in the rate of change of real output, which in turn will induce a flow demand (positve or negative) for real cash balances. Thus the term a in the bracketed part of equation (12) probably understates the monetary effect.

The fact that nominal interest rates in the various markets can differ under a system of floating exchange rates means that we can no longer assume constancy of the nominal interest rate in the face of monetary disturbances. The stock demand for money must therefore be dealt with directly. To maintain simplicity in the analysis, we will continue to assume that the demand for money depends upon the nominal rate of interest (as opposed to the expected rate of inflation) and that arbitrage causes differentials in nominal interest rates to be exactly equal to the rate of change in the exchange rate. The flow demand for money will be written as:

$$\frac{\Delta(\dot{M})^d}{P} = m\Delta\pi + \frac{\alpha\Delta M^d}{M} = m\Delta\pi - \alpha\beta\Delta i, \qquad \alpha > 0,\ \beta > 0; \qquad (15)$$

where M^d is the stock demand for nominal cash balances,

i is the nominal rate of interest,

α is a coefficient relating stock disequilibrium to flow demand, and

β is the semi-elasticity of demand for real cash balances with respect to the nominal interest rate.

The relationship between nominal interest rates is given by the interest-exchange rate parity theorem:

$$i = \frac{\dot{E}}{E} + i^*, \qquad (16)$$

where i^* is the foreign rate of interest which will be taken as fixed; hence

$$\Delta i = \frac{\Delta\dot{E}}{E}. \qquad (17)$$

Substituting equation (17) into (15) and the resulting equation into the differenced form of equation (3), we obtain the current account deficit equation.

$$\frac{\Delta D}{P} = \frac{(f_1\gamma - a)\Delta\dot{C}}{P} + f_2\Delta r + \frac{\alpha\beta\Delta\dot{E}}{E}, \qquad (18)$$

which corresponds to equation (8) in the fixed-exchange-rate case. As capital flows continue to be governed by the real rate of interest plus domestic private-sector credit creation, equation (10) remains unchanged.

$$\Delta K = Pf_2\Delta r - \Delta\dot{C}_p. \qquad (10)$$

To discuss the dynamics of exchange rate movements, an additional equation is needed. For current purposes, we will use an adjustment function of a Marshallian nature, in which the rate of change of the exchange rate is affected by the excess flow demand for foreign exchange.

$$\frac{\dot{E}}{E} = \left(\frac{\dot{E}}{E}\right)^{e} + \delta\left(\frac{D}{P} - \frac{K}{P}\right), \qquad \delta > 0. \tag{19}$$

The term $(\dot{E}/E)^{e}$ is the expected rate of change in the exchange rate based upon prior information; this will be the actual rate of change if it in fact produces balance-of-payments equilibrium. By substitution of equations (10) and (18) into (19), we obtain the behavior of the exchange rates.

$$\frac{P(\Delta\dot{E})}{E} = \frac{\delta(\Delta\dot{C})[(1-\gamma)+\gamma f_1 - a]}{1-\alpha\beta\delta}. \tag{20}$$

By substituting equation (20) into (9), we obtain the behavior of the balance of payments.

$$E(\Delta\dot{R}) = -\frac{\Delta\dot{C}\,[(1-\gamma)+\gamma f_1 - a]}{1-\alpha\beta\delta}. \tag{21}$$

The implications of equations (20) and (21) are as expected. An increase in the rate of expansion of domestic credit exerts *immediate* upward pressure on the exchange rate and *immediately* leads to a deterioration in the balance of payments. In addition, the three terms in the bracketed portions of equations (20) and (21) have the same interpretation as in the case of fixed rates. This is true despite the fact that the mechanism of adjustment is somewhat different.

An interesting question at this point concerns equation (21) versus (12)—the difference in the behavior of the balance of payments in going from floating to fixed rates. The two equations differ only in terms of the denominator, which is $1 - a$ with fixed rates and $1 - \alpha\beta\delta$ with floating rates. Obviously, stability requires that both terms be positive, but little more can be established on strictly a priori grounds. There is reason to believe, however, that the balance of payments will be more volatile under a system of floating rates than would be the case if rates were fixed; that is,

$\alpha\beta\delta > \alpha$.[9] This statement will sound counterintuitive to advocates of floating rates, some of whom can be expected to argue that movements in the rates themselves will discourage capital movements and hence add stability to the balance of payments. In fact, the opposite is the case, as a rising exchange rate signals a "shortage" of foreign exchange, but the increase in the exchange rate itself tends to draw capital out of the country.

The reason floating rates may well lead to more variation in the balance of payments than do fixed rates is quite simple. With fixed rates, there is a strong tendency for movements in the nominal interest rate to be confined to a small range around the rates of other countires (our assumption being that this range is zero); so changes in the quantity of money induced by changes in domestic credit do not significantly affect the demand for money through changes in the nominal rate of interest. Thus, fixed rates prevent a situation in which credit expansion increases nominal interest rates (by stimulating the rate of inflation), which in turn reduces the demand for real cash balances at the same time that the nominal supply is expanding at an increased rate. But this is precisely the situation that can develop under floating rates; a credit expansion causes the exchange rate to begin to rise, which implies that domestic interest rates must also rise relative to external rates, causing the movement out of money described in equation (15) above. That flight from money clearly exacerbates the already adverse movement in the balance of payments. An interesting conclusion to be drawn from this argument is that the monetary approach to the balance of payments is even more relevant to a world of floating rates than to one of fixed rates.

---

9. While it may sound queer to some to even discuss the balance of payments in a context of floating rates, much less the volatility thereof, it is clear that there is nothing about floating rates that guarantees that capital and current account will always compensate one another. Floating rates eliminate the possibility of a balance of payments *problem*, but at the cost of potential rate fluctuations.

SUMMARY

Under fixed exchange rates, a change in credit policy will have *immediate* effects upon the balance of payments, but the nature and magnitude of those effects depends upon the sources and uses of the credit. To the extent that commercial bank credit is a substitute for foreign credit (a capital inflow), an increase (decrease) in the rate of flow of that credit will generate an immediate worsening (improvement) of the capital account of the balance of payments and a loss (gain) of reserves. It is precisely this loss of reserves that sterilizes the flow of money created by the increment to the rate of credit creation. This effect will be present whether or not there was an excess supply of money prior to the change in credit policy.

A flow of credit to the public sector from the central bank simultaneously generates income and creates money. An increase in that flow, then, provokes an increase in spending and hence an immediate worsening of the current account; as there is no immediate improvement in the capital account, the balance of payments worsens. In this case, the reserve loss in the short run depends upon the marginal propensity to spend; if that propensity is less than unity, not all of the money creation will be sterilized by the current account deficit, and a further worsening of the balance of payments will occur over time in order to resolve potential stock disequilibrium in the money market. The only mechanism that can prevent the short-run effects of this sort of credit creation is a rapid response of the rate of inflation to the increase in spending, as such a response would "tax" away the income generated by the change in credit policy with respect to the public sector.

The analysis of the floating-rate case is less satisfactory because ad hoc assumptions were introduced with respect to the rate of resolution of monetary disequilibrium and the dynamics of the foreign exchange market. The results, however, were completely consistent with those obtained in the fixed-rate case. Credit creation causes the exchange rate to begin rising immediately and also causes immediate deterioration in the balance of payments. In this context, however, monetary factors play a more important role in the short run; indeed, monetary policy and the monetary approach in general is much more vital in the case of floating rates.

THE HYPOTHESIS OF OFFSETTING CAPITAL FLOWS

A Case Study of Germany*

Pentti J. K. Kouri**

International Monetary Fund, Washington, D.C.

"Imported inflation" and "offsetting capital flows" are two terms that have often been used to characterize the problem of monetary policy in the surplus countries of Europe during the period of fixed exchange rates.[1] The first proposition holds that the persistent deficits in the U.S. balance of payments in the past 15 years or so have been the main cause of world inflation. The deficits and changes in them have increased aggregate demand directly through the multiplier effects and directly through the effects of payments surpluses on the money supply. The second proposition holds that, because of highly integrated international capital markets, any independent tightening of monetary policy in European countries produces capital inflows that effectively offset the restrictive effect of the initial policy measures. If the central bank attempts to sterilize the liquidity effect of capital inflows, this will only serve to induce further inflows and eventually prompt speculative capital flows of unmanageable magnitude. The European countries—or any other non-reserve-currency-country—cannot

---

* Reprinted, with some changes, by permission of the author and North-Holland Publishing Co. from the JOURNAL OF MONETARY ECONOMICS 1 (1975): 21-39. An earlier version of the paper was presented at the 1973 Konstanz Seminar, and a German version appeared in KREDIT UND KAPITAL 8 (1975): 1-30.

** Economist, Research Department of International Monetary Fund. I wish to thank participants in the Konstanz Seminar, and David Walker, John Williamson, and Michael Porter for helpful comments. Mr. Fernando Santos of the International Monetary Fund provided valuable computational assistance. This paper represents the views of the author and not necessarily those of the International Monetary Fund.

1. The literature on this subject includes Baffi (1968); Goldstein (1972); Haberler (1972); Katz (1969); Logue (1969); Michaely (1970); Scott and Schmidt (1964). The view of the Bundesbank is explained in the Deutsche Bundesbank (1971, pp. 21-23).

pursue independent monetary policy with free capital movements and fixed exchange rates (while the United States can) because of the role of the U.S. dollar as a reserve currency. The fact that the U.S. dollar was a reserve currency in the system that existed until August 1971 ensured an automatic sterilization of the effects of private capital flows on the U.S. monetary base (and hence on the interest rate, if that was the target of monetary control). To the extent that central banks converted their dollar assets into primary reserves, the Federal Reserve System could easily offset the liquidity effect of these operations by adjusting the domestic component of the monetary base.[2]

The problem was made even more difficult for the main surplus countries—namely, Germany, Japan, and Italy—by the fact that countercyclical policy until very recently relied almost solely on monetary policy. In consequence, the central banks of these countries were often caught in the famous dilemma of a balance-of-payments surplus with domestic excess demand. This was, for instance, the case in Germany in the two periods of monetary contraction in 1959/60 and 1969/70 that culminated in revaluation of the Deutsche mark.[3]

This paper develops a framework for testing some of the hypotheses implied by this interpretation of the functioning of the Bretton Woods system. In particular, the relationship between monetary policy and capital flows in Germany in the period 1960:I-1972:II is examined. The theoretical basis of the empirical work is developed in section 1. The empirical results are presented in section 2, and the implications of the analysis are discussed in section 3.[4]

---

2. Discussions of the special role of the United States as a reserve currency country are given in McKinnon (1974) and Cooper (1974). A theoretical analysis of the operation of the world monetary system under alternative policy regimes is given in Girton and Henderson (1973).

3. A useful analysis of the experience of Italy, Japan, and Germany in the period 1960-72 is given in Thygesen (1973).

4. The pioneering study of "offsetting capital flows" in the case of Germany is Porter (1972). Willms (1971) approaches the problem from a different angle. A critical discussion of his approach is given in Porter (1972). This paper extends the work of Porter (1972) and Kouri and Porter (1974). For an alternative approach to explaining German capital flows, see Branson and Hill (1971).

1. DEVELOPMENT OF THE HYPOTHESIS

1.1. The Monetary Approach to the Balance of Payments

The theoretical basis of the above argument can be found in the monetary theory of the balance of payments developed by Mundell (1968, 1971), Johnson (1971, 1973), Dornbusch (1973*a*, *b*), and others. In the extreme version, the monetary model assumes a small country facing exogenously given prices and interest rates in the world goods and credit markets. In this situation, any domestic excess demand for goods or credit is eliminated by international flows of goods and securities rather than through domestic price or interest-rate adjustments. As a result, monetary policy becomes ineffective for the purposes of domestic stabilization: its only effect is to change the composition of central-bank assets between international reserves and domestic assets. If no country sterilizes the liquidity effect of payments deficits or surpluses, the effect of monetary policy of any country on the world interest rate depends on its relative size. If one country sterilizes, for whatever reason, it can in principle determine the world interest rate. If more than one country attempts to pursue independent monetary policy, the international monetary system becomes unstable. In particular, the role of the reserve currency country is to determine the world interest rate in the short run and the world inflation rate in the long run as long as fixed exchange rates are maintained. Given the world interest-rate level and prices, there is a given demand for money in the remaining countries. If this demand is not met by domestic credit creation, it will be met by surpluses (deficits) in the balance of payments.

There are very few empirical studies that test the various hypotheses implied by the above paradigm of the operation of the world monetary system. It is, however, clear from even superficial inspection of the data that it is not an accurate or sufficient description of the monetary system that prevailed until very recently. First, countries have had divergent inflation rates for sustained periods of time despite fixed exchange rates. An explanation for this is the existence of nontraded goods, as is shown in several papers, including those of Dornbusch (1973*b*), Krueger (1974) and Parkin (1974). Second, the theoretical models that appear in the literature all assume fully employed economies with flexible prices. Thus the theory of inflation that is implied is at best a long-run theory of inflation. It would seem clear that changes in unemployment can generate—at least temporarily—changes in wage and price inflation quite independently from what is happening in the other countries. If all of this is granted, the process through which inflation rates are equalized becomes of great importance. If one assumes no capital flows, as in Parkin (1974), there is a direct link between domestic inflation, the current account, and the money supply; and a specie-flow mechanism of a kind is in operation—of course, assuming no sterilization. If one assumes perfect capital mobility, however, there is no direct link between the current account and the money supply, since capital flows completely offset the liquidity effect of the current account—as is shown, for instance, in Kouri and Porter (1974). Brunner (1973, 1974) argues that completely offsetting capital flows and imported inflation are incompatible, since with offsetting capital flows the current account has no effect on the money supply. Clearly, the conventional view of the nature of imported inflation has to be altered with high capital mobility. The central proposition that with fixed exchange rates the inflation rates must be the same in the long run (allowing for index-number problems arising from changes in relative prices) still holds, but the adjustment process is no longer the same. The current account no longer has a liquidity effect, but it does have a wealth effect. In addition, as long as inflation rates are different among countries, the relative prices change continuously and, with that, the current account changes continuously. Changes in the current account have, of course, Keynesian multiplier effects on aggregate demand and thereby on the domestic rate of inflation. In addition to these two channels of "imported inflation" there is the direct effect of the costs of imported raw materials. Also, to the extent that internationally traded goods are close substitutes, one would expect their prices to be equalized quite fast.

What is the connection, then, between "imported inflation" and "offsetting capital flows"? The answer is twofold. On the one hand, capital flows accommodate inflation whether it is imported or domestic in origin. An increase in the domestic inflation rate will increase the demand for money. If this is not met by domestic credit creation, it will be met by capital inflows. Thus, domestic monetary policy is frustrated in its attempts to control inflation. On the other hand, inflation may be imported through the international capital market. An expansionary monetary policy in the reserve currency country will lower interest rates throughout the world. This increases aggregate demand, which is again accommodated by an increase in the money supply.

Finally, one should mention the role of the speculative capital flows. Suppose that the reserve currency country increases its rate of inflation. Its current account will move into a deficit. If the other countries attempt to maintain lower inflation rates, it will soon become obvious to speculators that this conflict can be resolved only by an adjustment in the exchange rate. As a result, capital will flow to the surplus countries, resulting in a lowering of the interest rate and an increase in the money supply. It is probably the speedy response of speculators that is the most effective equalizer of inflation rates as long as fixed exchange rates are adhered to.

1.2 Derivation of the Capital-Flow Equation

The central questions that emerge from the above discussion are: To what extent do capital flows offset measures of monetary policy? To what extent is it true that current account fluctuations are financed by private capital flows? What are the effects of changes in the world interest rate? To what extent do capital flows accommodate cyclical and secular movements in income? How much of capital flows is due to speculation? The remaining part of the paper will provide evidence on these questions for the Federal Republic of Germany in the period 1960-72. An answer to these questions will also give some idea of the feasibility of independent monetary policy by means of sterilization policies in an open economy that permits freedom of capital movement with fixed exchange rates.

The model that is used as a basis of the empirical analysis is developed and tested for Australia, Germany, Italy, and the Netherlands in Kouri and Porter (1974). The results presented here on Germany are more detailed than those presented in that paper. The derivation of the model is not presented here, but it is helpful to consider the limiting case of perfect capital mobility.

When domestic and foreign bonds are perfect substitutes, their interest rates can differ only by the cost of forward cover, abstracting from transactions costs. Taking the foreign interest rate, R^*, as exogenous, the domestic interest rate, R, is given by

$$R = R^* + \text{FP}, \tag{1}$$

where FP is the forward premium. The forward premium in turn is determined by the expected change in the exchange rate E, adjusted for risk, V:

$$\text{FP} = E + V. \tag{2}$$

Given the domestic interest rate and nominal income, Y, the demand for money, M^d, is determined. Without any loss of generality we can simplify the analysis and abstract from the banking system. The supply of money, M^s, is then equal to the sum of the central bank's net foreign and domestic assets, NFA and NDA. In equilibrium we have

$$M^d = L(Y, R) = M^s = \text{NFA} + \text{NDA}. \tag{3}$$

The foreign component of the base changes as a result of central-bank intervention in the foreign exchange market in support of the exchange rate. Thus

$$\Delta\,\text{NFA} = \text{TC} + \text{CAB}, \tag{4}$$

where TC is the net inflow of capital and CAB the current account balance.

In the short run we can take Y and CAB as given, while ΔNDA is determined by monetary policy. Thus the only variable that is left to equilibrate the financial markets is the net magnitude of capital flows, TC. Solving for TC we obtain:

$$\text{TC} = L_Y \Delta Y + L_R \Delta R^* + L_R \Delta E + L_R \Delta V - \Delta\text{NDA} - \text{CAB}. \tag{5}$$

This simply says that the magnitude of capital flows is equal to the excess flow demand for money. The sum of the first five terms is the stock-adjustment component of capital flows, while CAB is the flow component. To see why this is so, note that CAB is equal to the excess of domestic saving ("flow demand for wealth") over investment ("flow supply" of securities). With perfect capital mobility, the excess of new supply of securities over domestic acquisition of new securities is absorbed by the world capital market at a fixed rate of interest.

As such, equation (5) is of little use, since it assumes everything that we want to test. Its usefulness comes from the fact that in the general case the reduced-form capital-flow equation is of exactly the same form except for some additional variables. Furthermore, the reduced-form equation of the general case reduces to equation (5) as the degree of capital mobility becomes very high. In the general case, the reduced-form capital-flow equation is of the form[5]

$$\begin{aligned} TC = a_0 + a_1 \Delta W + a_2 \Delta Y + a_3 \Delta R^* + a_4 \Delta E + a_5 \Delta V \\ + a_6 \Delta NDA + a_7 \Delta W^* + a_8 \Delta Y^* + a_9 CAB + u, \end{aligned} \tag{6}$$

where ΔW is the change in the domestic stock of wealth,

ΔW^* is the change in the foreign stock of wealth, and

ΔY^* is the change in foreign income.

The foreign wealth and income variables enter the capital-flow equation because they affect foreign demand for domestic securities. The domestic wealth enters the equation because it affects domestic demand for securities. If the demand for money is a function of wealth, it would also have to be included in equation (5). With less than perfect capital mobility, the interest rate is no longer determined by equation (1). It adjusts to clear the demand for and supply of domestic securities. Thus, in the reduced form it is a function of the same variables as TC:

$$\begin{aligned} \Delta R = b_0 + b_1 \Delta W + b_2 \Delta Y + b_3 \Delta R^* + b_4 \Delta E + b_5 \Delta V \\ + b_6 \Delta NDA + b_7 \Delta W^* + b_8 \Delta Y^* + b_9 CAB + v. \end{aligned} \tag{7}$$

It should be noted that this derivation assumes, unrealistically, that domestic securities can be aggregated into a single security. Thus equation (7) determines the short-term (three-month) interest rate. The other interest rates are then determined by risk differentials and term-structure equations. To the extent that domestic markets are segmented, equation (7) is inadequate in explaining movements of the interest rate, since it explains a particular interest rate in terms of aggregate variables rather than variables pertaining to that particular market. Equation (6) is not similarly affected. Both left- and right-hand variables are aggregate quantities.

---

5. See Kouri and Porter (1974).

The degree of capital-market integration is measured by the offset coefficients a_6 and a_9. When capital mobility is infinite, the two coefficients are equal to minus one; when it is zero, they are also equal to zero. They should also be equal to each other. Also, coefficients a_7 and a_8 and possibly a_1 should also approach zero as capital mobility becomes very high. The same information is conveyed by the coefficients in the interest-rate equation. The b_3 coefficient varies between zero and one. In the limiting case it is equal to one, while b_1, b_6, b_7, b_8, and b_9 are equal to zero.

The a_3 coefficient on ΔR^* in equation (6) measures the effect of a 1 percent change in the world interest rate on the capital account when the domestic interest rate is allowed to adjust completely. A rough measure of the effect of a 1 percent change in the foreign interest rate on the capital account when the central bank maintains the domestic rate fixed by sterilization policies is given by $a_3/(1 + a_6)$. This is, in principle, an exact measure if the foreign interest rate does not enter the money-demand function.

In summary, the economic rationale for equations (6) and (7) is the following: In the short-run, equilibrium in the financial markets of an open economy with a fixed exchange rate is obtained through adjustments in the domestic interest rate and through capital inflows and outflows. With high capital mobility and an exogenous world interest rate, the adjustment takes place largely through the latter channel.

1.3 Estimation Problems

Equations (6) and (7) are the basis of the empirical results reported in the following sections. They were estimated in various forms by ordinary least squares on quarterly data for the period 1960:I-1972:II. While the reduced-form approach avoids the serious problem of simultaneity that occurs when capital flows are explained by interest-rate changes, it introduces new difficulties. First, there is a problem with sterilization policies. To the extent that ΔNDA is adjusted to offset the liquidity effect of payments surpluses or deficits, the estimates of equation (6) will be biased. The correct solution to this problem is a simultaneous model, which incorporates policy responses. An attempt along these lines is made by Argy and Kouri (1974), whose results were on the whole rather inconclusive. The main difficulty with this approach is in modeling central-bank behavior in any simple way. It is quite clear from reading the relevant history of central-bank policy that discretionary changes in policy tend to dominate regular response patterns. If this is so, the ordinary-least-squares estimates of equation (6) are not likely to be seriously biased. Second, there is a problem with the treatment of exchange-rate expectations. During the period of analysis there were substantial changes both in exchange-rate expectations and in exchange-rate risk. Two approaches are tried in this paper. In the first set of results, the speculative component of capital flows is captured by dummy variables introduced on the basis of a priori knowledge of speculative activity. In the subsequent results, the change in the forward premium is also introduced as an explanatory variable. This makes a difference in the results. Again, a potential problem with simultaneity is introduced. It should not be too serious a problem as long as the behavior of the forward premium is dominated by changes in expectations not directly induced by current capital flows. Third, there is the problem of what is the proper measure of monetary policy. The way the problem is taken care of in this paper is to try alternative specifications. On the whole the results are satisfactory. Fourth, there is a very difficult problem with adjustment lags. The model so far has been described as an equilibrium model because that is how it was estimated. There is no question that adjustment lags are important, but it proved to be impossible to detect them at this level of aggregation. It may be that short-term portfolios, which dominate the movement of the capital account, indeed adjust very quickly, but that remains a conjecture. Finally, one should remember not to expect too much from reduced-form aggregative analysis. For the purposes of this study, the reduced-form equation answers most of the interesting questions. There are many other interesting questions—such as the effects of capital controls, taxes on foreign investments, different effects of central-bank operations in the short-term and long-term, or equity, markets—which require structural models to be satisfactorily analyzed.

2. EMPIRICAL ANALYSIS

2.1 Explanatory Variables in the Capital-Flow Equation

The data on most variables appearing in the reduced-form equations (6) and (7) are readily available, with the exception of the wealth data, ΔW and

ΔW^*, and the foreign income series, ΔY^*. Since ΔW, and ΔW^* and ΔY^*, affect capital flows in opposite directions and since their variances relative to the variances of the other explanatory variables are likely to be small, the results should not be much affected by their exclusion. All the data are quarterly and seasonally nonadjusted for the period 1960:I-1972:II. A description of data sources is given in the Appendix.

A first approximation is made by taking the change in the Bundesbank's net domestic assets and the change in required reserves as the measures of monetary policy. The latter variable, ΔRR, is computed according to the formula

$$\Delta \mathrm{RR} = (r - r_{-1})L_{-1},$$

where ΔRR is the change in average required reserves,

r is the average reserve requirements ratio, and

L is the total bank liabilities subject to reserve requirements.

The difference of ΔNDA and ΔRR is equal to the domestic component of the extended monetary base.

The current account balance enters the capital-flow equation for the same reason as the change in the Bundesbank's net domestic assets, namely, because it is an autonomous source of change in the monetary base. For this reason, official capital flows are also added to the current account.

The world interest rate is taken to be the three-month Eurodollar rate. The coefficient on the Eurodollar rate does not measure the interest sensitivity of capital flows in the usual sense (i.e., assuming that the domestic rate is held constant). In the limiting case it measures the interest sensitivity of the demand for money; in the nonlimiting case it is a composite coefficient that measures the effect of a change in the Eurodollar rate on the capital account when the domestic component of the monetary base, rather than the domestic interest rate, is held fixed.

The expectations variable, ΔE, is approximated by a set of dummies designed to capture the pronounced capital inflows and outflows during a number of speculative episodes in the period 1960:I-1972:II. The dummy variables that are included on a priori grounds are:

D_1 = +1 in 1961:I,
= -1 in 1961:II.

D_2 = +1 in 1968:IV,
= -1 in 1969:I.

D_3 = +1 in 1969:III,
= -1 in 1969:IV.

D_4 = +1 in 1971:I,
= 0 in 1971:II,
= +1 in 1971:III,
= +1 in 1971:IV.

D_5 = +1 in 1972:II.

The first dummy captures the speculative inflow and subsequent outflow surrounding the revaluation of the Deutsche mark in March 1961. The second dummy accounts for the speculative inflow in the fourth quarter of 1968, which was prompted by an expectation of a revaluation of the Deutsche mark. The third dummy captures the massive inflow and outflow surrounding the revaluation of the DM in October 1969. The fourth dummy captures the continuing capital inflow during the crisis year of 1971. It takes the value of one in the first, third, and fourth quarters. In the first quarter there was a substantial inflow preceding the floating of the DM in May 1971. From the time of the dollar devaluation in August until the Smithsonian Agreement in December, capital continued to flow in for speculative reasons, and the Bundesbank had to intervene in the foreign exchange market to prevent undue appreciation of the DM. The fifth dummy captures the massive inflow prompted by the sterling crisis in mid-1972.

The change in domestic income enters the capital-flow equation because changes in income generate changes in the demand for money. As shown above in the limiting case, the income coefficient should equal the inverse of the marginal velocity of (base) money. In the absence of seasonally nonadjusted national income series, the Mass Income Series computed by the Bundesbank is used. The change in domestic wealth enters the equation for the same reason. If one assumes that the demand for money is a function of income only and not of wealth, then this term would disappear.

The changes in foreign income and wealth enter the capital-flow equation because they affect the foreign holdings of domestic securities. In the limiting case these two variables disappear: only domestic portfolio preferences matter. We have to drop these variables for more pragmatic reasons, since no data are easily available on them. The only direct link between external monetary impulses and the domestic monetary base is then the world interest rate.

In addition to these variables, a seasonal dummy is included to capture the pronounced end-of-year inflow and subsequent outflow.

2.2 Empirical Results

The capital-flow equation was estimated in this form on a quarterly basis for the period 1960:I-1972:II. The results are reported in table 1. The explanatory power of the equation is quite satisfactory, and there is no evidence of first-order serial correlation. With the exception of the Eurodollar rate and the dummy for the third quarter of 1972, all variables are statistically significant and have the expected signs.

The offset coefficients on ΔNDA and ΔRR are 0.72 and 0.75, respectively, and they are not statistically different from each other. In the second equation they are combined as a composite measure of monetary policy. The estimate of the offset coefficient is now 0.73, with a standard error of 0.04. The offset coefficient on the autonomous component of the balance of payments is somewhat higher, but it is not statistically different from that on ΔNDA - ΔRR. The coefficient on income is highly significant, indicating that an increase in income of 100 million Deutsche marks (at a quarterly rate) generates capital inflows of some 49 million Deutsche marks. The coefficient on the Eurodollar rate has the right sign but is not statistically significant. Although the interest-rate coefficient does not measure the interest sensitivity of capital flows (that is measured by the offset coefficients), it should still be significant as long as the demand for money is interest-sensitive.

All the dummies with the exception of the dummy for the third quarter of 1972 are statistically significant. It should be noted that the coefficients on the dummies take into account the fact that speculative inflows will

Table 1

Estimates of Capital-Flow Equation (1) for Germany

Dependent variable	Constant	ΔY	ΔR^*	A	ΔNDA	ΔRR	ΔNDA + ΔRR	D_1	D_2	D_3	D_4	D_5	ΔS_4	$\bar{R}^2$	$\overline{SE}$	DW
(1) TCP	237.11	0.48	-358.75	-0.90	-0.72	-0.75		1781.72	1744.78	3799.34	3331.56	5691.69	1786.52	0.953	912.78	2.303
	(1.17)	(4.06)	(1.45)	(8.95)	(12.88)	(8.42)		(2.59)	(2.40)	(3.73)	(5.76)	(4.70)	(6.46)			
(2) TCP	230.43	0.49	-333.71	-0.91			-0.73	1793.32	1766.04	3719.57	3312.54	5648.36	1791.09	0.955	901.63	2.339
	(1.16)	(4.28)	(1.52)	(9.39)			(17.32)	(2.64)	(2.48)	(3.93)	(5.86)	(4.77)	(6.57)			
(3) STCP	239.57	0.49	-335.44	-0.93	-0.70	-0.75		1827.61	1697.23	3863.36	3216.84	5158.91	1739.95	0.923	899.22	2.295
	(1.20)	(4.12)	(1.39)	(10.29)	(10.83)	(8.64)		(2.69)	(2.29)	(3.81)	(5.41)	(3.77)	(5.93)			
(4) STCP	227.05	0.50	-290.92	-0.94			-0.72	1855.22	1751.79	3705.66	3206.63	5170.35	1759.26	0.925	889.82	2.363
	(1.17)	(4.31)	(1.34)	(11.05)			(15.00)	(2.77)	(2.42)	(3.96)	(5.46)	(3.82)	(6.14)			

NOTE: The sample period is 1960:I-1972:II. The figures in the parentheses are the t-statistics. $\bar{R}^2$ and $\overline{SE}$ are the multiple correlation coefficient and standard error, respectively, corrected for the degrees of freedom. DW is the Durbin-Watson statistic. The variables are defined as follows: TCP = total private capital flows; STCP = total short-term private capital flows; Y = nominal income; R^* = three-month Eurodollar rate; A = current account plus official capital flows; when STCP is the dependent variable it also includes long-term private capital flows; NDA = net domestic assets of the Central Bank; ΔRR = policy-induced change in minimum required reserves; D_1, D_2, D_3, D_4, D_5, are speculation dummies; S_4 = seasonal dummy which is equal to one in the fourth quarter. TCP, STCP, Y, NDA, A, and RR are measured in millions of Deutsche marks.

increase the monetary base and reduce interest rates, thereby inducing capital outflow, which partially offsets the initial effect of the speculative inflow on the balance of payments. The net effect of speculation appears to have been substantially less than the actual inflow (or outflow) that occurred in 1969 and in 1972. The reason for this is that the liquidity effect of the speculative inflows has been in most cases sterilized. This point is illustrated by the following example. Suppose that there is an autonomous capital inflow of X million Deutsche marks. Without sterilization, this inflow will generate offsetting outflow of αX million DMs, where α is the offset coefficient. The net effect on the balance of payments is thus $(1 - \alpha)X$. With complete sterilization, the net effect will be X. In the fourth quarter of 1969 $(1 - \alpha)X$ was, according to the estimate of the coefficient on ΔD_3, some 3.7 billion DMs. Since α is roughly 0.73, the value of X is approximately 13.7 billion DMs, which is much closer to the magnitude of the outflow that actually occurred.

The coefficients of the dummies for 1971 and 1972 suggest that the inflow of speculative capital during this period amounted to some 16 billion DMs. In contrast to the earlier speculative episodes, there does not appear to have been any outflow of these speculative balances during the period covered in the analysis.

Equations (1) and (2) report the same results when total short-term private capital inflow is taken as the dependent variable and the basic balance (including short-term official flows) is taken as the autonomous component of the balance of payments. The results are essentially the same as those for the total capital flows, which indicates that in the short run the adjustment takes place largely through short-term flows.

2.3 Inclusion of the Forward Premium

The only variable that was not significant in the results discussed above was the change in the Eurodollar rate. The probable reason for this is that the behavior of the forward premium has not been incorporated. Since it often moves in a direction that is opposite to that of the Eurodollar rate (in particular, during speculative episodes), its exclusion is likely to suppress the coefficient on the Eurodollar rate. Table 2 reports the results when the

Table 2

Estimates of Capital-Flow Equation (2) for Germany

Dependent variable	Constant	ΔY	ΔR^*	ΔFP	A	ΔNDA	ΔRR	$\Delta NDA + \Delta RR$	D_1	D_2	D_3	D_4	D_5	ΔS_4	$\bar{R}^2$	$\overline{SE}$	DW
(1) TCP	287.66	0.44	-586.74	-389.38	-0.93	-0.68	-0.75		1601.35	1494.61	-448.42	3132.23	5171.15	1653.11	0.959	851.74	2.105
	(1.51)	(3.93)	(2.37)	(2.58)	(9.84)	(12.37)	(9.03)		(2.48)	(2.18)	(0.24)	(5.75)	(4.50)	(6.28)			
(2) TCP	260.05	0.47	-505.89	-340.27	-0.94			-0.70	1651.52	1576.32		3103.33	5106.57	1671.52	0.961	835.04	2.229
	(1.43)	(4.50)	(2.36)	(4.95)	(10.63)			(17.34)	(2.62)	(2.38)		(5.87)	(4.59)	(6.51)			
(3) STCP	319.13	0.41	-589.37	-470.41	-1.07	-0.70	-0.76		1871.71	1753.21	-1622.92	3258.67	5617.77	1749.56	0.934	833.14	2.067
	(1.71)	(3.53)	(2.42)	(2.70)	(10.79)	(11.71)	(9.42)		(2.97)	(2.55)	(0.72)	(5.92)	(4.39)	(6.44)			
(4) STCP	270.92	0.45	-492.05	-340.08	-1.04			-0.71	1886.44	1788.53		3206.57	5405.27	1739.83	0.936	821.56	2.250
	(1.53)	(4.34)	(2.31)	(5.01)	(13.41)			(16.81)	(3.05)	(2.68)		(5.93)	(4.39)	(6.64)			

NOTE: FP is the end-of-period forward premium. For other definitions, see table 1.

change in the forward premium is included as an explanatory variable in the capital-flow equation. All the variables are now statistically significant. The offset coefficients are almost the same as previously. The coefficient on income is also of similar magnitude. The only difference is that the Eurodollar rate is now significant: an increase of 1 percent in the Eurodollar rate will generate capital outflows of 0.5 billion DMs after allowing for adjustment in the domestic interest rate. (The domestic component of the monetary base is held constant.)

The coefficient on the forward premium is also significant, although it is slightly smaller than that on the Eurodollar rate. The probable reason for this is that the simultaneity of ΔFP tends to bias the ordinary-least-squares estimate of the coefficient downward. All the dummies with the exception of that for 1969 are significant and of the same magnitude as in the previous results. The fit of the net capital-flow equation [eq. (2) in table 2] is illustrated in figure 1. In addition to the sample period, three quarters are forecast and the actual values shown.

2.4 Partitioning of the Domestic Assets

In Germany the amount of commercial-bank borrowing from the Bundesbank is endogenous as long as the banks are within their rediscount quotas. For this reason, the capital-flow equation was also estimated by subtracting advances and loans from the net domestic assets of the Bundesbank. As a new instrument of policy, the change in the discount rate is introduced. Changes in rediscount quotas, which have been at times quite significant, should also be included. Unfortunately, no published data are available on this series prior to 1969.

The results of the estimation of the capital-flow equation in this form are reported in table 3. All the variables are highly significant, with the exception of some of the dummies. The offset coefficient on the change in the adjusted NDA is 0.69, while that on ΔRR is 0.65. When the two are combined, an offset coefficient of 0.68 is obtained. The offset coefficient on the autonomous component of the balance of payments is again very high. The income coefficient is also significant and of similar magnitude as in the

Figure 1

Total private capital flows in Germany from 1960:I to 1973:I.
Source: Eq. (2) of table 2. The estimated values for 1972:III-1973:I are post-sample forecasts.

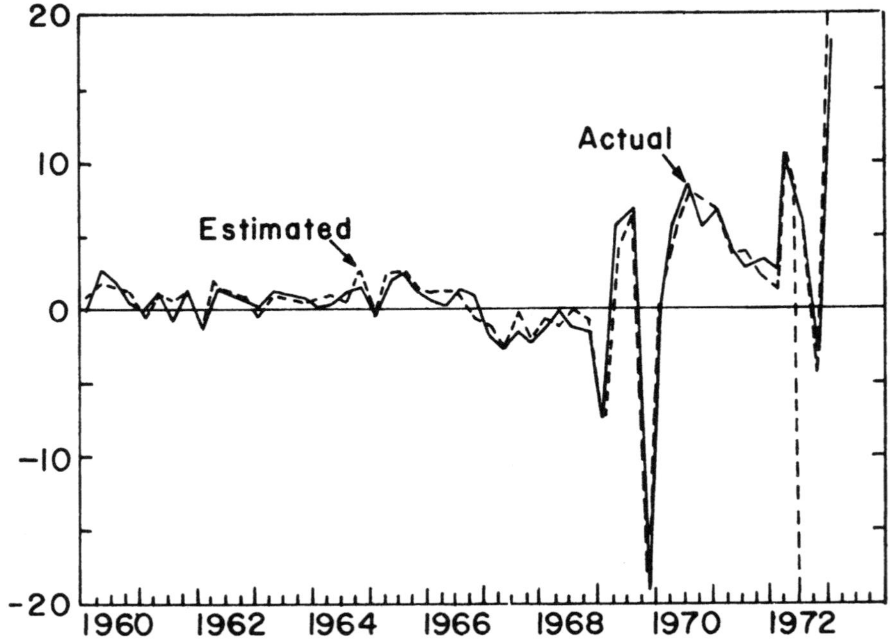

Table 3

Estimates of Capital-Flow Equation (3) for Germany

Dependent variable	Constant	ΔY	ΔR^*	ΔFP	A	ΔNDA*	ΔRR	ΔNDA* + ΔRR	ΔDISC	D_1	D_2	D_3	D_4	D_5	ΔS_4	$\bar{R}^2$	$\overline{SE}$	DW
(1) TCP	-29.16	0.50	-1598.77	-1253.68	-0.99	-0.69	-0.65		790.76	1582.58	1943.25	-6513.51	3127.00	5201.03	2183.57	0.9106	1263.51	2.0907
	(0.10)	(2.88)	(4.21)	(5.38)	(6.85)	(6.54)	(5.01)		(2.16)	(1.64)	(1.85)	(2.06)	(3.87)	(3.05)	(4.89)			
(2) TCP	-8.06	0.49	-1633.58	-1251.21	-0.98			-0.68	797.82	1554.75	1886.89	-6412.60	3142.80	5235.17	2151.54	0.9129	1247.17	2.0781
	(0.03)	(3.02)	(4.78)	(5.44)	(7.22)			(10.41)	(2.21)	(1.65)	(1.88)	(2.08)	(3.95)	(3.12)	(5.16)			
(3) STCP	22.15	0.55	-1627.79	-914.23	-0.61	-0.53	-0.69		1354.04	864.47	648.95	-2505.62	2592.03	2727.17	1803.45	0.8712	1165.37	2.2203
	(0.08)	(3.42)	(4.67)	(3.58)	(3.73)	(4.77)	(5.88)		(3.34)	(0.96)	(0.60)	(0.76)	(3.31)	(1.44)	(4.17)			
(4) STCP	-60.21	0.59	-1515.67	-959.67	-0.67			-0.61	1256.06	995.08	952.11	-3221.05	2626.40	2972.13	1943.44	0.8722	1161.01	2.2781
	(0.24)	(3.80)	(4.71)	(3.85)	(4.42)			(9.12)	(3.24)	(1.12)	(0.94)	(1.02)	(3.37)	(1.59)	(4.88)			

NOTE: NDA* is equal to NDA less Bundesbank claims on deposit money banks. For other definitions, see table 1.

previous results. The interesting aspect of the results is that the coefficients on the change in the Eurodollar rate and in the forward preimum are both significant and much higher than in the previous results— 1.6 and 1.3 billion Deutsche marks, respectively. This reflects the fact that if the discount rate is held constant while there is a change in the Eurodollar rate, the banks will adjust their borrowing from the Bundesbank and thus there is partial sterilization. In terms of the previous equation, the change in the Eurodollar rate is accompanied by a change in NDA. The change in the discount rate is also significant, indicating that an increase in the discount rate of 1 percent will generate capital inflows of some 0.8 billion Deutsche marks. It should be noted that the discount rate is also partly endogenous in that the Bundesbank has for most of the time adjusted the discount rate according to market developments.

2.5 Estimation of the Interest-Rate Equation

For the sake of comparison, the reduced-form interest-rate equation was also estimated for this period, with the change in the forward premium as one of the explanatory variables. The results are reported in table 4. In equation (1) the only variables that turned out significant are the change in the forward premium, the change in the Eurodollar rate, the dummy for the last two quarters of 1969, and the dummy capturing the pronounced end-of-year increase in short-term interest rates. The coefficient on the Eurodollar rate is 0.62 and that on the forward premium 0.45. The fact that these coefficients are less than one is consistent with the fact that the offset coefficients are less than one. It is, however, inconsistent with the fact that none of the other variables is statistically significant. Equation (3) reports the results when the change in the discount rate was included in the equation. The Eurodollar rate and the forward premium remain significant, but their coefficients are substantially less than the coefficient of 0.82 on the discount rate. This may reflect the fact that as long as the banks have unused rediscount quotas, the discount rate has a significant effect on the short-term money-market rate, while it also has a large effect on capital flows. Similarly, under these conditions a change in the Eurodollar rate has a relatively small effect on the domestic interest rate and a relatively large effect on capital flows.

Table 4

Estimates of the Interest-Rate Equation

Dependent variable	Constant	ΔR^*	ΔFP	ΔDISC	ΔY	A	A + LTCP	ΔNDA−ΔRR	ΔNDA*−ΔRR	ΔD_1	ΔD_2	ΔD_3	D_4	D_5	ΔS_4	$\bar{R}^2$	$\overline{SE}$	DW
(1) ΔMMR	-	0.62 (3.85)	0.45 (3.95)		+	-		+		+	+	5.78	+	+	0.74	0.562	0.653	1.83
(2) ΔMMR	+	0.56 (3.97)	0.37 (3.89)									5.47 (4.92)			0.88 (6.34)	0.577	0.642	1.91
(3) ΔMMR	+	0.29 (2.31)	0.24 (2.76)	0.82 (6.04)	+	-			+	+	+	2.93 (2.51)	+	+	0.93 (6.70)	0.771	0.473	2.24

NOTE: MMR is the three-month money-market rate. For other definitions, see table 1. Only the signs of the statistically insignificant coefficients are reported.

2.6 Summary of Results

The empirical results suggest that measures of monetary policy in Germany have, to a significant extent, been offset by capital inflows. The estimates of offset coefficients are, however, significantly less than one, which indicates that control of the monetary base is possible if the Bundesbank sterilizes the liquidity effect of the balance of payments. This policy, however, has a destabilizing effect on international reserves. The high offset coefficient on the current account indicates that private capital flows have, to a large extent, financed fluctuations of the current account. It also implies that the behavior of the overbalance of payments is dominated by the behavior of the capital flows.

3. IMPLICATIONS OF THE RESULTS

3.1 Behavior of the Balance of Payments

The results of the analysis confirm the view that the overall balance of payments behaves in a procyclical fashion. The reason for this is the cyclical behavior of the demand for money: the demand for money increases in a boom and decreases in a recession. Therefore, if the domestic component of the base is held constant, the overall balance of payments must be in surplus or deficit to accommodate the change in the demand for money. The same reasoning also explains why an increase in the rate of growth of income will, ceteris paribus, improve the balance of payments. Another conclusion that emerges from the analysis is that private capital flows finance, to a large extent, fluctuations in the current account in a country like Germany that is highly integrated into world credit markets. This implies that the need to intervene in the foreign exchange market--and hence the need for official reserve accumulation--does not arise so much from the need to finance trade imbalances as from the pursuit of independent monetary policy or from the need to offset disturbances of the capital account.

3.2 Effect of Speculative Disturbances

The results for Germany indicate that speculative capital flows have been very large at times. During some episodes--for instance, in 1961 and 1969--the speculative inflows were clearly related to expectations of a revaluation of the DM, which expectations in turn were induced at least partly by attempts to pursue independently tight monetary policy to cool off the booms of 1959/60 and 1968/69. In the latter period, the speculative inflows cannot so easily be traced to a disequilibrium in Germany. Rather, the inflows in 1971 and 1972 were related to the weakness of the dollar and, in 1972, of the U.K.-sterling. This illustrates how integrated capital markets rapidly transmit disturbances wherever they may originate.

Theoretically, an expectation of an exchange-rate adjustment should be reflected in the forward premiums and in international interest-rate differentials rather than in large movements of capital. However, if the expected exchange-rate change is even moderately large, the system breaks down for the reason that negative interest rates would be needed to eliminate speculative profit (for instance, prior to the October 1969 revaluation, the forward premium on the Deutsche mark was some 15 percent at an annual rate).

3.3 Independent Monetary Policy with a Fixed Exchange Rate

As long as the offset coefficient is less than minus one, which it appears to be for Germany, the central bank can in principle control the money supply if it sterilizes the effect of balance-of-payments deficits or surpluses on the monetary base. This policy, however, entails large fluctuations in the balance of payments. For instance, to maintain a fixed domestic interest rate in the event of a one percentage point decline in the Eurodollar rate, the Bundesbank would have to buy roughly 1.7 billion DMs of foreign exchange to peg the exchange rate.[6] This is only the short-run effect. In the long run, the magnitude is likely to be much larger for at least two reasons. First, a larger proportion of additions to wealth will be allocated to domestic securities. Unfortunately, we cannot obtain an estimate of this effect from the previous analysis. Second, it is likely that speculators will soon react to the accumulation of reserves by the central bank and make the pursuit of independent policy very difficult even in the short run. There is evidence that this was an important factor in the German experience.

---

6. This is a rough estimate obtained from eq. (2) in table 2; $1.7 \simeq 0.5/(1 - 0.7)$.

Another illustration of the difficulty of independent monetary policy is the fact that the results imply that to reduce the monetary base by 100 million DMs, ceteris paribus, the Bundesbank would have to reduce the domestic component of the base by 333 million DMs to offset the reserve accumulation of 233 million DMs.

3.4 Concluding Remarks

The analysis presented in this paper by and large supports the hypothesis of offsetting capital flows in the German case. Independent monetary policy, freedom of capital movement, and a fixed exchange rate are very difficult if not impossible to reconcile. This simple fact goes some way toward explaining the recurrent "crises" in the Bretton Woods system.

The analysis also suggests that the simple view that inflation is imported through the effect of current account surpluses on the money supply is valid. The process through which inflation rates are equalized under fixed exchange rates requires analysis that goes beyond the link between the money supply and the balance of payments.

APPENDIX: DATA SOURCES

All scale variables are in millions of Deutsche marks.

TCP = net private capital flows including errors and omissions; from various issues of the Monthly Report of the Deutsche Bundesbank (MRDB).

STCP = net short-term private capital flows including errors and omissions; from MRDB.

Y = mass income; from MRDB.

R^* = three-month Eurodollar rate; from various issues of International Financial Statistics (IFS).

A = the current account plus total official capital flows; from MRDB.

NDA = net domestic assets of the Deutsche Bundesbank; difference between line 134.14 and line 134.11 in IFS.

ΔRR = policy-induced change in required reserves; computed from $\Delta RR = (r - r_{-1})L_{-1}$.

L = total bank liabilities subject to reserve requirements; from MRDB.

r = average reserve requirements ratio; from MRDB.

FP = end-of-period forward premium on the Deutsche mark; computed from lines 134A and 134B in IFS.

DISC = Bundesbank discount rate; from MRDB.

NDA* = net domestic assets of the Bundesbank minus Bundesbank claims on banks; NDA minus line 134 12E in IFS.

REFERENCES

Argy, V., and Kouri, P. J. K. 1974. "Sterilization Policies and Volatility in International Reserves." In NATIONAL MONETARY POLICIES AND THE INTERNATIONAL FINANCIAL SYSTEM, edited by R. Z. Aliber. Chicago: University of Chicago Press.

Baffi, P. 1968. "Western European Inflation and the Reserve Currencies." Banca Nazionale del Lavoro QUARTERLY REVIEW 21 (Mar.): 3-22.

Branson, W., and Hill, R. D. 1971. "Capital Movements in the OECD Area." OECD Economic Outlook, Occasional Studies, Dec.

Brunner, K. 1973. "Money Supply Process and Monetary Policy in an Open Economy." In INTERNATIONAL TRADE AND MONEY, edited by M. Connolly and A. Swoboda. London: Allen & Unwin.

_____. 1974. "Monetary Management and the Central Banks: A Survey of Central Bank Thinking." In NATIONAL MONETARY POLICIES AND THE INTERNATIONAL FINANCIAL SYSTEM, edited by R. Z. Aliber. Chicago: University of Chicago Press.

Cooper, R. N. 1974. "Monetary Policy Implications of Eurodollars and the Balance of Payments Deficit." In NATIONAL MONETARY POLICIES AND THE INTERNATIONAL FINANCIAL SYSTEM, edited by R. Z. Aliber. Chicago: University of Chicago Press.

Deutsche Bundesbank. 1971. ANNUAL REPORT. Frankfurt: Deutsche Bundesbank.

Dornbusch, R. 1973*a*. "Currency Depreciation, Hoarding and Relative Prices." JOURNAL OF POLITICAL ECONOMY 81 (July/Aug.): 893-915.

_____. 1973*b*. "Devaluation, Money and Nontraded Goods." AMERICAN ECONOMIC REVIEW 63 (Dec.): 871-80.

Girton, L., and Henderson, D. 1973. "Financial Capital Movements and Central Bank Behavior in a Class of Two Country, Short Run Portfolio Balance Models." Unpublished. Washington, D.C.: Board of Governors of the Federal Reserve System.

Goldstein, N. H. 1972. "Imported Inflation—A Phrase in Search of a Phenomenon." Unpublished.

Haberler, G. 1972. "Prospects for the Dollar Standard." Lloyds Bank REVIEW 105 (July).

Johnson, H. G. 1971. "Inflation and the Monetarist Controversy." De Vries Lectures, Amsterdam.

_____. 1973. "The Monetary Approach to Balance of Payments Theory." In INTERNATIONAL TRADE AND MONEY, edited by M. Connolly and A. Swoboda. London: Allen & Unwin.

Katz, S. I. 1969. EXTERNAL SURPLUS, CAPITAL FLOWS, AND CREDIT POLICY IN THE EUROPEAN ECONOMIC COMMUNITY, 1958 TO 1967. Princeton Studies in International Finance, no. 22. Princeton, N.J.: Princeton University, International Finance Section.

Kouri, P. J. K., and Porter, M. G. 1974. "Portfolio Equilibrium and International Capital Flows." JOURNAL OF POLITICAL ECONOMY 82 (May/June): 443-67.

Krueger, A. D. 1974. "The Role of Home Goods in Exchange Rate Adjustments." In INTERNATIONAL TRADE AND FINANCE: ESSAYS IN HONOR OF JAN TINBERGEN, edited by W. Sellekaerts. White Plains, N.Y.: International Arts & Sciences Press.

Logue, R. 1969. IMPORTED INFLATION AND THE INTERNATIONAL ADJUSTMENT PROCESS. Federal Reserve System, Staff Economic Studies. Washington, D.C.: Board of Governors of the Federal Reserve System.

McKinnon, R. I. 1974. "Sterilization in Three Dimensions: Major Trading Countries, Eurocurrencies and the United States." In NATIONAL MONETARY POLICIES AND THE INTERNATIONAL FINANCIAL SYSTEM, edited by R. Z. Aliber. Chicago: University of Chicago Press.

Michaely, M. 1970. THE RESPONSIVENESS OF DEMAND POLICIES TO BALANCE OF PAYMENTS POST-WAR PATTERNS. New York: National Bureau of Economic Research.

Mundell, R. A. 1968. INTERNATIONAL ECONOMICS. New York: Macmillan.

_____. 1971. INFLATION, INTEREST AND GROWTH IN THE WORLD ECONOMY. Pacific Palisades, Calif.: Goodyear.

Parkin, M. 1974. "Inflation, the Balance of Payments, Domestic Credit Expansion and Exchange Rate Adjustments." In NATIONAL MONETARY POLICIES AND THE INTERNATIONAL FINANCIAL SYSTEM, edited by R. Z. Aliber. Chicago: University of Chicago Press.

Porter, M. G. 1972. "Capital Flows as an Offset to Monetary Policy." IMF STAFF PAPERS 19 (July): 395-424.

Scott, I. O., and Schmidt, W. E. 1964. "Imported Inflation and Monetary Policy." Banca Nazionale del Lavoro QUARTERLY REVIEW 17 (Dec.): 390-403.

Thygesen, N. 1973. "Monetary Policy, Capital Flows and Internal Stability: Some Experiences from Large Industrial Countries." SWEDISH JOURNAL OF ECONOMICS 75 (Mar.): 83-99.

Willms, M. 1971. "Controlling Money Supply in an Open Economy: The German Case." Federal Reserve Bank of St. Louis REVIEW 53 (Apr.).

THE DEMAND FOR MONEY IN AN OPEN ECONOMY:* GERMANY AND THE UNITED KINGDOM

Michael J. Hamburger**
Federal Reserve Bank of New York

Recently the role of money and monetary policy in an open economy has become a subject of increasing concern. This paper addresses the question by examining properties of the demand functions for money in Germany and the United Kingdom. The main purposes of the analysis are to contribute to our knowledge of these economies and, more generally, to inquire as to how the openness and the institutional setting of a country may influence the demand function for money and the definition of the quantity of money appropriate for that function. One of the principal issues to be considered is the stability of the demand function; another is the question of what interest rate or rates provide the most appropriate measures of the opportunity cost of holding money. Most frequently this dispute has

---

* Reprinted, with some changes, by permission of the author and North-Holland Publishing Co. from the JOURNAL OF MONETARY ECONOMICS 3 (1977): 25-40.

** The paper was completed while I served as visiting fellow, Carnegie-Mellon University. For helpful comments and criticism I am especially indebted to Charles Goodhart and Allan Meltzer. I am also grateful to Rona Stein for assistance with the research. Earlier versions of the paper were presented at the 1973 Konstanz Seminar; the meeting of the Federal Reserve System Committee on International Research and Analysis, Chicago, December 1973; and the meetings of the Econometric Society, New York, December 1973. Comments by participants at these sessions, as well as those of other colleagues--particularly Benjamin Friedman, Brian Griffiths, Laurence Meyer, Niels Thygesen, Manfred Willms, and Geoffrey Wood--also contributed to the paper. Needless to say, the views expressed are mine alone and do not necessarily reflect those of the individuals mentioned above, the Federal Reserve System, or the Federal Reserve Bank of New York.

centered on the problem of choosing between yields on short- and long-term government bonds and has neglected the possibility of including other domestic rates, e.g., the yield on equities (ordinary shares).[1]

Another important question in the case of an open economy concerns the role of foreign interest rates in the demand function and hence the substitutability between domestic and foreign assets. Resolution of this issue is important for determining the controllability of the domestic money stock. Under a regime of fixed exchange rates and close substitution between domestic and foreign assets, the impact of open-market operations (or other policy actions) will fall mainly on international capital flows and fluctuations in foreign exchange reserves rather than on the domestic money stock or the monetary base.[2]

The plan of the paper is as follows: section 1 presents a model to explain the demand for money in an open economy. The next two sections test the applicability of the model to Germany and Britain. In discussing the results, particular emphasis is placed on the similarities and differences between the demand functions for these countries and the United States and the ability of the estimated functions to explain movements outside the sample periods. A fifth and concluding section summarizes the results and indicates some of the more important implications.

---

1. Among those studies that find the yield (or price) of equities (ordinary shares) to be an important determinant of the demand for money are Alchian and Klein (1973), Hamburger (1966, 1969), Lee (1969), Penson (1971), and Thomson and Pierce (1971). Considering the purposes of the analyses, two conspicuous examples of studies in which the role of the equity rate is not investigated are Goldfeld (1973) and Goodhart and Crockett (1970).

2. Heretofore, the issue of the controllability of the domestic money stock has been approached almost entirely from the supply side (Kouri and Porter 1974; Porter 1972). A more extensive discussion of the problems of monetary management in an open economy is presented by Swoboda (1973).

1. THE DEMAND FOR MONEY IN AN OPEN ECONOMY

The general features of the model are quite standard. It posits that desired (equilibrium) money balances, M, are a function of interest rates, r, and a constraint, x:

$$\hat{M} = M(r, x). \tag{1}$$

In dealing with an open economy there are at least two modifications that must be considered. First, the list of possible components of the interest-rate vector, r, should be extended to include the yields on foreign as well as domestic assets. Our expectation is that the domestic rates are the more important variables. However, if these assets are perfect substitutes for one another, movements in their rates should be highly correlated, and it should make little difference which ones are included. Such a view is not beyond dispute. A number of economists have argued that the demand for money is primarily a "transactions" demand and that the only relevant measures of the opportunity cost of hold-money are the yields on very liquid assets, e.g., short-term government securities (Modigliani, Rasche, and Cooper 1970; Ando and Modigliani 1973). Foreign assets which involve the risk of exchange rate changes would presumably not be included in this category. Analysis of the data for open economies should, therefore, provide an additional means of discriminating between the so-called transactions approach to the demand for money and the more general wealth-adjustment models put forward by Brunner and Meltzer (1972) and Friedman and Schwartz (1973).

Another matter requiring special attention is the definition of money. In an open economy the problem is more complex than in a closed one, as decisions are required regarding the treatment of the domestic "money" holdings of foreigners and the holdings of foreign money balances by residents. The empirical analysis of this paper is based entirely on a fairly standard, narrow definition of money. For Germany, it is the sum of demand deposits of domestic nonbanks at commercial banks (denominated in marks) plus the currency holdings of all nonbanks, while for the United Kingdom it is currency in the hands of the public plus sterling current accounts (demand deposits) of the United Kingdom private sector. These specifications were chosen partially because of data considerations, partially because they correspond to the most commonly used definitions in other studies, and partially in the interest of employing similar money concepts for both countries. Some indication of the appropriateness of the measures should be provided when we examine the stability of the estimated demand functions.

Two other aspects of the model that require specification are (1) the level or constraint variable, x, and (2) the process by which actual money balances, M, approach their long-run equilibrium value, $\hat{M}$. For countries other than the United States, data limitations generally preclude the use of wealth as the constraint; hence the choice would seem to be restricted to either measured or permanent income. Since the latter is usually computed as a weighted average of current and past values of the former, our preference is to explicitly incorporate a distributed lag on measured income and let the data determine the nature of the weights. As far as estimation of the adjustment process is concerned, preliminary analysis suggested that the more appropriate approach was to include lagged values of the independent variables on the right-hand sides of the equations rather than the lagged dependent variable, as implied by the stock-adjustment model.

Consequently, equation (1) may be rewritten as

$$M_t = a + \sum_{i=o}^{T_1} b_i r_{t-i} + \sum_{i=o}^{T_2} c_i Y_{t-i} + v_t, \tag{2}$$

where M = the logarithm of the nominal money stock,

$\sum c_i Y_{t-i}$ = a distributed lag of the logarithm of nominal income,

$\sum b_i r_{t-i}$ = a distributed lag of the levels (as opposed to the logarithms) of interest rates, and

v_t = a random error term.

This specification, which has been employed in a number of recent studies (e.g., Goodhart and Crockett 1970; Feldstein and Eckstein 1970; and Klein 1974), implies that the elasticity of the demand for money with respect to income is constant, but that the absolute values of the interest-rate elasticities vary positively with the level of rates. Use of the nominal money stock as the dependent variable permits an examination of the homogeneity of the demand function with respect to the price level and thereby provides an additional means of evaluating the overall appropriateness of the model.[3]

2. THE EVIDENCE FROM GERMANY

2.1 Basic Results

Regression (3) presents the best results obtained when equation (2) is fit to quarterly observations of German data for the period 1963 through 1970 (t-statistics in parentheses).[4] The empirical definitions of the variables are as follows:[5]

---

3. Friedman (1959), on the other hand, prefers the use of the real money stock on the grounds that for a first approximation "it seems useful to regard the nominal quantity of money as determined primarily by conditions of supply, and the real quantity of money . . . as determined primarily by conditions of demand" (pp. 331-32). While the "exogeneity" of the nominal money stock in the United States is open to question (see Pierce and Thomson 1972), Friedman's distinction would seem to be of even less importance in an open economy, in a regime of fixed parities. Under such conditions, the most commonly held view is that both variants of the money stock, real and nominal, are demand-determined. For a more general discussion of the econometric consequences of using deflated variables, see Belsley (1972).

4. The choice of the sample period reflects (a) the lack of reliable data for some independent variables prior to 1963 (e.g., foreign interest rates) and (b) our interest in reconciling the German results with those for the United Kingdom, where the money-supply data are only available beginning in 1963. The period is terminated in 1970 to permit post-sample extrapolations.

5. The money-supply and interest-rate data are those collected by the Deutsche Bundesbank. Prior to 1968, the interest rates are from internal statistics of the bank. The money-supply series and the interest-rate data beginning in 1968 are taken from various issues of the bank's *Monthly Report*. The source for the income and price-level data is the Deutsche Institut für Wirtschaftsforschung. I am grateful to Dr. Manfred J. M. Neumann for providing the data.

   The specification of the interest rates, particularly the three-month loan rate, r_s, may require explanation. Being an interbank rate, it may be argued that r_s does not represent the most relevant short-term measure of the opportunity cost of holding money for the nonbank private sector. On the other hand, it is the only short-term market rate for which data are available. To the extent it is an inappropriate measure, the equations in which it appears should not fit the data as well as they otherwise might.

M = the logarithm of the domestically held narrow money stock (measured at the end of the quarter),

r = the interest rate on three-month loans in the Frankfurt money market (measured on a quarterly average basis), and

Y = the logarithm of nominal GNP.

All variables are unadjusted for seasonal variation; nevertheless, three dummy variables, $D1$, $D2$, and $D3$, are introduced to account for any residual seasonal variation in M.

$$M = \underset{(30.5)}{2.60} - \underset{(0.74)}{0.130 r_s} - \underset{(6.58)}{1.11 r_{s-1}} + \underset{(14.2)}{0.603\, Y} + \underset{(7.43)}{0.328} \left[1/7 \sum_{i=1}^{7} Y_{t-i} \right] \qquad (3)$$

$$- \underset{(0.66)}{0.004 D1} - \underset{(3.32)}{0.014 D2} - \underset{(5.58)}{0.022 D3}$$

$$\bar{R}^2 = 0.9983, \quad SE = 0.0065, \quad DW = 1.95$$

Several aspects of the results warrant comment. Note first that the statistical fit of the equation is exceedingly close and that the income and interest-rate elasticities have the anticipated signs and are significant at very high confidence levels. The standard error of the regression (0.0065) corresponds roughly to a 2.6 percentage point error in the seasonally adjusted annual growth rate in the money stock over a quarter, approximately one-seventh of the standard deviation in the series.

The equilibrium elasticity of the demand for money with respect to the short-term interest rate in Germany, evaluated at the sample mean of r, is -0.07. Although low in absolute value, this is within the range of estimates that have been obtained elsewhere.[6] Such a low value for this elasticity

6. For a survey of results for the United States and Britain, see Goodhart and Crockett (1970). If eq. (3) is reestimated using the more common constant interest-rate elasticity formulation (i.e., replacing r by its logarithm), the parameter estimates are essentially unchanged but the fit of the equation deteriorates somewhat, i.e., the equilibrium interest-rate elasticity remains at -0.07 but the standard error of the equation rises to 0.0072 and the Durbin-Watson statistic falls to 1.36.

casts some doubt on the view that money is primarily a substitute for other short-term liquid assets. On the other hand, it is difficult to find other interest rates that enter the equation significantly in the presence of the short-term rate.[7]

The long-run nominal income elasticity for Germany is one of the most robust statistics of the study: regardless of the specification of the demand function, all of the estimates of this parameter lie between 0.90 and 1.00. This finding is also in line with those that have been obtained for narrow definitions of the money supply in the United States and Britain. Of greater interest are the real income and price elasticities, which may be estimated by dividing nominal GNP into its two principal components. The summary statistics for this alternative formulation are similar to those for equation (3). More importantly, neither of the elasticities is significantly different from 1.0, which is consistent with one of the basic tenets of monetary theory, namely, that changes in the price level have no lasting effect on the demand for real balances.[8]

Turning to the dynamics of equation (3), we find that the response of aggregate money balances to changes in its determinants is much faster in Germany than in the United States. The adjustment to movements in short-term interest rates is apparently completed within two quarters, whereas two-thirds of the adjustment to changes in income occurs during the period in which there is a disturbance, with the rest distributed more or less evenly over the next seven quarters. Interpreted literally, the results suggest that the entire response to interest-rate changes occurs after a lag of one

---

7. If the yield on fully taxed, long-term bonds is substituted for the money-market rate in eq. (3), the equilibrium interest-rate elasticity is -0.35, with a t-statistic of 2.96, and the adjusted R^2 drops to 0.9953. When both rates are included in the same equation, the coefficient of the short rate remains significant at the 0.05 confidence level, but the bond-yield coefficient becomes insignificant even at very high confidence levels.

8. The estimates of the real income and price elasticities (and their t-statistics) are 0.986 (12.3) and 0.841 (6.5) respectively.

quarter, i.e., the current interest-rate coefficient in equation (3) is not significantly different from zero. While this is possible, it seems more likely that the regression suffers to some extent from simultaneous-equations bias because of efforts by the Bundesbank to influence interest rates. If this were the case, movements in interest rates would have a positive short-run effect on the *supply* of money, and this would tend to bias the estimated current-period interest-rate coefficient towards zero. The implications of the latter possibility are taken up in the next subsection.[9]

2.2 Alternative Interest Rates

The final question concerning the specification of the demand function is the relevance of interest rates other than those on domestic bonds. The two considered here are the dividend yield on equities (corporate shares--viewed as a proxy for the rate of return on real capital) and the covered yield on short-term foreign assets. The dividend-price ratio was chosen as the measure of the equity yield because it is the only readily available measure and because it has performed well in tests conducted with the United States data. All attempts to include the variable, either by itself or in addition to r_s, proved unsuccessful. Sometimes the coefficient had the anticipated (negative) sign, but it was never significantly different from zero. Thus, for Germany the dividend yield does not appear to be a useful indicator of the opportunity cost of holding money. There are at least two possible explanations for this finding, neither one of which excludes the other. First, the measurement problems associated with the variable may be more serious in Germany than in the United States. This view was expressed by several observers familiar with the financial markets in both countries. Second, given that the market for German equities is much smaller and does not appear to be nearly as well organized as its American counterpart, one might expect equities to be a poorer substitute for money in Germany than in the United States.

9. The specification of eq. (3) attributes the same coefficient to each lagged value of income. This simplifying restriction was imposed because all attempts to specify the lag pattern more precisely (by means of the Almon technique or completely unconstrained coefficieints) proved unsuccessful, i.e., the fits of these more complicated patterns were never significantly better than that of eq. (3). Finally, the addition of the lagged money stock actually tends to worsen the fit of the equation--the t-statistic for this variable is less than 1.0.

No comparable difficulty was encountered in incorporating the covered yield on short-term foreign assets, r_F, in the demand function—the rate on three-month Eurodollar deposits less the three-month forward premium on the Deutsche mark.[10] The objective here is to determine the degree of substitution between domestic and foreign assets and hence to test the hypothesis that in an open economy the domestic money stock may not be subject to central-bank control. If substitution is sufficiently close, an attempt to increase (decrease) the money stock will cause a temporary fall (rise) in interest rates, which will in turn stimulate an offsetting capital outflow (inflow) and return the money stock to its previous level. When r_F replaces r_s in equation (3), the two sets of results look very much alike:[11]

$$M = 2.53 - \underset{(2.17)}{0.529} r_F - \underset{(0.90)}{0.362} r_{F-1} - \underset{(1.66)}{0.452} r_{F-2} \tag{4}$$

$$+ \underset{(11.5)}{0.542} + \underset{(7.85)}{0.400} \left[1/7 \sum_{i=1}^{7} Y_{t-1} \right]$$

$$- \underset{(2.48)}{0.021} D1 - \underset{(2.92)}{0.013} D2 - \underset{(5.08)}{0.026} D3,$$

$$\bar{R}^2 = 0.9977, \quad SE = 0.0075, \quad DW = 1.91.$$

---

10. In those equations where these variables were included separately, their coefficients were always equal in absolute value and opposite in sign. The Eurodollar rate is that published in the Bank of England *Quarterly Bulletin*, while the three-month forward rate on the mark was obtained from the Board of Governors of the Federal Reserve System.

11. The high correlation among r_F, r_{F-1}, and r_{F-2} makes it inappropriate to evaluate the contribution of these variables by their individual t-statistics. The F-statistic, which measures the importance of the three variables taken together, exceeds 50.0.

Considering the close correspondence between short-term interest rates on German and foreign securities, such a finding may not be surprising.[12] There are, however, two differences in the results which suggest that the Bundesbank was able to exert some short-run control over the money stock even under the relatively fixed-exchange-rate regime of the 1960s. First, if r_S and r_F are included in the same equation, only the coefficients of the former remain statistically significant, implying that money is a closer substitute for domestic securities than it is for foreign securities. That is, although r_S and r_F generally move together, discrepancies arise; and when they do, it is r_S which determines the amount of money that is held.[13]

Further support for this view is provided by the pattern of the interest-rate lags in equations (3) and (4). While the response to movements in the domestic rate appears to be confined to the period following the one in which there is a change, the reaction to r_F is distributed evenly over the current and next two quarters. The evidence here is not very strong and is, of course, infested with multicolinearity. Nevertheless, it tends to confirm our earlier suspicion that (3) contains some simultaneous-equations bias. Such a finding could reflect the behavior of German commercial banks. However, given the importance central banks generally attach to stabilizing

---

12. The simple correlations between r_F and r_S for the 1963-70 period are 0.97 for the levels of the variables and 0.80 for their quarterly first differences. As a basis for comparison, the corresponding correlations between short- and long-term German rates, r_S and r_L, are 0.86 and 0.53, respectively.

13. The hypothesis being tested is that r_S and r_F are alternative measures of the same variable. If this is true, neither set of coefficients should be significant when the other variable is included. The fact that the coefficients of r_S are significant while those for r_F are not, suggests that the null hypothesis should be rejected. Once again the appropriate basis for judging the significance of the coefficients is the F-statistic. For r_S the value of the statistic is 3.90, while for r_F it is 0.90.

interest rates, it seems more likely that the results indicate some ability of the Bundesbank to accomplish this objective and to pursue an independent monetary policy, even if only for short periods.[14]

2.3 Stability

We turn next to the stability of the demand function, which provides an additional test of the appropriateness of the present specification, including the definition of money. Stability is measured here by how well (3) explains movements in the dependent variable: first, when the sample period is divided into two equal subperiods and second, in the six quarters immediately following the sample period. Taken together, the evidence suggests a very stable demand function. Application of the Chow (1960) test reveals that we are unable to reject the hypothesis that the data for the two halves of the sample period were generated by the same underlying structure, even at the 20 percent confidence level.

The post-sample period results are also impressive. Table 1 gives the predicted and actual levels of the money stock and the corresponding annual growth rates for the six quarters beginning in 1971:I. Aside from this quarter, equation (3) fits the data extremely well. The root mean square error for the money stock over the entire post-sample period is DM 1.4 billion, less than two-thirds of the smallest quarter-to-quarter change in the series. Even more striking is the sample correlation between the predicted and actual growth rates, 0.98.[15] Such stability in the estimated demand

---

14. The methodology employed here has a number of potential shortcomings. Nevertheless, it is encouraging to note that the present results, gleaned from the demand function for money, are almost identical to those obtained by Kouri and Porter (1974) and Porter (1972), who investigated the responsiveness of international capital flows in Germany to variations in Bundesbank policy instruments.

15. In natural logarithms, the root mean square error is 0.035, which is approximately two times the standard error of the equation over the sample period. However, as is apparent from table 1, the problem is confined solely to the first quarter of 1971. If this observation is eliminated, the root mean square error falls to 0.0084. The probability that this value could be obtained by chance, given that there were *no* changes in structure, is greater than 10 percent.

Table 1

Actual and Predicted Money-Stock Values Derived From Equation (3)
Germany, 1971:I—1972:II

	Levels (in millions of marks)			Growth rates* (at annual rates)		
	Actual	Predicted	Difference	Actual	Predicted	Difference
1971 I	101,514	104,325	-2,811	-23.4	-13.0	-10.4
II	109,650	111,111	-1,461	32.1	37.8	-5.7
III	111,994	113,222	-1,228	8.6	13.0	-4.4
IV	121,015	120,478	537	32.2	30.3	1.9
1972 I	116,765	116,967	-202	-14.0	-13.4	-0.6
II	125,516	124,775	741	30.0	27.4	2.6
Root mean square error			1,439			5.3
Simple correlation			1.00			0.98

*Predicted growth rates are calculated as the percentage change between the actual level of the money stock in quarter t-1 and the predicted value in quarter t.

function for money is similar to that observed for the United States, (Hamburger 1973; Goldfeld 1973). Considering the openness of the German economy and the disturbances that occurred in the foreign exchange markets in 1971 and 1972, the results amply demonstrate the usefulness of the present model.

3. THE EVIDENCE FROM THE UNITED KINGDOM

3.1 Basic Results

The best-fitting money-demand function for the United Kingdom is illustrated by equation (5). Since this formulation is unconventional, particularly in its specification of the opportunity cost of holding money, equation (6), which is more typical of the functions that have been estimated for the United Kingdom, is also reported. Finally, (7) presents the results when all of the variables are included in the same equation.

$$M = \underset{(74.6)}{5.89} - \underset{(5.40)}{1.20} r_E - \underset{(8.31)}{1.07} r_{E\$} + \underset{(39.2)}{0.672}\, Y, \qquad (5)$$

$$\bar{R}^2 = 0.9900, \quad SE = 0.0089, \quad DW = 1.96.$$

$$M = \underset{(2.70)}{2.25} - \underset{(4.17)}{0.959} r_{LA} + \underset{(4.36)}{0.328}\, Y + \underset{(4.46)}{0.582} M_{-1}, \qquad (6)$$

$$\bar{R}^2 = 0.9820, \quad SE = 0.0119, \quad DW = 1.71.$$

$$M = \underset{(5.97)}{4.68} - \underset{(0.62)}{0.156} r_{LA} - \underset{(3.97)}{1.01} r_E - \underset{(4.40)}{0.898} r_{E\$} + \underset{(7.71)}{0.562}\, Y, \qquad (7)$$

$$+ \underset{(1.55)}{0.192} M_{-1},$$

$$\bar{R}^2 = 0.9901, \quad SE = 0.0088, \quad DW = 2.24.$$

The definitions of the variables are as follows:

M = the logarithm of currency in the hands of the public plus sterling current accounts of the U.K. private sector, seasonally adjusted end-of-quarter values, millions;[16]

Y: = the logarithm of gross domestic product (GDP) at current prices, seasonally adjusted, millions;[17]

r_{LA} = the interest rate on local authority debt with three months to maturity;[18]

---

16. This is one of the few applications of this relatively new, narrow money-supply series published in the Bank of England *Quarterly Bulletin*. The more commonly used series includes only current account deposits of the London clearing banks (Fisher 1968; Goodhart and Crockett 1970). Both measures were examined in the analysis, and in no case would the conclusions reached below be reversed if they were based on the narrower series. The results are reported for the more inclusive measure because it yields the more appropriate specifications. A table showing selected regression results with the alternative series is available from the author on request.

17. Following general British practice, GDP is used instead of GNP as the measure of income. The difference between these alternative national-income concepts may, however, be worth investigating. If, as is frequently asserted, GDP corresponds more closely to a measure of domestic expenditure than to income, it would seem to be the appropriate variable to use if one takes a "transactions" as opposed to a "portfolio balance" approach to the demand for money.

18. The local authority rate is used here instead of the more common United Kingdom Treasury bill rate, following Goodhart and Crockett (1970) and Laidler (1971), who question the appropriateness of the latter as a measure of the opportunity cost of holding money. However, in the present investigation it made no important difference which of these rates was used; they both yielded essentially the same results. As before, all interest rates are measured as quarterly averages, and one percent equals 0.01.

r_E = the dividend-price ratio on ordinary shares;[19]

$r_{E\$}$ = the uncovered rate on three-month Eurodollar deposits.[20]

In many respects the results are similar to those for Germany. First, interest rates, regardless of how they are measured, are an important determinant of aggregate money holdings. Such a result has not always been obtained in studies of Britain for the postwar period (see Fisher 1968; Laidler and Parkin 1970). Second, although the differences are small, those formulations which allow for a positive relationship between the level of interest rates and the absolute values of the elasticities are generally superior to the constant elasticity formulations. Third, actual money balances respond very quickly to changes in their determinants. Indeed, according to equation (5) the adjustment is completed within a quarter. This finding constrasts sharply with the bulk of the evidence available for the United States and for this reason may be subject to question. Alternatively,

---

19. For Britain there are alternative measures of the equity yield. Three of those examined were: the earnings yield, the reciprocal of the share-price index, and the GDP deflator divided by share prices. Although there was considerable uniformity among the four sets of results, the best statistical fits were obtained with the dividend-price ratio, while the worst occurred with the earnings yield. One of the problems with the earnings yield is that current earnings is a fairly volatile series and consequently may not be the most useful measure of expected future earnings, which presumably is the relevant variable. To test this contention, the numerator of the earnings yield was replaced by an average of current earnings and its five lagged values. The fit was better than that for the conventional earnings yield but still poorer than that for the dividend yield. Longer lags for earnings are not possible because the series begins in 1962. Implicit in our use of the dividend-price ratio is the assumption that, on average, current dividends provide a better proxy of expected future earnings than some weighted average of current and past earnings. For a further discussion of this question and the United States evidence, see Hamburger (1966).

20. The Eurodollar rate is the same variable used earlier, but note that for the United Kingdom it is the uncovered, and not the covered, rate which seems appropriate.

one may question the accuracy of the United States estimates.[21] These considerations notwithstanding, I know of no compelling arguments as to why it should take wealthholders more than three months to equate their actual and desired money balances.[22]

The superiority of equation (5) relative to (6)—the more standard formulation—is based only partially on its superior fit. When nominal GDP is divided into its real-income and price-level components in equation (6), the real-income coefficient falls well short of statistical significance ($t = 0.8$). This problem is not encountered with equation (5), where the t-statistics for the real-income and price elasticities are 2.9 and 6.2 respectively. This difficulty with equations like (6) is not restricted to the present investigation. Almost identical results are reported by Goodhart and Crockett (1970) and Laidler (1971), and the latter attributes the problem specifically to the specification of the interest rate.

An important similarity between the United States and the United Kingdom money-demand functions is the significance of the dividend yield. This suggests that in countries where the equity markets are well developed and enjoy broad participation by individual wealthholders, the claims against

---

21. One potential source of bias in the United States estimates arises from the Federal Reserve's efforts, *and* its greater ability, relative to other central banks, to influence domestic yields. As noted earlier, such efforts introduce a positive short-run relation between money and interest rates (through the central bank's reaction function) that might be expected to lengthen OLS estimates of the lag in the demand function. In private correspondence, Ronald Teigen reports that his evidence tends to support this contention.

22. The only lagged variable that even approaches statistical significance when added to eq. (5) is Y_{-1}. The inclusion of this variable leaves unchanged the equilibrium elasticity of the demand for money with respect to income and the coefficients of the other variables and reduces the standard error of the regression to 0.0085. The estimates of Y and Y_{-1} (and their t-statistics) are 0.42 (2.98) and 0.26 (1.83) respectively. Recent United States studies using weekly and monthly data also indicate much shorter lags than those observed earlier (e.g., see Thomson and Pierce 1971; David and Schadrack 1974).

the earnings and real assets of firms are effective substitutes for money. Since this is the first time such a relationship has been isolated for the United Kingdom, our conclusions for it cannot be held with quite as much confidence as they can for the United States. Nevertheless, the evidence presented here would appear to be inconsistent with the view that the demand for money depends primarily on the level of income and the interest rate on some short-dated government security (Modigliani 1971).

Perhaps the most unexpected result is the overriding impact that changes in the Eurodollar rate have on the quantity of money demanded. This leaves little doubt that Britain is an open economy and that tight control of the domestic money stock may be difficult in a regime of fixed exchange rates. But it seems to go too far, suggesting that foreign bonds are closer substitutes for money than those denominated in sterling. An alternative explanation, which takes account of the control that the Bank of England exerted over the short-term money market, posits that during the period studied, the Eurodollar rate provided a better measure of the opportunity cost of holding money in Britain than did *published* domestic rates. Such a view, although unconventional, is consistent with other evidence (Hamburger 1971) and represents a modest extension of the arguments (cited earlier) by Goodhart and Crockett (1970) and Laidler (1971) concerning the specification of interest rates in Britain.[23]

---

23. For an excellent discussion of Bank of England policy during this period, see Goodhart (1973). Additional support for our interpretation is provided by replacing the three-month local authority rate (r_{LA}) in eq. (7) by the day-to-day interbank rate in London (r_{IB}). Since the latter would appear to be a less appropriate measure of the cost of holding money for the nonbank sector, but probably was also less subject to the controls of the monetary authorities, it is consistent with our view that r_{IB} outperforms r_{LA} in the estimated demand function. Over the period 1964:III to 1971:I (a continuous series for the interbank rate does not begin until June 1964), the t-statistics for r_{IB} and r_{LA} are 1.38 and 0.33 respectively.

Accepting this explanation, the question arises as to why British investors paid so much attention to the gross return on foreign securities (e.g., the Eurodollar rate) and so little to the cost of forward cover. When the three-month forward discount on sterling is added to equations (5) and (7) as a separate variable, its t-statistic never exceeds 0.50. Although this result may not be easy to rationalize, it is consistent with the views expressed by Marston (1974) and *The Economist*. According to Marston, "some investors, particularly nonfinancial institutions . . . , tend to ignore exchange rates in all but crisis periods. They are prepared to disregard the minor spot fluctuations that occur in normal periods and to make investment decisions solely on the basis of nominal returns." (P. 4) *The Economist* cites an extreme instance of this behavior. It reports that in the past British firms were so accustomed to ignoring exchange risk that they neglected to cover even when the dollar was allowed to float in August 1971 (*The Economist*, Aug. 28, 1971, pp. 59-60).

Furthermore, under existing foreign exchange controls, many United Kingdom investors are not free to buy and sell foreign securities in the open market. To invest abroad they must first acquire so-called investment dollars—foreign currency (expressed in United States dollars) which is available for the purchase of quoted foreign currency securities and for approved direct investment in nonsterling countries. During the period under consideration, these regulations apparently did have an impact on the price of foreign exchange in Britain. After correction for first-order serial correlation, the simple correlation between the official spot exchange rate and the price of investment dollars from 1963:II—1971:I is 0.45.[24] Thus, the poor performance of the three-month forward discount on sterling in the demand function for domestic money balances may be explained on the grounds that some investors do not cover forward; and for those that do, it may not be the relevant cost of cover.

---

24. The three-month forward discount on sterling, the official spot exchange rate, and the price of investment dollars are taken from the Bank of England *Quarterly Bulletin*; all are measured as quarterly averages.

Taken together, the evidence of this section indicates one of the serious problems that can arise when governments attempt to control interest rates (and other prices) by edict: published values cease to provide useful information to policymakers, investors, and econometricians.

3.2 Stability

Over the sample period, the preferred estimation equation for the United Kingdom, equation (5), is about as stable as its German counterpart. There is more than a 20 percent chance that the differences in specification between the two halves of the sample period could have occurred purely by chance. Beyond this period, however, the results for the two countries differ considerably.

Table 2 indicates that there is a close correspondence between the predicted and actual levels of the money stock during the first three post-sample period quarters, but thereafter the relationship deteriorates markedly.[25] Ordinarily such a breakdown in an empirical relationship would suggest some basic misspecification of the underlying economic structure. In the present instance, though, the empirical irregularities begin at the same time that the British monetary authorities instituted major reforms in their monetary control techniques and in the structure of the banking system.[26] While it is doubtful that all the errors can be attributed to these reforms, the coincidence of the two events makes it highly unlikely that they are unrelated. If correct, this suggests that one of the costs that must be set against the benefits derived from the reforms is that researchers may

---

25. In natural logarithms, the first three residuals are each less than the standard error of the regression over the sample period, while the last three are at least three times as large.

26. For a discussion of these and subsequent changes, introduced by the authorities, see Christelow (1974), Morgan and Harrington (1973), Parkin (1973), and Rowan (1973).

Table 2

Actual and Predicted Money-Stock Values Derived From Equation (5)
United Kingdom, 1971:II—1972:III

	Levels (millions of pounds)			Growth rates* (at annual rates)		
	Actual	Predicted	Difference	Actual	Predicted	Difference
1971 II	10,328	10,279	49	4.7	2.7	2.0
III	10,670	10,582	88	13.2	9.8	3.4
IV	10,875	10,806	69	7.7	5.1	2.6
1972 I	11,290	10,980	310	15.3	3.9	11.4
II	11,742	11,383	359	16.0	3.3	12.7
III	11,904	11,519	385	5.5	-7.6	13.1
Root mean square error			254			9.0
Simple correlation			0.99			0.51

*Predicted growth rates are calculated as the percentage change between the actual level of the money stock in quarter $t-1$ and the predicted value in quarter t.

no longer be able to combine observations for the 1960s and 1970s into a single data set.[27, 28]

4. CONCLUSION

In Germany and Britain, as in the United States, the quantity of money demanded appears to be a relatively stable function of two arguments: income and interest rates. There is considerable uniformity and stability in the parameter estimates. The standard narrow definition of money, which attributes little (or no) weight to the holdings of foreign deposits by

---

27. Author's note: For an updating of the research on the U.K. which suggests that the early-1922 deterioration in the money-demand function was not as large as it appeared at the time of the writing, see Hamburger and Wood (1978).

28. The problems reported here with the demand function for money after 1971 are not unique to our formulation. Indeed, as Charles Goodhart informs me (private correspondence), this has been the case with virtually all the demand-for-money functions, however specified, developed for the United Kingdom on the basis of the data for the 1960s. Similar results are also reported by Artis and Lewis (1974), who conclude "that either the demand for money is *inherently* unstable or the function has been lost to sight under a *succession* of shocks from the supply side of a scale not previously experienced" (p. 247, emphasis added). Such a judgment could ultimately prove to be correct, but at the moment it seems premature. First, it ignores the stability observed during the 1960s. Second, considering the nature of the errors in 1972, questions may be raised as to how important the changes in structure for the narrow money stock have actually been. The main problem with eq. (5) in 1972 is that it fails to "explain" the large increase in *M* during the first quarter. Thereafter, if the predicted growth rate is calculated using the predicted level of the money stock in the previous quarter instead of the actual value, the errors are not very large at all. The differences between the predicted and actual growth rates (at annual rates) are then 1.4 percent for 1972:II and 0.7 percent for 1972:III. Finally, if one accepts the proposition that the reforms introduced under "Competition and Credit Control" were sufficient to alter either the parameters or the arguments of the demand function, then some time will have to transpire before a new function can be estimated and its stability evaluated.

    One important difference between the present analysis and that of Artis and Lewis is that ours deals exclusively with the narrow money stock whereas theirs is based largely but not entirely on the broad money supply (M3 in Britain). For M3, the situation is even more complicated, as one must attempt to allow for a change in the specification of the variable after 1971 and for the adverse effects of the imposition of interest-rate ceilings.

residents and the domestic deposits of foreigners, is as appropriate for a moderately large, open economy as it is for a closed one. Thus, the demand function for the narrowly defined money stock appears quite robust despite considerable variation in the institutional setting and the openness of the economies examined. Such evidence stands in sharp opposition to the view that improvements in a country's payment mechanism and other forms of financial innovation are likely to require a broadening of the definition of money and perhaps a major reformulation of monetary analysis. This view was originally put forward by Gurley and Shaw (1960) and has recently been endorsed by a number of Federal Reserve officials (e.g., Mitchell 1972).

To be sure, the results are not entirely alike. In Germany, for example, where the market for corporate shares (equities) is relatively small and underdeveloped, such claims appear to be much poorer substitutes for money than they are in Britain and the United States. This suggests that the degree of substitution between money and other specific assets depends importantly on the nature of the markets in which the latter are traded. The lag in the adjustment of aggregate money balances to their determinants appears to be much shorter in Germany and the United Kingdom than in the United States. As discussed above, the magnitude of these discrepancies raises questions regarding the accuracy of the United States estimates.

We turn finally to the question of the control of the domestic money stock and the efficacy of monetary policy. For Germany, domestic and foreign securities appear to be close but not perfect substitutes for one another. This implies that even during the fixed-exchange-rate regime of the 1960s, the Bundesbank did, in principle, possess some ability to pursue an independent monetary policy over short time intervals. For the United Kingdom, the possibility that published domestic interest rates do not provide the most reliable measures of the opportunity cost of holding money complicates the interpretation of the results. However, the apparent substitutability between money and equities (claims against real capital) provides an avenue by which variations in the money stock could affect the real sector of the British economy even if they have only a negligible impact on the domestic bond rate.

REFERENCES

Alchian, A. A., and Klein, B. 1973. "On a Correct Measure of Inflation." JOURNAL OF MONEY, CREDIT AND BANKING, Feb., pp. 173-91.

Ando, A., and Modigliani, F. 1975. "Some Reflections on Describing Structures of Financial Sectors." In THE BROOKINGS MODEL: PERSPECTIVE AND DEVELOPMENT, edited by G. Fromm and L. R. Klein. Amsterdam: North-Holland.

Artis, M. J., and Lewis, M. K. 1974. "The Demand for Money: Stable or Unstable?" THE BANKER, Mar., pp. 239-47.

Belsley, D. A. 1972. "Specification with Deflated Variables and Specious Spurious Correlation." ECONOMETRICA, Sept., pp. 923-27.

Brunner, K., and Meltzer, A. H. 1972. "Money, Debt and Economic Activity." JOURNAL OF POLITICAL ECONOMY, Sept./Oct., pp. 951-77.

Chow, G. C. 1960. "Tests of Equality between Two Sets of Coefficients in Two Linear Regressions." ECONOMETRICA, July, pp. 591-605.

Christelow, D. B. 1974. "Britain's New Monetary Control System." Federal Reserve Bank of New York MONTHLY REVIEW, Jan., pp. 12-24.

Davis, R. G., and Schadrack, F. C. 1974. "Forecasting the Monetary Aggregates with Reduced-form Equations." In MONETARY AGGREGATES AND MONETARY POLICY. New York: Federal Reserve Bank of New York.

Feldstein, M., and Eckstein, O. 1970. "The Fundamental Determinants of the Interest Rate." REVIEW OF ECONOMICS AND STATISTICS, Nov., pp. 363-75.

Fisher, D. 1968. "The Demand for Money in Britain: Quarterly Results, 1951 to 1967." THE MANCHESTER SCHOOL, Dec., pp. 329-44.

Friedman, M. 1959. "The Demand for Money: Some Theoretical and Empirical Results." JOURNAL OF POLITICAL ECONOMY, Aug., pp. 327-51.

Friedman, M., and Schwartz, A. J. 1973. "Velocity and the Interrelations between the United States and the United Kingdom." Mimeographed. New York: National Bureau of Economic Research.

Goldfeld, S. M. 1973. "The Demand for Money Revisited." Brookings Papers on Economic Activity 3, pp. 577-638.

Goodhart, C. A. E. 1973. "Monetary Policy in the United Kingdom." In MONETARY POLICY IN TWELVE INDUSTRIAL COUNTRIES, edited by K. Holbik. Boston: Federal Reserve Bank of Boston.

Goodhart, C. A. E., and Crockett, A. D. 1970. "The Importance of Money." Bank of England QUARTERLY BULLETIN, June, pp. 159-98.

Gurley, J. G., and Shaw, E. S. 1960. MONEY IN A THEORY OF FINANCE. Washington, D.C.: Brookings Institution.

Hamburger, M. J. 1966. "The Demand for Money by Households, Money Substitutes, and Monetary Policy." JOURNAL OF POLITICAL ECONOMY, Dec., pp. 600-623.

_____. 1969. "Alternative Interest Rates and the Demand for Money: Comment." AMERICAN ECONOMIC REVIEW, June, pp. 407-11.

_____. 1971. "Expectations, Long-term Interest Rates and Monetary Policy in the United Kingdom." Bank of England QUARTERLY BULLETIN, Sept., pp. 354-71.

_____. 1973. "The Demand for Money in 1971: Was There a Shift?" JOURNAL OF MONEY, CREDIT AND BANKING, May, pp. 720-25.

Hamburger, M. J., and Wood, G. E. 1978. "Interest Rates and Monetary Policy in Open Economies." Federal Reserve Research Papers.

Klein, B. 1974. "Competitive Interest Payments on Bank Deposits and the Long-run Demand for Money." AMERICAN ECONOMIC REVIEW, Dec., pp. 931-49.

König, H.; Gaab, W.; and Walters, J. 1973. "An Econometric Model for the Financial Sector of the Federal Republic of Germany." Mimeographed. Mannheim: University of Mannheim.

Kouri, P. J. K., and Porter, M. G. 1974. "International Capital Flows and Portfolio Equilibrium." JOURNAL OF POLITICAL ECONOMY, May/June, pp. 443-68.

Laidler, D. E. W. 1971. "The Influence of Money on Economic Activity—A Survey of Some Current Problems." In MONETARY THEORY AND MONETARY POLICY IN THE 1970s, edited by G. Clayton, J. Gilbert, and R. Sedgwick. Oxford: Oxford University Press.

Laidler, D. E. W., and Parkin, M. 1970. "The Demand for Money in the United Kingdom, 1956-1967: Preliminary Estimates." THE MANCHESTER SCHOOL, Sept., pp. 187-208.

Lee, T. H. 1969. "Alternative Interest Rates and the Demand for Money." AMERICAN ECONOMIC REVIEW, June, pp. 412-17.

Marston, R. C. 1974. AMERICAN MONETARY POLICY AND THE STRUCTURE OF THE EURODOLLAR MARKET. Princeton: Princeton University, International Finance Section.

Mitchell, G. W. 1972. "Banking and the Payments Mechanism." Remarks at the Annual Meeting of the Association of Reserve City Bankers, April.

Modigliani, F. 1971. "Monetary Policy and Consumption." In CONSUMER SPENDING AND MONETARY POLICY: THE LINKAGES. Boston: Federal Reserve Bank of Boston.

Modigliani, F.; Rasche, R.; and Cooper, J. P. 1970. "Central Bank Policy, the Money Supply and the Short-term Rate of Interest." JOURNAL OF MONEY, CREDIT AND BANKING, May, pp. 166-218.

Morgan, E. V., and Harrington, R. L. 1973. "Reserve Assets and the Supply of Money." THE MANCHESTER SCHOOL, Mar., pp. 73-87.

Parkin, M. 1973. "The Discount Houses' Role in the Money Supply Control Process under the 'Competition and Credit Control' Regime." THE MANCHESTER SCHOOL, Mar., pp. 89-105.

Penson, J. E., Jr. 1971. "The Demand for Financial Assets in the Farm Sector: A Portfolio Balance Approach." Mimeographed. Urbana: University of Illinois.

Pierce, J. L., and Thomson, T. D. 1972. "Controling the Money Stock." In CONTROLING THE MONETARY AGGREGATES II: THE IMPLEMENTATION. Boston: Federal Reserve Bank of Boston.

Porter, M. G. 1972. "Capital Flows as an Offset to Monetary Policy: The German Experience." I.M.F. STAFF PAPERS, July, pp. 395-424.

Rowan, D. C. 1973. "The Monetary System in the Fifties and Sixties." THE MANCHESTER SCHOOL, Mar., pp. 19-42.

Swoboda, A. K. 1973. "Monetary Policy under Fixed Exchange Rates: Effectiveness, the Speed of Adjustment and Proper Use." ECONOMICA, May, pp. 136-54.

Thomson, T. D., and Pierce, J. L. 1971. "A Monthly Model of the Financial Sector." Paper presented at the Konstanzer Seminar on Monetary Theory and Policy, Konstanz, West Germany, June.

PRICE EXPECTATIONS AND THE INTEREST RATE IN AN OPEN ECONOMY: GERMANY, 1960-72*

Manfred J. M. Neumann**
Freie Universität, Berlin

Empirical investigations over the last decade into the determinants of the interest rate have concentrated on the search for the Fisher effect of anticipated price-level changes on the interest-rate level. In several studies it has been taken for granted that the real rate of interest is constant and that price expectations can be approximated by appropriate distributions of observed rates of inflation. Consequently, in those studies the nominal rate of interest has been regressed against current and past actual rates of inflation (Fisher 1930; Yohe and Karnosky 1969; Gibson 1970). Other studies have followed a broader approach by allowing for determinants such as real income and real balances, mostly derived from Keynes's theory of liquidity preference (Gibson and Kaufman 1968; Hamburger and Silber 1969; Hamburger and Platt 1975; Sargent 1969, 1972; Yohe and Karnosky 1969; Feldstein and Eckstein 1970; Roll 1972).

This study investigates the determinants of the nominal rate of interest for an open economy, given a fixed-exchange-rates regime. A credit-market model of the monetary sector is formulated, and a reduced-form solution for the interest rate is derived.

---

* Reprinted, with some changes, by permission of the author and the Ohio State University Press from the JOURNAL OF MONEY, CREDIT AND BANKING 9 (February 1977, pt. 2): 206-27. Copyright © 1977 by the Ohio State University Press.

** I am deeply indebted to Allan H. Meltzer for many discussions and valuable comments. Research support from the Graduate School of Industrial Administration, Carnegie-Mellon University, and from the Federal Reserve Bank of St. Louis is gratefully acknowledged. Earlier versions of the paper were presented at seminars at the University of Chicago, Ohio State University, the Federal Reserve Banks of New York and St. Louis, and at the 1976 Konstanz Seminar. Comments on those occasions were helpful.

Three features of the model may be noted. First, it incorporates a suitable formulation of the balance of payments and consequently introduces the foreign rate of interest as an important determinant of the domestic rate. Second, inflationary expectations enter the model through the anticipated rate of inflation and through the anticipated price level, dominantly emerging from the public's supply behavior with respect to domestic earning assets. This makes it unnecessary to supplement artificially a reduced-form equation by Fisher's anticipated rate of inflation.[1] Third, the model is concerned with short-run financial equilibria, holding the output market constant. Specifically, it is assumed that the quarterly time unit is sufficiently long to allow complete adjustment in financial markets but too short for the formation of a joint equilibrium of the financial and real sectors. Consequently, the model offers the short-run response of the interest rate to changes in the anticipated rate of inflation, and this response is found smaller than unity.

The solution for the interest rate serves for the estimation of regressions that explain the quarterly development of the long-term interest rate in Germany for 1960-72. Other authors have tried this before but have concentrated on catching the effect of adaptive price expectations without allowing for an alternative model of expectations formation or for additional determinants (Siebke and Willms 1972, 1973; Gebauer 1973; Jüttner 1975; Siebke 1976). In this study, particular attention is given to the role of the foreign interest rate and, more importantly, to a reliable measurement of the anticipated rate of inflation and its effect on the interest rate. Alternative proxies for the anticipated rate of inflation, based on either adaptive or rational expectations, are used in the estimation. A main finding of the study is that, as a proxy for the anticipated rate, the difference between the yields on paper and real assets is superior to polynomial distributed lags of actual rates of inflation.

---

1. See Feldstein and Eckstein (1970, p. 365). Sargent (1973*a*) has shown that adding a distributed lag in current and past actual rates of inflation to an inverted Keynesian demand function for real balances does not give a satisfactory synthesis of Keynes and Fisher.

1. THE MODEL

The model extends the Brunner-Meltzer theory of the monetary process to an open economy by adding the balance-of-payments constraint and reformulating the domestic credit market accordingly[2] for a fixed-exchange-rates regime. The core consists of a money market, a credit market, and a suitable balance-of-payments formulation. We will explain them in order.

In the *money market* the domestic public's stock demand for narrowly defined money, M^D, equals the stock supply of money, expressed as the product of the monetary base, B^A, and a money multiplier, m.

$$M^D(\ldots) = m(\ldots)B^A. \tag{1}$$

The stock demand for money is given by

$$M^D = L(i, i^*, p, p^a, P, e, W^N, W^H), \tag{2}$$

with $L_p, L_P, L_{W^N}, L_{W^H} > 0 > L_i, L_{i^*}, L_{p^a}, L_e$. It depends negatively on the domestic credit-market rate, i, the foreign interest rate, i^*, the anticipated level of output prices, p^a, and the anticipated net real return on real capital, e. It depends positively on the current output price level, p, the price level of existing real capital, P, and on human as well as nonhuman wealth, W^H and W^N.

The stock supply of money is described as a multiple of the monetary base, which is adjusted for net borrowing of commercial banks from the central bank. From the sources side, the adjusted base may be defined as the sum of two components:

$$B^A = B^X + C. \tag{3}$$

---

2. See Brunner and Meltzer (1968) and Brunner (1973*a*). Brunner and Meltzer (1976) themselves have extended their model to an open economy by using a differently formulated balance-of-payments constraint for the determination of foreign sources of the base and by lumping together the supply of domestic earning assets and foreign demand for such assets.

The first component, B^X, summarizes those sources that are exogenous or predetermined relative to the current monetary process, such as the central bank's bond holdings, its stock of credit to the government, and the cumulated surplus of the current account balance. The second component, C, denotes the cumulated net foreign position from private capital transactions. In a fixed-exchange-rate regime, the component C can be expected to be positive (negative) as long as the exchange rate parity is set such that the domestic currency is undervalued (overvalued).

Through the adjustment of the monetary base for net borrowing of commercial banks from the central bank, the money multiplier,[3]

$$m = m(i, i^*, d, r, P, e, W^N, W^H, p), \tag{4}$$

with $m_i, m_{i^*}, m_e > 0 > m_d, m_r$, is linked negatively with the discount rate, d, and positively with both the domestic and the foreign credit-market rate. Commercial bank borrowing from the central bank responds positively to changes in both rates, which in turn raises the money multiplier. An increase of reserve requirement ratios, r, decreases the multiplier.

In the *domestic credit market* the public's stock supply of domestic earning assets denominated in domestic currency, E, equalizes the sum of the stock demand for such assets by foreigners, F, and the respective stock demand by commercial banks, expressed as the product of the monetary base, B^A, and an asset multiplier, a^D.

$$E(\ldots) = a^D(\ldots)B^A + F(\ldots). \tag{5}$$

3. The money multiplier is defined by the expression

$$m = \frac{1 + k}{k + (rr + re - b)(1 + t)},$$

where k = public's currency ratio,
rr = required reserve ratio,
re = excess reserve ratio,
b = banks' net borrowing ratio, and
t = public's time and savings deposit ratio.

Banks' net borrowing is defined as gross borrowing through discounting and lombarding of eligible paper minus net purchase of money-market paper from the central bank.

Since the credit market aggregates domestic loan and bond markets, the public's stock supply of earning assets is defined as the sum of the public's desired stock demand for loans from banks and from foreigners, $L^B + L^F$, and its implicit stock supply of government bonds to commercial banks and foreigners, $S - S^P$:[4]

$$E = L^B + L^F + S - S^P. \tag{6}$$

The stock supply of domestic earning assets is given by

$$E = s(i - \pi, i^*, p^a, P, e, S, W^N, W^H), \tag{7}$$

with $s_{i^*}, s_{p^a}, s_e, s_S > 0 > s_{i-\pi}, s_P$. It responds positively to changes in the level and the rate of change of anticipated inflation, p^a and π, the foreign credit-market rate, the anticipated net return on real capital, and the total stock supply of government bonds, S; it responds negatively to changes in the credit-market rate and the price level of existing real capital.

The demand for domestic earning assets by commercial banks is again described as a multiple of the adjusted monetary base.[5] The asset multiplier, a^D, while depending on the same arguments as the money multiplier, responds differently. It depends positively on the domestic credit-market rate, i, but negatively on the foreign interest rate, i^*.

$$a^D = a^D(i, i^*, r, d, P, e, W^N, W^H, p), \tag{8}$$

---

4. By definition we have

$$S - S^P = S^B + S^F,$$

where S^B and S^F denote the holdings of domestic government bonds by domestic commercial banks and by foreigners, respectively. To be sure, the demand and supply of earning assets, denominated in foreign currency, do not belong to the domestic credit market described by eq. (5).

5. The domestic asset multiplier is defined by the expression

$$a^D = \frac{(1 + b - rr - re - f)(1 + t)}{k + (rr + re - b)(1 + t)},$$

where f = banks' ratio of foreign earning assets to total deposits.

with $a_i^D, a_P^D, a_{W^N}^D, a_{W^H}^D > 0 > a_{i*}^D, a_r^D, a_d^D, a_e^D, a_p^D$. The same holds for the foreign stock demand for domestic earning assets:

$$F = F(i, i^*, o^*), \tag{9}$$

with $F_i > 0 > F_{i*}$, where o^* serves as portmanteau variable for other non-specified foreign variables that need not concern us here.

The balance-of-payments formulation concentrates exclusively on private capital transactions. We treat the current account balance and capital transactions of the government as being given relative to current monetary processes. The cumulated net foreign position of the central bank from private capital transactions, C, may quite simply be defined as the difference between foreign holdings of domestic assets, F, and private domestic holdings of foreign assets, D:

$$C = F - D. \tag{10}$$

A more refined formulation would differentiate between the holdings of foreign assets by domestic banks and nonbanks as well as between foreign holdings of domestic nonbank and bank liabilities.[6]

The domestic stock demand for foreign financial assets is given by

$$D = D(i, i^*, P, p^a, e, W^N, W^H), \tag{11}$$

with $D_{i*}, D_P, D_{p^a}, D_{W^N}, D_{W^H} > 0 > D_i, D_e$. It depends positively on the foreign interest rate, the price level of existing real capital, the anticipated price level, and wealth; negatively on the domestic credit-market rate and the anticipated real net return on real capital.

Finally, to complete the model, there are three equations defining the wealth variables and the anticipated real net return on real capital:

6. It may be noted that such refinements would lead us to a reduced-form solution for the credit-market rate that would not be essentially different from the one we derive below.

$$W^N = PK + \nu(i)S + B^X, \text{ with } \nu_i < 0; \quad (12)$$

$$W^H = W^H(y, p^a), \text{ with } W^H_y, \; W^H_{p^a} > 0; \quad (13)$$

$$e = e(y, K), \text{ with } e_y > 0. \quad (14)$$

Nonhuman wealth includes the exogenous instead of the adjusted base. K denotes the existing stock of real capital and is treated as constant; y is real income.

The model can be reduced to three equations:

a money-market (MM) equation,

$$m(i, i^*, d, r, P, y)\,[B^X + C] - L(i, i^*, p, p^a, P, y, S, B^X) = 0; \quad (15)$$

a credit-market (CM) equation,

$$a^D(i, i^*, d, r, p, p^a, P, y, S, B^X)\,[B^X + C] + F(i, i^*) - (s - \pi, i^*, p^a, P, y, S) = 0; \quad (16)$$

and a capital-balance (CB) equation,

$$F(i, i^*) - D(i, i^*, p^a, P, y, S, B^X) - C = 0. \quad (17)$$

Assuming that the behavioral equations are linear in logarithms, it is convenient to rewrite the three equations such that responses of the same kind are lumped together into summary elasticities.[7] We denote relative rates of change by dots.

$$\begin{aligned} &\varepsilon(MM, i)\dot{i} + \varepsilon(MM, P)\dot{P} + \varepsilon(MM, C)\dot{C} + \varepsilon(MM, i^*)\dot{i}^* \\ &+ \varepsilon(MM, d)\dot{d} + \varepsilon(MM, r)\dot{r} + \varepsilon(MM, y)\dot{y} + \varepsilon(MM, p)\dot{p} \\ &+ \varepsilon(MM, p^a)\dot{p}^a + \varepsilon(MM, S)\dot{S} + \varepsilon(MM, B^X)\dot{B}^X = 0. \end{aligned} \quad (15a)$$

7. We acknowledge that the net foreign position of the central bank with respect to private capital transactions, C, *in principle* may become negative (usually in cases of heavily overvalued currencies). However, in the German case, C has almost always been positive, with the exception of a few quarters.

$$\varepsilon(CM, i)\dot{i} + \varepsilon(CM, P)\dot{P} + \varepsilon(CM, C)\dot{C} + \varepsilon(CM, i^*)\dot{i}^* \quad (16a)$$

$$+ \varepsilon(MM, d)\dot{d} + \varepsilon(MM, r)\dot{r} + \varepsilon(CM, y)\dot{y} + \varepsilon(CM, p)\dot{p}$$

$$+ \varepsilon(CM, p^a)\dot{p}^a + \varepsilon(CM, S)\dot{S} + \varepsilon(CM, B^X)\dot{B}^X$$

$$+ \varepsilon(CM, \pi)\dot{\pi} = 0.$$

$$\varepsilon(CB, i)\dot{i} + \varepsilon(CB, P)\dot{P} - \dot{C} + \varepsilon(CB, i^*)\dot{i}^* + \varepsilon(CB, y)\dot{y} \quad (17a)$$

$$+ \varepsilon(CB, p^a)\dot{p}^a + \varepsilon(CB, S)\dot{S} + \varepsilon(CB, B^X)\dot{B}^X = 0.$$

For the definitions and the hypothesized signs of these summary elasticities —denoted by $\varepsilon(MM, x)$, $\varepsilon(CM, x)$, and $\varepsilon(CB, x)$ —we refer the reader to appendix 2.

Solving the model gives reduced-form equations for $\dot{i}$, $\dot{P}$, and $\dot{C}$. The last two need not concern us here.[8] The solution for the relative rate of change of the credit-market rate is

$$\dot{i} = \varepsilon(i, B^X)\dot{B}^X + \varepsilon(i, d)\dot{d} + \varepsilon(i, r)\dot{r} + \varepsilon(i, S)\dot{S} + \varepsilon(i, i^*)\dot{i}^* \quad (18)$$

$$+ \varepsilon(i, \pi)\dot{\pi} + \varepsilon(i, p^a)\dot{p}^a + \varepsilon(i, p)\dot{p} + \varepsilon(i, y)\dot{y}.$$

---

8. In passing, we note that the model's reduced-form solution for C shows that interest-induced capital flows do not completely offset domestic policy actions in the short run. This contradicts an argument developed by Kouri and Porter (1974). On the basis of a Keynesian flow model—in essence consisting of a capital flow equation and a base-money-market flow equation—they concluded that in the utopian state of perfect capital-market integration, with information and adjustment costs zero, the offset coefficient would become minus unity.

   Our model gives the following offset coefficient:

$$\frac{\delta C}{\delta B^X} = \frac{-Z_2}{Z_1(B^A/C) + Z_2},$$

   with $Z_1 < 0$, $Z_2 < 0$, $B^A/C > 1$. The Zs are summary expressions of financial asset-market elasticities. For the offset coefficient to become minus unity, the adjusted base, B^A, must be zero.

Table 1 gives the definitions and signs of the elasticities. The signs of the elasticities with respect to d, r, S, π, p^a, and p are unambigously determined. The signs of the remaining elasticities are identified by order constraints listed in appendix 2.

The credit-market rate responds positively to changes in the discount rate, reserve requirement ratios, and government debt but negatively to changes in the exogenous base. Thus, for the response of the credit-market rate to changes in policy instruments under a fixed-exchange-rates regime, the model gives the same results one would expect for a closed economy, although with numerically smaller elasticities.

Table 1

Responses of the Credit-Market Rate

Elasticities	Definitions	Sign
$\varepsilon(i, B^X)$	$-[Q_1\,\varepsilon(CB, B^X) - Q_2\,\varepsilon(MM, B^X) + Q_3\,\varepsilon(CM, B^X)]/\Delta$	-
$\varepsilon(i, d)$	$-[-Q_2\,\varepsilon(MM, d) + Q_3\,\varepsilon(CM, d)]/\Delta$	+
$\varepsilon(i, r)$	$-[-Q_2\,\varepsilon(MM, r) + Q_3\,\varepsilon(CM, r)]/\Delta$	+
$\varepsilon(i, S)$	$-[Q_1\,\varepsilon(CB, S) - Q_2\,\varepsilon(MM, S) + Q_3\,\varepsilon(CM, S)]/\Delta$	+
$\varepsilon(i, i^*)$	$-[Q_1\,\varepsilon(CB, i^*) - Q_2\,\varepsilon(MM, i^*) + Q_3\,\varepsilon(CM, i^*)]/\Delta$	+
$\varepsilon(i, \pi)$	$Q_3\,\varepsilon(CM, \pi)/\Delta$	+
$\varepsilon(i, p)$	$-[-Q_2\,\varepsilon(MM, p) + Q_3\,\varepsilon(CM, p)]/\Delta$	+
$\varepsilon(i, p^a)$	$-[Q_1\,\varepsilon(CB, p^a) - Q_2\,\varepsilon(MM, p^a) + Q_3\,\varepsilon(CM, p^a)]/\Delta$	+
$\varepsilon(i, y)$	$-[Q_1\,\varepsilon(CB, y) - Q_2\,\varepsilon(MM, y) + Q_3\,\varepsilon(CM, y)]/\Delta$	+

with $Q_1 = [\varepsilon(MM, P)(1-\alpha) - \varepsilon(CM, P)]\,C/B^A < 0,$

$Q_2 = \varepsilon(CM, P) + \varepsilon(CB, P)(1-\alpha)\,C/B^A > 0,$

$Q_3 = \varepsilon(MM, P) + \varepsilon(CB, P)\,C/B^A < 0;$

where $\alpha = F/E,$

$$\Delta = Q_1\varepsilon(CB, i) - Q_2\varepsilon(MM, i)\,Q_3\,\varepsilon(CM, i) < 0.$$

Anticipation of inflation affects the credit-market rate through two channels: the rate of inflation anticipated in the credit market, π, and the anticipated price level in the output market, p^a. Both the acceleration, π, and the velocity of anticipated inflation, p^a, induce the credit-market rate to change into the same direction (see also Brunner 1973a, p. 385). It also responds positively to changes in the foreign interest rate, i^*.[9] The elasticity is smaller than unity in the shorter run if $|\varepsilon(CM, i^*)| \leq \varepsilon(CM, i)$.

2. EMPIRICAL ANALYSIS

A Specific Hypothesis of Interest-Rate Determination

For the estimation of the reduced-form equation (18), we choose a semilogarithmic formulation:[10]

$$i = g(\pi, i^*, d, \ln B^X, \ln S, \ln y, \ln p, \ln p^a). \tag{19}$$

Specifically, we assume that: (a) first derivatives of the credit-market rate with respect to rates of return but not necessarily the respective elasticities are constant, and (b) elasticities of the credit-market rate with respect to real and nominal quantities increase numerically with a decreasing level of the credit-market rate. The last assumption is intuitively appealing, since it implies that relative responses in quantities to relative changes in rates of return increase numerically with the level of those rates.[11] Of particular interest is the numerical magnitude of the response of the credit-market rate to changes in the acceleration of anticipated inflation. Our model of the financial sector implies that the response is less than unity in the short run.

---

9. The foreign interest rate is treated as exogenous.

10. At the presentation of an earlier version of this paper, Laidler and Parkin pointed out that this, like any reduced form, is compatible with a wide class of models. In principle, we cannot rule out that eq. (19) is derivable from a Keynesian model, provided the model takes care of the channels of inflation anticipation and imports a suitable money-supply function.

11. In a recent study on the German money demand, Hamburger (1974, p. 12) found a semilogarithmic formulation superior to a log-linear formulation, though the improvement of the estimates was modest.

From the expression for $\varepsilon(i, \pi)$ in table 1 we obtain

$$\frac{\delta i}{\delta \pi} = \frac{Q_3 \varepsilon(CM, \pi) i/\pi}{Q_1 \varepsilon(CB, i) - Q_2 \varepsilon(MM, i) + Q_3 \varepsilon(CM, i)} \quad .$$

Since (see appendix 2)

$$\varepsilon(CM, i) = (1 - \alpha) \varepsilon(a^D, i) + \alpha\varepsilon(F, i) + \varepsilon (CM, \pi)\, i/\pi \, ,$$

and

$$| \, Q_1 \varepsilon(CB, i) - Q_2 \varepsilon(MM, i) + Q_3 [(1 - \alpha) \bar{\varepsilon}(a^D, i) + \alpha\varepsilon(F, i)] \, | > 0,$$

it follows that

$$\frac{\delta i}{\delta \pi} < 1.$$

In the short run, the anticipated rate of inflation affects the nominal rate of interest positively but by less than unity and therefore affects the real rate on financial assets negatively (see also Brunner 1973 *a*, p. 385). This result is not surprising, as the model concentrates on the interaction of asset markets while holding the output market constant. In the long run, of course, the Fisher effect holds, i.e., $\delta i / \delta \pi = 1$.

Measurement of Anticipated Inflation

Rate and level of anticipated inflation, π and p^a, are not directly observable. Price expectations may be either adaptive or rational. To avoid any prejudice, we employ both the adaptive- and the rational-expectations approach for the construction of alternative proxies for π and p^a.

The widely used adaptive modeling of price expectations assumes that economic agents base their expectations about future rates of inflation on no other information than observed rates of inflation. Consequently, expected future rates of inflation are represented by a distributed lag of past rates of inflation with declining weights, as given by

$$\pi = \lambda \, \dot{p}_{-1} + (1 - \lambda) \pi_{-1} .$$

Instead of trying to estimate the expectation parameter, λ, we choose a priori two alternative values:

$\lambda_1 = 1$; hence, $\pi_1 = \dot{p}_{-1}$.

$\lambda_2 = 0.62$; hence, $\pi_2 \simeq 0.620\dot{p}_{-1} + 0.236\dot{p}_{-2} + 0.090\dot{p}_{-3} + 0.034\dot{p}_{-4}$.

The value λ_2 is arbitrary. It still implies a relatively short distributed lag. The computations are based on the official cost-of-living index.

Since the λ 's are arbitrarily chosen, we cannot rule out that a λ less than 0.62 might be more appropriate. On the other hand, the widely used procedure of searching for an Almon-distributed lag for π that gives a sum of the weights as close to unity as possible is inappropriate. First, if this is done in regressions that focus exclusively on the anticipated rate of inflation as the determinant of the nominal rate of interest, it presupposes constant real rates of interest on financial assets even in the short run, which is unreasonable. Second, if the Almon-based search is carried out in regressions that allow for additional determinants, this procedure introduces a bias against the remaining explanatory variables, as has been pointed out by Roll (1972). The bias is that the remaining explanatory variables enter only once and therefore do not benefit from the search over an essentially infinite number of transformations.

The adaptive-expectations approach extrapolates the history of inflation and may work satisfactorily whenever the actual rate of inflation moves on a constant trend. But it will perform badly when the economy undergoes pronounced swings. In that case it would be irrational for economic agents to continue to form their price expectations adaptively.[12] The rational-expectations approach assumes that economic agents use all the information available to them and learn that the actual development of inflation is conditioned by the structure of the economy and the policies applied (Muth 1961; Shiller 1975). The approach suggests "that expectations, since they are informed predictions of future events, are essentially the same as the predictions of the relevant economic theory" (Muth 1961, p. 316). As Muth pointed out, this implies neither that all economic agents

12. An adaptive formation of expectation is not irrational per se (Sargent 1973*b*).

hold the same expectations nor that predictions are perfect. All that is required is that any hypothesis we set up about the formation of expectations about future values of a particular economic variable be consistent with the hypothesis we hold about the determination of actual future values of that variable.

If we extend the model set up above by an explicit formulation of the output market and allow for time lags, we could derive a reduced form explaining changes in the actual rates of inflation by lagged accelerations or decelerations of the money stock, government spending, real exports, and import prices for a given trend rate of real growth.

$$\Delta \dot{p}_t^c = p(\Delta \dot{M}_{t-1}, \Delta \dot{G}_{t-1}, \Delta \dot{x}_{t-1}, \Delta \dot{P}_{t-1}^I, \dot{y}_{t-1}),$$

where p^c = the cost-of-living index,

M = the money stock (currency plus demand deposits),

G = a fiscal stimulus measure (a linear combination of government spending and cumulated initial revenue effects, resulting from changes in tax rates),

x = real exports,

P^I = an index of import prices converted into domestic currency, and

y = output of the private sector.

Estimating the equation for the sample period 1960 through 1974 with annual data, we found considerable multicollinearity between $\Delta \dot{P}^I$ and $\Delta \dot{x}$, and we therefore eliminated the export variable. Searching over the surrounding lag specifications, the following estimate appeared to be the best (t -ratios in parentheses):

$$\underset{}{\Delta \dot{p}^c} = \underset{(-0.98)}{-\,0.33} + \underset{(2.89)}{0.15\,\Delta \dot{M}_{-2}} + \underset{(2.37)}{0.08\,\Delta \dot{G}_{-1}} + \underset{(3.20)}{0.20\,\Delta \dot{P}_{-2}^I} + \underset{(2.26)}{0.13\dot{y}_{-1}},$$

$$\bar{R}^2 = 0.70, \qquad DW = 1.82.$$

This estimate serves for computing the proxy π_3 for quarterly data.

Finally, differences between yields on nominal and real assets may also be used to measure the anticipated rate of inflation (Fisher 1930, pp. 401-7; Friedman and Schwartz 1963, pp. 583-84). Therefore, we select as a fourth proxy, π_4, the difference between the bond yield and the dividend yield on all German common stock traded on stock exchanges. The advantage of this proxy is that it requires no hypothesis about the way in which expectations are formed. Its weakness is that it reflects the sum of the rates of anticipated inflation and anticipated real growth of dividends, and we have no procedure for separating these components (Roll 1972, p. 270).

Alternative proxies for the anticipated price level, p^a, can be derived by assuming that participants in the output market hold the same anticipations of inflation as participants in the credit market. This simplification allows us to use the four constructed time series for π_1, π_2, π_3, and π_4 for computing corresponding alternative time series for anticipated price levels p_1^a to p_4^a by applying, observation for observation, the definition $\ln p_t^a = \ln p_t + \pi/100$, where π is measured in percentage points and p_t^a denotes the year-later price level expected at time t.

Estimates

Estimates of the reduced-form equation (19) are presented in tables 2 and 3. They are based on quarterly observations from 1960 through 1972. A brief identification of the empirical variables may be useful. (A more detailed description of the data appears in appendix 1.) The proxy for the dependent variable i is the average yield on long-term public bonds. The alternative π_s's and p_s^a's have already been described above. i_f^* is a short-term Eurodollar rate, adjusted for the forward premium on holding dollar claims, and d is the discount rate. B^X denotes the exogenous monetary base, including reserves liberated or impounded by changes in reserve requirements, and B_R^X the corresponding real base. S is nominal government debt, S_R the corresponding real debt. Y and y are nominal and real gross national product, respectively.

Table 2 gives estimates that comparably employ the alternative proxies for π and p^a. We have left out government debt, S, and the concurrent price level, p, as explanatory variables. The reason for this is high multicollinearity between these variables and the alternative proxies for the anticipated price level. The respective coefficients of correlation range between 0.95 and 0.98 for variables measured in logarithms.

Table 2

Regressions of the Nominal Rate of Interest on Alternative Proxies for Inflation and Other Determinants
(t-ratios in parentheses)

Period: 1960:I—1972:IV

Regression Number	Variables Changed	π	i_f^*	d	$\ln B^X$	$\ln y$	$\ln p^a$	Const.	$\bar{R}^2$	SE	DW
2.1.1	$\pi = \pi_1, p^a = p_1^a$	-0.01 (-0.28)	0.09 (3.19)	0.30 (7.06)	-1.46 (-8.57)	1.22 (1.69)	2.52 (2.18)	-7.45 (-1.78)	0.944	0.215	1.65
2.1.2	$\pi = \pi_1, p^a = p_1^a, d = d_1$	0.02 (0.49)	0.25 (12.92)	same as above				-7.09 (-1.69)	0.944	0.215	1.65
2.2.1	$\pi = \pi_2, p^a = p_2^a$	-0.01 (-0.13)	0.09 (3.19)	0.30 (7.06)	-1.45 (-8.05)	1.25 (1.73)	2.46 (2.10)	-7.57 (-1.82)	0.944	0.215	1.64
2.2.2	$\pi = \pi_2, p^a = p_2^a, d = d_2$	0.03 (0.54)	0.25 (12.89)	same as above				-7.21 (-1.73)	0.944	0.215	1.64
2.3.1	$\pi = \pi_3, p^a = p_3^a$	-0.04 (-1.34)	0.09 (2.86)	0.32 (6.41)	-1.54 -10.77)	1.34 (1.86)	2.62 (2.29)	-11.34 (-3.34	0.944	0.215	1.71
2.3.2	$\pi = \pi_3, p^a = p_3^a, d = d_3$	0.04 (1.55)	0.24 (12.35)	same as above				-11.05 (-3.26)	0.944	0.215	1.71
2.4.1	$\pi = \pi_4, p^a = p_4^a$	0.08 (1.47)	0.12 (3.83)	0.24 (4.82)	-1.47 -10.64)	1.30 (1.88)	2.25 (2.07)	-7.28 (-1.82)	0.948	0.207	1.69
2.4.2	$\pi = \pi_4, p^a = p_4^a, d = d_4$	0.23 (4.96)	0.23 (12.71)	same as above				-7.39 (-1.84)	0.948	0.207	1.69

Table 3

Regressions of the Nominal Rate of Interest on the Difference between Bond and Dividend Yield and Other Determinants
(t-ratios in parentheses)

Period: 1960:I—1972:IV

Regression Number	π_4	i_f^*	d_4	$\ln B^X$	$\ln B_R^X$	$\ln S$	$\ln S_R$	$\ln Y$	$\ln y$	Const.	$\bar{R}^2$	SE	DW
3.1	0.26	0.23	0.24	-1.47				1.51		0.23	0.947	0.209	1.57
	(5.97)	(13.17)	(4.72)	(-11.36)				(13.46)		(0.12)			
3.2	0.25	0.23	0.24	-1.54		0.38		1.08		2.57	0.949	0.205	1.80
	(5.72)	(13.45)	(4.84)	(-11.40)		(1.56)		(3.59)		(1.07)			
3.3	0.26	0.23	0.24		-1.51				1.75	-2.34	0.949	0.206	1.66
	(6.00)	(13.05)	(4.82)		(-12.48)				(8.56)	(-0.74)			
3.4	0.25	0.23	0.24		-1.54		0.29		1.33	0.43	0.949	0.205	1.81
	(5.72)	(13.10)	(4.85)		(-12.45)		(1.12)		(3.09)	(0.10)			

Regressions 2.1.1, 2.2.1, 2.3.1, and 2.4.1 are direct estimates of the reduced-form equation (19). All four provide a relatively good fit for the variation of the German long-term interest rate. The standard errors of estimate are less than 22 basis points, and the Durbin-Watson coefficients reflect no significant serial correlation at the 0.01 level. With the exception of the regression coefficients of the proxies for the anticipated rate of inflation, all regression coefficients have the expected sign and most are significant at the 0.05 significance level.

Two properties of the four regressions require special attention. First, the estimated parameter of the adjusted foreign interest rate, i_f^*, while significant, is unconvincingly small. However, the smallness of this parameter is not due to our selection of the short-term Eurodollar rate as the foreign interest rate. Substituting the adjusted average yield on all U.S. "seasoned" A-grade corporate bonds, one finds almost exactly the same coefficient for i_f^*. Second, the estimated parameters of the alternative proxies for the anticipated rate of inflation are either zero or negligibly small. In fact, the regressions do not lose any explanatory power when the π's are left out in estimation.

Both properties of the four regressions are unexpected but are not to be taken at face value. They may have a common cause that lies in the working of discount-rate policy. Though set at the discretion of policy-makers, the discount rate to a major extent may reflect the trend movements of the anticipated rate of inflation and the adjusted foreign interest rate. The supporting hypothesis is: to prevent a runaway inflation as well as a cumulative deflation, monetary authorities had to set the discount rate more or less in line with the developments of the domestic credit-market rate; thus with the anticipated rate of inflation, and the foreign interest rate when exchange rates were fixed.[13] We have tested this hypothesis by running four regressions of the discount rate on the adjusted

13. Within the limits of rediscount quotas that are related to their capital, banks in Germany have automatic access to central-bank credit. Though this borrowing has always been an important proximate determinant of cyclical fluctuations in the money supply, banks in total never utilized more than 50 percent of the quotas during the sixties. In the early seventies, the utilization rate temporarily rose to about 80 percent.

foreign interest rate, each containing a different π as the second determinant. The best estimate was as follows:

$$d = 0.48 i_f^* + 0.60 \pi_4 - 0.43,$$
$$(10.45) \quad (5.25) \quad (-1.00)$$
$$\bar{R}^2 = 0.77, \qquad DW = 1.65.$$

It tends to confirm our hypothesis. The estimated residuals of this regression may be identified with the autonomous part of discount-rate variation. On this interpretation we derive from the four discount-rate regressions four alternative proxy variables for the autonomous part of discount-rate variation, d_1 to d_4, where the numbering corresponds to the numbering of π_s's in the discount-rate regressions.[14]

We have reestimated the interest-rate regressions 2.1.1, 2.2.1, 2.3.1, and 2.4.1 of table 2 with the proxies d_1 to d_4 replacing the actual discount rate (see regressions 2.1.2, 2.2.2, 2.3.2, and 2.4.2). This leaves the explanatory power of the regressions unchanged, but it raises the estimated parameters of i_f^* and π, without affecting those of the remaining determinants of the interest rate.

The parameters estimated for i_f^* more than doubled in all reestimates. A similar significant increase of the parameter of π can only be observed in regression 2.4.2, where the proxy for the anticipated rate of inflation is π_4, the difference between bond and dividend yield. There we find a highly significant regression coefficient of 0.23, while in regressions 2.1.2, 2.2.2, and 2.3.2 the coefficients remain close to zero and insignificant. This is an indication that our measures π_1 to π_3 that were based on the assumption of either adaptive or rational price expectations measure equally badly the true anticipated rate of inflation.

---

14. It would be misleading to substitute the actual rate of inflation for the proxies for the anticipated rate. It is the anticipated and not the actual rate that influences the discount rate through changing the credit-market rate.

The comparative success of proxy π_4 in regression 2.4.2 is not surprising. Whatever the true process of the formation of price expectations, if the anticipated rate of inflation affects the nominal rate of interest positively and in the short run affects the real rate negatively, then changes of this unobservable must be reflected by changes in the difference between bond and dividend yield. Nevertheless, we do not know how well they are reflected. That would require information about the correlation between anticipated real growth of corporate earnings and anticipated rate of inflation.

Regression 2.4.2 provides a parameter estimate of 0.23 for π. This parameter does not represent the total effect of the anticipated rate of inflation on the nominal rate of interest. There are two additional effects. One results from the simultaneous change in p^a. This is a minor effect of 0.02. The other one is ten times larger, 0.23. It arises from the induced change in the adjusted foreign interest rate, i_f^*. In an open economy, a change in the anticipated domestic rate of inflation simultaneously changes the forward premium on holding foreign currency assets—in the same direction and, if both variables are measured in percent per year, by the same amount, since efficient foreign currency markets imply a respective partial derivative of unity.

According to regression 2.4.2, the total effect on the nominal rate of interest of an increase of the anticipated rate of inflation by one percentage point is 48 basis points during the same quarter.[15] This result is in accordance with the prediction of our model that $\delta i / \delta \pi < 1$ in the short run. It does not appear to be unreasonably small if one considers that the average level of nominal rate of interest measured over the period 1970 through 1975 exceeded its average level of the sixties by no more than 0.7 times the increase in the respective average rate of inflation.

---

15. If the risk differential is disregarded, the difference between bond and dividend yield is equal to the sum of the anticipated rate of inflation and the anticipated real growth rate of dividends or corporate net earnings plus a compounding term. Depending on whether the changes in these two anticipated rates are positively or negatively correlated, the true total effect of π on i is larger or small than 0.48 in the short run.

Even the best estimate of table 2, regression 2.4.2, is not completely satisfactory. Since the estimated parameter of $\ln p^a$ is numerically larger than the parameter of $\ln B^X$, the regression implies that any increase in the actual or the anticipated price level will permanently raise the nominal rate of interest. This nonhomogeneity has no backing in monetary theory and can be avoided in estimation by a constraint that equates the responses of the interest rate to changes in real income and in the anticipated or the actual price level.

Consider regressions 3.1 and 3.2 of table 3, where nominal income has replaced real income and the price level. Both regressions reveal the desired homogeneity property: in regression 3.1 the numerical values of the estimated parameters of the logs of the nominal base and nominal income are not significantly different from each other; in regression 3.2 the numerical value of the parameter of the base is not significantly different from the sum of the parameters of nominal income and nominal debt. Note that the introduction of nominal debt led to the expected positive sign, but the parameter is not significant at the 0.05 significance level, presumably due to the presence of multicollinearity with nominal income. In regressions 3.3 and 3.4, finally, the homogeneity property is simply imposed on the estimates by replacing the nominal stock variables by their deflated counterparts. This did not result in major changes of the estimates.

In all four regressions of table 3, the proxy for the anticipated rate of inflation is π_4, the difference between bond and dividend yield. Uniformly, for changes in π we find a total effect on i of about 0.5 in the short run.

A Further Alternative: Distributed Lags of the Rate of Inflation

The estimates presented above suggest that the difference between bond and dividend yield, π_4, is a more appropriate proxy for the anticipated rate of inflation than the proxies π_1 and π_3 that were based on either adaptive or rational price expectations. One might wonder whether an approximation of the anticipated rate of inflation by an explicitly estimated distributed lag of past rates of inflation would lead to superior estimates of the nominal rate of interest. Yohe and Karnosky (1969, p. 38) found for U.S.

quarterly data (1961-69) that when they regressed the long-term rate on a distributed lag of current and past rates of inflation only the sum of the weights reached 0.8 for the best estimate. When they included additional nonlagged variables, the sum of the weights of the distributed lag variable remained almost unchanged. Feldstein and Eckstein (1970), on the other hand, produced a sum of the weights of unity by estimating an equation resulting from what they considered to be a proper synthesis of Keynes and Fisher.[16] Both studies relied on the polynomial lag technique.

Similar estimates for the German data are presented in table 4. In all regressions, the distributed lags of past rates of inflation are based on polynomials of third degree without end-point constraints. Though the length of the lag is varied, the period of estimation is identical for all regressions.

The first three regressions, 4.1.1 to 4.3.1, follow the narrow Fisher approach, explaining the interest rate solely by a distributed lag of current and past rates of inflation. Searching over lags of up to 28 quarters, we have chosen the lags of 8, 14, and 24 quarters, using the following criteria: regression 4.1.1 gives a sum of weights of the same size found, if one regresses i on proxy π_1 or π_2, while regression 4.2.1 offers the conventionally searched-for result of a sum of weights that is closest to unity. The best statistical explanation is provided by regression 4.3.1, whose standard error of estimate is the lowest. This regression, on the other hand, is nonsensical, as the sum of the weights is significantly above unity.

The next three regressions, 4.1.2 to 4.3.2, include the additional variables suggested by our model's solution for the interest rate.[17] The more extensive specification not only raises the adjusted $\bar{R}^2$'s considerably but also substantially reduces, at least for the shorter lags, the sum of

16. See note 1.

17. Note that the discount rate again is represented by suitable estimates of its autonomous component. See the definitions of d_8, d_{14}, and d_{24} in appendix 1.

Table 4

Regressions of the Nominal Rate of Interest on Almon-distributed Lags of Rates of Inflation and Other Determinants
(t-ratios in parentheses)

Period: 1960:I—1972:IV

Regression Number	Lag	Variable Changed	$\sum_{j=o}^{n} w_j p_{t-j}^c$	i_f^*	d	$\ln B^X$	$\ln B_R^X$	$\ln y$	$\ln p^c$	Const.	$\bar{R}^2$	SE	DW
4.1.1	$n = 8$,		0.57							5.34	0.450	0.656	0.24
			(5.25)							(18.28)			
4.2.1	$n = 14$,		0.87							4.65	0.551	0.610	0.32
			(5.70)							(12.31)			
4.3.1	$n = 24$,		1.58							2.96	0.863	0.336	0.89
			(12.99)							(10.37)			
4.1.2	$n = 8$,	$d = d_8$	0.10	0.25	0.35	-1.34		1.55	1.26	-6.70	0.949	0.205	1.63
			(1.21)	(13.01)	(7.41)	(-6.67)		(2.23)	(0.97)	(-1.64)			
4.2.2	$n = 14$,	$d = d_{14}$	0.36	0.26	0.38	-1.04		1.10	0.58	-1.53	0.947	0.209	1.44
			(2.03)	(12.15)	(7.28)	(-3.94)		(1.54)	(0.40)	(-0.31)			
4.3.2	$n = 24$,	$d = d_{24}$	1.43	0.15	0.30	-0.55		1.19	-2.33	3.97	0.958	0.187	1.48
			(4.53)	(7.39)	(5.83)	(-2.16)		(1.90)	(-1.37)	(10.28)			
4.1.3	$n = 8$,	$d = d_8$	0.10	0.25	0.35		-1.34	1.51		-0.38	0.950	0.202	1.63
			(1.34)	(13.22)	(7.72)		(-6.74)	(5.04)		(-0.11)			
4.2.3	$n = 14$,	$d = d_{14}$	0.33	0.26	0.37		-1.07	0.92		3.83	0.948	0.207	1.48
			(2.17)	(12.24)	(7.61)		(-4.19)	(2.04)		(0.92)			
4.3.3	$n = 24$,	$d = d_{24}$	0.97	0.16	0.28		-0.82	0.50		5.62	0.954	0.194	1.60
			(4.50)	(7.77)	(5.39)		(-3.31)	(1.03)		(1.15)			

weights of the distributed lag variable. These results run counter to findings by Yohe and Karnosky (1969, p. 38). Again the regression with the longest lag and the smallest standard error, regression 4.3.2, makes no sense. The total effect of the anticipated rate of inflation is estimated to be significantly above unity, and the price level affects the interest rate negatively. This regression, as well as regressions 4.2.1 and 4.2.2, apparently suffer from serious multicollinearity due to the joint inclusion of the price level and a distributed lag of its past rates of change. Apart from that, regressions 4.1.2 and 4.2.2 do not appear unreasonable. However, neither provides a closer fit for the interest rate than does the comparable regression 2.4.2 of table 2, nor do they point to a significantly larger total effect of π on i.

In the last three regressions of table 4, the nominal exogenous monetary base is replaced by its real counterpart, and the price-level variable is excluded. The smallest standard error was obtained for regression 4.3.3. Like the estimates of Feldstein and Eckstein (1970) for the United States, this regression identifies a total lag in adaptive-expectations formation of 24 quarters and a total effect of the anticipated rate of inflation on the interest rate not significantly different from unity. This result does not appear to be reliable because we cannot discriminate between this estimate and regressions 4.1.3 or 4.2.3 that are based on shorter lags. The predictive power of regression 4.1.3 is not significantly different from that of regression 4.3.3, but in contrast, it assigns to the distributed lag variable a negligible effect of 0.10. Also noteworthy is the observation that while the sum of the weights of the distributed lag variable increases with an increasing length of the lag, the parameter of real income decreases and becomes insignificant in regression 4.3.3.

We conclude that the conventional approximation of the anticipated rate of inflation by an estimated polynomial distributed lag of actual rates of inflation is inferior to the use of the difference between bond and dividend yield.[18] Regression 3.3 of table 3, where this proxy is employed,

18. One frequently observes that in the estimation of polynomial distributed lags, end-point constraints are imposed. We have checked whether this would lead to more favorable results for the conventional approach but found the opposite. Most noteworthy, the sum of weights of the distributed lag variable appeared to be significantly smaller for the same lag length than in the case of no end-point constraints.

has predictive power equal to regressions 4.1.2 to 4.3.3 but is less affected by serial correlation and multicollinearity and therefore appears to be more trustworthy.

3. CONCLUSIONS

The main objective of this study has been to clarify for an open economy the role of price expectations as a short-run determinant of the nominal rate of interest, given a fixed-exchange-rates regime. Under these conditions, anticipated domestic inflation affects the rate of interest through two main channels: the familiar substitution between domestic nominal and real assets, and the substitution between domestic and foreign nominal assets.

It has been shown that the direct effect of the anticipated rate of inflation on the interest rate is smaller than unity in the short run. We have tested this hypothesis and found it confirmed by reduced-form estimates that employed alternative proxies for the anticipated rate of inflation based on either adaptive or rational expectations. The most reliable estimate was obtained with neither of these alternatives, but by introducing the observable difference between the yield on newly issued bonds and the dividend yield on common stocks as a proxy for the anticipated rate of inflation. According to our estimates, an increase of the anticipated rate of inflation by one percentage point raises the nominal rate of interest by about 50 basis points during the same quarter and symmetrically depresses the real rate on financial assets.

In assessing this result, one must presume that the chosen proxy is not an ideal indicator of the true anticipated rate of inflation. On the other hand, we have found that the conventional approach—assuming adaptive expectations and using an estimated polnomial distributed lag of actual rates of inflation as a proxy for the anticipated rate of inflation—led to estimates of the interest rate that appear to be less trustworthy. A systematic variation of the length of the distributed lag between 4 and 28 quarters showed that a lengthening of the lag increased the sum of weights of the distributed lag variable considerably while decreasing the parameter values of the remaining explanatory variables. The adjusted R^2 was only negligibly affected. A reliable discrimination between these estimates appeared to be impossible due to serial correlation.

Finally, we note that the foreign interest rate appeared to be an important determinant of the German long-term interest rate during the period of fixed exchange rates. According to our estimates, changes in the Eurodollar rate had exactly the same effect on the domestic interest rate as did changes in the central bank's discount rate.

APPENDIX 1

Symbols

B^A = monetary base adjusted for net borrowing from the central bank

B^X = exogenous source component of monetary base

B^X_R = B^X deflated by p^c

C = net foreign postion of central bank resulting exclusively from private capital transactions

D = holdings of foreign assets by domestic banks and nonbanks

E = domestic earning assets, denominated in domestic currency

F = foreign holdings of domestic earning assets

G = fiscal stimulus variable

K = existing stock of real capital

M = money stock excluding time deposits

P = price level of existing stock of real capital

S = total circulation of government bonds

S_R = S deflated by p^c

W^H = human wealth

W^N = nonhuman wealth

a^D = asset multiplier

d = discount rate

d_1 = residuals from the regression $d = d(\pi_1, i_f^*)$

d_2 = residuals from the regression $d = d(\pi_2, i_f^*)$

d_3 = residuals from the regression $d = d(\pi_3, i_f^*)$

d_4 = residuals from the regression $d = d(\pi_4, i_f^*)$

d_8, d_{14}, and d_{24} are residuals from regressions of d on i_f^* and polynomial distributed lags (of degree three) of $\dot{p}^c$, where the length of the lags was 8, 14, and 24 quarters, respectively

e = anticipated real net return on real capital

i = credit-market rate

i^* = foreign interest rate

i_f^* = Eurodollar rate on three-month deposits, adjusted for forward premium

m = money multiplier

p = current price level

p^a = price level anticipated to be existent one year later

p_1^a = $(1 + \pi_1/100)\, p^c$

p_2^a = $(1 + \pi_2/100)\, p^c$

p_3^a = $(1 + \pi_3/100)\, p^c$

p_4^a = $(1 + \pi_4/100)\, p^c$

p^c = cost-of-living index

p^I = index of import prices

r = reserve requirement ratio

x = real exports

y = output of private sector

α = F/E

β = D/F

π = anticipated rate of inflation, measured in percentage points

$\pi_1 = \dot{p}^c_{-1}$

$\pi_2 = 0.620\,\dot{p}^c_{-1} + 0.236\,\dot{p}^c_{-2} + 0.090\,\dot{p}^c_{-3} + 0.034\,\dot{p}^c_{-4}$

π_3 = proxy for the anticipated rate of inflation based on rational expectations

π_4 = difference between current bond yield and current dividend yield

Description of the Data

The proxy for the credit-market rate, i, is the daily average yield to maturity on public bonds in circulation. These bonds have the largest daily turnover. Their average maturity is six years.

The foreign interest-rate variable i^*_f, is the rate on three-month Eurodollar deposits in London (averages of all Fridays) plus the forward premium on holding three-month dollar contracts (daily averages). Both rates are measured in percent per year.

The discount-rate variable, d, is the daily average of the official discount rate set by the Deutsche Bundesbank.

The monetary-base variable, B^X, is the monetary base adjusted for (1) liberated reserves, (2) net borrowing of banks from the Deutsche Bundesbank, and (3) the cumulated capital inflow due to private capital transactions. Starting period of the cumulation is 1950.

The government debt variable, S, is total debt minus the debt held by the Deutsche Bundesbank.

The income variables, Y and y, are nominal and real gross national income as published by the Deutsche Institut für Wirtschaftsforschung, Berlin.

The price index used is the most broadly based cost-of-living index. It serves for deflating the monetary base and government debt as well as for computing the actual rate of inflation, the proxies π_1 and π_2 for the anticipated rate of inflation, and the four proxies for the anticipated price level.

Computation of π_4 is based on the daily average yield to maturity on all newly issued bonds and on the dividend yield on all common stock admitted to the trade on stock exchanges.

Note that the interest-rate data are averages of the last month of each quarter, while the stock variables are measured at the end of each quarter. No series is seasonally adjusted. Generally, the introduction of seasonal dummies did not significantly improve the estimates. Therefore, only results using unadjusted data are reported.

APPENDIX 2

Definitions of Elasticities of Equations (15a), (16a), (17a)

$$\varepsilon(MM, i) = \varepsilon(m, i) - \varepsilon(L, i) - \varepsilon(L, W^N)\varepsilon(\nu, i)\, \nu S/W^N > 0$$

$$\varepsilon(CM, i) = (1-\alpha)[\varepsilon(a^D, i) + \varepsilon(a^D, W^N)\varepsilon(\nu, i)\, \nu S/W^N] + \alpha\varepsilon(F, i)$$
$$- \varepsilon(s, i-\pi)\, i/(i-\pi) > 0$$

$$\varepsilon(CB, i) = [\varepsilon(F, i) - \beta\varepsilon(D, i) - \beta\varepsilon(D, W^N)\varepsilon(\nu, i)\, \nu S/W^N]/(1-\beta) > 0$$

$$\varepsilon(MM, P) = \varepsilon(m, P) - \varepsilon(L, P) - \varepsilon(L, W^N)\, PK/W^N < 0$$

$$\varepsilon(CM, P) = (1-\alpha)[\varepsilon(a^D, P) + \varepsilon(a^D, W^N)\, PK/W^N] - \varepsilon(s, P) > 0$$

$$\varepsilon(CB, P) = -\beta[\varepsilon(D, P) + \varepsilon(D, W^N)\, PK/W^N]/(1-\beta) < 0$$

$$\varepsilon(MM, C) = C/B^A > 0$$

$$\varepsilon(CM, C) = (1-\alpha)\varepsilon(MM, C) > 0$$

$$\varepsilon(MM, B^X) = B^X/B^A - \varepsilon(L, W^N)\, B^X/W^N > 0$$

$$\varepsilon(CM, B^X) = (1-\alpha)[B^X/B^A + \varepsilon(a^D, W^N)\, B^X/W^N] > 0$$

$$\varepsilon(CB, B^X) = -\beta\varepsilon(D, W^N)\, B^X/W^N (1-\beta) < 0$$

$$\varepsilon(MM, d) = \varepsilon(m, d) < 0, \quad \varepsilon(MM, r) = (m, r) < 0$$

$$\varepsilon(CM, d) = (1-\alpha)\varepsilon(a^D, d) < 0, \quad \varepsilon(CM, r) = (1-\alpha)\varepsilon(a^D, r) < 0$$

$$\varepsilon(MM, i^*) = \varepsilon(m, i^*) - \varepsilon(L, i^*) > 0$$

$$\varepsilon(CM, i^*) = (1-\alpha)\varepsilon(a^D, i^*) + \alpha\varepsilon(F, i^*) - \varepsilon(s, i^*) < 0$$

$$\varepsilon(CB, i^*) = [\varepsilon(F, i^*) - \beta\varepsilon(D, i^*)]/(1-\beta) < 0$$

$$\varepsilon(CM, \pi) = -\varepsilon(s, i-\pi)\, \pi/(i-\pi) > 0$$

$$\varepsilon(MM, p) = -\varepsilon(L, p) < 0$$

$$\varepsilon(CM, p) = \varepsilon(a^D, p) < 0$$

$$\varepsilon(MM, p^a) = -\varepsilon(L, p^a) - \varepsilon(L, W^H)\varepsilon(W^H, p^a) > 0$$

$$\varepsilon(CM, p^a) = (1-\alpha)\varepsilon(a^D, W^H)\varepsilon(W^H, p^a) - \varepsilon(s, p^a) < 0$$

$$\varepsilon(CB, p^a) = [\varepsilon(F, p^a) - \beta\varepsilon(D, p^a) + \beta\varepsilon(D, W^H)\varepsilon(W^H, p^a)]/(1-\beta) < 0$$

$$\varepsilon(MM, y) = [\varepsilon(m, e) - \varepsilon(L, e)]\varepsilon(e, y) - \varepsilon(L, W^H)\varepsilon(W^H, y) > 0$$

$$\varepsilon(CM, y) = (1-\alpha)[\varepsilon(a^D, e)\varepsilon(e, y) + \varepsilon(a^D, W^H)\varepsilon(W^H, y)] - \varepsilon(s, e)\varepsilon(e, y) <$$

$$\varepsilon(CB, y) = -\beta[\varepsilon(D, e)\varepsilon(e, y) + \varepsilon(D, W^H)\varepsilon(W^H, y)]/(1-\beta) > 0$$

$$\varepsilon(MM, S) = -\varepsilon(L, W^N)\, vS/W^N < 0$$

$$\varepsilon(CM, S) = (1-\alpha)\varepsilon(a^D, W^N)\, vS/W^N - \varepsilon(s, S) < 0$$

$$\varepsilon(CB, S) = -\beta\varepsilon(D, W^N)\, vS/W^N (1-\beta) < 0$$

Note: (a) $\alpha = F/D$, $\beta = D/F$, $1 - \beta = C/F$. (b) The positive signs of the elasticities $\varepsilon(MM, C)$ and $\varepsilon(CM, C)$ are defined for $C > 0$, an assumption which generally holds in the German case. (c) We assume that the net response of money demand to an increase in the anticipated price level is negative, while the net response of the domestic demand for foreign assets is positive. We also hypothesize that in all financial markets the partial response to a change in y via the anticipated net yield on real capital dominates the partial response to the change in y via human wealth. (d) To increase the empirical content of the model, we introduce the following order constraints:

$$\varepsilon(CM, i),\ \varepsilon(CB, i) > \varepsilon(MM, i)$$
$$|\varepsilon(MM, P)| > \varepsilon(CM, P),\ |\varepsilon(CB, P)|$$
$$|\varepsilon(CB, i^*)|, |\varepsilon(CM, i^*)| > \varepsilon(MM, i^*)$$
$$|\varepsilon(CM, y)| > \varepsilon(MM, y),\ \varepsilon(CB, y).$$

REFERENCES

Andersen, L. C., and Jordan, J. L. 1968. "The Monetary Base—Explanation and Analytical Use." Federal Reserve Bank of St. Louis REVIEW, Aug., pp. 7-14.

Brunner, K. 1973*a*. "Credit Market, Interest Rate, and Three Types of Inflation." KREDIT UND KAPITAL 6: 375-414.

_____. 1973*b*. "Money Supply Process and Monetary Policy in an Open Economy." In INTERNATIONAL TRADE AND MONEY, edited by M. B. Conolly and A. K. Swoboda. London: Allen & Unwin.

Brunner, K., and Meltzer, A. H. 1968. "Liquidity Traps for Money, Bank Credit, and Interest Rates." JOURNAL OF POLITICAL ECONOMY 76: 1-37.

_____. 1976. "Monetary and Fiscal Policy in Open Interdependent Economies with Fixed Exchange Rates." In RECENT ISSUES IN INTERNATIONAL MONETARY ECONOMICS, edited by E. M. Claassen and P. Salin. Amsterdam: North-Holland.

Feldstein, M., and Eckstein, O. 1970. "The Fundamental Determinants of the Interest Rate." REVIEW OF ECONOMICS AND STATISTICS 52: 363-76.

Fisher, I. 1930. THE THEORY OF INTEREST. New York: Macmillan.

Friedman, M., and Schwartz, A. J. 1963. A MONETARY HISTORY OF THE UNITED STATES, 1867-1960. Princeton: Princeton University Press (for National Bureau of Economic Research).

Gebauer, W. 1973. "Die Determinanten des Zinsniveaus in der Bundesrepublik Deutschland." KREDIT UND KAPITAL 6: 187-202.

Gibson, W. E. 1970. "Price Expectations Effects on Interest Rates." JOURNAL OF FINANCE 25: 19-34.

Gibson, W. E., and Kaufman, G. C. 1968. "The Sensitivity of Interest Rates to Changes in Money and Income." JOURNAL OF POLITICAL ECONOMY 76: 472-78.

Hamburger, M. J. 1974. "The Demand for Money in an Open Economy: Germany and the United Kingdom." JOURNAL OF MONETARY ECONOMICS 3 (1977): 25-40. Reprinted in this volume.

Hamburger, M. J., and Platt, E. N. 1975. "The Expectations Hypothesis and the Efficiency of the Treasury Bill Market." REVIEW OF ECONOMICS AND STATISTICS 57: 190-99.

Hamburger, M. J., and Silber, W. L. 1969. "An Empirical Study of Interest Rate Determination." REVIEW OF ECONOMICS AND STATISTICS 51: 369-73.

Jüttner, J. 1975. "Zinssätze und Inflationserwartungen in der Bundesrepublik." JAHRBUCHER FÜR NATIONALÖKONOMIE UND STATISTIK 188: 385-95.

Kouri, P. J. K., and Porter, M. G. 1974. "International Capital Flows and Portfolio Equilibrium." JOURNAL OF POLITICAL ECONOMY 82: 443-66.

Meiselman, D. 1963. "Bond Yields and the Price Level: The Gibson Paradox Regained." In BANKING AND MONETARY STUDIES, edited by D. Carson. Homewood, Ill.: Irwin.

Muth, J. F. 1961. "Rational Expectations and the Theory of Price Movements." ECONOMETRICA 29: 315-35.

Roll, R. 1972. "Interest Rates on Monetary Assets and Commodity Price Index Changes." JOURNAL OF FINANCE 27: 251-77.

Sargent, T. J. 1969. "Commodity Price Expectations and the Interest Rate." QUARTERLY JOURNAL OF ECONOMICS 83: 127-40.

_____. 1972. "Anticipated Inflation and the Nominal Rate of Interest." QUARTERLY JOURNAL OF ECONOMICS 86: 121-227.

_____. 1973*a*. "The Fundamental Determinants of the Interest Rate: A Comment." REVIEW OF ECONOMICS AND STATISTICS 55: 391-93.

_____. 1973*b*. "Rational Expectations and the Dynamics of Hyperinflation." INTERNATIONAL ECONOMIC REVIEW 14: 328-50.

_____. 1973*c*. "What Do Regressions of Interest on Inflation Show?" ANNALS OF ECONOMIC AND SOCIAL MEASUREMENT 2: 289-301.

Shiller, R. 1975. "Rational Expectations and the Dynamic Structure of Macroeconomic Models: A Critical Review." Paper presented at the Helsinki Conference on the Monetary Mechanism in Open Economies, Aug.

Siebke, J. 1977. "Price Expectations and the Interest Rate in the Federal Republic of Germany." In MONETARY POLICY AND ECONOMIC ACTIVITY IN WEST GERMANY, edited by S. F. Frowen, A. S. Courakis, and M. H. Miller. Surrey: University of Surrey Press.

Siebke, J., and Willms, M. 1972. "Zinsniveau, Geldpolitik und Inflation." KREDIT UND KAPITAL 5: 171-205.

_____. 1973. "Die Determinanten des Zinsniveaus in der Bundesrepublik Deutschland." KREDIT UND KAPITAL 6: 203-19.

Yohe, W. P., and Karnosky, D. S. 1969. "Interest Rates and Price Level Changes, 1952-1969." Federal Reserve Bank of St. Louis REVIEW, Dec., pp. 18-38.

TRANSACTION COSTS AND THE EFFICIENCY OF INTERNATIONAL CAPITAL MARKETS: TRANQUIL VERSUS TURBULENT PERIODS*

Jacob A. Frenkel & Richard M. Levich
University of Chicago, New York University

Numerous economic phenomena would not exist in a world in which the cost of transacting is zero. The existence of money, the distortions associated with monopolies, externalities, and the like, cannot be explained in the absence of some cost of negotiations, search, information, or other forms of transaction costs. The existence of such costs might be responsible for what otherwise would be inefficient allocations. In particular, various parity conditions based on the assumption of costless arbitrage need not be exact if the activity of arbitrage entails cost.

This paper deals with transaction costs and the efficiency of short-term capital movements. Our prime purpose is to examine whether, and to what extent, the efficiency of short-term capital movements have been affected by different economic environments generated by the varying exchange rate regimes.

In a previous paper (Frenkel and Levich 1975), we suggested a method for estimating the cost of transactions associated with covered interest arbitrage. The period studied was from January 1962 to November 1967—a period which was relatively homogeneous in terms of the extent of volatility in the foreign exchange markets. We refer to that period as the "tranquil pegged exchange rate period." The British devaluation in November 1967 terminated the "tranquil period" and set the stage for extremely turbulent times in the foreign exchange markets during 1968 and 1969, a period that may be referred to as the "turbulent pegged exchange rate period." Following a transitional phase, the system evolved into its present state, referred to as the "managed (or dirty) float."

---

* The paper is an expanded version of "Transaction Costs and Interest Arbitrage: Tranquil versus Turbulent Periods," JOURNAL OF POLITICAL ECONOMY 85, no. 6 (December 1977): 1207-24. Printed by permission of the authors and the University of Chicago Press. An earlier version of the paper was presented at the 1975 Konstanz Seminar and at the Helsinki Conference on Monetary Mechanism in Open Economies, August 1975.

In the present paper we apply the method of estimation to the abovementioned three phases of the exchange rate system, concentrating on a comparison of the results obtained for these three periods. One of the conclusions emerging from such a comparison is reflected in the title of this paper and relates to the classification of periods; it suggests that for the study of covered interest arbitrage, it might be preferable to classify periods by the extent of turbulence rather than by the legal and institutional arrangements of the exchange rate regime (e.g., pegged or flexible-exchange rate systems). In section 1 we outline some of the theoretical aspects associated with incorporating the cost of transactions into the standard formulae for covered interest arbitrage. Section 2 contains a description of the methodology and the estimates of the cost of transactions. In section 3 we use the estimated cost of transactions to assess their significance in accounting for the observed deviations from the parity condition during the three periods under examination. In section 4 we discuss the concept of "unexploited profit opportunities" and examine the implications of following a simple trading rule. In section 5 we proceed to compare some of the characteristics of the three periods by examining the time-series properties of the various exchange rates. Some concluding remarks are contained in section 6.

1. INTEREST ARBITRAGE AND TRANSACTION COSTS: THEORETICAL ASPECTS

The interest-parity theory states that the equilibrium forward premium on foreign exchange is

$$\frac{F - S}{S} = \frac{i - i^*}{1 + i^*}, \tag{1}$$

where F and S are, respectively, the forward and spot exchange rates and i and i^* are the domestic and the foreign rates of interest on securities that are identical in all respects except for the currency of denomination.[1] The formulation in equation (1) ignores any transaction costs in the security and the foreign exchange markets. In Frenkel and Levich (1975) we have shown

1. For an early formulation of the interest-parity theory, see Keynes (1923).

that in the presence of such costs the equilibrium condition is modified. To facilitate the empirical estimation of the costs, we simplify the formulation by assuming that the various costs are proportional to the value of the amount transacted. Thus, we ignore any lumpy cost that is independent of the quantity transacted.

In executing covered interest arbitrage, it is convenient to distinguish between two classes of transactions: those involving the security markets and those involving the foreign exchange markets. The security markets can be further classified into domestic and foreign, while the foreign exchange markets can be classified into spot and forward markets.

To derive the equilibrium conditions that allow for transaction costs, consider first the transactions involved in covered *outflow* of arbitrage funds from the domestic to the foreign economy. If arbitrageurs do not hold cash, then covered outflow requires the execution of four transactions; (a) sale of domestic securities with transaction costs of t percent, (b) spot purchase of foreign currency with transaction costs of t_S percent, (c) purchase of foreign securities with transaction costs of t^* percent, and (d) forward sale of foreign currency with transaction costs of t_F percent.

The cost, C, of transferring the amount χ from domestic to foreign securities is the foregone earnings:

$$C = \chi(1 + i). \tag{2}$$

In turn, the revenue, R, derived from the (covered) investment of these funds in foreign securities is

$$R = \chi\Omega(1 + i^*)F/S, \tag{3}$$

where $\Omega = (1 - t)(1 - t_S)(1 - t^*)(1 - t_F)$.

From (2) the marginal cost is $1 + i$, and from (3) the marginal revenue is $\Omega\,(1 + i^*)F/S$. Equating the marginal cost with the marginal revenue yields the *lower* limit on the forward premium, $p = (F - S)/S$, for which covered outflow is profitable:

$$\underline{p} = \frac{(1 + i) - \Omega(1 + i^*)}{\Omega\,(1 + i^*)} \; . \tag{4}$$

In (4), Ω summarizes the various costs of transactions. As long as there are any transaction costs, $\Omega < 1$ and p exceeds the value that is indicated by equation (1). In other words, the presence of costs implies that in order to induce marginal outflow, the forward premium on foreign exchange must be higher than otherwise so as to compensate for the costs.

Consider now the transactions involved in covered *inflow* of arbitrage funds from the foreign to the domestic economy. The corresponding chain of transactions are (a) sale of foreign securities with transaction costs of t^* percent, (b) spot sale of foreign currency with transaction costs of t_S percent, (c) purchase of domestic securities with transaction costs of t percent, and (d) forward purchase of foreign currency with transaction costs of t_F percent. By symmetric reasoning, the cost (or foregone earnings) of the inflow is

$$C = \chi(1 + i^*), \tag{5}$$

and the revenue is

$$R = \chi\Omega(1 + i)S/F. \tag{6}$$

Equating the marginal cost, $1 + i^*$, with the marginal revenue, $\Omega(1 + i)S/F$, yields the *upper* limit on the forward premium for which covered inflow is profitable:

$$\bar{p} = \frac{\Omega(1 + i) - (1 + i^*)}{1 + i^*} \; . \tag{7}$$

Notice that $\bar{p}$ is smaller than the value indicated from equation (1). Thus, to induce marginal capital inflow the forward discount must be larger (or equivalently, the forward premium must be smaller) so as to compensate for the various costs associated with the transactions.

Equations (4) and (7) set the limits for a neutral band within which covered interest arbitrage is not profitable. Whenever the forward premium falls within the neutral band such that

$$\frac{\Omega(1 + i) - (1 + i^*)}{1 + i^*} \leq p \leq \frac{(1 + i) - \Omega(1 + i^*)}{\Omega(1 + i^*)} \; , \tag{8}$$

there will be no incentive for covered interest arbitrage. Thus, points that are bounded within the neutral band may be viewed as equilibrium points even though the condition of equation (1) is not satisfied. The width of the neutral band increases with the cost of transactions; therefore, the higher the costs, the more likely it is that situations that seem to entail profit opportunities are in fact equilibrium positions that are bounded within the band. To enable such an analysis it is necessary, therefore, to estimate these costs.[2] The above formulation assumes that potential arbitrageurs always hold securities; as a result, the initial transaction has to be a sale of securities for cash. Since, however, at each period, some fraction of the existing stock of securities matures, some arbitrageurs may initially hold cash. Allowing for this possibility in the above formulae results in a more conservative measure of the cost of transactions, where in equation (4) we replace Ω by $\Omega_1 = \Omega/(1 - t)^2$ and in equation (7) we replace Ω by $\Omega_2 = \Omega/(1 - t^*)^2$, with the corresponding modification of condition (8). Our framework corresponds to the typical textbook description, which views arbitrage as a "round trip" activity. For example, U.S. artibrageurs begin and end with dollar-denominated assets and avoid exchange risk by covering in the forward market. To the extent that holders of a specific currency wish to purchase another currency without completing the round trip, some of the costly transactions could be avoided. In this case, the resulting band will be narrower than indicated by equation (4). For an elaboration of this case, see Deardorff (1977).

2. TRANSACTION COSTS: METHODOLOGY AND ESTIMATES

There are no direct estimates of the cost of transactions in either the market for foreign exchange or the security market. If deviations from the interest-parity condition were due only to the cost of arbitrage, then the

2. Observed deviations from the arbitrage condition induced various attempts to reconcile the theoretical expectations with the empirical facts. In addition to analyzing covered interest arbitrage, the modern theory of forward exchange considers the activities of hedging and speculation as factors determining the forward rate (e.g., Tsiang 1959; Kenen 1965; Grubel 1966). Other attempts to account for the persisting deviations have emphasized the role of transaction costs (Branson 1969; Frenkel and Levich 1975), political risk (Aliber 1973), the elasticities of demand and supply in the capital markets (Prachowny 1970; Frenkel 1973), and differential tax treatments (Levi 1977). For a survey, see Officer and Willet (1970).

existing deviations would provide a measure of the cost. This approach to the measurement of the cost of transactions is clearly unsatisfactory, since the assumption is that all profit opportunities are exploited. Thus, the answer to the basic question under consideration is being assumed without verification. An estimate of the cost should be deduced from data other than the existing deviations from covered interest parity.

In an earlier paper (Frenkel and Levich 1975), we proposed a procedure for the estimation of the cost of transactions in the market for foreign exchange by using data on triangular arbitrage. Briefly, the essence of triangular arbitrage is to ensure consistency of cross exchange rates.[3] As an example, consider the exchange rates between the U.S. dollar and the U.K. pound, the U.S. dollar and the German mark, and the German mark and the U.K. pound. In the absence of transaction costs, arbitrage among currencies ensures that equation (9) holds.

$$(\$/£)_\tau = (\$/DM)_\tau \, (DM/£)_\tau, \tag{9}$$

where the terms in parentheses indicate the corresponding exchange rates, and the subscript τ indicates that these prices are for foreign exchange delivered at the same maturity, τ.[4] If transactions in the foreign exchange market are costly, the two sides of equation (9) could differ, and the maximum discrepancy would correspond to the differential costs involved in executing the two types of exchange. Furthermore, if the cost of transacting is approximately equal across leading currencies, then one would expect the maximum discrepancy between the two sides of equation (9) to

3. For an analysis and measurement of triangular arbitrage, see Grubel (1966).

4. This formulation assumes that the various exchange rates reflect a direct exchange of one currency for another. In practice, many exchanges between two convertible currencies may use another vehicle currency as an intermediary. Since all of the exchange rates in eqs. (9) and (9') involve either the U.K. pound or the U.S. dollar (both being vehicle currencies), it seems that the assumption of a direct exchange is satisfied. It should be noted that our method may not be generalized for cases that do not involve vehicle currencies, since not all exchange rates will reflect meaningful direct quotations.

correspond to the cost of one transaction. Accordingly, this is the way we estimate the cost of transactions in the market for foreign exchange. This estimate should be interpreted to encompass the total cost associated with a transaction. Thus, it includes elements like brokerage fees, time cost, subscription costs, and all other components that enter into the cost of being informed.[5]

When we take the cost of transactions in the market for foreign exchange as the upper limit of the discrepancy from triangular arbitrage, we assume that the structure of the cost remains stable throughout the period under examination. It is only under this assumption that we can interpret smaller deviations from triangular arbitrage as being within a neutral band such that the cost of transaction exceeds arbitrage profits. Therefore, it is necessary to identify periods during which market conditions were approximately homogeneous. In identifying such periods, we follow the suggestion of Leamer and Stern (1972) and inspect the ratio of the forward rates to the spot exchange rates for various currencies. A forward rate lying outside the support limits may indicate (under a regime of pegged

---

5. This suggested procedure could be criticized on the gounds that it presumes that arbitrage in currencies is efficient and therefore that the upper limit of the deviations from the equality implied by triangular arbitrage measures the cost of transaction. It seems, however, that if there is a market for which this presumption is justified, it is the market for foreign exchange. This was also the market used by Walras in developing the concept of arbitrage, as well as the notion that discrepancies from parity in that market correspond to the cost of transactions:

> Whenever this state of general equilibrium is disturbed, it will be restored by arbitrage operations in bills of exchange exactly like arbitrage operations in commodities. . . . Bills of exchange are *par excellence* the most suitable commodity for arbitrage operations. At every commercial center there are special bankers, called *cambists*, whose business it is to keep continual watch on the rates of exchange and to restore general equilibrium in foreign exchange by taking advantage of the possibility of any profit to be made by making indirect rather than direct purchases. . . . There is a limit of the loss and premium on exchange; and this limit is the total cost. . . . If the limit were exceeded, the debtor would prefer to send species. Hence the limit cannot be exceeded. [Walras 1870, Lesson 34]

Similar concepts of the operation of the foreign exchange market can be found in Ricardo (1811, pp. 9-10) and Cournot (1838, chap. 3).

exchange rates) pressures reflecting lack of confidence in the government's ability to maintain the peg. When the exchange rate is flexible, there is no obligation to maintain a specific rate; in this case, periods may be classified according to the degree of volatility of the ratio of the forward to the spot exchange rate.

In figure 1 we plot the ratio of the 90-day forward to the spot exchange rates for two pairs of currencies: the mark-dollar and the pound-dollar rates. As is evident, several periods emerge: (a) 1962-67—which we identify as the tranquil peg; (b) 1968-69—which we identify as the turbulent peg; and (c) 1973-75—the managed float. We chose not to analyze the period from January 1970 to June 1973, which marks the breakdown of the pegged rate system and the transition toward the current regime. As can be seen from figure 1, the various peaks and troughs correspond to the major crises in the international financial markets.[6] To further explore the relative homogeneity of the three periods, we have examined the deviations from triangular arbitrage; while these deviations differ markedly among periods, their structure is relatively stable within each period. Accordingly, we have concluded that there are three distinct periods for which we need to estimate the cost of transactions in the market for foreign exchange.

To estimate the cost of transactions, we have analyzed the series of weekly observations of the spot and the 90-day forward exchange rates. Using these observations, we have computed for each period two series of weekly percentage deviations from the triangular arbitrage of equation (5) for the spot and the forward rates. The upper limits of these series of deviations correspond to t_S and t_F, respectively—the cost of transactions in the spot and the forward markets. To allow for errors in measurement and other data inaccuracies, we have taken a more conservative measure: our estimates of t_S and t_F for the various periods are the percentage deviation which bounds 95 percent of the weekly deviations from triangular arbitrage.

---

6. A more comprehensive Crisis Index that provides for a similar classification is developed by Stokes (1972).

Figure 1

Ratio of 90-Day Forward Rates to Spot Exchange Rates, Weekly Observations (for data source, see Appendix).

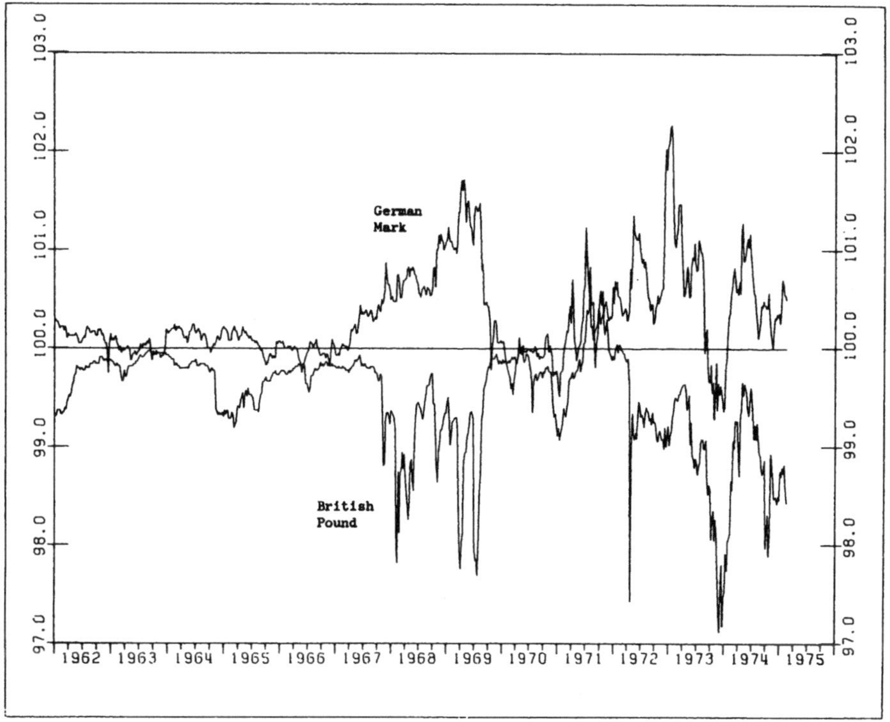

The indirect exchange between the U.S. dollar and the U.K. pound in equation (9) was assumed to occur through the German mark. In principle, other currencies could be used as intermediaries. It is expected that competition will assure that the cost of transacting will tend to be equalized among leading vehicle currencies. To allow, however, for possible differences in transaction costs as a function of the intermediate currency, we have also computed the cost for the case in which the Canadian dollar (C$) replaces the German mark as the vehicle of arbitrage, as in equation (9').[7]

$$(\$/\pounds)_\tau = (\$/C\$)_\tau (C\$/\pounds)_\tau \quad (9')$$

The various estimates of the cost of transactions in the market for foreign exchange are summarized in table 1. As can be seen, these estimates differ significantly among the different periods under consideration, while within each period the estimates show much less variation with respect to the choice of the intermediate currency.

Table 1

Estimates of the Percentage Cost of Transactions
in the Market for Foreign Exchange
(Spot and 90-Day Forward)

Period	Arbitrage Between Securities	Intermediate Currency	t_S	t_F	$t_S + t_F$
Jan. 1962-	U.S.$ and £	DM	0.051	0.076	0.127
Nov. 1967	U.S.$ and £	C$	0.058	0.068	0.126
Jan. 1968-	U.S.$ and £	DM	0.102	0.160	0.262
Dec. 1969	U.S.$ and £	C$	0.085	0.112	0.197
July 1973-	U.S.$ and £	DM	0.523	0.507	1.030
May 1975	U.S.$ and £	C$	0.438	0.442	0.920

SOURCE: See Appendix.

7. For a related discussion on the role of the cost of transactions in the determination of vehicle currencies, see Swoboda (1969).

The changes in the cost of transactions are also related to the pattern depicted in figure 1. The British devaluation in November 1967 signified the start of the turbulent period, which manifested itself in lack of confidence and increased uncertainty. In the face of these developments, dealers required a larger compensation for carrying inventory of various currencies and for standing ready to take immediate positions. In addition, the period following the British devaluation witnessed a lower degree of communications and harmonization among central banks, resulting in wider bands, and larger uncertainty.

In the most recent, managed-float period, the cost of transactions in foreign exchange has risen to unprecedented heights. Depending on the currency and on the maturity of the contract, the cost during the period is from six to ten times higher than the corresponding cost during the tranquil peg. In the face of increased uncertaintly concerning the evolution of the system and the financial collapse of some institutions, many banks are reluctant to take positions even for a short period, which results in larger deviations from triangular arbitrage.[8]

It should be emphasized, however, that these developments need not be interpreted as a necessary characteristic of the flexible-exchange-rate regime. They may have been just coincidental to the timing of the system's evolution into the current regime, or they may have reflected the friction associated with the transition toward and the familiarization with a new

8. The financial collapse of some institutions due to losses from foreign exchange operations encouraged governments to tighten controls over such operations and thereby to further increase the cost of transactions. An instructive example to this effect is provided by the market and governmental reactions to the failure of the German Herstatt bank. This reaction is described in the *Weekly Review* of the Harris Bank (June 28, 1974):

> The Bundesbank's closing of a large German bank due to foreign exchange losses was received with nervous uncertainty in all exchange markets. ... Starting next month, all German banks will be required to report their foreign currency positions up to the month's end in one month, three months, and over three months categories. ... By weekend, most exchanges settled back to a thin but restrained trading with unusually wide trade margins.

exchange rate system. There is, however, a presumption that ask-bid spreads, which are components of the cost of transactions, are higher during periods of uncertainty. Volatility of price series may imply that price changes contain new information. Dealers, wishing to protect themselves against the superior information that may be possessed by several traders, will quote a wider ask-bid spread and thereby raise the cost of transactions. Indeed, evidence on the early float indicates the close link between the extent of uncertainty and the ask-bid spread.[9] In addition, if transaction costs include fixed components, the average cost of transactions is inversely related to the size of transactions. To the extent that the rise in uncertainty reduced the average size of transactions, it may have contributed to the higher cost.

The second class of transactions required for covered interest arbitrage involves the security markets. We adopt Demsetz's (1968) estimate, according to which total costs are about 2.5 times the ask-bid spread. Since the ask-bid spread corresponds to the cost of two transactions (a round trip), our estimate of the cost of a *single* transactions is 1.25 times the ask-bid spread.

In the next section we explore the impact of transaction costs on the efficacy of covered interest arbitrage among various groups of securities. One group comprises traditional pairs of securities: the U.S.-U.K. treasury bills and the U.S.-Canadian treasury bills. The second group comprises

---

9. Using daily observations on the ask-bid spread for various currencies during the early float in 1971, Fieleke (1975) found a close link between the spread and some proxies for the extent of uncertainty. Our approach to the estimation of the cost of transactions in the market for foreign exchange differs in that we do not interpret the size of the daily deviation from triangular arbitrage as the daily cost. Rather we prefer to provide an estimate for a longer period that is more or less homogeneous. We do observe, however, a close relationship between our estimates and the estimates derived from the ask-bid spread. Lack of data on the various currencies for the whole of the three periods prevented a complete comparison of the two approaches. Further evidence of the pattern displayed by the ask-bid spread is provided in Aliber (1975), McKinnon (1976), and McCormick (1975). An interesting theoretical analysis on the relationship between uncertainty and the ask-bid spread is contained in Allen (1977).

external pairs of securities, e.g., securities that are issued in the Euromarket.[10] Since we did not have a uniform source of information on the spreads in the Euro-currency markets for the period as a whole, we report estimates only for the latter two periods. The modal values of these costs for the various periods are reported in table 2. As can be seen, the cost of transactions in the U.S. treasury bills increased over the period under examination, while the cost in the Euro-dollar market remained stable as between the last two periods. The cost in the thinnest market—the Euro-sterling market—exceeded the corresponding cost in the other markets in the last two periods.

Table 2

Estimates of the Percentage Cost of Transactions in the Markets for 90-Day Securities

Period	U.S. Treasury Bills—t	Euro-$ Rate t (external)	Euro-£ Rate t^* (external)
Jan. 1962-Nov. 1967	0.0095	N.A.	N.A.
Jan. 1968-Dec. 1969	0.0132	0.0381	0.1172
July 1973-May 1975	0.0299	0.0381	0.1175

SOURCE: See Appendix.

10. Aliber (1973) has argued that the traditional pair does not always satisfy the comparability criterion, since treasury bills are issued in financial centers that may differ in political risks. In that respect, the Euro-market securities are more comparable, since both are issued in an external center. There is some evidence that banks use the Euro-currency interest rates in making their quotations of the forward exchange rate. To this extent, the interest-parity relation in the Euro-market will be extremely robust.

3. INTEREST ARBITRAGE AND TRANSACTION COSTS: EMPIRICAL ASPECTS

In this section, we use the formulae developed in section 1 together with the estimates of the cost of transactions to examine their quantitative impact on the operation of covered interest arbitrage. Of special interest is the comparison of the efficacy of covered interest arbitrage--when allowance is made for the cost of transactions--in exploiting profit opportunities during the specified periods. Prior to that examination, a preliminary note on transformation of data in the presence of transaction costs is pertinent.

3.1 Transformation of Data and Transaction Costs

Virtually all studies of covered interest arbitrage that we are familiar with have examined arbitrage of short-term securities—typically, 90-day securities—but have expressed the rates of interest and the forward premium on foreign exchange on an annual basis. Similarly, published sources of data report their annualized values. The process of annualizing rates of return on 90-day contracts amounts basically to quadrupling the 90-day magnitudes. This procedure introduces noise into the data, since there is no presumption that the premium on a one-year forward contract for foreign exchange should be four times the premium on a 90-day forward contract. By the same taken, the structure of the various yield curves may be such that interest-rate differentials on one-year securities are not exactly equal to four times the corresponding differential on 90-day securities.

More fundamentally, in dealing with annualized data of instruments that are of 90-day maturity, the implicit assumption that is being made is that the proceeds of the 90-day loan are reinvested three more times at the same rate of return. In the presence of transaction costs, this implies that one has to take account of four transactions rather than only one. It is clear that the method of annualizing the data increases all deviations fourfold, thereby, if the financial instruments are 90-day securities, creating illusory profit margins. Similarly, if the data collector were to choose to decadize rather than annualize the 90-day data, the profit margins would have been multiplied by forty. Since our estimates of the costs are specific to the 90-day maturity contracts, it is important to associate them with contracts of this length only. Applying these estimates to the annualized data raises the important question of the relationship between the cost of transactions and the maturity of the arbitraged assets. Some preliminary evidence on the term structure of the cost of transactions suggests that the cost tends to rise with the length of the contract (while it tends to decline with the width of the market), but we have not yet analyzed the exact relationship between the cost and the term to maturity.

The basic model of the covered interest arbitrage is a one-period model; it is clear, therefore, that the introduction of annualized data for contracts of maturities differing from one year may, in the presence of transaction costs, introduce confusion and leave the impression of illusory profit opportunities.[11] Consequently, to conform to the 90-day, one-period model, we have transformed the annualized data back into their 90-day counterparts by dividing the published premia and interest rates by four. The following empirical analysis of covered interest arbitrage is based on the transformed data.

---

11. It is interesting to note that similar issues were dealt with (more than a century ago) by George Goschen in *The Theory of the Foreign Exchanges* in his attempt to reconcile what seemed to be unexploited profit opportunities:

> ... it may well be inquired—How is it possible that ... such a difference in the rates of interest can exist between two countries. ... This is a mystery which has puzzled many during periods. ... It is a question, however, which can be solved with the greatest ease. ... It must not be forgotten that—the interest being taken at a percentage calculated per annum, and the probable profit having, when an operation in three-month bills is contemplated, to be divided by four, whereas, the percentage of expense has to be wholly borne by the one transaction—a very slight expense becomes a great impediment. If the cost is only ½ percent, there must be a profit of 2 percent per annum in the rate of interest, or ½ percent on three months, before any advantage commences. [Goschen 1864, pp. 139-43]

3.2 Deviations from Parity: Tranquil versus Turbulent Periods

We turn now to examine, for the various periods, the role of the cost of transactions in accounting for deviations from the interest-parity condition. The traditional pairs are analyzed by examining weekly data on arbitrage between 90-day U.S. and U.K. treasury bills as well as between 90-day U.S. and Canadian bills. The external pair is analyzed by examining weekly data on arbitrage between 90-day Euro-dollar and Euro-sterling securities.

The neutral band around the interest-parity line was computed by using the various estimates of the cost of transactions in foreign exchange—t_S and t_F—and the modal estimates of the cost of transactions in securities—t and t^*.

The fraction of the observations bound within the neutral band generated by the cost of transactions during the various periods is reported in table 3. The computations were made for the traditional as well as the external pairs of securities, using the alternative estimates of the cost from tables 1 and 2. In computing the neutral band, arbitrageurs were assumed to start from two alternative initial positions: first, where the initial position is in securities, so that the cost corresponds to Ω ; and second, where the initial position is in cash, so that the cost corresponds to Ω_1 and Ω_2. The latter case is reported in table 3 under the column headed by Ω'. Due to lack of data on external Canadian interest rates, a similar analysis could not be applied to arbitrage between U.S. and Canadian yields in the external market.

Table 3 reveals that the cost of transactions played a very similar and significant role during the tranquil peg (1962-67) and the managed-float (1973-75) periods. In both, the cost of transactions accounted for a similar fraction of the apparent profit opportunities implied by deviations from the interest-parity condition. This result is striking in view of the vast differences in the estimates of the cost of transactions during these two periods. Within each of these periods, the proportion of the deviations from the U.S.-U.K. parity line explained by the cost of transactions is similar to the proportion of the deviations from the U.S.-Canada parity line explained by these costs. Thus, during these two periods the role played by transaction costs in accounting for deviations from the interest-parity line was almost invariant with respect to the arbitraged assets. The observation that similar fractions of the deviations from parity are explained by the cost of transactions leads to a conclusion that, in spite of the large differences in the estimates of the cost, there has been no fundamental structural change concerning the relative role of the cost of transactions. This result is of some interest in view of the basic changes that took place in the international financial system as well as in the exchange rate regime between the 1962-67 and 1973-75 periods.

Table 3

Transaction Costs and Neutral Band for 90-Day Covered Arbitrage

Period	Arbitraged Securities' Denominations	Intermediate Currency for Estimating t_S and t_F	Observations Bounded within Neutral Band (%)			
			Traditional Pair		External Pair	
			Ω	Ω'	Ω	Ω'
Jan. 1962-	U.S.$ and £	DM	87.0	82.4	99.7	99.3
Nov. 1967	U.S.$ and £	C$	87.0	82.1	99.7	99.3
	U.S.$ and C$	C$	87.6	82.1	N.A.	N.A.
Jan. 1968-	U.S.$ and £	DM	36.9	35.0	97.1	87.4
Dec. 1969	U.S.$ and £	C$	33.0	30.1	94.2	69.9
	U.S.$ and C$	C$	67.0	63.1	N.A.	N.A.
July 1973-	U.S.$ and £	DM	89.7	87.6	100.0	99.0
May 1975	U.S.$ and £	C$	84.5	81.4	99.0	99.0
	U.S.$ and C$	C$	100.0	99.0	100.0	100.0

SOURCE: See Appendix

The intermediate period of the turbulent peg, 1968-69, seems to differ fundamentally. During that period the cost of transactions accounts for a much smaller proportion of the deviations from parity. Moreover, the fraction of the deviations that is explained by transaction costs differs between the pairs of arbitraged assets. However, when we consider the deviations from parity of a different pair of securities—the external pair—

almost all of the deviations are accounted for. It thus seems that, unlike the periods 1962-67 and 1973-75, the traditional pairs of securities were not comparable during the period 1968-69. That turbulent period was characterized by financial uncertainty, a reduced cooperation among central banks, and related phenomena which make up the concept of "political risk."[12] Many of these elements of incomparability are removed when the arbitrage is within the Euro-currency market. What remains to be seen, however, is whether the observed deviations from parity (after allowance for transaction costs) imply some sort of market imperfections in the sense of unexploited profit opportunities; this issue is analyzed in the following section.

The comparison of the various periods also suggests that for the study of covered interest arbitrage, periods should be classified by the extent of turbulence, speculative pressures, and the like rather than by the legal arrangement of the exchange rate regime. We will return to examine this implication in section 5.

4. UNEXPLOITED PROFITS AND A SIMPLE TRADING RULE

The previous analysis suggests that a significant fraction of the deviations from parity is accounted for by allowing for cost of transactions. Since the remaining observations (most abundant during the period 1968-69) indicate the possibility of unexploited profit opportunities, a closer examination of this phenomenon might be useful.

---

12. Viewing the period 1968-69 as a turbulent, speculative period suggests that, on theoretical grounds, the exact parity condition need not hold even when due account is given to the cost of transactions (Tsiang 1959; Kenen 1965). In addition to the cost of transactions, the width of the neutral band around the interest-parity line depends on the size of the elasticities of the demand and supply in the capital markets and in the foreign exchange markets. The lower the elasticities, the wider becomes the neutral bank. In Frenkel and Levich (1975), we have developed the formulae which take account of the possibility that the various elasticities are finite. Applying these formulae to the various periods revealed that, given the cost of transactions, the implied elasticities were very high (reaching at least the value of 100) even during the period 1968-69.

The concept of unexploited profit opportunities should be understood in an ex ante sense. The notion that the operation of an efficient market eliminated unexploited profits does not imply that, ex post, one could not identify situations in which profits could be found. Rather, it implies that ex ante, in the expected-value sense, investors behave—subject to the information they possess—so as to eliminate all profit opportunities. Investors may, of course, be wrong by either undertaking investments that prove to carry losses or by neglecting opportunities that prove profitable. An efficient market ensures that such mistakes do not occur systematically. Therefore, in analyzing ex post data, one needs to verify that (a) the reported prices correspond to actual transaction prices, and (b) the information conveyed ex post was available ex ante.

The first point pertains to aspects of data collection and reporting. Typically, the data that is being reported (e.g., by the Federal Reserve *Bulletin*), is already "consensus data"; i.e., the data collector, having various sources, uses a sampling and averaging technique in reporting forward premia and rates of interest. It cannot be inferred that investors actually transacted and therefore made profits at these reported prices. Moreover, a further misspecification is frequently introduced by using mid-point quotations rather than the ask or bid quotations which correspond more closely to actual transaction prices.

The second point relates to the timing of transactions and to the stock of information available at each point in time. To the extent that the technology of information gathering and processing introduces a lag between the receipt of information signaling arbitrage profit opportunities and the actual execution of the arbitrage transactions, prices might change to bid away profts. Ex post computations showing that on some dates there were some profit opportunities, do not necessarily imply that an investor could have designed an ex ante trading rule which would then yield *sure* profits. The adjective "sure" in the previous sentence is stressed because, in the presence of a lag, prices may change so as to introduce a discrepancy between quoted prices and actual transaction prices; under these circumstances covered interest arbitrage is not risk-free but rather contains an element of speculation.

To explore the consequences of a possible lag, we have examined the implications of an extremely simple trading rule: investors receive information at period t, and whenever there is a possibility of a profit opportunity (after allowing for transaction cost), a transaction is executed at period $t + 1$ (at the prices prevailing at $t + 1$). Table 4 summarizes the implications of such a simple trading rule for the alternative measures of the cost of transactions and for the alternative assumptions concerning the initial positions of arbitrageurs. If investors were able to transact in quoted prices at period t, there would be N profit opportunities. The implied mean percentage profit is indicated in the corresponding entry with a t-statistic in parentheses below the mean. For example, during the tranquil period 1962-67, the mean percentage profit would have been about 0.05 percent; while from 1973 to 1975 it would have been about 0.3 percent. However, when actual transactions are executed at period $t + 1$, some of the profit opportunities turn out to be illusory, and the mean percentage profit is reduced to about 0.04 percent for 1962-67 and to about 0.1 percent for 1973-75. The turbulent period 1968-69 proves again to be somewhat of an exception. During that period the number of apparent profit opportunities and the mean rate of profit are high, and the simple trading rule still leaves relatively high and statistically significant profits. However, as argued before, during that period the traditional pairs of securities do not seem to be comparable and thus do not seem to be appropriate for the analysis of covered interest arbitrage. Indeed, when the same computation is applied to the external pair of securities (see the lower panel of table 4) the positive and significant mean percentage profit that would have been implied, if transactions could be executed at t, turn out to entail significant losses under the simple trading rule.[13]

---

13. While the above results illustrate the relevance of distinguishing between the ex ante and ex post concepts of profit opportunities and the possible implications of a simple trading rule, they should be viewed with caution. A conclusive test of the trading rule requires much more refined data than that used in the present computation. Ideally, the difference between t and $t + 1$ should correspond to consecutive transactions or, at most, to daily data. Since the results of table 4 are based on weekly data, they should be viewed only as illustrative.

Table 4

Mean Percentage Profits of a Simple Trading Rule
(Traditional Pair)

Period	Arbitraged Securities' Denominations	Intermediate Currency for Estimating t_S and t_F	N		t Mean Profit		$t+1$ Mean Profit	
			Ω	Ω'	Ω	Ω'	Ω	Ω'
Jan. 1962– Nov. 1967	U.S.$ and £	DM	40	54	0.055 (7.2)	0.058 (8.4)	0.038 (3.7)	0.045 (5.4)
	U.S.$ and £	C$	40	55	0.056 (7.3)	0.058 (8.4)	0.039 (3.8)	0.044 (5.4)
	U.S.$ and C$	C$	38	55	0.058 (7.8)	0.058 (8.7)	0.046 (3.8)	0.041 (4.2)
Jan. 1968– Dec. 1969	U.S.$ and £	DM	65	67	0.577 (9.6)	0.585 (9.8)	0.540 (8.3)	0.550 (8.6)
	U.S.$ and £	C$	69	72	0.606 (10.2)	0.607 (10.4)	0.572 (9.1.)	0.586 (9.4)
	U.S.$ and C$	C$	34	38	0.107 (6.8)	0.120 (7.9)	0.086 (4.1)	0.102 (5.2)
July 1973– May 1975	U.S.$ and £	DM	10	12	0.261 (4.3)	0.272 (4.6)	0.076 (0.8)	0.097 (1.1)
	U.S.$ and £	C$	15	18	0.304 (5.1)	0.306 (5.3)	0.115 (1.2)	0.187 (2.0)
Jan. 1968– Dec. 1969	U.S.$ and £	DM	3	13	0.310 (4.1)	0.154 (3.2)	-0.319 (6.4)	-0.210 (2.7)
(External Pair)	U.S.$ and £	C$	6	31	0.193 (2.2)	0.104 (3.9)	-0.357 (3.08)	-0.055 (1.5)

SOURCE: See Appendix,
NOTE: t-statistics in parentheses

5. A TIME-SERIES APPROACH

One of the themes of discussion in section 3 was a comparison among the various periods. The implication of that comparison was that it might be preferable to classify periods according to the degree of turbulence rather than the legal arrangements of the exchange rate regime. In the present section we pursue further the comparison among periods by examining the time-series processes of the various exchange rates.[14]

In estimating these processes, we apply the Box-Jenkins time-series approach. We first differenced the series of the logarithms of the various exchange rates and then estimated the sample autocorrelation functions so as to identify the models, which were then estimated. The maximum likelihood parameter estimates for the spot and the forward exchange rates are reported in tables 5 and 6. As can be inferred from the Q-statistics, the residuals are not serially correlated (except for one case), and thus the transformation reduced the observed data to random noise.[15]

In comparing the general characteristics of the time-series properties of spot and forward rates, the first pattern to notice is that in the first and last periods the random walk hypothesis is rejected at the 5 percent level in nine of the twelve series (as is evident from the Zellner-Palm test). On the other hand, during the turbulent peg period (1968-69) we cannot reject the random walk model for any of the six series.[16]

---

14. A more detailed analysis of the time-series models is contained in Levich (1977). For a clear introduction to the applications of the approach, see Nelson (1973).

15. In fitting the series and deciding whether to add additional terms, we have used the Zellner-Palm (1974) likelihood ratio analysis, which objectively tests the hypothesis that additional terms reduce the residual variance. The Zellner-Palm test statistic is reported in the last column of tables 5 and 6.

16. Since exchange rates reflect the outcomes of economic policies, there is nothing special in the random walk hypothesis, and no inference concerning efficiency may be inferred from rejecting the random walk. Our purpose in this section is more descriptive, with the intent of showing that the first and the third periods are similar.

Table 5

Time-Series Models for Spot Exchange in Three Periods

Time Period	Country	Moving-Average Coefficients θ_1	θ_2	θ_3	$10^{-5}\hat{\sigma}_a^2$	Q (k)	$2 \ln \lambda$ (r)
1962-67	England	-0.06	-0.06	-0.11	0.021	22.8	1.46
(N = 306)		(1.0)	(1.1)	(1.9)		(21)	(3)
	Germany	-0.10	-0.14	---	0.050	17.2	6.08*
		(1.6)	(2.3)			(22)	(2)
	Canada	-0.10	-0.17	---	0.334	12.4	9.92*
		(1.6)	(3.1)			(22)	(2)
1968-69	England	-0.10	-0.07	+0.15	0.167	16.2	1.18
(N = 99)		(0.9)	(0.7)	(1.5)		(21)	(3)
	Germany	-0.10	---	---	3.420	6.9	-2.05
		(0.9)				(23)	(1)
	Canada	+0.14	-0.16	---	0.123	12.3	1.60
		(1.4)	(1.7)			(22)	(2)
1973-75	England	-0.16	+0.10	-0.40	7.480	16.3	10.22*
(N = 96)		(1.6)	(1.0)	(4.1)		(21)	(3)
	Germany	+0.10	-0.47	+0.18	20.500	18.4	16.32*
		(1.0)	(5.5)	(2.0)		(21)	(3)
	Canada	-0.10	-0.24	---	0.852	18.1	4.19**
		(1.0)	(2.3)			(22)	(2)

NOTE: Moving-average coefficients in the model

$$\ln (S_t/S_{t-1}) = a_t - \theta_1 a_{t-1} - \theta_2 a_{t-2} - \theta_3 a_{t-3},$$

with t-statistics in parentheses.

$\hat{\sigma}_a^2$ = residual variance in series.

Q = Box-Pierce test statistic for autocorrelation of residuals. Distributed as χ^2 with k degrees of freedom.

$2 \ln \lambda$ = Zellner-Palm test statistic for significance of fitted model against null hypothesis that the series is a random walk. Distributed as χ^2 with r degrees of freedom.

* = significant at 5% level.

** = significant at 20% level.

Table 6

Time-Series Models for Forward Exchange in Three Periods

Time Period	Country	Moving-Average Coefficients θ_1	θ_2	θ_3	$10^{-5}\hat{\sigma}_a^2$	Q (k)	2 ln λ (r)
1962-67	England	-0.08	+0.02	-0.25	0.033	31.3*	12.60*
(N = 306)		(1.4)	(0.4)	(4.5)		(21)	(3)
	Germany	-0.13	---	---	0.041	20.3	4.42*
		(2.2)				(23)	(1)
	Canada	-0.05	-0.16	---	0.354	11.0	6.84*
		(0.9)	(2.9)			(22)	(2)
1968-69	England	-0.05	-0.04	-0.05	1.900	18.9	-2.64
(N = 99)		(0.5)	(0.4)	(0.5)		(21)	(3)
	Germany	-0.07	---	---	3.180	14.6	-2.20
		(0.7)				(23)	(1)
	Canada	+0.07	---	---	1.690	16.2	-0.59
		(0.7)				(23)	(1)
1973-75	England	-0.06	+0.02	-0.37	9.800	19.4	8.43*
(N = 96)		(0.6)	(0.2)	(3.8)		(21)	(3)
	Germany	+0.05	-0.40	---	2.230	14.3	16.38*
		(0.5)	(4.5)			(22)	(2)
	Canada	-0.10	-0.22	---	0.788	18.2	3.12
		(1.0)	(2.1)			(22)	(2)

NOTE: For explanation, see table 5 note.

A closer examination reveals further similarities between the tranquil peg and the managed float periods. Consider, for example, the pound spot rate: both the tranquil peg and the managed float periods contain a significant third moving-average term which is not significant in the turbulent peg period. This phenomenon is even more striking when we compare the estimates for the British pound's forward rates in table 6: during the tranquil peg, the estimates of the moving-average coefficients are -0.08, +0.02, -0.25; while during the managed float, the respective coefficients are -0.06, +0.02, -0.37, with significant third moving-average terms.[17] The similarity in the sign and magnitude of these coefficients for these two periods stands in contrast with the estimated time-series process for the turbulent peg, which appears to follow a random walk.

The Canadian exchange rate also provides an example: during the tranquil peg and the managed float periods, the second moving-average coefficients are significant for both the spot and the forward rates—in contrast with the turbulent peg period, for which the exchange rates series may be characterized as random walk. The German-mark case is somewhat weaker, although the 1962-67 and 1973-75 periods seem to have more in common with each other than with the 1968-69 period.

To sum up, the evidence from the time-series analysis seems to be consistent with the interpretation that the tranquil peg and the managed float periods are similar to each other, while both differ from the turbulent peg period.

6. CONCLUDING REMARKS

In this paper we examined the effects of transaction costs on the efficacy of covered interest arbitrage during three periods: 1962-67—the tranquil peg; 1968-69—the turbulent peg; and 1973-75—the managed float.

---

17. The appearance of what seems to be a three-week cycle in the British pound has also been recorded by Grubel (1966) and more recently by Upson (1972), who applies a spectral analysis.

Several conclusions emerge. First, the cost of executing transactions associated with covered interest arbitrage has risen dramatically during the managed float period as compared with the previous periods. Second, in spite of the vast differences in the estimates of the cost, they played a similar quantitative role in accounting for deviations from parity during the tranquil peg and the managed float periods. The exceptional period was that of the turbulent peg. This pattern is also consistent with evidence provided by the time-series characteristics of the various exchange rates. It suggests that for the purpose of analyzing covered interest arbitrage, it might be preferable to classify periods by the degree of turbulence rather than by the legal arrangement of the exchange rate regime. The third conclusion concerns the efficacy of arbitrage in eliminating profit opportunities. The data suggest that—after allowing for transaction costs and ensuring that the arbitraged assets are comparable—covered interest arbitrage does not seem to entail unexploited opportunities for profit.

Our conclusion on the empirical validity of the interest-parity relationship is of significance for the recently developed asset-market approach to exchange rate determination. An important characteristic of this approach is the hypothesis that interest parity holds and that the speed of adjustment is relativley high.[18] Our paper provides evidence that is consistent with this building block of the asset approach to the determination of exchange rates.

We turn now to some of the policy implications of the foregoing analysis. The evolution of the system into a new regime of managed float is expected to increase the need for forward cover. The smooth operation of the system requires the development of hedging facilities that could be provided automatically in response to the rise in demand for such services (see Friedman 1953; Johnson 1969). A relevant question, however, is

18. See, for example, Bilson (1978), Frenkel (1976), Dornbusch (1976), and related papers in the *Scandinavian Journal of Economics* 78, no. 2 (May 1976).

whether the competitive system will provide for the socially optimal amount of these services. To the extent that private and social costs of the provision of these services differ, a case may be made for some governmental intervention. Private and social cost may differ in aspects of collecting, processing, identifying, and securing relevant information.

The case for governments' actively encouraging the development of forward markets and hedging facilities may be especially relevant for the period of transition toward a well-functioning floating rate system. It seems quite obvious that what might have been optimal depth and breadth of the forward markets during the tranquil peg period would be suboptimal for a floating rate regime. During the tranquil peg period, exchange rates were relatively stable, and the expected rate of return from investment in precise forecasting of future exchange rates was relatively low. Under these conditions, the demand for hedging services could be met by relatively thin markets. The transition toward a system of floating rates associated with a larger variability of exchange rates increases the expected rate of return from accurate forecasting and increases the demand for forward cover. The existing facilities, inherited from the pegged rate regime, could not, in the short run, supply the larger amount of services without rising cost. Thus, the sharp rise in cost might reflect short-run adjustment.

Even if perfect competition were to result in the optimal provision of hedging facilities, it is the role of government to secure a legal framework conducive to the operation of such a competitive system. To secure a competitive environment among dealers, some legislation may be required concerning entry into the trade, licensing, and enforcement of antitrust laws. The role of government becomes even more important in view of the imperfect competition among dealers outside the United States. Cartel-like agreements among leading banks are widespread in the various European financial centers. Even Switzerland, with its highly developed foreign exchange market, tolerated monopolistic practices among the leading banks, which cooperate in fixing the margins between buying and selling prices.[19]

---

19. For further evidence on restrictive practices, see Machlup (1970).

In view of the monopolistic practices prevailing in the various financial centers, it is unlikely that, in the absence of some intervention, the market will provide the optimal amount of hedging services. An active role taken by the U.S. government is in the interest of both the international community and the U.S. economy. The breadth and depth of the New York capital market makes it a natural place for the development of the world center for a futures market.[20] The special role of the dollar in international transactions, and the existing legal structure together with financial stability, provide a presumption that the United States may possess a comparative advantage in the provision of the services of forward markets. To the extent that monopolistic competition from abroad, coupled with uncertainty about the evolution of the international monetary system, deters the private sector from providing the optimal amount of hedging facilities, a case can be made for governmental intervention.[21] This case for intervention is analytically similar to the infant-industry argument for protection and calls for eliminating the discrepancy between private and social costs. Governmental intervention should provide the information and secure the legal structure that is conducive to the development of a competitive environment capable of providing the socially optimal size and diversity of a futures market in foreign currencies.

20. For further details of these arguments, see Friedman (1971).

21. One method to promote competition would be to remove reserve requirements, interest ceilings, and restraints on short-term capital movements so that all national financial markets would become more like the Euro-markets.

APPENDIX ON DATA

1. Foreign Exchange Market

Exchange rates involving the U.S. dollar and used to display the behavior of the series (figure 1) and to calculate the cost of transactions (table 1) for the period 1962-69 are taken from the *International Financial Statistics* (*IFS*) (Washington, D.C.: International Monetary Fund). These data were collected by the IMF as follows: the U.S.$/£ rates are the closing prices in London as reported in the *Financial Times* ; the U.S.$/C$ rates are the noon-time interbank prices in Toronto as reported by the Bank of Canada; and the U.S.$/DM rates are the 11:00 A.M. Official Session Quotation of the Bundesbank in Frankfurt. Data on the latter period used in figure 1 are from the *Weekly Review of International Money Markets* (Chicago, Ill.: Harris Bank). These data are the closing bid prices from the New York interbank market for the last trading day of the week. For the purpose of computing transaction costs for 1973-75, data involving the U.S.$ are closing mid-points and are from the *International Money Market Year Book* and the *Daily Information Bulletin* (Chicago, Ill.: International Monetary Market, Chicago Mercantile Exchange).

The exchange rates involving the U.K. pound sterling (DM/£) and (C$/£) are from the *Montagu Monthly Review* (London: Samuel Montagu & Co.). The spot rates are the mid-points of the daily range. The forward rates were obtained by adding the mid-points of the closing forward spreads to the estimates of the spot rates (described above).

Ideally, in computing transaction costs one should allow for the fact that some transactions use the ask price while some use the bid price. Our use of the mid-points may introduce some noise but need not introduce a systematic bias. Similarly, the various exchange rates should be quotations at the same moment in time; since our data sources report prices that are a few hours apart, an additional source of noise is introduced. To allow for these inaccuracies, we have used conservative measures that bound 95 percent of the deviations from triangular arbitrage.

2. Security Market

All three-month treasury bill rates used in the analysis of the interest parity for the traditional pairs of securities for the period 1962-69 are taken from the Federal Reserve *Bulletin*. In fact, since the Federal Reserve *Bulletin* reports the latest three-month rate, some of the rates used are for bills that are slightly less than three months by two or three days. For the period 1973-75, the data source was the *Weekly Review of International Money Markets*.

The external rates used for the period 1962-69 are Euro-sterling deposits in Paris and Euro-dollar deposits in London; both are three-month middle closing rates taken from the Bank of England *Quarterly Bulletin*. For the period 1973-75, these rates are three-month deposits in Frankfurt taken from the *Money Manager* (New York).

The computation of the cost of transactions in securities (table 2) is based on the percentage ask-bid spread. The bid price and the ask price (expressed as a percentage of par) were computed according to: (1) bid price = 100 - (bid yield x days to maturity)/360; (2) ask price = 100 - (ask yield x days to maturity)/360. The percentage spread is (ask price - bid price)/ask price. The data on the bid yield and ask yield on U.S. treasury bills for the period 1962-69 are from *Solomon Brothers Monthly Bond Report*, while for the later period they are from the *Money Manager*. Since 90-day treasury bills are not issued on every day, for each observation date we have computed the ask-bid spread on the treasury bill whose maturity was closest to 90 days. The range of maturities accepted was between 87 and 93 days. The ask-bid spreads on the external deposits for the period 1973-75 were taken from the *Money Manager*, and for the period 1968-69 from the *Bond Buyer* (which in 1972 changed its name to the *Money Manager*).

In the absence of information on ask-bid spreads on U.K. and Canadian treasury bills, we have assumed that those are equal to the spread on the U.S. bills and thus that, for the traditional pairs of securities, $t = t^*$. Since transaction costs are expected to be inversely related to the width of the market, the assumption that $t = t^*$ might have introduced a downward bias in the estimate of the cost. As indicated in the discussion of table 2, we had no estimates, for the period 1962-67, of the cost of transactions in Euro-dollar and Euro-sterling deposits. In tables 3 and 4 for that period we have used, instead, the cost of transactions in 90-day U.S. treasury bills. For the reason indicated above, this might have resulted in a conservative estimate of the cost of transactions in the external market for the early subperiod.

REFERENCES

Aliber, R. Z. 1973. "The Interest Rate Parity Theorem: A Reinterpretation." JOURNAL OF POLITICAL ECONOMY 81, no. 6 (Nov./Dec.): 1451-59.

_____. 1975. "Monetary Independence under Floating Exchange Rates." JOURNAL OF FINANCE, (May): 365-76.

Allen, W. A. 1977. "A Note on Uncertainty, Transaction Costs and Interest Parity." JOURNAL OF MONETARY ECONOMICS 3, no. 3 (July): 367-73.

Bilson, J. F. O. 1978. "Rational Expectations and the Exchange Rate." In Frenkel and Johnson (1978).

Branson, W. H. 1969. "The Minimum Covered Interest Differential Needed for International Arbitrage Activity." JOURNAL OF POLITICAL ECONOMY 77, no. 6 (Nov./Dec.): 1028-35.

Cournot, A. 1838. MATHEMATICAL PRINCIPLES OF THE THEORY OF WEALTH. Reprint. New York: Kelly, 1971.

Deardorff,A. V. 1977. "Do Transactions Costs Really Account for Departures from Interest Parity?" Unpublished. Ann Arbor: University of Michigan.

Demsetz, H. 1968. "The Cost of Transacting." QUARTERLY JOURNAL OF ECONOMICS 82, no. 1 (Feb.): 33-53.

Dornbusch, R. 1976. "The Theory of Flexible Exchange Rate Regimes and Macroeconomic Policy." SCANDINAVIAN JOURNAL OF ECONOMICS 78, no. 2 (May): 255-75. Reprinted in Frenkel and Johnson (1978).

Fieleke, N. S. 1975. "Exchange Rate Flexibility and the Efficiency of the Foreign Exchange Markets." JOURNAL OF FINANCIAL AND QUANTITATIVE ANALYSIS 10, nos. 3-5 (Sept.): 409-26.

Frenkel, J. A. 1973. "Elasticities and the Interest Parity Theory." JOURNAL OF POLITICAL ECONOMY 81, no. 3 (May/June): 741-47.

_____. 1976. "A Monetary Approach to the Exchange Rate: Doctrinal Aspects and Empirical Evidence." SCANDINAVIAN JOURNAL OF ECONOMICS 78, no. 2 (May): 200-224. Reprinted in Frenkel and Johnson (1978).

Frenkel, J. A. and Johnson, H. G., eds. 1978. THE ECONOMICS OF EXCHANGE RATES: SELECTED STUDIES. Reading, Mass.: Addison-Wesley.

Frenkel, J. A., and Levich, R. M. 1975. "Covered Interest Arbitrage: Unexploited Profits?" JOURNAL OF POLITICAL ECONOMY 83, no. 2 (April): 325-38.

_____. 1977. "Transaction Costs and Interest Arbitrage: Tranquil versus Turbulent Periods." JOURNAL OF POLITICAL ECONOMY 85, no. 6 (Dec.): 1207-24.

Friedman, M. 1953. "The Case for Flexible Exchange Rates." In his ESSAYS IN POSITIVE ECONOMICS. Chicago: University of Chicago Press.

_____. 1971. "The Need for Futures Markets in Currencies." Prepared for the Chicago Mercantile Exchange.

Goschen, George. 1864. THE THEORY OF THE FOREIGN EXCHANGES. 3rd ed. Reprint (4th ed.). London: Pitman House, 1932.

Grubel, H. G. 1966. FORWARD EXCHANGE SPECULATION AND THE INTERNATIONAL FLOW OF CAPITAL. Stanford: Stanford University Press.

Johnson, H. G. 1969. "The Case for Flexible Exchange Rates, 1969." ST. LOUIS FEDERAL RESERVE BANK REVIEW 51, no. 6. Reprinted in his FURTHER ESSAYS IN MONETARY ECONOMICS. London: Allen & Unwin.

Kenen, P. B. 1965. "Trade, Speculation and the Forward Exchange Rate." In TRADE, GROWTH AND THE BALANCE OF PAYMENTS, edited by R. Baldwin et al. Amsterdam: North-Holland.

Keynes, J. M. 1923. A TRACT ON MONETARY REFORM. London: Macmillan.

Leamer, E. E., and Stern, R. M. 1972. "Problems in the Theory and Empirical Estimation of International Capital Movements." In INTERNATIONAL MOBILITY AND MOVEMENT OF CAPITAL, edited by F. Machlup et al. New York: National Bureau of Economic Research.

Levi, M. D. 1977. "Taxation and 'Abnormal' International Capital Flows." JOURNAL OF POLITICAL ECONOMY 85, no. 3 (June): 635-46.

Levich, R. M. 1977. "The International Money Market: Tests of Forecasting Models and Market Efficiency." Ph.D. diss. University of Chicago.

McCormick, F. 1975. "Transaction Costs in the Foreign Exchange Market under Fixed and Floating Exchange Rates." Paper presented to the Western Economic Association, San Diego, Calif.

McKinnon, R. I. 1976. "Floating Foreign Exchange Rates, 1973-74: The Emperor's New Clothes." In Carnegie-Rochester Conference Series on Public Policy, vol. 3, supp. to the JOURNAL OF MONETARY ECONOMICS 2: 79-114.

Machlup, F. 1970. "The Forward-Exchange Market: Misunderstanding between Practitioners and Economists." In APPROACHES TO GREATER FLEXIBILITY OF EXCHANGE RATES, edited by G. N. Halm. Princeton: Princeton University Press.

Nelson, C. R. 1973. APPLIED TIME SERIES ANALYSIS. San Francisco: Holden-Day.

Officer, L. H., and Willet, T. D. 1970. "The Covered-Arbitrage Schedule: A Critical Survey of Recent Developments." JOURNAL OF MONEY, CREDIT AND BANKING 2, no. 2 (May): 247-57.

Prachowny, M. F. 1970. "A Note on Interest Parity and the Supply of Arbitrage Funds." JOURNAL OF POLITICAL ECONOMY 78, no. 3 (May/June): 540-45.

Ricardo, D. 1811. REPLY TO MR. BOSANQUET'S PRACTICAL OBSERVATIONS ON THE REPORT OF THE BULLION COMMITTEE. London.

Stein, J. L. 1962. THE NATURE AND EFFICIENCY OF THE FOREIGN EXCHANGE MARKET. Essays in International Finance, no. 40. Princeton: Princeton University Press.

Stokes, H. H. 1972. "The Crisis Index: An Empirical Test of the Degree of Tension in the Foreign Exchange Market." ECONOMIC NOTES 1, no. 1 (Jan./Apr.): 72-91.

Swoboda, A. K. 1969. "Vehicle Currencies: The Case of the Dollar." In THE INTERNATIONAL MARKET FOR FOREIGN EXCHANGE, edited by R. Z. Aliber. New York: Praeger.

Tsiang, S. C. 1959. "The Theory of Forward Exchange and the Effects of Government Intervention on the Forward Market." I.M.F. STAFF PAPERS 7, no. 1 (Apr.): 75-106.

Upson, R. B. 1972. "Randon Walk and Forward Exchange Rates: A Spectral Analysis." JOURNAL OF FINANCIAL AND QUANTITATIVE ANALYSIS 7, nos. 3-5 (Sept.): 1897-1905.

Walras, L. 1870. ELEMENTS OF PURE ECONOMICS. Translated by W. Jaffé. New York: Kelly, 1969.

Zellner, A., and Palm, F. 1974. "Time Series Analysis and Simultaneous Equation Econometric Models." JOURNAL OF ECONOMETRICS 2: 17-54.

UNANTICIPATED MONEY GROWTH AND UNEMPLOYMENT IN THE UNITED STATES*

Robert J. Barro**
University of Rochester

The hypothesis that forms the basis of this empirical study is that only unanticipated movements in money affect real economic variables like the unemployment rate or the level of output. This hypothesis is explicit in "rational expectation" monetary models, such as those of Lucas (1972, 1973), Sargent and Wallace (1975), and Barro (1976*b*). However, the proposition that only the unanticipated part of money movements has real effects is clearly more general than the specific setting of these models.

In order to implement and test the hypothesis empirically, it is necessary to quantify the notions of anticipated and unanticipated money movements. Accordingly, the first part of the analysis specifies a simple model of the money growth process. The variables that turn out empirically to have a systematic effect on U.S. money growth, using annual observations from 1941 to 1973, are a measure of federal government expenditure relative to "normal," a lagged unemployment rate, and two lagged values of money growth. Anticipated money growth is then viewed as the prediction that could have been obtained by exploiting the systematic relation between money growth and this set of independent variables.

---

* Reprinted, with some changes, by permission of the author and the American Economic Association from THE AMERICAN ECONOMIC REVIEW 67 (1977): 101-15. An earlier version of the paper was presented at the 1976 Konstanz Seminar.

** The National Science Foundation has supported this research. I have benefitted from comments on earlier drafts by Jack Carr, Bob Hodrick, Pieter Korteweg, Bob Lucas, Michael Parkin, and Chris Sims.

The measure of unanticipated money growth—actual growth less the anticipated portion—that is obtained in section 1 is used in section 2 as an explanatory variable for the unemployment rate—the real economic variable that is focused on in the present study. Over the 1946-73 period, the contemporaneous and two annual lag values of unanticipated money growth turn out to have effects on unemployment that are significantly negative. Further, the hypothesis that only the unanticipated part of money expansion influences unemployment receives strong support from some empirical tests.

The final sections discuss unemployment predictions, implications for policy, and some possibilities for extension of the research.

1. ANALYSIS OF MONEY GROWTH

Setup of the Equation

The money growth rate equation used in this study applies to annual observations for the 1941-73 period. The equation includes the following variables: a measure of federal government expenditure relative to normal, the lagged unemployment rate, and two lagged values of money growth. The government expenditure variable captures an aspect of the revenue motive for money creation. In Barro (1976 *a*) I describe a theoretical model in which an exogenous level of government expenditure is financed by a combination of taxes and money issue. (Extensions to include public debt and nongovernment money do not alter the main conclusions.) Each method of finance involves administrative and other deadweight costs that increase, *ceteris paribus*, at an increasing rate with the amount of revenue raised by that method. However, the costs of raising a given amount of revenue by either method are assumed to decline with an increase in national income. In addition, the costs associated with taxation are assumed to depend negatively on the amount of fixed "capital" that has been accumulated in tax-raising capacity. For example, the setting up of an income tax and of an institutional apparatus for administering this tax are viewed as increases in tax-raising capital that reduce the collection costs imputed by the government to any particular amount of revenue raised by taxes. The amount of capital invested in the tax-raising "industry" is, itself, endogenous to the model, but adjustment-type costs associated with changes in taxing capacity imply that the current amount of capital will depend on "long-run" values of such variables as government expenditure and national income, rather than simply on the current values.

The breakdown of the total government budget between the two revenue components—and therefore the rate of money growth—is determined to minimize the total costs associated with raising revenue.[1] With a fixed amount of tax-raising capital—which depends, among other things, on the long-run level of government expenditure—an increase in the current government budget leads to increases in both types of revenue and hence to an increase in the growth rate of money. This type of response would apply especially to periods of wartime during which there are sharp, temporary increases in the size of the government budget. The long-run response of money to an increase in the government budget—for example, to the secular growth of federal government spending relative to GNP that occurred from the 1930s to the 1960s—would be different because it would lead also to an increase in tax-raising capital. Since "permanent" expansions in the share of GNP that is absorbed by government leads to an expansion of taxing capacity, it is possible—depending on the form of the "production function" that generates tax revenues—that no change in the money growth rate would occur. In this situation, it is only increases in government expenditure relative to normal that would induce monetary expansion.

Specifically, my equation for money growth uses the variable

$$FEDV \equiv \log(FED) - [\log(FED)]^*$$

where ***FED*** is real expenditure of the federal government and $[\log(FED)]^*$ refers to the normal value of this expenditure. Empirically, $[\log(FED)]^*$ was generated from the adaptive formula

$$[\log(FED)]^*_t = \beta[\log(FED)]_t + (1 - \beta)[\log(FED)]^*_{t-1} \, ;$$

---

1. Phelps (1973) has a theoretical discussion of inflation within a public-finance context.

Table 1

Values of Money Growth and Unemployment

	DM	$\hat{DM}$	DMR	U	$\hat{U}$	U-U	$UNAT$
1939	0.114	--	--	--	--	--	--
1940	0.151	--	--	0.095	--	--	--
1	0.160	0.166	-0.007	0.058	--	--	--
2	0.180	0.212	-0.032	0.029	--	--	--
3	0.265	0.201	0.064	0.015	--	--	--
4	0.162	0.192	-0.031	0.010	--	--	--
1945	0.150	0.158	-0.008	0.016	--	--	--
6	0.068	0.055	0.013	0.037	0.039	-0.002	0.034
7	0.047	0.038	0.009	0.038	0.043	-0.005	0.051
8	0.004	0.017	-0.012	0.037	0.044	-0.007	0.048
9	-0.010	0.013	-0.023	0.057	0.053	0.004	0.042
1950	0.026	0.006	0.019	0.052	0.059	-0.007	0.048
1	0.044	0.026	0.018	0.031	0.031	0.000	0.039
2	0.049	0.037	0.012	0.028	0.025	0.003	0.036
3	0.024	0.041	-0.017	0.027	0.032	-0.005	0.035
4	0.015	0.024	-0.008	0.052	0.044	0.008	0.036
1955	0.031	0.027	0.004	0.042	0.043	-0.001	0.037
6	0.012	0.021	-0.009	0.039	0.042	-0.003	0.040
7	0.005	0.023	-0.018	0.041	0.049	-0.008	0.041
8	0.012	0.020	-0.007	0.065	0.054	0.011	0.041
9	0.037	0.030	0.007	0.053	0.046	0.007	0.041
1960	-0.001	0.030	-0.031	0.053	0.046	0.007	0.041
1	0.021	0.033	-0.013	0.065	0.062	0.003	0.042
2	0.022	0.033	-0.012	0.053	0.059	-0.006	0.042
3	0.029	0.033	-0.004	0.055	0.053	0.002	0.043
4	0.039	0.035	0.004	0.050	0.047	0.003	0.044
1965	0.042	0.037	0.005	0.043	0.041	0.002	0.043
6	0.044	0.042	0.002	0.037	0.038	-0.001	0.042
7	0.039	0.043	-0.004	0.036	0.042	-0.006	0.043
8	0.068	0.042	0.026	0.034	0.040	-0.006	0.044
9	0.061	0.041	0.020	0.034	0.030	0.004	0.044
1970	0.044	0.047	-0.004	0.047	0.046	0.001	0.064
1	0.067	0.049	0.018	0.057	0.054	0.003	0.062
2	0.063	0.056	0.006	0.054	0.048	0.006	0.060
3	0.071	0.061	0.010	0.048	0.049	-0.001	0.059
4	0.055	0.056	-0.001	0.055	0.056	-0.001	0.064
1975	0.042	0.062	-0.020	0.083	0.071	0.012	0.065
6	--	0.065	--	--	0.081	--	0.065
7	--	0.065	--	--	0.068	--	0.063
8	--	0.069	--	--	0.061	--	0.061

SOURCES: M_1 data are from the Federal Reserve BULLETIN, various issues; unemployment data are from U.S. Council of Economic Advisers, ECONOMIC REPORT OF THE PRESIDENT, various issues.

NOTES: $DM_t \equiv \log(M_t) - \log(M_{t-1})$, where M is an annual average of M_1.

$\hat{DM}$ = the estimated value from eq. (2).

$DMR \equiv DM - \hat{DM}$.

U = the annual average unemployment rate, based on the total labor force, which includes military personnel.

$\hat{U}$ = an estimated value from eq. (4).

$UNAT$ = an estimated value from eq. (4) with all DMR values set equal to zero.

Unemployment data from 1940-43 were adjusted for treatment of government "emergency workers," as discussed in Darby (1976).

Values of $\hat{DM}$ for 1976-78 are based on the value $FEDV$ = 0.18. The 1977-78 values of DM use the value of $\hat{U}$ from the preceding year. The values of $\hat{U}$ (and $UNAT$) subsequent to 1975 are based on DMR = 0 for 1976 and beyond, MIL = 0, and the $MINW$ values indicated in table 2.

that is, $[\log(FED)]^*$ is an exponentially declining distributed lag of $\log(FED)$.[2] The equation reported below uses the value of the adaptation coefficient, $\beta = 0.2$ per year (see note 4). Values of *FEDV* corresponding to this value of β are tabulated from 1941 to 1975 in table 2.

In the empirical analysis, I test the hypothesis that it is only the difference between $\log(FED)$ and $[\log(FED)]^*$ that influences money expansion, with no separate effect of the level of federal expenditure. This hypothesis is supported by the empirical evidence over 1941 to 1973, so that the main analysis includes only the *FEDV* variable.

The money growth equation also includes a measure of lagged unemployment. A positive response of money growth to this variable could reflect two elements. First, there could be a countercyclical policy response of money to the level of economic activity. (The subsequent analysis has important implications for the efficacy of this type of policy.) Second, a decline in real income lowers holdings of real balances, which would reduce the amount of government revenue from money issue for a given value of the money growth rate. As shown in an earlier paper (Barro, 1976*a*), the optimal response to a decline in income below its normal level would be an increase in the money growth rate. My empirical analysis does not separate out these two possible sources of countercyclical money response.

Finally, the money growth equation includes two lagged values of money growth as "explanatory" variables. Presumably, these lagged dependent variables pick up any elements of serial dependence or lagged adjustment that have not been captured by the other independent variables.

---

2. It would be preferable to generate $[\log(FED)]^*$ from a prediction relation based on the time-series properties of $\log(FED)$. Costs of adjustment in taxing capacity would then also have to be taken into account in specifying the reaction of money growth to optimal predictions of future values of $\log(FED)$. I have not yet proceeded along these lines.

Table 2

Values of the Federal Expenditure, Military Personnel and Minimum Wage Variables

	FEDV (β = 0.2)	*MIL*		*MINW*
1941	0.803	--		--
2	1.356	--		--
3	1.369	--		--
4	1.161	--		--
1945	0.812	--		--
6	-0.131	0.105		0.228
7	-0.338	0.012	(0.048)	0.203
8	-0.196	0.022	(0.044)	0.191
9	-0.016	0.048		0.180
1950	-0.033	0.049		0.323
1	0.199	0.092		0.301
2	0.307	0.106		0.284
3	0.303	0.105		0.269
4	0.151	0.099		0.258
1955	0.090	0.090		0.248
6	0.089	0.083		0.307
7	0.123	0.081		0.298
8	0.167	0.075		0.283
9	0.139	0.073		0.273
1960	0.116	0.071		0.262
1	0.157	0.071		0.283
2	0.179	0.077		0.328
3	0.157	0.073		0.325
4	0.143	0.072		0.334
1965	0.136	0.071		0.325
6	0.204	0.079		0.315
7	0.245	0.086		0.392
8	0.248	0.087		0.426
9	0.195	0.085		0.421
1970	0.173	0	(0.075)	0.402
1	0.165	0	(0.065)	0.367
2	0.188	0	(0.056)	0.344
3	0.172	0	(0.052)	0.322
4	0.154	0	(0.048)	0.408
1975	0.195	0	(0.046)	0.426
6	(0.18)	(0)		(0.42)
7	(0.18)	(0)		(0.39)
8	(0.18)	(0)		(0.36)

SOURCES: *FEDV* data are from U.S. Council of Economic Advisers, ECONOMIC REPORT OF THE PRESIDENT, various issues. *MIL* data are from U.S. Bureau of the Census, HISTORICAL STATISTICS OF THE UNITED STATES, 1960, pp. 736, 8, 10; and STATISTICAL ABSTRACT OF THE UNITED STATES, various issues. *MINW* data for 1947-68 were calculated by the U.S. Bureau of Labor Statistics and reported in Mincer (1976, table 1.6); for 1946 and 1969-75, *MINW* is estimated from data contained in Weiss (1973, tables 1-3).

NOTES: In calculating *FEDV*, figures on the nominal federal budget were divided by the GNP deflator (1958 = 1.0). The *MIL* values shown in parentheses for certain years are the actual ratios of military personnel to the male population aged 15-44, ignoring the absence of a selective draft for all or part of those years.

The *FEDV* value of 0.18, shown in parentheses for 1976-78, corresponds to the average value for 1960-75. The *MINW* value shown in parentheses for 1976 is an estimated value that takes account of the rise in the nominal minimum wage on January 1, 1976. The 1978 value of 0.36 is the sample average for 1960-75. For purposes of predicting unemployment for 1977 and beyond, it is assumed that the *MINW* variable will fall over a two-year period from its 1976 value to the average value of 0.36.

The form of the systematic part of the money growth equation is

$$DM_t = \alpha_o + \alpha_1 DM_{t-1} + \alpha_2 DM_{t-2} + \alpha_3 FEDV_t + \alpha_4 UN_{t-1}, \tag{1}$$

where M_t = an annual average of M_1 (see note 18 below on the money definition),

$DM_t \equiv \log(M)_t - \log(M)_{t-1}$ measures the annual average money growth rate,

$FEDV_t \equiv \log(FED)_t - [\log(FED)]^*_t$, as defined above, and

$UN_{t-1} = \log[U/(1-U)]_{t-1}$, where U is the annual average unemployment rate in the total labor force (which includes military personnel).

The form in which the unemployment rate enters corresponds to the form of the unemployment equation given below.

Estimated Equation

The estimated money growth equation for the 1941-73 period is, with standard errors in parentheses,

$$\underset{(0.031)}{DM_t = 0.087} + \underset{(0.15)}{0.24} DM_{t-1} + \underset{(0.13)}{0.35} DM_{t-2} \tag{2}$$

$$+ \underset{(0.015)}{0.082} \cdot FEDV_t + \underset{(0.010)}{0.027} \cdot UN_{t-1},$$

$$R^2 = 0.90, \quad \hat{\sigma} = 0.020, \quad DW = 2.39$$

(sample average of $DM = 0.057$),

where $\hat{\sigma}$ is the standard error of estimate.[3]

3. A measure of the contemporaneous or lagged value of the federal government deficit relative to GNP is insignificant when added to eq. (2). A lagged value of the inflation rate (based on the GNP deflator) or of the interest rate on prime commercial paper is also insignificant.

Consider, first, the coefficient on the federal expenditure variable, *FEDV*.[4] The estimated value of 0.08 implies that a 10 percent increase in real federal expenditure—holding fixed the normal expenditure and lagged values of *DM*—would raise DM_t by 0.8 percentage point per year. Historically, the extreme values of *FEDV* have occurred during and just after wartime periods. For example, the 1943 value of *FEDV* = 1.37 implies (with DM_{t-1} and DM_{t-2} held fixed, so that 0.08 is the applicable coefficient) that DM_t would be 11 percentage points per year higher than when *FEDV* is zero, while the 1947 value of *FEDV* = - 0.34 implies that DM_t would be 3 percentage points per year less than otherwise.[5]

The hypothesis that government expenditure enters into the determination of money growth only as the difference, $FEDV \equiv \log(FED) - [\log(FED)]^*$ has been tested by entering *FEDV* and log(*FED*) separately into the *DM* equation. The estimated coefficient of log(*FED*) (0.01, standard error = 0.01) differs insignificantly from zero, and there is little change in the estimated coefficients on the other variables. (The results are similar if *FED* is measured as a ratio to a trend value of real GNP.) Accordingly, the results are consistent with the view that only temporary movements in federal expenditure stimulate monetary expansion.

---

4. Based on the fit of the money growth equation, the maximum likelihood estimate of the adaptation coefficient β is in the interval between 0.15 and 0.20, with an asymptotic 95 percent confidence interval of (0.1, 0.4). Since the unemployment results showed little sensitivity to variations in β over the interval from 0.15 to 0.30, I have limited the reported results to the case of $\beta = 0.20$.

5. Note, however, that *FEDV* has not been normalized to make the long-run average value equal to zero. Since the normal value of government expenditure is generated by a distributed lag of actual values, secular growth of the public sector implies that the typical measured value of *FEDV* will be positive. It turns out that constant growth of real expenditures at rate g would generate an *FEDV* value of $g(1 - \beta)/\beta$, which equals $4g$ at $\beta = 0.20$. From 1949 to 1973 the average annual growth rate g is 0.05, so that the corresponding "long-run average" value of *FEDV* is 0.20. However, growth of the public sector at 5 percent per year would not seem to be permanently sustainable.

Consider next the coefficient on the lagged unemployment variable. The estimated value of 0.03 imples that a 10 percent increase in U--that is, an increase by 0.5 percentage point starting from $U = 5$ percent--would imply a reaction of next year's money growth by about 0.3 percentage point per year. Hence, an increase by 1 percentage point in the unemployment rate induces an increase in next year's money growth rate by about 0.6 percentage point per year.[6]

Finally, the regression results indicate persistence effects with an estimated DM_{t-1} coefficient of 0.24 and an estimated DM_{t-2} coefficient of 0.35. If the error term in equation (2) is assumed to follow a first-order Markov process $u_t = \rho u_{t-1} + \varepsilon_t$, the maximum likelihood estimate of ρ is -0.35 (the estimated coefficient on DM_{t-1} is then 0.45 and that on DM_{t-2} is 0.21). However, the estimated value of ρ differs insignificantly from zero at the 5 percent level--the asymptotic chi-square value is 2.6 with a critical value of 3.8. Since the inclusion of a nonzero value for ρ also has a negligible impact on the subsequent analysis of unemployment, I have limited the main analysis to the case where $\rho = 0$.

A notable aspect of the estimated DM equation is that it implies a normal, or long-run average, money growth rate. For a given value of the constant term and the federal expenditure and unemployment variables, the equation specifies the mean value of DM (both in a short-run sense, conditioned on given values of DM_{t-1} and DM_{t-2}, and also in a long-run unconditional sense). For example, if the unemployment rate is 4.3 percent, the average estimated "natural rate" during the 1960s (as discussed below), and if the $FEDV$ variable takes on an "average" value of 0.20 (see note 5), the implied long-run mean value of DM is 4.4 percent per year.

---

6. From either the countercyclical policy or optimal revenue-raising viewpoints, it would seem preferable to enter the unemployment variable relative to its perceived long-run average value. The results on unemployment over 1946 to 1973, below, suggest that the principal movement in this long-run average value may have occurred since 1970. However, I have not yet attempted to adjust the unemployment variable along these lines.

If the *DM* equation had contained a distributed lag of past *DM* values with the lag coefficients summing to one, as is true in the adaptive-expectations formula developed by Cagan (1956), then the model would not have the property of possessing a natural or long-run mean value of the money growth rate. Presumably, the formulation with lag weights summing to unity would provide a satisfactory framework for predicting *DM* only if money growth were in fact generated by a nonstationary process (for example, a random walk, or a random walk observed with error, as in Muth [1960]) for which a long-run mean did not exist. If the money growth process is stationary, it would not be expected that the sum of the lag weights in money growth predictions would equal one. It follows that any implicit tests of expectation formation concerning money growth that are based on lag weights summing to one would not generally be meaningful--a point that was made in a general context by Sargent (1971).

Prior Predictions of Money Growth

For the present analysis, the purpose of fitting a money growth equation is to obtain a division of money growth into anticipated and unanticipated components. The theoretical proposition then is that only the unanticipated part of money growth will influence unemployment. There is a basic problem to consider in using an estimated money growth equation to specify the concept of anticipated money growth. Consider the formulation of this anticipation for date *t*, $\hat{DM}_t$. This anticipation could be based on information that was available up to date $t - 1$ and might also include partial information applicable to date *t*. However, $\hat{DM}_t$ should not be based on any information that becomes available only after date *t*. For example, if the estimated values from the *DM* regression for the 1941-73 period were used to obtain $\hat{DM}$ for 1950, then information subsequent to 1950 would be used to "predict" that year's money growth. Specifically, later observations on *DM*, *FEDV*, and *UN* would be used to estimate the coefficients of the *DM* relation and these coefficients would then be applied to the 1950 values of the independent variables to obtain $\hat{DM}$ for 1950. However, it should be noted that the manner in which later observations affect earlier values of $\hat{DM}$ is solely through pinning down the estimates of the coefficients in the *DM* equation. If individuals have information about the money growth structure beyond that conveyed in prior observations (for example, from the experiences of other countries or on theoretical grounds), then the use of the overall sample period, 1941-73, may be reasonable even for the earlier dates.

A procedure that avoids the use of later observations to generate earlier predictions involves obtaining $\hat{DM}_t$ from a regression in which the coefficients are estimated from data only up to date $t-1$. In this approach there would be as many DM equations (each incorporating data up to $t-1$) as there were predicted values, $\hat{DM}_t$. In this context, it would also be natural to consider the possibility of weighting the observations so that more recent information was counted more heavily in forming predictions.[7]

In an earlier study Barro (1975), which is available on request, I devoted a good deal of space to estimations that based money growth predictions solely on prior observations. Since it turned out that the implications for the analysis of unemployment were minor, I have not included this discussion. For the present analysis I use the estimated values of DM from the 1941-73 regression, equation (2), to form a time-series of anticipated money growth, $\hat{DM}$. Unanticipated money growth, $DMR \equiv DM - \hat{DM}$, then corresponds to the residuals from the equation. The values of $\hat{DM}$ and DMR from equation (2) are indicated in table 1.[8]

2. ANALYSIS OF UNEMPLOYMENT

Setup of the Equation

The effects of monetary expansion on unemployment are measured by the impact of current and lagged values of unanticipated money growth, $DMR \equiv DM - \hat{DM}$. The number of lags to introduce was not established from a priori reasoning, although Lucas (1975) presents a theoretical rationale for

7. Heavier weighting of recent observations can be rationalized along the lines of the adaptive regression model (Cooley and Prescott 1973).

8. Note that $\hat{DM}_t$ is calculated from the contemporaneous value of *FEDV*, rather than from a lagged value. The rationale is that the principal movements in *FEDV*, which are dominated by changes in wartime activity, would be perceived sufficiently rapidly to influence $\hat{DM}$ without a lag. For example, in 1946 the value of $\hat{DM}$ is much lower than in 1945 because of the contemporaneous downward movement in *FEDV*.

persistence effects of monetary shocks in this type of model. Empirically, it turned out that the current and two annual lag values of *DMR* had significant effects on unemployment.

Aside from monetary variables, the unemployment equation includes two "real" variables. The first is a measure of military conscription. The specific variable is

$$MIL \equiv \frac{\text{Military personnel}}{\text{Male population aged 15-44}}$$

for years in which a "selective" military draft law was in effect (all years since 1946 except for April 1947 to June 1948 and 1970-73).[9] The value $MIL = 0$ was entered for the nonselective draft law years. Values of *MIL* are tabulated from 1946 to 1975 in table 2. Aside from the possible direct employment effect of conscription on draftees, a selective draft would provide incentives for eligible civilians to enter a low draft probability status. One effect would involve the choice of remaining in school rather than entering the labor force—an effect that would reduce the measured unemployment rate if the affected individuals had an above-average tendency toward unemployment. A second effect involves the choice between working and unemployment for labor-market participants. On this count, conscription would work toward reducing the unemployment rate if draft probabilities were highest, *ceteris paribus*, for unemployed persons.

The second real variable measures the impact of the minimum wage rate. This variable, tabulated for 1946-75 under the heading *MINW* in table 2, is defined as the ratio of the applicable minimum wage to private, nonfarm average hourly earnings, multiplied by the proportion of covered nonsupervisory employment. The *MINW* variable would have a positive

---

9. A discussion of the draft law in the United States up to 1970 is contained in Rafuse (1970). The lottery draft period from 1970 to June 1973 (during which there were draft calls for 1970-71) was taken out, since the lottery draft does not provide the same incentives to avoid unemployment as appear to operate during a selective draft. See the discussion below. Periods with zero draft calls, but with a selective draft law in effect (February 1949 to June 1950), were included with the draft period.

effect on the unemployment rate if the negative impact of the minimum wage on employment dominates the probable negative effect on labor-force participation.[10]

The form for the systematic part of the unemployment equation[11] used for annual observations for 1946-73 is

$$\log[U/(1-U)]_t = a_1 DMR_t + a_2 DMR_{t-1} + a_3 DMR_{t-2} + a_4 MIL_t + a_5 MINW_t. \tag{3}$$

---

10. I also considered an unemployment compensation variable, which was defined as average benefits per recipient relative to average hourly earnings multiplied by the fraction of covered employment. In my initial investigations this variable was insignificant in the unemployment equation. However, I have recently recalculated the unemployment compensation variable to take account of taxes on earnings and to incorporate a fuller measure of unemployment compensation coverage. This revised variable does turn out to have a significantly positive effect on the unemployment rate. The other coefficients in the estimated unemployment equation are insensitive to the inclusion of this variable, except that the minimum wage variable becomes less important. I plan to report on these results more fully at a later time.

11. The form confines the unemployment rate to the interval (0, 1).

    Since *DMR* is based on estimated coefficients of the *DM* relation, eq. (2), there would be small-sample problems of errors in the independent variables in eq. (3). The main impact would seem to be a bias toward zero in the estimated *DMR* coefficients. In obtaining estimates of the a-coefficients in eq. (3), and the α-coefficients in eq. (1), it would be preferable to carry out a joint maximum likelihood estimation. In contrast with my two-stage procedure, the choice of the α-estimates in the money growth equation would then give some weight to the effect on the fit of the unemployment equation, through the selection of the *DMR* values that enter into eq. (3). In my procedure the α-estimates are chosen solely to obtain a least-squares fit in eq. (1). For the case of normally distributed error terms, the a-estimates would be chosen in both cases to obtain a least-squares fit in eq. (3), conditional on the *DMR* values. Since my procedure yields consistent estimates (assuming serially independent error terms) and the alternative, nonlinear procedure requires a large amount of numerical calculation, I have not carried out the joint maximum likelihood estimation.

Since the sample period begins in 1946, the values for *DMR* start in 1944. It may be worth noting that, since the dependent variable in equation (3) depends on a distributed lag of *DMR* values, the unemployment rate can be serially correlated even if the *DMR* (and the *MIL* and *MINW* variables) were not. (The *DMR* values would not be serially correlated if $\hat{DM}_t$ were an efficient predictor of DM_t, based on information that included an observation of DM_{t-1}.)

Results with Unanticipated Money Growth Rates

With *DMR* measured as the residuals from equation (2), the estimated unemployment equation is,[12] with standard errors in parentheses,

$$\log[U/(1-U)]_t = -\underset{(0.15)}{3.07} - \underset{(2.1)}{5.8}DMR_t - \underset{(1.9)}{12.1}DMR_{t-1} \quad (4)$$

$$- \underset{(1.9)}{4.2}DMR_{t-2} - \underset{(0.8)}{4.7}MIL_t + \underset{(0.46)}{0.95}MINW_t,$$

$$R^2 = 0.78, \quad \hat{\sigma} = 0.13, \quad DW = 1.96$$

(average of $|U - U| = 0.0043$).

Equation (4) includes a contemporaneous and two annual lag values of *DMR*. Additional lag terms were insignificant. The implied lag pattern (the form of which was not constrained ex ante) for unemployment behind unanticipated money growth has a triangular shape, with the strongest effect appearing after a one-year lag. The contemporaneous and two-year

12. The results of a similar analysis (Barro 1975) using the log of output (real GNP) instead of the unemployment rate as a dependent variable (with a time trend included as an additional explanatory variable) correspond in major respects to those discussed below for unemployment.

lag effects are of about equal size.[13] The t -values associated with a null hypothesis of a zero coefficient are 6.4 for DMR_{t-1}, 2.8 for DMR_t, and 2.2 for DMR_{t-2}. The F-values for the three DMR coefficients jointly is F^3_{22} = 21.0 (5 percent critical value = 3.1). More detailed aspects of the estimated DMR coefficients and of the estimated coefficients for the MIL and $MINW$ variables will be discussed below.

In evaluating the fit of equation (4), a useful measure is the average absolute residual for implied estimates of the unemployment rate (generated from a straightforward, though not quite statistically valid, transformation of the dependent variable, $\log[U/(1-U)]$). This average value is 0.0043—that is, the average error in estimated unemployment rates is somewhat more than 0.4 percentage point.[14]

The Durbin-Watson statistic of 1.96 from equation (4) indicates absence of first-order serial correlation in the residuals. This result is surprising, given the autocorrelated nature of the U-series,[15] since a lagged dependent variable was not included to soak up the serial correlation.[16] In

---

13. The estimated coefficient of DMR_t could be biased toward zero if there is a contemporaneous policy feedback from U_t (current period unemployment) to DM_t. The response of money growth to lagged unemployment was already taken into account in forming the anticipated money growth rate $\hat{DM}_t$. Presumably, this problem of within-period policy response would be lessened if the length of the observation period were reduced by moving to quarterly data. I plan to carry out that extension at a later time.

14. I have redone the unemployment analysis with two alternative definitions of the money stock, M_2 and high-powered money (see Barro 1975 for details). It turns out that the M_1 definition is superior in terms of the fit for unemployment. In a form parallel to eq. (4), the M_2 definition yields an R^2 of 0.31 with an average absolute error for U of 0.0076—about twice that of the M_1 form. For high-powered money the R^2 is 0.49 with an average absolute error for U of 0.0066.

15. An autoregression of UN_t on UN_{t-1} yields the estimated coefficient 0.40, standard error = 0.14.

16. Except for the indirect effect of lagged U on $\hat{DM}$. However, that effect was estimated from a separate equation, so that the usual problem of correlation between a lagged dependent variable and a serially correlated error term would not arise here.

fact, if $\log(U/1 - U)_{t-1}$ is added to equation (4), its estimated coefficient is 0.09, standard error = 0.10, which differs insignificantly from zero.

Results with Total Money Growth Rates

Unemployment regressions have also been run based on total money growth rates, *DM*, rather than on the unanticipated part of growth, *DMR*. For a regression that includes a contemporaneous and two lagged values of *DM* along with the military and minimum wage variables, none of the estimated *DM* coefficients turns out to be individually significantly different from zero, and an *F*-test for joint significance yields the statistic $F^3_{22} = 2.6$, which is below the 5 percent critical value of 3.1. The fit of the regression is indicated by $R^2 = 0.38$—half that of the *DMR* equation. The inclusion of a third lag of *DM* into the unemployment equation has a negligible impact. When DM_{t-4} is included the fit improves noticeably, although the estimated coefficients on DM_{t-2} and DM_{t-3} are positive. The estimated equation with four lags is

$$\log[U/(1 - U)]_t = \underset{(0.34)}{-\,2.46} \underset{(2.9)}{-\,1.2DM_t} \underset{(2.7)}{-\,5.7DM_{t-1}} \underset{(2.5)}{+\,0.7DM_{t-2}} \quad (5)$$

$$\underset{(1.8)}{+\,3.5DM_{t-3}} \underset{(1.5)}{-\,3.2DM_{t-4}} \underset{(1.4)}{-\,4.5MIL_t} \underset{(1.0)}{-\,0.3MINW_t},$$

$$R^2 = 0.52, \quad \hat{\sigma} = 0.20, \quad DW = 1.68$$

$$(\text{average of } |U - \hat{U}| = 0.0059).$$

The *F*-value for the joint hypothesis that all five *DM* coefficients are zero is $F^5_{20} = 3.0$, which is above the 5 percent critical value of 2.7. The fit of the equation with four lagged values of *DM* is indicated by $R^2 = 0.52$, average absolute error for $U = 0.0059$. Hence, the fit is still considerably poorer than that obtained in equation (4) with two lagged values of the *DMR* variable.

Tests That Only Unanticipated Money Growth Affects Unemployment

A key hypothesis of this study is that only the unanticipated part of money growth influences unemployment. This hypothesis can be tested by running a regression that simultaneously includes sets of *DMR* and *DM* variables and then seeing whether the deletion of the *DM* variables, which amounts to a set of linear restrictions on the coefficients, produces a significant worsening of the fit. The resulting test statistic is $F^{3}_{19} = 1.4$ (5 percent critical value = 3.1) when two lagged values of DMR and DM are included, and $F^{5}_{15} = 2.0$ (5 percent critical value = 2.9) when four lagged values of each are included. Hence, the hypothesis that only the unanticipated part of money growth is relevant to unemployment is accepted by these tests.

The procedure can also be carried out in reverse by deleting the DMR values while retaining the DM values. When two lagged values of DMR and DM are included, the test statistic is $F^{3}_{19} = 15.7$. In the four-lag case the result is $F^{5}_{15} = 8.2$. Therefore, the reverse hypothesis that the DMR values are irrelevant to unemployment, given the DM values, can easily be rejected.

A point to stress about these tests is that they can be carried out at all only because predictors of DM_t other than its own history—DM_{t-1}, DM_{t-2}, etc.—have been included in the money growth equation. For example, suppose that $\hat{DM}_t$ were generated solely as a function of DM_{t-1}, say, $\hat{DM}_t = \alpha_0 + \alpha_1 DM_{t-1}$. In this case a regression of unemployment on a series of DMR ($\equiv DM - \hat{DM}$) values could not possibly fit better than a regression of the same form on a series of DM values that included one additional lagged term. The use of DMR values would amount, in this situation, solely to imposing a restriction on the coefficients that describe the effect of the DM variables on unemployment, so that (if no adjustment is made for the difference in degrees of freedom) the DMR regression would necessarily show a poorer fit. Hence, the superior fit of the DMR form of the unemployment equation reflects the impact of the additional predictors—namely, the federal expenditure and lagged unemployment variables—that were included in the money growth equation.

To make this point directly, I have obtained DMR values from money growth equations that involve solely the history of DM. An illustrative case, which includes 3 lagged values of DM over the 1941-73 period, is the following:

$$DM_t = 0.011 + 0.76DM_{t-1} + 0.30\,DM_{t-2} - 0.30DM_{t-3}, \qquad (6)$$
$$(0.008)\ (0.17) \qquad (0.21) \qquad (0.14)$$
$$R^2 = 0.77, \quad \hat{\sigma} = 0.031, \quad DW = 2.16.$$

Calculating DMR values as the residuals from the above equation leads to the estimated unemployment equation for 1946-73,

$$\log[U/(1-U)]_t = -3.00 + 1.2DMR_t - 4.9DMR_{t-1} - 1.9DMR_{t-2} \qquad (7)$$
$$(0.31)\ (2.9) \qquad (2.7) \qquad (2.4)$$
$$- 2.6MIL_t + 0.2MINW_t,$$
$$(1.3) \qquad (0.9)$$
$$R^2 = 0.31, \quad \hat{\sigma} = 0.23, \quad DW = 0.95,$$

which shows a substantially poorer fit than that obtained with the alternative DMR values from equation (2). Hence, a "naive" model that bases $\hat{DM}_t$ solely on the history of money growth would be inadequate for explaining unemployment.[17]

Further perspective on the distinction between actual and unanticipated money growth can be obtained by substituting into the estimated unemployment relation, equation (4), from the condition $DMR_t \equiv DM_t - \hat{DM}_t$, where $\hat{DM}_t$ is generated from the estimated money growth relation, equation (2). The resulting "reduced form" expresses unemployment as a function of $DM_t, \ldots DM_{t-4}$; $FEDV_t, \ldots FEDV_{t-2}$; $UN_{t-1}, \ldots UN_{t-3}$; MIL_t; and $MINW_t$. Specifically, the coefficients that derive from this substitution are indicated as hypothesized values in the first column of table 3.

17. If lagged values up to DM_{t-10} are included, the R^2 of the DM equation rises to 0.89 and that of the unemployment equation rises to 0.35. Allowing for first-order serial correlation of the error term in the DM equation does not materially affect any of these results.

Table 3

Hypothesized and Estimated Coefficients of Reduced Form for Unemployment

	Hypothesized	Estimated	Standard Error
C	-1.2	-1.1	(0.5)
DM_t	-5.8	-2.5	(2.6)
DM_{t-1}	-10.7	-12.5	(2.9)
DM_{t-2}	0.8	-5.8	(4.6)
DM_{t-3}	5.2	4.4	(1.8)
DM_{t-4}	1.5	2.3	(1.6)
$FEDV_t$	0.5	0.3	(0.7)
$FEDV_{t-1}$	1.0	1.3	(0.4)
$FEDV_{t-2}$	0.3	0.8	(0.5)
UN_{t-1}	0.2	-0.3	(0.4)
UN_{t-2}	0.3	0.5	(0.2)
UN_{t-3}	0.1	0.2	(0.2)
MIL_t	-4.7	-8.8	(2.2)
$MINW_t$	0.9	-0.6	(0.7)

It is also possible to estimate the reduced form for unemployment in a direct, unconstrained manner—a process that yields the estimated coefficients and standard errors that are also shown in table 3.

The use of the *DMR* form of the unemployment relation, equation (3), corresponds to a set of constraints on the manner in which the reduced-form independent variables influence unemployment. Specifically, the use of equation (3) with *DMR* values generated from equation (2) amounts to reducing the number of independent coefficients to be estimated in the unemployment relation from 14 in the unconstrained reduced form to 6 in the *DMR* form.[18] If the *DMR* specification in equation (3) is appropriate, then these 8 coefficient constraints should not significantly worsen the fit of the unemployment equation—heuristically, the hypothesized coefficients in table 3 should not differ "too much" from the estimated ones (taking account of standard errors). An overall test of the hypothesis is based on a comparison of restricted and unrestricted sums of squared residuals, which leads to the statistic $F^{8}_{14} = 1.4$, which is less than the 5 percent critical value of 2.7. Hence, this test also supports the use of the *DMR* form of the unemployment equation.

This listing of the reduced-form coefficients in table 3 brings out another point, which relates to the discussion of observational equivalence in Sargent (1976). Namely, the *DMR* form of the unemployment equation is equivalent to a form that contains *DM* values (in this case up to DM_{t-4}), along with the *FEDV* and lagged *UN* variables (up to $FEDV_{t-2}$ and UN_{t-3}, respectively) that were included in the *DM* relation. The exclusion of the *FEDV* and lagged *UN* variables from the form of the unemployment relation, equation (3), constitutes a set of identifying restrictions that permits an observational separation between the *DMR* and *DM* forms of the unemployment equation. The above tests of the distinction between these two forms then amount to tests of the joint hypothesis that (a) $\hat{DM}$ is generated in accordance with equation (2); (b) *DM* influences unemployment only in the form $DMR \equiv DM - \hat{DM}$; and (c) the *FEDV* and lagged *UN* variables that appear in equation (2) do not enter directly in equation (3). Of course, the acceptance of the joint null hypothesis by the above statistical tests provides support for each element of the hypothesis, namely for (a) and (b), which were the main objects of interest.

---

18. There are also 5 coefficients to be estimated in the *DM* equation, but this estimation was carried out separately from the fitting of the unemployment relation.

It would be possible, nevertheless, to interpret the estimated reduced form for unemployment (table 3, col. 2) as indicating the influence of actual money growth, *DM*, along with direct influences of the *FEDV*, lagged *UN*, *MIL*, and *MINW* variables (with the coefficients of the *DM*, *FEDV*, and lagged *UN* variables satisfying the restrictions implied by the *DMR* form out of pure coincidence). However, this interpretation leaves a number of results that require a theoretical explanation: (a) the *positive* effect of the *FEDV* variables on unemployment, in contrast with the negative effect that would be predicted along Keynesian lines; (b) the presence of positive coefficients on DM_{t-3} and DM_{t-4}; and (c) the stronger (positive) contribution of UN_{t-2} than of UN_{t-1}. These three sets of results are readily explained by the theory that relates unemployment to *DMR* values.

Properties of the Estimated Unemployment Equation

I will now discuss some detailed properties of the estimated *DMR* form of the unemployment relation, which is rewritten here for convenience.

$$\log[U/(1-U)]_t = \underset{(0.15)}{-3.07} \; \underset{(2.1)}{-5.8DMR_t} \; \underset{(1.9)}{-12.1DMR_{t-1}} \qquad (4)$$

$$\underset{(1.9)}{-4.2DMR_{t-2}} \; \underset{(0.8)}{-4.7MIL_t} \; \underset{(0.46)}{+0.95MINW_t}$$

Consider the magnitudes of the estimated *DMR* coefficients. The coefficient of -12 on DMR_{t-1} implies that an increase by 1 percentage point per year in the unanticipated money growth rate would reduce next year's unemployment rate by a proportion of about 12 percent, or by about 0.6 percentage point at an initial unemployment rate of 5 percent. However, the contemporaneous impact of this *DMR* shift would be only about half as large. If the increase in *DMR* by 1 percentage point per year were sustained over a three-year period (which would be an unusual event), then the full effect would be a reduction of the unemployment rate by about 1 percentage point.

It should be stressed that the lag pattern for money growth that is described in equation (4) refers to unanticipated rather than actual money growth. The implied lag pattern in terms of actual money growth—given the money growth relation as estimated in equation (2)—is shown as the hypothesized coefficients in table 3. Because of the positive effects of DM_{t-1} and DM_{t-2} on the current value of anticipated money growth, the lag pattern for unemployment in terms of DM differs markedly from that in terms of DMR. Two important differences are, first, the "mean" lag effect from DM to unemployment is shorter than that associated with DMR; and, second, there are positive coefficients in the DM form even when the DMR form is restricted to negative coefficients. Quantitatively, the lag pattern for DM that is shown in column 1 of table 3 accords with the well-known 6- to 18-month lag between (actual) money growth and economic activity that has been reported by Friedman (1969, p. 180). A lack of distinction between actual and unanticipated money growth can also account for some of the apparent variablility of the lag in Friedman's results (pp. 180-81).

Equation (4) also indicates the importance of the military variable (t-value of 5.9). The magnitude of the effect implied by the coefficient of -4.7 is that an increase by 1 percentage point in the ratio of military personnel to the male population aged 15-44 would reduce the unemployment rate by a proportion of about 4.7 percent, that is, by about 0.2 percentage point at U = 5 percent. Expressed alternatively, if changes in the labor force are neglected, an increase by an amount X in the number of military personnel would reduce the number of unemployed by about $0.5X$ (assuming that U = 0.05 and that the ratio of the labor force to the male population aged 15-44 takes on its 1973 value of 2.0).[19]

---

19. If the distinction between selective draft and nonselective draft years is dropped (which affects 1947-48 and 1970-73), the estimated unemployment rate equation becomes

$$\log[U/(1-U)]_t = \underset{(0.20)}{-2.88} \underset{(2.5)}{-4.5DMR_t} \underset{(2.3)}{-10.1DMR_{t-1}} \underset{(2.2)}{-1.5DMR_{t-2}}$$
$$\underset{(1.6)}{-7.1MIL_t} \underset{(0.56)}{+1.11MINW_t}, \quad R^2 = 0.68, \quad \hat{\sigma} = 0.16$$
$$DW = 1.38 \text{ (average of } |U - \hat{U}| = 0.0049).$$

The fit of the equation is poorer than that of equation (4), but the general implications are not altered.

The estimated minimum wage coefficient in equation (4) is positive and has a t-value of 2.1. Using the 1973 values of average hourly earnings ($3.92) and fraction covered (0.79), and starting from $U = 0.05$, the implication is that an increase by $1 in the minimum wage would raise the unemployment rate by about 1 percentage point. Viewed alternatively, if the minimum wage ($1.60 in 1973) were set to zero, the estimated fall in the unemployment rate would be by about 1.33 percentage points.

Given the estimated relation from equation (4), it is possible to calculate values of unemployment associated with $DMR = 0$ for all t—that is, with fully anticipated current and past monetary expansion. I will refer to these unemployment rates as natural values, *UNAT*.[20] In the present setup, the natural unemployment rate depends on the values of the military and minimum wage variables and on the constant term. Values of *UNAT* derived from equation (4) and from the values of *MIL* and *MINW* shown in table 2 are indicated for 1946-75 in table 1. This table also contains actual unemployment rates and the estimated values and residuals from equation (4). The pattern of results in this table is as follows.

With the end of World War II and the associated drop in military personnel, the estimated natural unemployment rate rose from about 1.5 percent to about 3.5 percent in 1946 and 5 percent for 1947-48 (partially non-draft law years). Although there was a large cutback in money growth, from rates about 15 percent per year during World War II to 6.8 percent in 1946 and 4.7 percent in 1947, the money growth equation implies that this cutback was anticipated because of the sharp decline in federal expenditure. In fact, the estimated values, $D\hat{M} = 5.5$ percent in 1946 and 3.8 percent in 1947, imply that these two years were characterized by unanticipated monetary expansion. Accordingly, the unemployment rates for 1946-48 remained at about 4 percent—below the natural rate for 1947-48. The unanticipated monetary contraction of 1948-49 ($DMR = -0.012$ and -0.023, respectively) implied increases in the unemployment rate for 1949 and 1950.

---

20. Because of nonlinearities, these values differ from expected unemployment rates derived from eq. (4) with an additive, constant variance error term. The (positive) gap between the expected unemployment rate and the natural rate, as defined, increases with the variance of the error term and with the variance of *DMR*.

For the Korean War years of 1951-53, an expansionary element was an increase in the military variable that lowered the natural unemployment rate to 3.5-4 percent. This factor, combined with unanticipated monetary expansion from 1950 to 1952 (*DMR* values of 0.019, 0.018, and 0.012, respectively), led to unemployment rates in the neighborhood of 3 percent for 1951-53. From the end of the Korean War through 1969, the maintenance of a selective draft law with high levels of military personnel implied small variations in the natural unemployment rate. In particular, with *UNAT* confined to a range of 4.0-4.4 percent from 1956 to 1969, movements in the natural rate have a minor effect on estimated unemployment rates during this period.

In 1954 the unanticipated monetary contraction of 1953 (-0.017) was the main contributor to the rise in unemployment (though my *U*-estimate of 0.044 is below the actual value of 0.052). For 1954-55, the unanticipated parts of money growth were small, implying values of *U* near the natural rate of 4 percent for 1955-56. The unanticipated monetary contraction in 1956 (-0.009) led to an estimated *U*-value for 1957 of 4.9 percent, although the actual value was only 4.1 percent. On the other hand, my estimate for *U* in 1958 is 5.4 percent (reflecting the additional monetary contraction of -0.018 in 1957), which substantially underestimates the actual value of 6.5 percent. For 1959-60, the estimates are about 0.5 percentage point below the actual values, which were themselves about 1 percentage point above the natural rates.

Perhaps the most interesting monetary behavior of the post-World War II period is the absolute contraction of money that occurred during 1960. This behavior represented the first absolute decline in money since 1949; but more significantly, the estimate for anticipated money growth in 1960 is 3.0 percent, as contrasted with 1.3 percent for 1949. Hence, the unanticipated monetary contraction for 1960 was -3.1 percent—the largest absolute value of *DMR* for the entire post-World War II period. According to the estimated equation, this large negative value of *DMR* for 1960 accounted for the sharp rise in the unemployment rate in 1961 to over 6 percent—about 2 percentage points above the natural rate.

From 1963 to 1967 there was a period of monetary stability, in the sense of small deviations between actual and anticipated values of *DM*. The response in *U* was a gradual downward movement, first to the natural rate in 1965, and then slightly below for 1966-67. There was then a sharp monetary expansion in 1968 (*DMR* = 0.026), which ended the brief period of "constant growth rate rule" for money.[21] For 1968-69 the unemployment rate of 3.4 percent was about 1 percentage point below the natural rate.

The explanation of behavior in 1970 is complicated, since it hinges on the treatment of the switch to the lottery draft as equivalent, in terms of unemployment effects, to a removal of conscription (see note 19). The assumption that the military variable was zero from 1970 on implies a natural rate, since 1970, of 6-6.5 percent (depending on the value of the *MINW* variable)—an increase of 1.5-2.0 percentage points from the 4.4 percent value for 1969. Given the rise in the natural rate, the maintenance of 1970 unemployment at only 4.7 percent of the labor force reflected the continuing impact of the strong 1968-69 monetary expansion. The monetary behavior from 1971 to 1973 was expansionary, and the unemployment rate remained 0.5-1.0 percentage point below the natural rate during this period.

Unemployment Predictions

The unemployment and money growth rate relations, estimated from data up to 1973, can be used to form projections for 1974 and beyond. For 1974, the predicted value of *DM* is 5.6 percent per year, as compared to an actual value of 5.5 percent. Hence, the *DMR* value for 1974 is close to zero. The prediction from equation (4) for the 1974 unemployment rate is 5.6 percent, which almost coincides with the actual value of 5.5 percent.

For 1975, the predicted value of *DM* (conditioned on the value DM_{t-1} = 0.005 for 1974) is 6.2 percent per year. Since the actual value of *DM* for 1975 is 4.2 percent, the monetary contraction during this year is measured by *DMR* = -2.0 percent. Using the ex post values *DMR* = -0.001 for 1974 and -0.020 for 1975, the "predicted" value for 1975 unemployment turns out to

---

21. I use this expression to signify predictability of *DM*, rather than constancy per se.

be 7.1 percent. Since the actual average of unemployment rates during 1975 is 8.3 percent, there is an underprediction of unemployment by about the same magnitude as for the 1958 contraction.

For 1976 and 1977 (using the value *FEDV* = 0.18, which is the average over the 1960-75 period), the predicted value for *DM* is 6.5 percent per year.[22] Using values of *DMR* = 0 for 1976 and beyond (which is appropriate ex ante), assuming a zero value for *MIL* and using the values of *MINW* that are shown in table 2, the predicted unemployment rates are 8.1 percent for 1976, 6.8 percent for 1977, and 6.1 percent (the natural rate) for 1978 and beyond. Based on observations for the first few months, it appears that the model will overpredict 1976 unemployment.

3. SOME POLICY IMPLICATIONS

Acceptance of the hypothesis that only the unanticipated part of money growth affects unemployment has some important policy implications. One result is that the systematic feedback from unemployment to money growth that appears in equation (2) has no implications for the time path of unemployment itself—a result that accords with the theoretical propositions in Sargent and Wallace (1975) and Barro (1976*b*). Only movements in money that depart from the usual countercyclical response affect subsequent unemployment rates.[23] This observation raises questions concerning the rationality of the countercyclical policy response that appears in equation (2). One possibility is that the reaction of money to lagged unemployment reflects optimal public finance considerations (see section 1 and Barro 1976*a*), rather than an attempt at economic stabilization.

---

22. This high value of $\hat{DM}$ reflects the high value of lagged unemployment. It may be preferable to measure unemployment relative to its perceived long-run value, which has apparently increased since 1970 (see n. 6). This modification would lower the values of $\hat{DM}$ for the 1970s, but a quantitative adjustment would require a measure of the perceived long-run value of unemployment.

23. However, the present analysis has not dealt with the possible temporary impact of structural shifts in the money growth process, as discussed theoretically in Taylor (1975). Such shifts did not appear to be important over the 1941-73 period (see Barro 1975).

Similar conclusions apply to the response of money to the federal budget variable, *FEDV*. Increases in federal expenditure above its normal level (with the military variable held fixed) reduce unemployment only if the accompanying increase in money is larger than the usual amount.[24] In fact, if actual money growth is held constant, an increase in *FEDV* raises unemployment because of the associated increase in anticipated money growth. (Some preliminary results indicate that this effect is important during the middle 1930s.)

4. CONCLUSIONS AND EXTENSIONS

The starting point for this study was the hypothesis that only unanticipated movements in money would affect economic activity. That hypothesis was quantified by interpreting anticipated money growth as the amount that could have been predicted based on the historical relation between money growth and a specified set of explanatory variables. For the United States from 1941 to 1973 these variables included a measure of federal expenditure relative to normal, a lagged unemployment rate, and two annual lag values of money growth. Unanticipated money growth was then measured as actual growth less the amount obtained from this predictive relationship. The current and two annual lag values of unanticipated money growth were shown to have considerable explanatory value for unemployment. Further, some statistical tests confirmed the underlying hypothesis that actual money growth is irrelevant for unemployment, given the values of unanticipated money growth.

The results reported in this paper would be more reliable if they could be replicated for other experiences. For the United States, I am currently working on the unemployment and output experiences back to 1890. Since the structure of the money growth process prior to World War II appears different from that estimated for the 1941-73 period, the long-period evidence will permit a much more powerful test of the hypothesis that only

24. I attempted to find a direct fiscal effect on unemployment by entering into the unemployment equation the full-employment federal government deficit (measured as a ratio to the outstanding stock of privately held public debt). This variable was insignificant (estimated coefficient of -0.7, standard error = 1.0), as were lagged values of the deficit and measures of the deficit relative to its "anticipated" value.

unanticipated money growth affects unemployment. Further, it will be possible to test the hypothesis advanced by Lucas (1973) that shifts in the prediction variance of money would alter the response of unemployment to monetary shocks.

Finally, although the present analysis was directed toward the effects of money on unemployment (with related implications for output), the division of money growth into anticipated and unanticipated parts also has important implications for inflation. I plan to deal with this topic in a subsequent paper.

REFERENCES

Barro, R. J. 1975. "Unanticipated Money Growth and Unemployment in the United States." Working Paper. Rochester: University of Rochester.

_____. 1976*a*. "Optimal Revenue Collection and the Money Growth Rate." Unpublished.

_____. 1976*b*. "Rational Expectations and the Role of Monetary Policy." JOURNAL OF MONETARY ECONOMICS 2 (Jan.): 1-32.

Cagan, P. 1956. "The Monetary Dynamics of Hyperinflation." In STUDIES IN THE QUANTITY THEORY OF MONEY, edited by M. Friedman. Chicago: University of Chicago Press.

Cooley, T. F., and Prescott, E. 1973. "Varying Parameter Regression: A Theory and Some Applications." ANNALS OF ECONOMIC AND SOCIAL MEASUREMENT 2: 463-74.

Darby, M. R. 1976. "Three-and-a-half Million U.S. Employees Have Been Mislaid; or, an Explanation of Unemployment, 1934-1941." JOURNAL OF POLITICAL ECONOMY 84 (Feb.): 1-17.

Friedman, M. 1969. "The Supply of Money and Changes in Prices and Output." In his THE OPTIMUM QUANTITY OF MONEY AND OTHER ESSAYS. Chicago: University of Chicago Press.

Lucas, R. E. 1972. "Expectations and the Neutrality of Money." JOURNAL OF ECONOMIC THEORY 4 (Apr.): 103-24.

_____. 1973. "Some International Evidence on Output-Inflation Tradeoffs." AMERICAN ECONOMIC REVIEW 63 (June): 326-34.

_____. 1975. "An Equilibrium Model of the Business Cycle." JOURNAL OF POLITICAL ECONOMY 83 (Dec.): 1113-44.

Mincer, J. 1976. "Unemployment Effects of Minimum Wages." JOURNAL OF POLITICAL ECONOMY 84 (Aug.), pt. 2: S87-104.

Muth, J. F. 1960. "Optimal Properties of Exponentially Weighted Forecasts." JOURNAL OF THE AMERICAN STATISTICAL ASSOCATION 55 (June): 299-306.

Phelps, E. S. 1973. "Inflation in the Theory of Public Finance." SWEDISH JOURNAL OF ECONOMICS 75 (Mar.): 67-82.

Rafuse, J. L. 1970. "United States' Experience with Volunteer and Conscript Forces." In STUDIES PREPARED FOR THE PRESIDENT'S COMMISSION ON AN ALL-VOLUNTEER ARMED FORCE, vol. 2. Washington, D. C.: Government Printing Office.

Sargent, T. J. 1971. "A Note on the 'Accelerationist' Controversy." JOURNAL OF MONEY, CREDIT AND BANKING 3 (Aug.): 721-25.

_____. 1976. "The Observational Equivalence of Natural and Unnatural Rate Theories of Macroeconomics." JOURNAL OF POLITICAL ECONOMY 84 (June): 631-40.

Sargent, T. J., and Wallace, N. 1975. "'Rational' Expectations, the Optimal Monetary Instrument and the Optimal Money Supply Rule." JOURNAL OF POLITICAL ECONOMY 83 (Apr.): 241-54.

Taylor, J. B. 1975. "Monetary Policy during a Transition to Rational Expectations." JOURNAL OF POLITICAL ECONOMY 83 (Oct.): 1009-21.

U.S. Bureau of the Census. 1960. HISTORICAL STATISTICS OF THE UNITED STATES, COLONIAL TIMES TO 1957. Washington, D. C.: Government Printing Office.

_____. STATISTICAL ABSTRACT OF THE UNITED STATES, various issues. Washington, D. C.: Government Printing Office.

U.S. Council of Economic Advisers. ECONOMIC REPORT OF THE PRESIDENT, various issues. Washington, D. C.: Government Printing Office.

Weiss, A. 1973. Statement before the Subcommittee on Labor Standards, House Education and Labor Committee, Nov.

ANTICIPATED INFLATION AND UNANTICIPATED PRICE CHANGE*

A Test of the Price-Specie Flow Theory and the Phillips Curve

Allan H. Meltzer**

Carnegie-Mellon University

The Phillips curve is widely accepted as the maintained theory of inflation. In the standard version of the theory, current inflation depends on some measure of anticipated inflation and on the deviation of current output from full-employment output. Most recent studies of inflation report the continuing search for variables that increase the accuracy with which the theory predicts or forecasts. Recent surveys by Laidler and Parkin (1975) and Gordon (1976) summarize these developments. An entirely different direction has been taken by Lucas (1972, 1975, 1977) and Phelps (1972). These authors seek to provide a firm micro-foundation for the relation.

The Phillips curve differs from earlier explanations of price fluctuations. Hume, Thornton, and other early exponents of the price-specie flow theory relate price levels to output, so that the short-run rate of price change depends on the rate of change of output and not on the current or past level of output. Producers respond to changes in demand by moving

* Reprinted, with some changes, by permission of the author and the Ohio State University Press, from the JOURNAL OF MONEY, CREDIT AND BANKING 9 (February 1977, pt. 2): 182-205. Copyright © 1977 by the Ohio State University Press. An earlier version of the paper was presented at the 1976 Konstanz Seminar.

** Much of the work appearing here has developed from the discussion that I have had for many years with Karl Brunner and from our joint work. Brunner's long-time interest in the problems addressed is well known. I am pleased that this attempt at explanation appears as an essay in his honor. As teacher, collaborator, and friend, he stimulated my interest in the problems addressed and in the importance of economic analysis and evidence for correct conclusions. I am indebted to Timothy McGuire for helpful suggestions and to Walter Dolde, William Dewald, Helmut Frisch, John Bryant, Robert Hodrick, and Claudio Haddad for criticisms of previous drafts and to the participants in the 1976 Konstanz Seminar for helpful comments.

along positively sloped supply curves. Aggregate supply is the appropriately weighted sum of individual producers' supplies. Prices and output respond positively to changes in demand. I know of no recent effort to develop the Hume-Thornton analysis as an alternative to the Phillips curve or to test the Phillips curve by comparison with the alternative theory.[1]

There are, moreover, reasons for skepticism about much of the evidence used to support Phillips curves. First, economic theory implies that agents respond differently to one-time price changes and maintained rates of price change. This distinction is ignored in every empirical study of inflation that uses past rates of price change to measure anticipated inflation. Most studies (Gordon 1976; Laidler and Parkin 1975; Modigliani and Papademos 1975) include one-time changes in the price level in measures of anticipated inflation, contrary to economic theory.

Second, much of the evidence is drawn from a brief period with a particular type of international monetary arrangement. The formation of price anticipations depends on the prevalent type of monetary arrangements. Under a gold standard, a rise in the domestic price level relative to prices abroad implies that domestic prices must fall in the future. Under the dollar standard, as Klein (1976) has suggested, an increase in the current rate of inflation carries no implication of later deflation. Little evidence has been produced to show that Phillips curves are capable of explaining price changes in the interwar period or under the gold standard.

There has been much discussion of Friedman's (1970) proposition that inflation is always a monetary phenomenon. Standard theory (Metzler 1951) implies that the price level changes with a one-time change in tastes, the degree of monopoly, or other real variables. Empirical observation suggests that, generally, real changes do not occur at a steady rate but occur discretely and therefore affect the price level and not inflation. Hence,

---

1. Lucas (1975, 1977) develops an equilibrium model in which the aggregate supply curve relates output to the rate of price change.

Friedman's proposition cannot be falsified by showing that some changes in the price level result from nonmonetary causes. To reject the proposition, we require a theory that distinguishes between once-and-for-all price changes and maintained rates of price change. The model developed here makes the distinction, thereby permitting a test of Friedman's proposition.[2]

The term "inflation," as used here, means the rate of price change maintained for a period of time (to be defined more precisely below). The "rate of price change" includes inflation and all changes in the price level.[3]

In the following sections, I develop a model relating output, inflation, and rates of price change to monetary and fiscal variables and to anticipations. I estimate anticipated inflation and output using a procedure similar to McGuire's (1976). Then I use the estimates to separate the effects of anticipated inflation on the current rate of price change from the effects of random and systematic changes in the price level.

Phillips curves attribute inflation to excess demand and excess demand to government policies (Cross and Laidler 1976; Gordon 1976; Laidler and Parkin 1975). Evidence of the effect of policies is rarely presented. In contrast, the model developed here provides estimates of the responses to government policies and tests some central propositions about the effects of the growth of money and other variables on inflation and output.

A THEORY OF INCOME, INFLATION, AND PRICES

The economy I consider has many of the features found in classical or neoclassical theory. The steady-state path of aggregate, anticipated income is determined by real resources. Wealth consists of tangible real assets,

---

2. Helmut Frisch points out that when rates of change dominate and the effect of levels is small, Friedman's (1974) adjustment equation is closer to what I have called the price-specie flow model than to the Phillips curve.

3. The use of "inflation" to refer to current rates of price change and maintained inflation creates a problem analogous to the use of "growth" to refer to the rate of change of output during a finite interval that includes a recovery or a recession. Rather than my terminology, some may prefer the terms short- and long-term inflation, current and maintained inflation, or even permanent and transitory inflation.

government debt, and money balances. The steady-state growth path of the economy, obtained from the quantity equation, is

$$\mu = \hat{p}^a + g, \tag{1}$$

where μ is the maintained rate of monetary expansion,

$\hat{p}^a$ is the fully anticipated rate of inflation,[4] and

g is the rate of change of fully anticipated output or real income.

The economy does not remain on the steady-state path, so current receipts and income differ. The term "income" refers to the realizations along the path; "receipts" refers to the actual or anticipated current value of aggregate output available for spending. Spending is the rate of purchase of durables and nondurables and depends on receipts; consumption is the rate of use and depends on income. When consumers' receipts are less than their income, consumers reduce spending, maintain consumption, reduce inventories of assets, and lower replacement relative to depreciation. Friedman (1957) gave the name "transitory income" to the difference between income and current receipts and provided an explanation of the relation of consumption to income and receipts, but he did not investigate differences between consumption and spending or indicate how receipts are determined. Fluctuations in receipts relative to income constitute most of the movements known as the business cycle.

I assume that each individual acts as if his anticipated current receipts depend on his total wealth and the way in which society uses available resources. Anticipated aggregate *receipts*, y^a, is obtained by summing individual anticipations, y^a/L:

$$\frac{y^a}{L} = H\left[\left(\frac{K}{L}\right)^{\alpha}\left(\frac{L}{N}\right)^{\beta}(L_g)^{\gamma}\left(\frac{S}{p}\right)^{\delta} e^{kB/p}\right], \tag{2}$$

$$\alpha, \gamma, k > 0, \quad \beta < 0.$$

4. Throughout, the symbol "^" denotes the relative rate of change, and the superscript "a" denotes the anticipated or planned value.

The H function is assumed to be homogeneous of degree one in population N, capital, and labor force. Anticipated receipts per worker depend on capital per worker, K/L, the proportion of the population in the labor force, L/N, the absorption of labor by government, L_g, and on real government debt, S/p, and base money held by the public, B/p. Per capita receipts vary directly with capital per worker and inversely with participation in the labor force. Absorption of labor by government reduces the supply of labor to the private sector. Privately produced output falls, but government services increase. Since there is no force equating the marginal social product of government service to the wage rate paid by government, real wages and anticipated receipts change when L_g changes (Coulter 1976).

The financing of past government budgets and balances of payments determines the current stocks of financial assets, S and B. Current values of financial stocks are known, but future increments are unknown and subject to variations that are a principal cause of fluctuations in output and prices (Brunner and Meltzer 1976; Christ 1968; Friedman 1970; Mayer 1975). I assume that fluctuations in policy are so erratic that rational individuals forecast neither the timing nor the magnitude of current *changes* in B and S.[5] Once the changes occur, however, agents adjust.

Equation (2) permits agents to respond to changes in the composition of wealth. By issuing or withdrawing base money and debt, the government affects anticipated output, changing relative prices and the composition of spending (Brunner and Meltzer 1976; Christ 1968; Tobin 1961). Budget deficits financed by issuing debt increase wealth and raise interest rates. As in Brunner and Meltzer (1976), I have assumed that the effect of S/p on y or

5. To state the point in a way that is more consistent with recent discussions of rational expectations, individuals may hold anticipations about long-run tax rates and the size of government, but the costs of predicting the *timing* of policy actions are high relative to the costs of monitoring current operations. I assume that, as the evidence in Hamburger and Platt (1975) suggests, individuals monitor policy actions, and every policy action is "known" up to a random component when it occurs. The assumptions about the lag structure of eq. (2) are introduced when estimation is discussed below.

y^a is positive. Increases in the base raise wealth and lower interest rates. If prices do not fully adjust, real base-money balances and anticipated real receipts (or output) rise and fall together.

Real base-money balances change, also, when there are technological changes in the payments system. Improvements in payments technology permit agents to reallocate effort from making payments to both production and leisure, so anticipated receipts (and output) rise. If the change in payment arrangements increases the demand for *nominal* base money, real base-money balances and real anticipated receipts (output) are positively related.[6]

The value of aggregate current receipts (output) is a random variable that fluctuates around anticipated receipts.

$$y_t = y_t^a \nu_{1,t}. \tag{3}$$

Equation (3) recognizes two types of disturbances. First, differences between y^a and *income* describe the position of the economy in the business cycle. Second, agents make errors using equations (2) and (3) to forecast anticipated receipts. The forecast error $\nu_{1,t}$ in equation (3) includes real shocks and unanticipated changes in government policies.

The rate of change of anticipated receipts fluctuates around the economy's growth path. When the rate of change of anticipated receipts is above or below the growth rate of income, the rate of change of planned spending is above or below the growth rate of steady-state consumption and investment. Equation (4) describes the relation between the anticipated rate of change of aggregate spending in nominal terms, $\mu + \hat{V}^a$, and the current anticipated rate of change of receipts, $\hat{y}^a + \hat{p}^a$. The anticipated rate of change of velocity, $\hat{V}^a$, depends on changes in the anticipated rate of price

6. This interpretation of productive monetary arrangements is developed in Brunner and Meltzer (1971). The contribution of money balances is not, as in Sinai and Stokes (1972) a "direct" contribution of money balances to output. Some notable changes in exchange arrangements are the introduction of the Federal Reserve System and the breakdown of the international gold standard in the '30s.

change, $\hat{\pi} = d\hat{p}^a/\hat{p}^a$, and on the rate of change of anticipated receipts, $\hat{y}^a$. When $\hat{p}^a$ is constant ($\hat{\pi} = 0$) and $\hat{y}^a = g$, velocity is constant and agents expect the economy to move along the steady-state path shown in equation (1).

$$\mu + \hat{V}^a(\hat{\pi}, \hat{y}^a) = \hat{y}^a + \hat{p}^a. \tag{4}$$

The actual rate of price change, $\hat{p}$, is not identical to $\hat{p}^a$, and current spending is not identical to planned spending. Current ***private*** spending is MV, and current receipts is the sum of the receipts of individual agents, $py = \Sigma\, p_i y_i$. The growth of actual private spending and receipts in any year is obtained by taking logarithms of the quantity equation $MV = py$ and differentiating to obtain relative rates of change. Fluctuations in government services are measured by the growth rate of public employment, $\hat{L}_g$, so $\hat{y} - \hat{L}_g$ is the rate of change of private output.

$$\hat{M} + \hat{V} = \hat{p} + \hat{y} - \hat{L}_g, \tag{5}$$

where $\hat{M}$ and $\hat{V}$ are the relative rates of change of money and actual velocity and $\hat{p}$ and $\hat{y}$ are relative rates of change of prices and total current real receipts. By subtracting equation (5) from equation (4) and rearranging terms, we obtain an equation for the difference between the actual and anticipated rate of price change.[7]

$$\hat{p} - \hat{p}^a = \hat{y}^a - \hat{y} + \hat{M} - \mu + \hat{L}_g + \hat{V} - \hat{V}^a.$$

To test Friedman's (1970) proposition that inflation is a "monetary phenomenon," assume that $\hat{p}^a = \mu - g$ and that g is constant. Observed rates of price change differ from anticipated inflation whenever there are adjustments in velocity or errors in forecasting current receipts. Adjustments of velocity and errors are one-time events that affect the price level but not the maintained rate of inflation.

---

7. At first glance, it appears that I have adjusted $\hat{y}$ but not $\hat{y}^a$ for government absorption of labor, $\hat{L}_g$. The effect of L_g on y^a is given by eq. (2), which is used to compute y^a.

$$\hat{p} = \hat{M} + \hat{V} - \hat{V}^a - \hat{y} + \hat{L}_g + \hat{y}^a - g. \qquad (6)$$

To complete the hypothesis, we require information about the response of velocity. The demand function for money provides the underlying analysis. As in Brunner and Meltzer (1976), the demand for money balances depends on total wealth, the market rate of interest, and the prices of assets and output. The market value of wealth is the sum of base money, government debt, and real capital at market prices. In a full equilibrium, assets sell at replacement cost and the output price level differs from the anticipated level by anticipated price change. Fluctuations in the economy induce changes in the prices of assets and output. I assume that wealth owners use the anticipated price level, p^a, as an index of the anticipated cost of withdrawing output for use as capital, so that $c_o p^a$ is a measure of the replacement cost of assets. Further, to avoid later problems of measurement, I use nominal income as a measure of the combined effect of nominal human wealth and nominal real capital. With these adjustments, the demand function for money is

$$M = \lambda(r + \hat{p}^a, p, c_o p^a, yp, S, B),$$

$$\lambda_1, \lambda_3 < 0, \qquad \lambda_2, \lambda_4, \lambda_5, \lambda_6 > 0.$$

The demand function is homogeneous of first degree in prices and the value of financial assets. For velocity and current y to be positively related, the income elasticity of the demand for money must be less than unity. I have left the sign of y open. Velocity, the ratio of real income to real balances, is

$$V = V\left(r + \hat{p}^a, c_o \frac{p^a}{p}, y, \frac{S}{p}, \frac{B}{p}\right), \qquad (7)$$

$$V_1, V_2 > 0, \qquad V_4, V_5 < 0.$$

Differentiating (7) and multiplying to form elasticities makes $\hat{V}$, the relative rate of change of current velocity, depend on the relative rates of change of its determinants. Elasticities are denoted ε and, as before, relative rates of change are shown by a circumflex. $\hat{\pi}$ is the relative rate of price acceleration.

$$\hat{V} = \varepsilon(V, r)\hat{r} + \varepsilon(V, \hat{p}^a)\hat{\pi} + \varepsilon(V, p^a)\hat{p}^a + \varepsilon(V, S)\hat{S} + \varepsilon(V, B)\hat{B}$$
$$- \varepsilon(V, p)\hat{p} + \varepsilon(V, y)\hat{y}.$$

The real rate of interest is neither constant nor given in the determination of $\hat{V}$. The real rate that governs portfolio choice and intertemporal resource allocation in any year is the product of an expected return to capital per unit of capital, n, and the ratio of the price level of current output to the price level of existing assets (Brunner and Meltzer 1976). As before, the anticipated price level, p^a, is an index of the anticipated cost of using a unit of output to replace or increase capital and is assumed to be proportional ($1/c_o$) to the replacement cost of capital. The real rate of interest is, then,

$$r = \frac{p}{c_o p^a} n,$$

where $n = n(y - y^a, B/p, S/p, L_g, y^a)$, $n_1, n_3 > 0$ and $n_2, n_4, n_5 < 0$.

The expected return to capital, n, depends on the capital stock; the effect is shown by n_5. The expected return depends, also, on the real value of financial assets and on the amount of labor absorbed by government. The current return to capital rises when agents receive information that they have underestimated the current expansion ($y < y^a$), and n falls if $y > y^a$. Absorption of labor by government raises the marginal product of labor in private production and lowers the anticipated return to capital.

Differentiating r and multiplying throughout to express the results as elasticities and relative rates of change yields

$$\hat{r} = [\, 1 - \varepsilon(n, p)\,]\hat{p} - \hat{p}^a + \varepsilon(n, y^a)\hat{y}^a + \varepsilon(n, L_g)\hat{L}_g \tag{8}$$
$$+ \varepsilon(n, B)\hat{B} + \varepsilon(n, S)\hat{S}.$$

By replacing $\hat{r}$ with equation (8), rewriting $\hat{V}^a(\hat{\pi}, \hat{y}^a)$ from (4) in terms of elasticities and relative rates of change, and substituting in equation (6), we obtain a solution for $\hat{p}$.

$$\hat{p} = w_o + w_1\hat{p}^a + w_2\hat{B} + w_3\hat{S} + w_4\hat{\pi} + w_5\hat{L}_g + w_6\hat{y} \tag{9}$$
$$+ w_7\hat{y}^a + v_2, \qquad w_1, w_2, w_5, w_7 > 0.$$

The current rate of monetary expansion is measured by $\hat{B}$, the growth rate of the monetary base. The responses to $\hat{S}$, $\hat{\pi}$, and $\hat{y}$ are ambiguous. The derivation of the signs is shown in appendix 2.

ESTIMATES OF ANTICIPATED INFLATION AND REAL RECEIPTS

To test the theory of the rate of price change developed in the previous section, I require estimates of the anticipated rate of inflation and the rate of change of current real receipts. In this section, the anticipated values are estimated from past data, and propositions about the formation of anticipations are tested. In later sections, I use the estimates developed in this section to test propositions about monetary and other sources of price changes.

Anticipated Receipts, y^a

Equations (2) and (3) form a hypothesis about the formation of anticipated current receipts and the relation of anticipated to observed receipts (measured real output). Three problems arise in implementing the hypothesis. First, consistent data for the private capital stock are not available for the entire century. I combined two available series on the stock of capital to form a not entirely consistent set of data for the relevant years.[8] I assume that anticipated receipts in year t depend only on information available at the start of the year. Agents have more information than the equation permits, but some evidence (Hamburger and Platt 1975) suggests that the net benefit of monitoring current policy actions is high relative to the benefits of predicting the timing of events. Third, I have found no way to separate the effect of lifetime *income* on current anticipated receipts from the effects of current receipts and current activity. The responses to K, L, L_g, etc., combine the response to long-term growth with the response to recovery and recession. This problem is of particular importance because the years 1929-40 are a significant part of the sample period.

8. A complete list of sources and procedures is given in appendix 1. Note that debt is the outstanding stock of government debt minus net foreign debt and debt owned by the Federal Reserve.

Using gross private domestic product as the measure of receipts, least-squares estimates for the period 1900-1974, omitting the years of price and interest-rate controls, 1941-52, suggest that agents estimated aggregate receipts according to[9]

$$\frac{y_t^a}{L_{t-1}} = e^{-9.64} \left(\frac{K}{L}\right)_{t-1}^{0.41} \left(\frac{L}{N}\right)_{t-1}^{-2.40} (L_g)_{t-1}^{0.09} \left(\frac{B}{p}\right)_{t-1}^{0.36} N_t^{0.25}.$$

The point estimates imply that as population grows, aggregate anticipated receipts rise relative to labor force. Anticipated receipts increase with capital per worker and decline with increased labor-force participation.

Anticipated Rate of Inflation

Anticipations of inflation depend on the prevailing monetary standard. Under a pure gold standard, maintained growth or contraction of the monetary gold stock brings inflation or deflation. Rational agents in the gold-standard countries base anticipations of world inflation on the

---

9. The coefficient of S/p is close to zero (see below) and is omitted in the text. The Durbin-Watson statistic shows substantial serial correlation, but I made no effort to adjust the estimates. Little is known about aggregate anticipated output. It is not unreasonable for the aggregation of individual forecasts to yield forecasts that remain above or below actual output for several years in succession. The least-squares estimates are shown with t-statistics in parentheses, the Durbin-Watson statistic (DW) and $\bar{R}^2$ adjusted for degrees of freedom. A dummy variable was used for World War I (1917-19), and a second dummy was used to adjust for the break in the capital stock series (1925) and the break in the data series (1953). The regression equation is

$$\ln y_t = -9.64 + \underset{(5.54)}{0.409} \ln K_{t-1} - \underset{(4.02)}{1.802} \ln L_{t-1} + \underset{(0.83)}{0.090} \ln L_{gt-1}$$

$$+ \underset{(7.55)}{1.300} \left(\frac{B}{p}\right)_{t-1} - \underset{(0.24)}{0.004} \ln \left(\frac{S}{p}\right)_{t-1} + \underset{(6.21)}{2.646} \ln N_t,$$

$$\bar{R}^2 = 0.99, \quad DW = 0.72.$$

The equation was estimated with none of the variables in per capita terms. If the lagged values of K and L are deflated by labor force and population, an equiproportionate increase in K, L, and N raises y more than proportionally.

maintained rate of change of the world gold stock. Maintained change in domestic money at rates inconsistent with the growth of the world gold stock generates anticipations of domestic inflation and devaluation or deflation and revaluation. Persistent difference between domestic and foreign price levels requires the central bank to pay out or absorb gold, adjust the stock of money, and devalue or revalue currency in terms of gold.

The international gold standard ended after Britain gave up the standard in 1931. The United States devalued in 1934 and ended the formal link between gold and the dollar in 1971. Following World War II, dollars became the principal component of international base money.

Under the dollar standard, maintained expansion of the U.S. money stock did not set off a process that reduced the growth rate of money. Most foreign central banks did not insist on the convertibility of dollars into gold and did not revalue. Instead, they purchased dollar securities, expanded stocks of money, and permitted prices to rise. When after 1970 foreign governments chose to separate domestic inflation from U.S. inflation, the dollar standard ended, and an era of fluctuating exchange rates began.

If rational agents use information about the monetary standard when estimating the anticipated rate of inflation, changes in the stock of money should not have the same effect on maintained inflation for 1901-31 as for 1954-71. The years 1932-40 are a mixture that I have treated separately in my estimates and in subsequent tests. I have included 1971-74 with the years of the dollar standard.

Equation (10) is a restatement of equation (1); g is constant, and μ, the fully anticipated rate of monetary expansion, is defined as the weighted sum of recent and "maintained" monetary growth. A three-year, unweighted, moving average of rates of monetary change, lagged one year, is used to measure "maintained" monetary growth. The mean lag of two years does not differ markedly from some recent estimates (Mayer 1975).

The anticipated rate of inflation and the *anticipated* one-year rate of price change are identical.[10]

$$\hat{p}_t = a_o + a_1\hat{M}_{t-1} + a_2\hat{\bar{M}}_{t-1} + a_3D + \nu_3, \qquad (10)$$

where $\hat{p}$ is the actual rate of price change,

$\hat{M}_{t-1}$ is the growth of money in the previous year,

$\hat{\bar{M}}_{t-1}$ is the average growth rate of money in the three years ending in $t-1$,

D is a dummy variable, and

ν_3 is the difference between anticipated and actual rates of price change.

Table 1 shows least-squares estimates of equation (10).

The regressions suggest that, if equation (10) is a correct representation of agents' behavior, a considerable part of the observed rate of price change is unanticipated. Agents did less well, on average, anticipating the rate of price change under the gold standard, 1901-31, than under the dollar standard. One reason is that the variance of the rate of price change was greater (0.14) for 1901-31 than for 1954-74 (0.08). A second, related, reason is that monetary growth has two effects on $\hat{p}^a$ under the gold standard. The rate of price change is expected to respond first positively, then negatively, to monetary growth. The timing of the anticipated reversal is not fixed and uniform but is uncertain.

The estimates in table 1 show that deviations from the maintained average rate of change—accelerations and decelerations of money in the recent past--have much greater effect on $\hat{p}^a$ under the gold standard than under the dollar standard. The estimates suggest that, under the dollar

10. This is very restrictive. Agents may anticipate once-and-for-all price changes or distinguish such changes from the rate of inflation, or they may form a term structure of anticipated inflation instead of a mean rate. Silveria (1973) has shown that the length of the lag depends on the rate of monetary expansion. All such problems are neglected. In passing, I note that the response of $\hat{p}$ to $\hat{M}_{t-1}$ is 0.62 for 1901-31 and 0.47 for 1901-40.

Table 1

Estimating Equations for $\hat{p}^a$

Variable	1901-31	1901-40	1954-74
$\hat{M}_{t-1}$	0.83 (3.19)	0.54 (2.97)	-0.02 (1.33)
$\hat{\bar{M}}_{t-1}$	-0.45 (1.18)	-0.17 (0.65)	0.99 (6.08)
Dummy for avg.	0.02 (0.79)	0.03 (1.00)	-0.003 (0.36)
Dummy for gold revaluation		0.10 (1.56)	
Constant	-0.001 (0.08)	-0.01 (0.67)	0.001 (0.18)
R^2/DW	0.26/2.08	0.23/1.79	0.64/1.02

NOTE: A bar over the variable indicates a three-year moving average. t-statistics are shown in parentheses. The dummy for avg. is 1 for 1917-22 and for 1954-56 to allow for any effect of World War 1 and the Korean War; the dummy for revaluation is 1 in 1934 to allow for revaluation at the end of 1933.

standard, the rate of inflation anticipated at the start of the year is approximately the maintained average rate of monetary expansion plus a constant that is considerably smaller than g. Accelerations and decelerations have no independent effect on anticipations. Since anticipations of inflation formed and decayed more slowly under the dollar standard, sudden changes in monetary policy—stop-and-go policies—had their principal effect on inflation by changing the maintained rate of monetary expansion.

The three sets of estimates for equation (10) provide three interpretations of $\hat{p}^a$. I used the 1901-31 and 1954-74 regressions as the measure of $\hat{p}^a$ for those years and used the 1901-40 regression for the years 1932-40.

INFLATION AND THE CURRENT RATE OF PRICE CHANGE

The current rate of price change fluctuates around the anticipated rate of inflation whenever there are random or systematic changes in the price level. If the price level does not respond instantly, the measured rate of price change during any finite interval includes the anticipated rate of inflation, unanticipated inflation, and any once-and-for-all adjustment that occurs during the interval. The estimates of the rate of inflation anticipated at the start of the year, $\hat{p}^a$, permit a test of the effect of anticipated inflation and other variables on the current rate of price change.

In this section, I estimate parameters of equation (9) to test the proposition that inflation is principally a monetary phenomenon. By construction, the anticipated rate of inflation at the start of the year, $\hat{p}^a$, given by equation (10), measures the effect of past monetary expansion. The growth rate of the monetary base is a measure of the current rate of monetary expansion. The current rate of growth of the base affects the current rate of price change and, by changing the growth rate of money, changes the anticipated rate of inflation in subsequent periods.

Variables other than the growth rate of the base and $\hat{p}^a$ affect the current rate of price change, but, by assumption, they can affect the anticipated rate of inflation only by changing the rate of monetary expansion. Effects of wealth, income, rates of interest, and other variables on the money stock are small relative to the effect of the base (Brunner and Meltzer 1968). The potentially more powerful effect of some of these variables is on the rate of price change, as shown in equation (9).

Table 2 shows estimates of two forms of equation (9) for each of the periods used to form $\hat{p}^a$ and for the period as a whole.[11] The first set of estimates uses all of the variables in equation (9). The second set recognizes

---

11. The procedure used is equivalent to using instrument variables as measures of anticipations, $\hat{p}^a$ and y^a, in the regressions for the rate of price change. The procedure would be comparable to two-stage least-squares if the regressions in tables 1 and 2 are regarded as the first stage. The regressions for $\hat{p}$ would then be the second stage. However, I have interpreted Friedman's (1970) hypothesis as $p^a = \mu - g$ and have not used any other information about anticipated inflation in the system. Note that the "first-stage" estimate would be y^a, not $\hat{y}^a$.

Table 2

Current Rate of Price Change

Equation	Period	$\hat{p}^a$	$\hat{B}$	$\hat{S}$	$\hat{\pi}$	$\hat{L}_g$	$\hat{y}$	$\hat{y}^a$	Intercept	$\bar{R}^2/DW$
(9.11)	1901-31	0.28 (1.23)	0.71 (4.87)	0.09* (0.22)	0.01* (0.26)	0.08 (1.77)	0.16 (1.48)	0.38 (1.94)	-0.03 (3.26)	0.70/2.16
(9.12)	1901-40	0.65 (2.95)	0.17 (1.51)	0.20* (0.40)	0.001* (0.02)	0.07 (1.24)	0.14 (1.10)	0.35 (1.52)	-0.02 (2.04)	0.40/1.83
(9.13)	1955-74	0.60 (3.96)	0.24 (1.74)	-0.10 (2.74)	-0.53* (1.20)	-0.12 (1.39)	-0.28 (3.69)	-0.19 (1.17)	0.02 (2.86)	0.87/1.58
(9.14)	combined	0.66 (3.34)	0.24 (2.82)	0.14* (0.33)	0.01* (0.11)	0.09 (2.00)	0.11 (1.15)	0.58 (4.44)	-0.03 (4.15)	0.83/1.87
(9.21)	1901-31	0.29 (1.36)	0.73 (5.16)			0.09 (2.19)		0.40 (2.09)	-0.03 (3.06)	0.71/2.27
(9.22)	1901-40	0.72 (3.57)	0.18 (1.65)			0.09 (1.69)		0.40 (1.82)	-0.02 (2.08)	0.44/1.96
(9.23)	1955-74	0.87 (3.02)	0.02 (0.22)			-0.16 (1.28)		-0.38 (1.74)	0.02 (1.67)	0.69/1.16
(9.24)	combined	0.69 (4.44)	0.25 (3.09)			0.11 (2.61)		0.65 (5.65)	-0.03 (4.36)	0.84/1.98

NOTE: t-statistics are in parentheses; * indicates that the number shown is 100 times the computed coefficient.

that, as shown in appendix 2, responses to $\hat{S}$, $\hat{\pi}$, and $\hat{y}$ contain offsetting elements. Since the estimated responses are small and not significant by the usual tests, I omit these variables and retest.

The two sets of estimates have similar implications about the role of money. Current monetary growth has a larger and more reliable effect under the gold standard than under the dollar standard. This difference is consistent with the earlier finding (table 1) that acceleration and deceleration of the money stock has a large effect on $\hat{p}^a$ under the gold standard and almost no effect under the dollar standard. The difference is consistent also with evidence that the lag of the rate of price change behind the rate of monetary growth has lengthened in recent years.

The hypothesis suggests a reason for the longer lag. Under the gold standard, price movements were dominantly price changes, not maintained inflation. Expectations were firmly held that the price-specie flow mechanism would reverse the rate of price change. The dollar standard changed performance and anticipations. The rate of price change became less variable and more dependent on the anticipated rate of inflation. Under the dollar standard, rates of price change are much less dependent on changes in money and much more dependent on maintained monetary growth. In this respect, recent price changes are "different," as much of the popular and some academic discussion of inflation insists.

There is another sense in which recent price changes are different. The price-specie flow mechanism predicts a positive relation between prices and output and between rates of price changes and rates of change of output or anticipated output. Table 2 shows that under the gold standard, and for the period as a whole, the data support this implication of the theory. During the years of the dollar standard (equations 9.13 and 9.23), the data reject the proposition. Rates of change of output and anticipated output are negatively related to rates of price change.

We might dismiss the evidence for the dollar standard as an aberration caused by the small number of degrees of freedom. However, the period of the dollar standard has been a main source of evidence in support of Phillips curves, so I am reluctant to dismiss this evidence. One alternative is to use the coefficients in appendix 2 to interpret the evidence. If the interest elasticity of the demand for money or the response of real rates of interest to y and y^a was smaller under the dollar standard than under the gold standard, positive terms in the coefficients of $\hat{y}$ and $\hat{y}^a$ in equation (9) are reduced. Reinforcing these effects was the commitment of foreigners to acquire dollar securities and sell goods to maintain the dollar exchange rate. Lucas's (1976) proposition implies that a change from the gold to the dollar standard changes the structural coefficients, so changes in the coefficients arising from changes in the monetary standard and reduced fluctuation in real returns provide one plausible explanation. A second alternative is to treat the model as misspecified either because of the presence of an endogenous variable $\hat{y}$ or the omission of some measure of excess capacity.

Equations (9.21)-(9.24) omit $\hat{y}$. The explanatory power of the hypothesis falls only during the period of the dollar standard. The negative coefficient of $\hat{y}^a$ in that period remains. The presence of $\hat{y}$ in (9.13) does not explain the difference between the dollar standard and other periods.

Popular discussions of inflation suggest that recent inflation is different in yet another respect. Growth of monopoly power in product and factor markets is alleged to be a cause of the "new inflation." The intercept of the $\hat{p}$ equation has shifted from negative to positive in the recent sample, so the annual rate of price change is now higher for the same rates of change in money and output. Whether the shift is explained by a bias in the price index or by some systematic change in the degree of monopoly has not been studied, but it is clear that the shift cannot explain the acceleration of prices after 1965. Moreover, the evidence in table 2 suggests that the rate of price change is no less predictable than in the past without allowing for any change in monopoly power.

INFLATION, DEFLATION, AND THE PHILLIPS CURVE

The Phillips curve relates the current rate of price change to the fully anticipated rate of inflation and some measure of unemployed resources, such as the percentage of the labor force unemployed or the gap between current and full employment output. Fully anticipated steady inflation raises the price level at a steady rate but, except in the late stage of hyperinflation, has little effect on real output. Unanticipated inflation increases output by encouraging workers to accept real wages lower than the wages they anticipate. In various forms, this explanation, offered in simple or more complex ways, dominates current discussion of the way in which the economy responds to inflation (Cross and Laidler 1976; Gordon 1976; Laidler and Parkin 1975; Modigliani and Papademos 1975).

The price-specie flow model, as presented here, denies that the full-employment "gap" is a significant determinant of the current rate of price change. Rational agents form anticipations of output, and current prices reflect those anticipations. When random shocks and unanticipated changes in government policies shift demand, agents revise their anticipations of output and receipts. Actual prices and output adjust to anticipations.

In this section I compare the two explanations for the four sample periods. Comparison of the subperiods provides evidence of any difference between the years of the dollar standard, from which much of the evidence to support Phillips curves has been drawn, and other periods.

Equation (11) is a standard Phillips curve. When current unemployment, U, equals the "natural" rate, $\bar{U}$, the actual and anticipated rates of price change coincide.

$$\hat{p} = h_1(U - \bar{U}) + \hat{p}^a, \qquad h_1 < 0. \tag{11}$$

Since the price-specie flow theory distinguishes between income and anticipated receipts in the determination of current spending, it seems appropriate to distinguish between the anticipated rate of unemployment, U^a, and the "natural" or full-employment rate, $\bar{U}$. U^a is the rate of unemployment consistent with agents' anticipated receipts and decisions to spend. Anticipated unemployment rises as output falls below full-employment output, y_f. Rational agents use information about the current position of the economy to form anticipations of unemployment up to the point at which the marginal benefit equals the marginal cost of acquiring information.[12] Let

$$U^a - \bar{U} = h_2(y - y_f), \qquad h_2 < 0.$$

Unemployment falls below anticipated unemployment whenever receipts grow faster than anticipated, and unemployment rises when receipts are below anticipations. The reason is that unanticipated changes in receipts change spending and employment.

$$U - U^a = h_3(\hat{y} - \hat{y}^a), \qquad h_3 < 0.$$

Substituting in equation (11), we obtain

$$\hat{p} = h_1 h_3(\hat{y} - \hat{y}^a) + h_1 h_2(y - y_f) + \hat{p}^a + Z, \tag{12}$$

where Z includes current government policies and random shocks. Equation (12) permits a test of the alternatives. If the price-specie flow theory is correct, the principal effects of unemployment are anticipated; $h_1 h_2$ is zero, and the full-employment gap has no independent effect on current $\hat{p}$. The omission of the gap is not a misspecification, and omission of the short-run Phillips curve cannot explain the negative response of $\hat{p}$ to $\hat{y}$ for 1955-74. A positive coefficient $(h_1 h_2)$ on the gap and a positive or insignificant response to $\hat{y}^a$ would support the Phillips curve and strongly suggest misspecification of equation (9).

Table 3 shows the results of the test. Equations (12.11)-(12.14) include the full-employment gap as an addition to equation (9.11)-(9.14) of table 2. In all important respects, the estimates are unchanged. The response of $\hat{p}$ to the gap is small and insignificant for the period as a whole and during the

---

12. Under my hypothesis, it is more appropriate to equate $U^a - U$ to $y^a - y_f$. The reason for not proceeding in this way is to retain the type of measure proposed by those who claim to have isolated a short-run Phillips curve. This introduces endogeneity in the "gap" as measured here, but the response to the "gap" is so small and the significance of the coefficient so tenuous that it is doubtful that the use of lags or other steps to remove endogeneity will change the economic implications.

Table 3

Tests of the Short-Run Phillips Curve

Equation	Period	$\hat{p}^a$	$\hat{B}$	$\hat{S}$	$\hat{\pi}$	L_g	$\hat{y}$	$\hat{y}^a$	$y - y_f$	Intercept	$\bar{R}^2/DW$
(12.11)	1901-31	0.26 (1.06)	0.71 (4.78)	0.07* (0.16)	0.01* (0.19)	0.08 (1.76)	0.13 (0.78)	0.36 (1.76)	0.29 (0.31)	-0.02 (1.12)	0.68/2.17
(12.12)	1901-40	0.50 (2.30)	0.27 (2.34)	0.18* (0.38)	-0.01* (0.20)	0.08 (1.52)	0.06 (0.46)	0.29 (1.30)	0.85 (2.21)	-0.01 (0.05)	0.47/2.08
(12.13)	1955-74	0.66 (3.08)	0.18 (1.08)	-0.11 (2.93)	-0.57* (1.28)	-0.09 (1.02)	-0.23 (2.60)	-0.14 (0.84)	0.12 (1.03)	0.01 (0.94)	0.87/1.52
(12.14)	combined	0.66 (3.94)	0.24 (2.81)	0.13* (0.31)	-0.01* (0.16)	0.10 (2.00)	0.10 (1.04)	0.59 (4.41)	0.05 (0.29)	-0.03 (2.67)	0.83/1.88
(12.21)	1901-31	1.00 (3.67)					0.24 (1.15)	0.43 (1.57)	-0.03 (0.02)	-0.02 (0.56)	0.37/1.89
(12.22)	1901-40	0.80 (3.88)					0.14 (1.13)	0.25 (1.14)	0.35 (0.93)	-0.001 (0.08)	0.37/1.80
(12.23)	1955-74	0.82 (5.83)					-0.24 (2.87)	-0.03 (0.16)	-0.09 (0.81)	0.01 (0.67)	0.81/1.53
(12.24)	combined	0.82 (4.65)					0.23 (2.26)	0.83 (7.59)	-0.05 (0.27)	-0.03 (2.58)	0.78/1.73

NOTE: y_f = potential GNP; $y - y_f$ is trillions of 1958 dollars; t-statistics are in parentheses; * indicates that the number shown is 100 times the computed coefficient.

years of the gold and dollar standards. The importance of the gap increases only when the 1930s are included with the gold standard. The full-employment gap appears to have lowered the rate of price change in the '30s.

Under the gold standard, unemployment reduces imports and increases exports. The trade balance changes from deficit toward surplus; the base increases, the economy expands, and the gap declines. In the years of the dollar standard, reliance on current-cyclical government policy relates $\hat{L}_g$ and $\hat{B}$ to the size of the gap if the government increased the absorption of labor and the rate of monetary expansion when unemployment increased. Equations (12.21)-(12.24) retest the response of $\hat{p}$ to the gap, omitting the rates of changes in policy variables. The principal effect is an increase in the coefficient of $\hat{p}^a$ to include most of the response to $\hat{B}$ in (12.11)-(12.14). The effect of the gap falls during the years of the gold standard and remains small and insignificant during the dollar standard and in the period as a whole.[13]

The estimates of equation (12) suggest that the gap contains little information that is not included in the rate of change of receipts anticipated at the start of the year. Since $\hat{y} = \hat{y}^a + \hat{v}_1$, we can interpret the response to $\hat{y}$, given $\hat{y}^a$, as the effect on $\hat{p}$ of errors in estimating the growth of current receipts. As new information accumulates, both $\hat{p}$ and $\hat{y}$ adjust. The size of the "gap" between current output and full employment contains no additional information useful for predicting the adjustment, except in years of severe depression.

Recent work by Gordon (1976) and by Modigliani and Papademos (1975) claims that, beyond a point often reached in moderate recessions, additions to unemployment have very little effect on inflation. These authors point to the 1930s as evidence to support their conclusion and to argue that rapid

13. I estimated several other sets of equations: (a) using only $\hat{p}^a$ and the gap, (b) adding the gap to eqq. (9.21)-(9.24) in table 2, and (c) substituting the gap for $\hat{y}$ and $\hat{y}^a$ in eqq. (9.21)-(9.24). Although the detail differs, the principal conclusions are unaffected. Substituting the gap for $\hat{y}$ and $\hat{y}^a$ gives a result similar to (12.12) for the period 1901-40. $\bar{R}^2$ increases to 0.50; each billion dollars of gap lowers $\hat{p}$ by 0.001 on average.

monetary growth can be used to raise employment without increasing the rate of price change. The findings here suggest, on the contrary, that $\hat{p}$ responded to $\hat{B}$, the current rate of monetary expansion in the '30s. Moreover, the annual data show no evidence of any reliable short-run Phillips curve under the dollar standard. For the peirod 1955-74, the response of $\hat{p}$ to $\hat{y}$ or $\hat{y}^a$ is negative. Table 3 shows that the negative response cannot be explained as misspecification resulting from the omission of the full-employment gap.

Three explanations occur to account for the difference between the present findings and earlier evidence in support of Phillips curves. First, much of the evidence for the Phillips curve may reflect the way in which the dollar standard operated. Second, larger samples, the use of quarterly or semiannual data, or an alternative measure of the gap may reconcile my results with previous studies. Third, further work may show that the gap is a proxy for the rate of change of anticipated receipts, so that the Phillips curve is a misspecified version of the price-specie flow theory. The last explanation seems most consistent with the results of this study, but until the alternatives are tested further, some doubt remains.

IMPLICATIONS FOR ECONOMIC THEORY AND POLICY

The two principal relations of the model are the equations determining anticipated receipts and the current rate of price change. Each specifies a relation between p and y^a (or $\hat{p}$ and $\hat{y}^a$). To make the dimensions comparable, differentiate the equation for $\ln y = \ln y^a$ in note 9 and solve for $\hat{p}$ using the elasticity of y^a with respect to B/p evaluated at the sample mean 0.36. The result is denoted AA and is shown in figure 1.

$$AA:\ \hat{p} = -2.8\hat{y}^a + 1.14K - 5.00\hat{L} + 0.25\hat{L}_g + 7.36\hat{N} + \hat{B}.$$

The slope of the AA curve is relatively steep (-2.8). The position of the curve depends on endowments of capital and labor, monetary policy, and absorption of labor by the government.

The second relation is denoted BB. For this relation I have chosen equation (9.24) in table 2, although the principal results are not greatly changed if (9.14) is used instead. The BB curve has a slope of 0.65; its position depends on $\hat{p}^a$, $\hat{B}$, and $\hat{L}_g$.

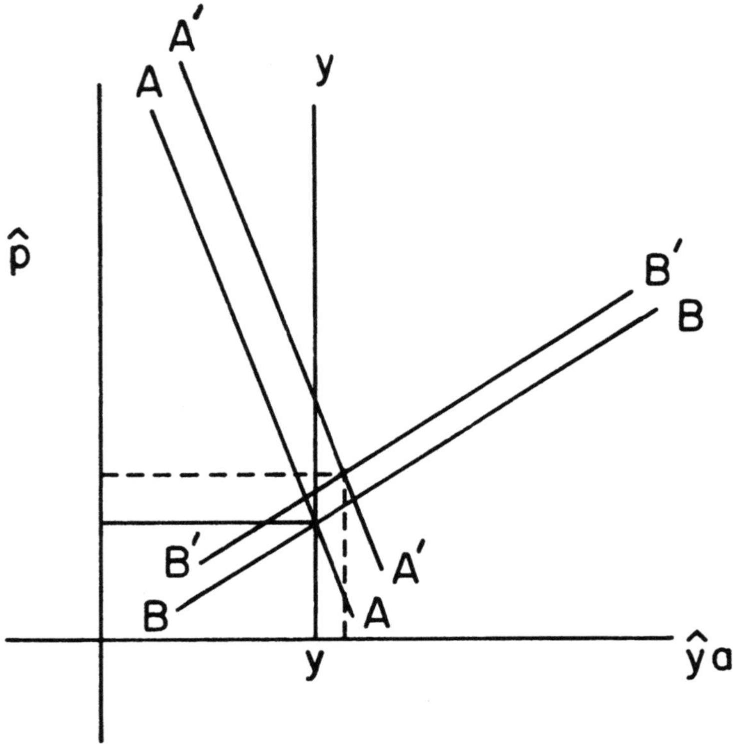

Figure 1

$$BB: \hat{p} = 0.69\hat{p}^a + 0.25\hat{B} + 0.11\hat{L}_g + 0.65\hat{y}^a.$$

The two curves determine a position of equilibrium at the intersection of *AA* and *BB* in figure 1. With given anticipations, maintained growth of endowments, a constant rate of participation in the labor force, and constant monetary and fiscal policy, the economy remains in equilibrium.

Suppose, however, the growth rate of the base increases. The *AA* line initially shifts by a multiple of the shift in *BB*; the elasticity of *p* with respect to *B* is unity in the *AA* equation and 0.25 in the *BB* equation. The public appears to act on the knowledge that periods of increased monetary expansion are, at first, periods of economic expansion, as the price-specie flow theory implies. Output and anticipated receipts accelerate, and the rate of price change increases.

Maintaining the higher growth of B increases the growth rate of money. The anticipated rate of price change, $\hat{p}^a$, depends on the maintained rate of monetary expansion. As $\hat{p}^a$ rises, the BB curve shifts along AA, raising the rate of price change and lowering the anticipated and actual rate of change of output. Adjustment of $\hat{p}$ and $\hat{y}^a$ continues until full equilibrium is restored. The AA and BB relations can be solved to obtain the equilibrium output, yy, and price, pp, relations.

$$yy: \; \hat{y}^a = 0.22\hat{B} - 0.20\hat{p}^a + 0.04\hat{L}_g + 0.33\hat{K} - 1.45\hat{L} + 2.13\hat{N}.$$

$$pp: \; \hat{p} = 0.39\hat{B} + 0.56\hat{p}^a + 0.14\hat{L}_g + 0.22\hat{K} - 0.94\hat{L} + 1.40\hat{N}.$$

The yy equation is shown as the vertical line in figure 1.

The pp and yy equations imply that maintained monetary expansion raises the rate of price change proportionally but has no effect on anticipated or actual output. The reason is that the coefficients of $\hat{B}$ and $\hat{p}^a$ are (approximately) equal but of opposite sign in the yy equation and sum to unity in the pp equation. If maintained growth of the base induces a corresponding rate of change of money (Brunner and Meltzer 1968), $\hat{p}^a$ and $\hat{B}$ are equal in equilibrium. The steady-state value of $\hat{y}^a(g)$ depends on real variables and is independent of the maintained rate of monetary expansion. The rate of price change rises with the rate of monetary expansion.

The evidence is consistent with some principal propositions of monetary theory. Changes in the rate of monetary expansion induce temporary changes in the growth rate of output--anticipated and actual--but have no permanent effect. Maintained changes in the rate of monetary expansion affect the anticipated and actual rate of price change.

However, the maintained rate of inflation does not depend on the growth rate of money. Absorption of labor by government contributes to inflation. The steady-state effect of labor absorption shown in the equation is slightly smaller than the estimated effect on $\hat{p}$ in equation (9.24), but both equations suggest that changes in L_g change the price level and changes in $\hat{L}_g$ change the rate of price change.

The pp and yy equations imply that balanced growth in capital and labor with unchanged monetary and fiscal policy is accompanied by rising prices. From the coefficients of the yy equations, we see that whenever K, L, N, and L_g grow at the same rate, y^a (and y) increases equiproportionally. The yy equation satisfies this standard property of economic models. However, prices rise with constant money stock and balanced growth in capital and labor.[14] The coefficients of the pp equation imply that equiproportionate growth of K, L, N, and L_g raises $\hat{p}$ approximately 0.8 percent for each 1 percent increase in endowments and unchagned distribution of labor between the private and the public sectors.

The estimates make clear that velocity has increased during the period used for estimation. Attempts to interpret the increase as an adjustment of average cash balances to anticipated inflation are not supported by evidence.[15] An alternative interpretation is that innovations in cash management are, in part, induced by growth of capital and output. If the productivity of the payments system grows with the economy, improvements in payments arrangements lower the demand for money relative to the demand for capital and relative to output. Steady-state velocity rises as wealth owners equate the marginal product of labor or capital in transactions with the marginal products of labor in the production of goods and services. This explanation has not been tested.

Since the rise in velocity has not been explained as a response to inflation, we cannot conclude that inflation has been entirely a response to money growth. Secular growth in velocity and secular inflation appear to result from maintained growth in capital and labor with unchanged distribution of labor between the public and private sector and from growth in the public sector relative to the private sector.

---

14. Claudio Haddad points out that the positive coefficient of $\hat{K}$ in the pp equation may reflect the assumption that g is constant.

15. The response of $\hat{p}$ to $\hat{\pi}$ in eqq. (9) and (12) is a measure of the effect of adjustment of cash balances to inflation. The effect is zero according to the estimate in tables 2 and 3. The sign of the coefficients depends on the difference between short- and long-term adjustment, as shown by w_4 in appendix 2. A zero value does not deny that long-term adjustment of velocity occurs, but it provides no evidence of the response.

CONCLUSION

The principal conclusions of this paper come from comparison of a standard Phillips curve to the price-specie flow model. The former implies that the rate of inflation depends on some measure of the gap between current output and full-employment output. The latter implies that agents are not surprised by the existence of a full-employment gap and do not respond to the gap. Instead, producers move along their supply curves, changing output in response to actual and anticipated spending. When spending increases, prices rise and output increases. The rate of price change varies directly with the rate of change of output or anticipated output and is independent of the level of output. The price-specie flow theory is broadly consistent with propositions advanced in recent work by Friedman (1974) and Lucas (1975, 1977) and with much earlier work by Hume and Thornton.

Data for the century as a whole and for subperiods distinguish between the alternatives. There is substantial support for the price-specie flow theory and less support for the Phillips curve when the theories of inflation are compared. Price changes in the inflation of the '60s and '70s and under the gold standard appear to have resulted from a process that the price-specie flow theory summarizes. Both processes appear to have operated during the depression of the '30s.

There are other differences between periods. A principal difference is in the way anticipations of inflation formed and decayed. Under the gold standard, the anticipated rate of price change rose in periods of monetary and economic expansion and fell during monetary contractions and recessions. Maintained inflation depended on the growth of the world gold stock, not on fluctuations in money resulting from temporary redistribution of the existing stock between countries. Once the gold standard was abandoned, the determinants of the money stock changed, and the relation of money growth to anticipated inflation changed also. The data suggest that the rate of price change became more predictable and the mean rate of change—anticipated and actual--rose.

Several recent discussions of inflation suggest that monetary policy has very little influence on the current rate of price change once unemployment reaches a critical level (Gordon 1976; Modigliani and Papademos 1975; Tobin 1975). Conclusions of this kind are often based on a Phillips curve in which some measure of the full-employment gap is related to the rate of price change. A finding that the effect of the gap on the rate of price change falls as the gap increases is, at best, indirect evidence. The evidence here shows that during the depression of the '30s the mean response of the rate of price change to current and past monetary growth was slightly lower than the response in the rest of the century, but the effect of money on prices did not vanish.

Economic theory implies that sustained monetary expansion, at rates in excess of the growth of output, raises the rate of inflation but has no effect on the steady-state growth of output. My estimates suggest that the growth rate of output is homogeneous of zero degree in the rate of price change, but the rate of price change does not appear to be independent of the rate of growth of output. With steady growth of money and output, the price level rises at a steady rate.

To test Friedman's (1970) proposition that inflation is always "a monetary phenomenon," I define anticipated inflation as the maintained average rate of monetary expansion and distinguish between the current rate of price change and anticipated inflation. I find that current and past monetary growth are principal determinants of the current rate of price change. However, if maintained inflation is defined as the average rate of price change, the results deny that inflation has been entirely a response to growth in money. The government contributed to inflation by maintaining the growth rate of public employment above the growth rate of real output. Further, the evidence suggests that rising prices accompanied growth of capital and labor. Velocity appears to have increased at approximately the rate of growth of output per man. Keeping prices stable, under the circumstances of this century, would have required a reduction of 0.8 percent in stock of base money for each 1 percent increase in capital, labor, and population.

APPENDIX 1

Symbol	Description	Source
B	Monetary base in billions of dollars	1900-1917: Friedman and Schwartz (1963, table B3), June dates; 1918-40: Brunner and Meltzer series including adjustment for changes in reserve requirement ratio, unpublished; 1953-74: Federal Reserve Bank of St. Louis
y_f	Potential GNP adjusted to billions of 1958 dollars	1897-1908: exponential trend fitted between 1897 and 1909 to GNP fromU.S., Bureau of Economic Analysis, LONG-TERM ECONOMIC GROWTH, 1860-1970 (1973 series A1, p. 182) (hereafter cited as LTEG); 1909-40: LTEG (series A4, p. 182); 1953-73: U.S., Bureau of Economic Analysis, BUSINESS CONDITIONS DIGEST (Jan. 1975, p. 109); 1974: U.S., Bureau of Economic Analysis, BUSINESS CONDITIONS DIGEST (Dec. 1975, p. 5).
K	Private, nonfarm, nonresidential stock adjusted to 1958 dollars	1900-1924: Kendrick, PRODUCTIVITY TRENDS, (1961, table A15, p. 320); 1925-73: U.S., Bureau of Economic Analysis, SURVEY OF CURRENT BUSINESS (Mar. 1974, table 1, p. 25).
L	Total labor force in thousands	1900-1929: LTEG (Lebergott series, table A107, p. 198); 1930-70: LTEG (table A108, p. 700); 1971-74: U.S., Bureau of Labor Statistics, HANDBOOK OF LABOR STATISTICS (1975, p. 26).
L_g	Government labor force = persons engaged in national economy minus persons engaged in private economy (in thousands)	1900-1928: LTEG (tables A80, A82, p. 194); 1929-70: LTEG (tables A81, A83, p. 194); 1971-74: U.S., Bureau of Labor Statistics, HANDBOOK OF LABOR STATISTICS (1975, p. 119).

M	Money, currency, and demand deposits in billions of dollars	1900-1914: U.S., Bureau of the Census, HSUS (1970, table X267, p. 646); 1915-70: LTEG (tables B109, B110, p. 230); 1971-74: U.S., Council of Economic Advisers, ERP (1975, p. 310).
N	Population residing in the United States in thousands	1900-1939: LTEG (table A2, p. 7); 1940-74: U.S., Bureau of the Census, SAUS (1975, table 2, p. 5).
P	Implicit price deflator for GNP, 1958 = 100	1900-1970: LTEG (tables B61, B62, p. 222); 1971-74: U.S., Bureau of Economic Analysis, BUSINESS CONDITIONS DIGEST (Dec. 1973, table 1, p. 5; Dec. 1975, table 1, p. 5).
S	Total stock of government debt held by private investors minus net foreign positions (S_f - S^*), see below, in billions	Stock of government debt: 1900-1915: Phillip Cagan's unpublished worksheets listing interest-bearing debt held outside Treasury and, in 1915, outside Federal Reserve; June dates, 1900-1915; Dec. dates, 1906-15; 1916-38; U.S., Bureau of the Census, HSUS (1960 series X425 minus series X429, pp. 664, 642); 1939-74: U.S., Council of Economic Advisers, ERP (1975, p. 333).
$S_f - S^*$	Net foreign position in billions	1900-1940: Kendrick (1961, table A15, p.321), for 1916, net value is negative but value set at $1 million; 1953-67: U.S., Federal Reserve Board of Governors, FLOW OF FUNDS ACCOUNTS (Aug. 1973, pp. 106-7); 1968-74: U.S., Councilof Economic Advisers, ERP (various issues), net international investment less assets and liabilities of U.S. government.
y	Gross private domestic product in billions of 1958 dollars	1900-1940: LTEG (Table A6, p. 182); 1953-74: U.S., Council of Economic Advisers, ERP (1975, table C2, p. 250); 1900-1970 (GPDP): LTEG (tables A13, A14, p. 184, 185); 1971-74 (GPDP): U.S., Council of Economic Advisers, ERP (1975, table C10, p. 261).

APPENDIX 2: COEFFICIENT OF $\hat{p}$

The signs of the coefficients in equation (9) are expressed in terms of the elasticities of the text to make my assumptions explicit.

$$\hat{p} = w_o + w_1\hat{p}^a + w_2\hat{B} + w_3\hat{S} + w_4\hat{\pi} + w_5\hat{L}_g + w_6\hat{y} \tag{9}$$

$$+ w_7\hat{y}^a + v_2.$$

The denominators of the w_i are

$$1 - \{\varepsilon(V, p) + \varepsilon(V, r)\ [1 - \varepsilon(n, p)]\} \ > \ 0.$$

The numerators are

$$w_1 = \varepsilon(V, p^a) - \varepsilon(V, r) \ > \ 0$$

$$w_2 = 1 + [\varepsilon(V, B) + \varepsilon(V, r)\varepsilon(n, B)] \ > \ 0$$

$$w_3 = \varepsilon(V, S) + \varepsilon(V, r)\varepsilon(n, S)$$

$$w_4 = \varepsilon(V, p^a) - \varepsilon(V^a, p^a) \ \sim \ 0$$

$$w_5 = 1 + \varepsilon(V, r)\varepsilon(n, L_g) \ > \ 0$$

$$w_6 = \varepsilon(V, y) + \varepsilon(V, r)\varepsilon(n, y) - 1$$

$$w_7 = 1 + \varepsilon(V, r)\varepsilon(n, y^a) - \varepsilon(V^a, y^a) \ > \ 0.$$

I have assumed that $\varepsilon(V, p^a)$ is greater than $\varepsilon(V, r)$ in w_i and that the bracketed expression in w_2 is between 0 and -1. $\hat{B}$ is used as the measure of current monetary growth.

A value of $\varepsilon(n, y)$ substantially above unity makes w_6 positive. This occurs if the anticipated return to capital is very sensitive to unanticipated changes in current receipts. In this case $\hat{p}$ and $\hat{y}$ are positively related in equation (9).

REFERENCES

Brunner, K., and Meltzer, A. H. 1968. "Liquidity Traps for Money, Bank Credit, and Interest Rates." JOURNAL OF POLITICAL ECONOMY 76 (Jan.): 1-37.

_____. 1971. "The Uses of Money: Money in the Theory of an Exchange Economy." AMERICAN ECONOMIC REVIEW 61 (Dec.): 784-805.

_____. 1976. "An Aggregative Theory for a Closed Economy." In MONETARISM, edited by J. Stein. Amsterdam: North-Holland.

Christ, C. 1968. "A Simple Macroeconomic Model with a Government Budget Constraint." JOURNAL OF POLITICAL ECONOMY 76 (Jan.): 53-67.

Cross, R., and Laidler, D. 1976. "Inflation, Excess Demand, and Expectations in Fixed Exchange Rate Open Economies." In INFLATION IN THE WORLD ECONOMY, edited by M. Parkin and G. Zis. Manchester: University of Manchester Press.

Coulter, D. 1976. "A Two-Sector Model of the Labor Market." Multilithed. Pittsburgh: Carnegie-Mellon University.

Friedman, M. 1957. A THEORY OF THE CONSUMPTION FUNCTION. Princeton: Princeton University Press, for the National Bureau of Economic Research.

_____. 1970. THE COUNTER-REVOLUTION IN MONETARY THEORY. London: International Economic Association.

_____. 1974. "A Theoretical Framework for Monetary Analysis." In MILTON FRIEDMAN'S MONETARY FRAMEWORK, edited by Robert J. Gordon. Chicago: University of Chicago Press.

Friedman, M. and Schwartz, A. J. 1963. A MONETARY HISTORY OF THE UNITED STATES, 1867-1960. Princeton: Princeton University Press, for the National Bureau of Economic Research.

Gordon, R. J. 1976. "Recent Developments in the Theory of Inflation and Unemployment." JOURNAL OF MONETARY ECONOMICS 2 (Apr.): 185-220.

Hamburger, M. J., and Platt, E. 1975. "The Expectations Hypothesis and the Efficiency of the Treasury Bill Market." REVIEW OF ECONOMICS AND STATISTICS 57 (May): 190-99.

Klein, B. 1976. "The Social Costs of the Recent Inflation: The Mirage of Steady, Anticipated Inflation." Carnegie-Rochester Conference Series on Public Policy 3. JOURNAL OF MONETARY ECONOMICS 2 (suppl., Aug.): 185-212.

Laidler, D., and Parkin, M. 1975. "Inflation: A Survey." ECONOMIC JOURNAL 85 (Dec.): 741-809.

Lucas, R. E., Jr. 1972. "Expectations and the Neutrality of Money." JOURNAL OF ECONOMIC THEORY 4 (Apr.): 103-24.

_____. 1975. "An Equilibrium Model of the Business Cycle." JOURNAL OF POLITICAL ECONOMY 83 (Dec.): 1113-44.

_____. 1976. "Econometric Policy Evaluation: A Critique." Carnegie-Rochester Conference Series on Public Policy 1. JOURNAL OF MONETARY ECONOMICS 2 (suppl., Jan.): 19-46.

_____. 1977. "Understanding Business Cycles." Carnegie-Rochester Conference Series on Public Policy 5. JOURNAL OF MONETARY ECONOMICS 3 (suppl., Feb): 7-29.

Mayer, T. 1975. "The Structure of Monetarism." KREDIT UND KAPITAL 8 (Apr./July): 190-218, 293-316.
McGuire, T. W. 1976. "On Estimating the Effects of Controls." Carnegie-Rochester Conference Series on Public Policy 2. JOURNAL OF MONETARY ECONOMICS (suppl., Apr.): 115-57.
Metzler, L. 1951. "Wealth, Saving, and the Rate of Interest." JOURNAL OF POLITICAL ECONOMY 59 (Apr.): 93-116.
Modigliani, F., and Papademos, L. 1975. "Targets for Monetary Policy in the Coming Year." BROOKINGS PAPER ON ECONOMIC ACTIVITY (Winter): 141-63.
Phelps, E. S. 1972. INFLATION POLICY AND UNEMPLOYMENT THEORY. New York: Norton.
Silveria, A. M. 1973. "The Demand for Money: The Evidence from the Brazilian Economy." JOURNAL OF MONEY, CREDIT AND BANKING 5 (Feb.): 113-40.
Sinai, A., and Stokes, H. 1972. "Real Money Balances: An Omitted Variable in the Production Function?" REVIEW OF ECONOMICS AND STATISTICS 54 (Aug.): 290-96.
Tobin, J. 1961. "Money, Capital, and Other Stores of Value." AMERICAN ECONOMIC REVIEW (May): 26-37.
_____. 1975. "Monetary Policy, Inflation and Unemployment." Multilithed. New Haven: Yale University.
U.S., Bureau of Economic Analysis. 1973. LONG-TERM ECONOMIC GROWTH, 1860-1970 (LTEG). Washington, D.C.: Government Printing Office.
U.S., Bureau of the Census. 1960, 1970. HISTORICAL STATISTICS OF THE UNITED STATES (HSUS). Washington, D.C.: Government Printing Office.
_____. 1975. STATISTICAL ABSTRACT OF THE UNITED STATES (SAUS). Washington, D.C.: Government Printing Office.
U.S., Council of Economic Advisers. Various issues. ECONOMIC REPORT OF THE PRESIDENT (ERP). Washington, D.C.: Government Printing Office.

TARGETS, INSTRUMENTS, AND INDICATORS OF MONETARY POLICY*

Benjamin M. Friedman**
Harvard University

Keeping one's eye on the ball is often an important precept, familiar in games of skill and games of chance alike. The making of monetary policy, an activity at which success involves both skill and chance, is no exception. For monetary policy, however, a recurring problem has been the difficulty of determining what is the real ball. Indeed, the problem is yet more serious. Monetary policymakers, even with the assistance of monetary economists, have often not known how to set about discovering what is the real ball.

Within the past decade economists have developed two approaches for trying to find the ball that monetary policymakers should watch. First, the literature of targets and indicators of monetary policy (e.g., Brunner 1969; Brunner and Meltzer 1967; Davis 1971; Dewald 1963; Hamburger 1970; Hendershott 1968; Hendershott and Horwich 1969; Holbrook and Shapiro 1970; Kaufman 1967; Saving 1967; Starleaf and Stephenson 1969; Zecher 1970) suggested watching not one but two balls simultaneously, suggested how both to characterize and to use these two balls, and attempted to identify the most likely candidates for each. More recently, the application of control methodologies to problems of monetary policy has attracted widespread attention (e.g., B. Friedman 1971; Kareken 1970; Kareken et al.

---

* Reprinted, with some changes, by permission of the author and North-Holland Publishing Co., from the JOURNAL OF MONETARY ECONOMICS 1 (1975): 443-73. An earlier version of the paper was presented at the 1974 Konstanz Seminar.

** The author is grateful to the Subcommittee on Monetary Research of the Social Science Research Council for research support and to Vincent Fitzgerald, George Kaufman, Edward Leamer, John Lintner, Thomas Mayer, and Janet Yellen for helpful discussion.

1971; Parkin 1973; Pindyck and Roberts 1974; Poole 1970, 1971; Shupp 1972); such applications have typically relied on the familiar structure of targets and instruments (alternatively called state and controller variables, respectively).

Because of the complex nature of the monetary policy process, however, the resulting literature has at times been somewhat confused. The relationship between the recent literature of target and instrument variables and the previous discussions of target and indicator variables, for example, has remained unclear. The distinction between targets as ultimate goals and targets as intermediate operating devices is straightforward enough, but how do instruments and indicators fit into the pattern? Can an instrument be an indicator? Can an intermediate operating target be an instrument?

Even within the recent control applications literature itself, apparent contradictions abound.[1] Is the stock of money a target (e.g., Federal Reserve Bank of Boston 1972) or an instrument (e.g., Federal Reserve Bank of Boston 1969)? Should the policy planning framework treat income (or employment) as endogenous (e.g., Poole 1970) or exogenous (e.g., Pindyck and Roberts 1974)? Must the central bank manipulate reserve management so as to exert indirect control over interest rates (e.g., Pindyck and Roberts 1974), or can it control interest rates directly (e.g., Kareken 1970)? What is the true menu of available instruments?

The objects of this paper are, first, to set forth clearly the basic targets-and-instruments structure of the monetary policy control problem and, second, to explore the relationship between this targets-and-instruments structure and the targets-and-indicators discussions. As developed below, the basic targets-and-instruments structure provides a useful framework for defining and understanding the targets-and-indicators concepts.

---

1. The literature of targets and indicators also has its unclear aspects, but it is not the purpose of this paper to rehash them yet again; the references cited above are sufficient.

Section 1 uses a static deterministic model to define the basic elements of the targets-and-instruments structure of the monetary policy control problem. Section 2 shows how the *instrument problem*, which is trivial in the context of the model of section 1, becomes nontrivial when that model is generalized to be stochastic. Section 3 briefly reviews some of the previous literature that has implicitly or explicitly treated the operation of monetary policy as a two-stage control process, showing that some of the confusions and apparent inconsistencies in this literature result from the two-stage representation itself—an approach that may be invalid under actually prevailing conditions. Section 4 uses the targets-and-instruments framework to analyze the *intermediate target problem* in its usual context of lags in the receipt of information about the policy targets themselves. This section first recasts the model of sections 1 and 2 to incorporate the major implications of such a data lag; it then illustrates the use of the money stock as an intermediate target variable and compares this procedure with optimal operating procedures in the presence of information lags. Section 5 briefly shows that, although the intermediate target problem has typically been associated with data lags, structural lags in the effects of monetary policy may lead to the same considerations as those discussed at length in section 4. Section 6 shows that use of the targets-and-instruments framework renders the *indicator problem* a relatively unimportant aspect of monetary policymaking. Section 7 briefly summarizes the paper's principal conclusions.

1. ELEMENTARY CONCEPTS

Tinbergen's (1956) conception of a policy problem in terms of targets and instruments provides a useful starting point for analyzing the structure of the monetary policy control problem. For a linear deterministic system, Tinbergen's expression of the reduced form is

$$\begin{bmatrix} y_1 \\ \hline y_2 \end{bmatrix} = \Gamma \begin{bmatrix} x \\ \hline z \end{bmatrix}, \qquad (1)$$

where y_1 = a vector of values of endogenous variables that policymakers seek to control (*target* variables),

y_2 = a vector of values of the remaining endogenous variables in the system (*irrelevant* variables), x = a vector of values of exogenous variables subject to direct control by policymakers (*instrument* variables),

z = a vector of values of the remaining predetermined variables in the system, including any lagged values (*data* variables), and

Γ = the reduced-form matrix of coefficients that describe the system's behavior.

A simple linear model of an economy with a goods-and-services market and a money market consists of Hicks's (1937) *IS* relation,

$$Y = a_1 r + a'z ; \tag{2}$$

Hicks's *LM*, or money demand, relation,

$$M = b_1 Y + b_2 r + b'z ; \tag{3}$$

and a money supply relation,

$$M = c_1 R + c_2 r + c'z ; \tag{4}$$

where Y = income,

r = the nominal interest rate,

z = a vector of values of variables exogenous to the monetary policy process (including fiscal policy variables),

M = the money stock, and

R = the stock of nonborrowed bank reserves.

The anticipated values of the scalar coefficients are $a_1, b_2 < 0$ and $b_1, c_1, c_2 > 0$; a, b, and c are vectors of coefficients applicable to all exogenous variables in z, including zeroes for cases in which individual exogenous variables do not appear in individual structural equations.

This three-equation model is determined with any one of the four variables (Y, r, M, R) taken as exogenous.[2] In practice, central bank

2. It is also possible to preserve the endogeneity of all four of these variables and to render the model determined by adding another constraint. One example of such an additional constraint is a rule requiring that r and R bear some fixed relation to one another. See, e.g., Poole (1970, 1971) and Parkin (1973); Brainard (1967) also discussed the use of a "package" consisting of constrained joint movements of multiple instruments. Another example is a feedback rule directly relating movements of either r or R to income or other endogenous variables of the system.

operations may exert control directly over the interest rate or over the stock of nonborrowed reserves.[3] Taking income as the endogenous variable that monetary policymakers seek to control, the choice of instrument variables leads to two alternative ways of fitting this model into Tinbergen's format.

Variable	"Rate" alternative	"Reserves" alternative
Y	target	target
r	instrument	irrelevant
M	irrelevant	irrelevant
R	irrelevant	instrument
z	data	data

Either of these policy alternatives possesses a distinct reduced-form solution corresponding to equation (1). For the "rate" alternative, the reduced form is

$$\begin{bmatrix} Y \\ M \\ R \end{bmatrix} = \begin{bmatrix} \gamma_{11} & \gamma'_1 \\ \gamma_{21} & \gamma'_2 \\ \gamma_{31} & \gamma'_3 \end{bmatrix} \begin{bmatrix} r \\ z \end{bmatrix} , \qquad (5)$$

where $\gamma_{11} = a_1, \quad \gamma_{21} = b_2 + b_1 a_1, \quad \gamma_{31} = c_1^{-1}(b_1 a_1 + b_2 - c_2);$ (6a)

$$\gamma_1 = a, \quad \gamma_2 = b + b_1 a, \quad \gamma_3 = c_1^{-1}(b_1 a + b - c). \qquad (6b)$$

For the "reserves" alternative, the reduced form is

$$\begin{bmatrix} Y \\ M \\ r \end{bmatrix} = \begin{bmatrix} g_{11} & g'_1 \\ g_{21} & g'_2 \\ g_{31} & g'_3 \end{bmatrix} \begin{bmatrix} R \\ z \end{bmatrix} , \qquad (7)$$

---

3. The ability of the central bank to set the nominal interest rate implicitly reflects the focus of the control applications literature on relatively short-run stabilization policy. It also probably indicates an assumption that "the interest rate" is the yield on a short-maturity debt instrument, although opinions differ on the central bank's ability to influence yields on long-maturity assets. In a more general model it would be useful to distinguish between the role of the short-term interest rate in eqq. (3) and (4) and that of the long-term interest rate in eq. (2); the resulting five-variable model would then require an additional constraint, such as a "term-structure" equation relating the values of the two interest-rate variables.

where $$g_{11} = (b_1 a_1 + b_2 - c_2)^{-1} a_1 c_1, \tag{8a}$$

$$g_{21} = c_1 + (b_1 a_1 + b_2 - c_2)^{-1} c_1 c_2,$$

$$g_{31} = (b_1 a_1 + b_2 - c_2)^{-1} c_1;$$

$$g_1 = a - (b_1 a_1 + b_2 - c_2)^{-1} a_1 (b_1 a + b - c), \tag{8b}$$

$$g_2 = c - (b_1 a_1 + b_2 - c_2)^{-1} c_2 (b_1 a + b - c),$$

$$g_3 = (b_1 a_1 + b_2 - c_2)^{-1} (b_1 a + b - c).$$

In the context of the deterministic model, it makes no difference which one of these two operating alternatives the central bank chooses to follow. For desired income value Y^* and known data values z^0, the optimal value of the interest rate instrument under the rate alternative is

$$r^*|_r = \gamma_{11}^{-1}(Y^* - \gamma_1 z^0) = a_1^{-1} Y^* - a_1^{-1} a' z^0, \tag{9}$$

and from equation (5) the associated value of the stock of reserves is

$$\begin{aligned} R^*|_r &= \gamma_{31} r^*|_r + \gamma_3' z^0 \\ &= (a_1 c_1)^{-1}(b_1 a_1 + b_2 - c_2) Y^* \\ &\quad + (a_1 c_1)^{-1}\{(c_2 - b_2) a + a_1 (b - c)\}' z^0. \end{aligned} \tag{10}$$

Similarly, the optimal value of the stock of reserves under the reserves alternative is

$$\begin{aligned} R^*|_R &= g_{11}^{-1}(Y^* - g_1' z^0) \\ &= (a_1 c_1)^{-1}(b_1 a_1 + b_2 - c_2) Y^* \\ &\quad + (a_1 c_1)^{-1} \{(c_2 - b_2) a + a_1 (b - c)\}' z^0, \end{aligned} \tag{11}$$

and from equation (7) the associated value of the interest rate is

$$r^*|_R = g_{31} R^*|_R + g_3' z^0 = a_1^{-1} Y^* - a_1^{-1} a' z^0. \tag{12}$$

Since $r^*|_r = r^*|_R$ and $R^*|_R = R^*|_r$, the central bank in fact carries out the same actions regardless of whether it operates in the first instance by controlling the interest rate or the stock of reserves.

2. THE INSTRUMENT PROBLEM

Within the context of the monetary policy control problem, the *instrument problem* is the choice of the variable(s) over which the central bank will exert direct control. For the four-variable, three-equation model developed in section 1, the instrument problem is the choice between the rate alternative with r exogenous and the reserves alternative with R exogenous.

For the deterministic model of equations (2) to (4), equations (9) to (12) indicate that the central bank's choice of instrument variables makes no real difference either for the policy actions it takes or for the results of these actions for the system's endogenous variables. If the model is stochastic, however, and if an object of monetary policy is to minimize the variance of income about the desired value Y^*, then the instrument problem is nontrivial.

Rewriting structural equations (2) to (4) to include additive disturbance terms yields

$$Y = a_1 r + a'z + u_Y, \qquad (2')$$

$$M = b_1 Y + b_2 r + b'z + u_{MD}, \qquad (3')$$

$$M = c_1 R + c_2 r + c'z + u_{MS}. \qquad (4')$$

For the rate alternative, the reduced form of this stochastic system is

$$\begin{bmatrix} Y \\ M \\ R \end{bmatrix} = \begin{bmatrix} \gamma_{11} & \gamma'_1 \\ \gamma_{21} & \gamma'_2 \\ \gamma_{31} & \gamma'_3 \end{bmatrix} \begin{bmatrix} r \\ z \end{bmatrix} + \begin{bmatrix} \varepsilon_Y \\ \varepsilon_M \\ \varepsilon_R \end{bmatrix}, \qquad (5')$$

where the γ_{ij} and γ_i are as defined in equations (6a) and (6b) and

$$\varepsilon_Y = u_Y, \qquad \varepsilon_M = u_{MD} + b_1 u_Y, \qquad (6')$$

$$\varepsilon_R = c_1^{-1}(b_1 u_Y + u_{MD} - u_{MS}).$$

For the reserves alternative, the reduced form of the stochastic system is

$$\begin{bmatrix} Y \\ M \\ r \end{bmatrix} = \begin{bmatrix} g_{11} & g'_1 \\ g_{21} & g'_2 \\ g_{31} & g'_3 \end{bmatrix} \begin{bmatrix} R \\ z \end{bmatrix} + \begin{bmatrix} e_Y \\ e_M \\ e_r \end{bmatrix}, \qquad (7')$$

where the g_{ij} and g_i are as defined in equations (8a) and (8b), and

$$e_Y = u_Y - (b_1 a_1 + b_2 - c_2)^{-1} a_1 (b_1 u_Y + u_{MD} - u_{MS}), \tag{8'}$$

$$e_M = u_{MS} - (b_1 a_1 + b_2 - c_2)^{-1} c_2 (b_1 u_Y + u_{MD} - u_{MS}),$$

$$e_r = - (b_1 a_1 + b_2 - c_2)^{-1} (b_1 u_Y + u_{MD} - u_{MS}).$$

The solution to the instrument problem emerges from the comparison of ε_Y and e_Y. If the structural disturbances (u_Y, u_{MD}, u_{MS}) each have zero mean, then

$$E(\varepsilon_Y) = E(e_Y) = 0. \tag{13}$$

Hence the optimal instrument variable values under the rate and reserves alternatives—$r^*|_r$ and $R^*|_R$, respectively—will be certainty equivalents, identical to the values given by equations (9) and (11), and

$$E(Y)|_r = E(Y)|_R = Y^*. \tag{14}$$

If, in addition, the structural disturbances have respective nonzero variances $(\sigma^2_Y, \sigma^2_{MD}, \sigma^2_{MS})$ and covariances $(\sigma_{Y,MD}, \sigma_{Y,MS}, \sigma_{MD,MS})$, then

$$E(Y - Y^*)^2|_r = E(\varepsilon_Y)^2 = \sigma^2_Y, \tag{15}$$

and

$$E(Y - Y^*)^2|_R = E(e_Y)^2 \tag{16}$$

$$= (b_1 a_1 + b_2 - c_2)^{-2} \{(b_2 - c_2)^2 \sigma^2_Y + a_1^2 \sigma^2_{MD}$$

$$+ a_1^2 \sigma^2_{MS} - 2a_1(b_2 - c_2)\sigma_{Y,MD}$$

$$+ 2a_1(b_2 - c_2)\sigma_{Y,MS} - 2a_1^2 \sigma_{MD,MS}\}.$$

The solution to the instrument problem is to choose the rate alternative if $E(\varepsilon_Y)^2 < E(e_Y)^2$ and to choose the reserves alternative if

$E(\epsilon_Y)^2 > E(e_Y)^2$. Hence the choice of instruments depends upon the coefficients of equations (2') to (4') and upon the joint distribution of the structural disturbance terms (u_Y, u_{MD}, u_{MS}).[4]

3. LEVELS OF THE MONETARY POLICY CONTROL PROBLEM

For several operational reasons, the current central bank approach to monetary policy planning is essentially a two-level, or two-stage, process.[5] Numerous writers have applied control methodologies to monetary policy, and each has typically focused on only one of these two levels. The result has been some confusion in the literature, including a number of specific apparent contradictions, over the precise relationship among the economic variables that appear as targets and instruments in these formulations of the monetary policy control problem. In particular, within the framework of equations (2') to (4') the interest rate, money stock, and income variables all constitute distinct sources of confusion and apparent contradiction.

Clearing up this confusion should, in the first instance, facilitate understanding of how the Federal Reserve System plans and implements open-market policy, as well as understanding of how the seemingly divergent elements of the monetary policy control literature relate to one another; to

4. This treatment is not fully general for several reasons. First, it admits additive uncertainty only, i.e., it assumes that the coefficients of eqq. (2') to (4') are nonrandom and known with certainty; hence the certainty equivalence result of Simon (1956) and Theil (1957) holds. If the model's coefficients were uncertain, the variance expressions in eqq. (15) and (16) would contain an additional term in the difference between the instrument value and its historical or sample-period mean, and the resulting optimal r^*, R^*, and $E(Y)$ values would all be different. (See the references cited in note 31 below, on the implications of multiplicative uncertainty.) Second, in a dynamic model, a case of Holbrook's (1972) "instrument instability" may render one instrument inferior to another; this one-period model does not analyze dynamic results. Third, the policy authorities may have some preferences about the values of r or R per se, wholly apart from the impact of these variables on the target variable(s).

5. See Axilrod (1971) and Davis (1973) for an account of the current implementation of central bank open market policy.

this end, the discussion of this section indicates the nature of the key inconsistencies involved. In addition, the clarification of these issues permits the more fundamental identification of the conditions required for the usual two-level approach to the monetary policy process to be valid and useful.

At the broadest macroeconomic level, Poole (1970) has posed the alternative of monetary policy control of nominal income by means of direct control over either the interest rate or the money stock. Poole examined this question by using the *IS-LM* framework consisting of equations (2') and (3') above. This two-equation model, which does not include a reserves variable, is determined with any one of the three variables (Y, r, M) taken as exogenous. Again with income as the endogenous variable that monetary policymakers seek to control, Poole's two alternatives are as follows.

Variable	"Rate" alternative	"Money" alternative
Y	target	target
r	instrument	irrelevant
M	irrelevant	instrument
z	data	data

This formulation of the monetary policy control problem, shown in panel (a) of figure 1, is especially interesting because it not only indicates a pair of alternatives that policymakers have openly confronted (e.g., Federal Reserve Bank of Boston 1969) but also corresponds to familiar bodies of literature of empirical economics. As Poole has shown in an analysis similar to that of section 2, the choice between the two alternatives depends in general upon the coefficients of equations (2') and (3') and upon the joint distributions of the structural disturbance terms u_Y and u_{MD}. The consideration of the (dynamic) coefficients of equations (2') and (3') was the subject of the Andersen-Jordan (1968) St. Louis equation and the subsequent literature (e.g., de Leeuw and Kalchbrenner 1969; Davis 1969; Hamburger 1971), as well as of investigations performed with complete macroeconometric models such as the FRB-MIT model (de Leeuw and Gramlich 1968). The comparison of u_Y and u_{MD} was the subject of the

Friedman-Meiselman (1963) CMC paper and the subsequent literature (e.g., Ando and Modigliani 1965; De Prano and Mayer 1965; M. Friedman and Meiselman 1965).

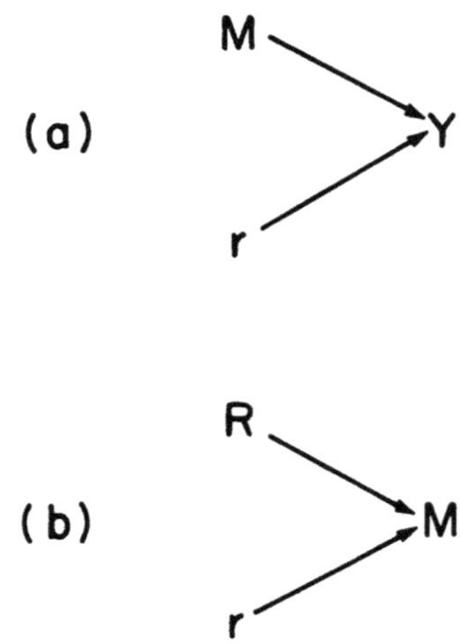

Levels of the monetary policy control problem

Figure 1

In a more realistic sense than that of this broad macroeconomic approach, however, the money stock is not an exogenous variable in the strict sense required for the control problem. The Federal Reserve System cannot set the money stock directly but, rather, must affect it indirectly by influencing the actions of commercial banks and the deposit-holding public. The true instruments that it has available for this purpose are open market operations (i.e., purchases or sales of securities in the portfolio of the System Open Market Account), member bank reserve requirements, and the discount rate. If an analysis of equations (2') and (3') indicates that the "money" alternative is preferable to the "rate" alternative at the broad macroeconomic level, control of the money stock itself therefore constitutes a separate stage of the monetary policy process and hence a second control problem.

At this second, money market level, Pierce and Thomson (Federal Reserve Bank of Boston 1972, pp. 115-36) have posed the alternative of control of the money stock by means of direct control over either the interest rate or the stock of nonborrowed reserves. They examined this question by using a market-clearing model of the money market consisting of equations (3') and (4') above. This two-equation model is determined with any two of the four variables (Y, r, M, R) taken as exogenous. In formulating this second stage of the monetary policy control problem, Pierce and Thomson took the money stock as the endogenous variable that policymakers seek to control and assumed that, for purposes of short-term management of the money market, income is exogenous with respect to contemporaneous central bank actions. Their two alternatives, shown in panel (b) of figure 1, are as follows.

Variable	"Rate" alternative	"Reserves" alternative
Y	data	data
r	instrument	irrelevant
M	target	target
R	irrelevant	instrument
z	data	data

Pierce and Thomson showed that the same analytical methods of section 2, which Poole used, also apply to their formulation of this prior stage of the monetary policy control problem, and so the choice between the two alternatives depends upon the coefficients of equations (3') and (4') and upon disturbance terms u_{MD} and u_{MS}. Like Poole's formulation, this formulation of the problem also indicates a pair of alternatives that policymakers have actually confronted (e.g., Federal Reserve Bank of Boston 1972) and also corresponds to at least some nascent body of empirical work.[6]

As set forth by Poole and by Pierce and Thomson, these two formulations of the monetary policy control problem are distinct, referring to two possible stages of the policy planning process. For at least three reasons, however, there has been much confusion between the two formulations.

6. See the list of papers cited by Pierce and Thomson.

One source of confusion is the fact that "the interest rate" enters both formulations in approximately parallel ways. Some writers have distinguished between the two appearances of the interest rate by referring to the three-month Treasury bill or commercial paper rate in the *IS-LM* formulation and to the federal funds rate in the money market formulation, so that the relationship between the two is as in panel (a) of figure 2. Such a distinction simply clouds the issue, however, since there is no a priori reason for preferring the federal funds rate to either the Treasury bill rate or the commercial paper rate in equations (3') or (4').[7] Hence figure 3 is a more accurate representation of the relationship between these two formulations.

An example of this confusion caused by the presence of the interest rate in both formulations of the control problem is the set of experiments in which Pindyck and Roberts (1974) used a monthly model of the money market to examine the relative controllability of the Treasury bill rate and the money stock. Their formulation of the monetary policy control problem, shown in panel (b) of figure 2, supposed a symmetrical treatment of the Treasury bill rate and the money stock as alternative target variables, either of which might in turn be controlled alternatively by the federal funds rate or the stock of nonborrowed reserves. Despite the appeal of the symmetrical decision tree, this formulation is misleading. Since the Federal Reserve System Open Market Account has a portfolio of over $75 billion of U.S. Treasury securities (mostly short maturities) in comparison with only $39 billion of Treasury bills held by nonofficial investors,[8] it is unnecessary for the central bank to use some other variable, such as the federal funds rate or the stock of reserves, to control the Treasury bill rate indirectly. The Federal Reserve's willingness to buy or sell large amounts of bills at an appropriately narrow bid-ask spread is sufficient to determine the Treasury bill rate directly, within the relatively short time horizon employed by Pindyck and Roberts.

---

7. In fact, the empirical evidence seems to favor either the Treasury bill rate or the commercial paper rate. See de Leeuw (1965), de Leeuw and Gramlich (1968), and Thomson, Pierce, and Parry (1975); Davis's (1972) use of the federal funds rate is something of an exception.

8. Data, which are for June 1973, are from the Federal Reserve *Bulletin*.

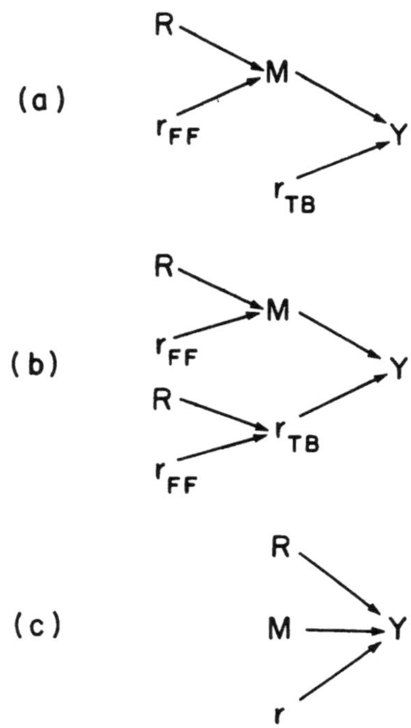

Incorrect structures of the monetary policy control problem

Figure 2

A second source of confusion in this two-stage representation of the monetary policy process is the role of the money stock as an instrument variable at the broad macroeconomic level and as a target variable at the money market level. Holbrook and Shapiro (1970) and Parkin (1973), for example, have posited the model shown in panel (c) of figure 2, in which the target variable is income and three available instrument variables are the interest rate, the money stock, and the stock of reserves. This conception of the monetary policy control problem is internally inconsistent, however, since money and reserves are not instrument variables in the same sense. Reserves and the interest rate may be parallel variables in that both are subject to direct policy control, and money and the interest rate may be parallel variables with respect to their respective roles in the *IS-LM* framework; but reserves and money are not parallel variables in a meaningful control sense.[9]

The contradiction implied by the two roles of the money stock in the two formulations shows clearly that the two stages of the monetary policy process are in fact not totally independent in the presence of uncertainty. The solution to the problem of equations (2') and (3'), based on the assumption that the money stock may be made exogenous, may indicate that the money alternative is the better approach to controlling income. The solution to the problem of equations (3') and (4'), however, will in general yield a nonzero variance of the endogenous money stock about the desired value M^*. If that variance is sufficiently large, allowing for it may render the interest-rate alternative the better solution to the problem of equations (2') and (3') after all.

A potential third source of confusion in the two-stage formulation of the monetary policy process is the role of income as a target variable at the broad macroeconomic level and as a data variable at the money market level. In other words, income is endogenous with respect to events in the money market at the former level but exogenous with respect to the same events at the latter level. One trend in the literature to date has been to resolve this discrepancy by using different time units for examining the two stages of the problem—using a monthly (e.g., Thomson, Pierce, and Parry 1975), or even a weekly (e.g., Farr, Roberts, and Thomson 1972), model at the money market level and the familiar quarterly model at the broad macroeconomic level. Nevertheless, there has been little research to evaluate the adequacy of this schizophrenic approach, which is at best only an approximation to reality. Although some models, such as the FRB-MIT model and the Wharton model (Evans and Klein 1968), may suggest that central bank actions in the money market have only a negligible impact on income in the contemporaneous quarter, the Andersen-Carlson (1970) model indicates that a $1 billion addition to the money stock in any quarter yields a

---

9. Holbrook and Shapiro (1970) acknowledged this inconsistency in a footnote (p. 46) but reported the results of their full analysis anyway.

$1.22 billion addition to income in the same quarter.[10] If this increase in income occurs throughout the quarter, with personal income correspondingly increasing, the monthly money market model used by Pindyck and Roberts indicates that the feedback in terms of additional demand for money will be of the order of $160 million, or about one-sixth of the initial addition to the money stock.[11] In short, the two-stage representation of the monetary policy process in figure 3 is incomplete in that it lacks an arrow leading from *Y* to *M*.

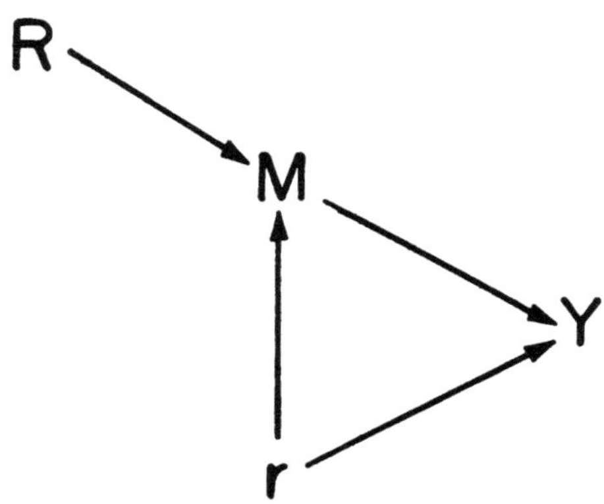

Two-stage structure of the monetary policy control problem

Figure 3

Like the dual role of the money stock in these two formulations, the endogeneity of income with respect to central bank actions in the money market calls into question the two-stage representation of the monetary policy process. Under what conditions is it appropriate to separate the

10. Andersen and Jordan (1968) found estimates of the current-quarter impact as large as $1.58 billion.

11. This rough calculation assumes that personal income, which in 1972 was approximately eighty percent of total gross income, rises by $980 million with the $1.22 billion rise income. In the Thomson-Pierce-Parry monthly money-market model, a form of which provided the base for Pindyck and Roberts's experiments, the demand for money is a function of current and lagged values of personal income.

monetary policy control problem into a broad macroeconomic level and a money market level, as is the custom in current central bank practice? As the discussion of this section indicates, at least two conditions required to justify absolutely such a separation are, first, absolute controllability of the money stock within each time period and, second, a lag structure that renders income absolutely independent of contemporaneous central bank activity in the money market within each time period. It is unlikely that either condition holds absolutely in reality, and so the errors introduced by using the two-stage approach to monetary policy depend upon the degree to which the assumption of these two conditions may be a close approximation to reality. The closeness of such approximations is itself not a logical question but a proper object of empirical research.

If these two assumptions are not at great variance with the true workings of the economic system, at least the qualitative choices of the rate or the money alternative at the broad macroeconomic level and the rate or the reserves alternative at the money-market level will still be valid. The true optimal instrument variable values, however, will still differ from the values yielded in the analysis based on the two-stage representation of the monetary policy process. If the two assumptions are further away from reality, then even the qualitative choices of rate or money and rate or reserves may be wrong; in this case the two-stage approach would be counterproductive, and policy analysis would do better to rely on a straightforward unified reduced-form framework such as that set forth in section 2.

4. THE INTERMEDIATE TARGET PROBLEM

4.1. The Problem

A major issue, faced in one form or another during the past decade by central bankers, monetary economists, and financial market participants and observers, has been the role of intermediate operating targets of monetary policy. The targets-and-instruments framework developed in sections 1 and 2 provides a useful vehicle for analyzing the role of such intermediate target variables.

The *intermediate target problem*[12] is the choice of a variable, usually a readily observable financial market price or quantity, that the central bank will treat, for purposes of a short-run operating guide, as if it were the true ultimate target of monetary policy. The two-stage representation of the monetary policy control problem in figure 3 shows clearly how such an intermediate target variable can fit into the planning and implementation of monetary policy; at the same time, it raises useful questions about why an intermediate target variable should play such a role.

Suppose, for example, that empirical and other research on the problem of equations (2') and (3') indicated that the money alternative is optimal for controlling income, and that similar research on the problem of equations (3') and (4') indicated that the reserves alternative is optimal for controlling the money stock. If the central bank were then to act, in one stage of the policy process, to manipulate the stock of reserves as if the money stock were the ultimate goal of policy, then the money stock would be playing the role of an intermediate target variable.

Several troublesome questions arise at this point. In the light of the uncertain validity of the two-stage representation of the monetary policy process, discussed in section 3, would it be better simply to apply the target-and-instrument methodology based on reduced-form equation (7') and ignore the irrelevant (in Tinbergen's sense) variable M? Similarly, if research on the problem of equations (3') and (4') indicated that the rate alternative is optimal for controlling the money stock, would it be better to apply the targets-and-instruments methodology based on reduced-form equation (5')? In terms of figure 3, why is the roundabout policy procedure based on the intermediate target variable M preferable to simply following the conceptual arrow from r to Y? In short, what is the purpose of using the money stock (or any other variable) as an intermediate target variable?

---

12. Most writers on this subject have simply called this problem the "target problem." The purpose of the extra word "intermediate" or "operating," both of which are typical of more recent usage, is to distinguish this problem from that of identifying the targets of policy in the sense of section 1—i.e., those variables, such as employment and price stability, that enter directly into policymakers' preference functions. The targets-and-indicators literature typically referred to the latter variables as policy "goals."

Brunner and Meltzer (Brunner 1969, p. 2) defined the intermediate target problem as "the problem of choosing an optimal strategy or strategies to guide monetary policy under the conditions of uncertainty and lags in the receipt of information about the more remote goals of policy." Subsequent writers have also cited both uncertainty and information lags as either necessary or sufficient conditions for the usefulness of an intermediate target variable (e.g., Saving 1967, p. 448; Holbrook and Shapiro 1970, p. 40). The model used in section 2 is stochastic, but its one-period structure precludes the incorporation of information lags. Rewriting equation (5') by inserting a time subscript to emphasize that the single time period in question is one of a series of time periods,[13] yields

$$\begin{bmatrix} Y_t \\ M_t \\ R_t \end{bmatrix} = \begin{bmatrix} \gamma_{11} & \gamma'_1 \\ \gamma_{21} & \gamma'_2 \\ \gamma_{31} & \gamma'_3 \end{bmatrix} \begin{bmatrix} r_t \\ z_t \end{bmatrix} + \begin{bmatrix} \varepsilon_{Yt} \\ \varepsilon_{Mt} \\ \varepsilon_{Rt} \end{bmatrix} . \tag{17}$$

For simplicity, again let the objective of monetary policy be to minimize the expected variance of the target variable Y_t in each time period about the corresponding desired value of Y_t^*.[14] Given zero expectation for the structural disturbance terms (u_{Yt}, u_{MDt}, u_{MSt}) and therefore zero expectation for the reduced-form disturbance terms (ε_{Yt}, ε_{Mt}, ε_{Rt}), the optimal policy in the presence of additive uncertainty is the certainty equivalent

$$r_t^* = \gamma_{11}^{-1} (Y_t^* - \gamma'_1 z_t), \tag{18}$$

13. The analysis of this section proceeds in the context of the rate alternative for the problem of eqq. (2'), (3'), and (4'). The key results are equally applicable to the reserves alternatives.

14. See B. Friedman (1971) for an analysis of time-linked objectives in which differences between the target variables and their desired values in separate time periods may offset one another.

and the resulting expectations of the three endogenous variables are

$$E(Y_t) = \gamma_{11} r^*_t + \gamma'_1 z_t = Y^*_t, \tag{19}$$

$$E(M_t) = \gamma_{21} r^*_t + \gamma'_2 z_t,$$

$$E(R_t) = \gamma_{31} r^*_t + \gamma'_3 z_t.$$

If the model's structural disturbances are autocorrelated, that is, if

$$u_{Yt} = \rho_Y \cdot u_{Y,t-1} + \nu_{Yt}, \tag{20}$$

$$u_{MDt} = \rho_{MD} \cdot u_{MD,t-1} + \nu_{MDt},$$

$$u_{MSt} = \rho_{MS} \cdot u_{MS,t-1} + \nu_{MSt},$$

where the ρ_i are nonzero, $-1 < \rho_i < 1$, and if the ν_{it} are serially uncorrelated variables with zero expectation and variances $(s^2_Y, s^2_{MD}, s^2_{MS})$ and covariances $(s_{Y,MD}, s_{Y,MS}, s_{MD,MS})$, then the reduced-form disturbances are also autocorrelated in a related way. In particular, from equations (6') and (20)

$$E(\varepsilon_{Yt}) = \rho_Y \cdot u_{Y,t-1}, \tag{21}$$

$$E(\varepsilon_{Mt}) = \rho_{MD} \cdot u_{MD,t-1} + b_1 \rho_Y \cdot u_{Y,t-1},$$

$$E(\varepsilon_{Rt}) = c_1^{-1}(b_1 \rho_Y \cdot u_{Y,t-1} + \rho_{MD} \cdot u_{MD,t-1}$$

$$- \rho_{MS} \cdot u_{MS,t-1}).$$

Given observations of Y_{t-1}, M_{t-1}, and R_{t-1} at the beginning of time period t, it would be straightforward to calculate the reduced-form disturbances $(\varepsilon_{Y,t-1}, \varepsilon_{M,t-1}, \varepsilon_{R,t-1})$ as the differences between these observations and the corresponding expectations in the analogue of equation (19) from the previous period. Knowledge of these reduced-form disturbances would, in turn, be sufficient to solve equations (6') for the structural disturbances $(u_{Y,t-1}, u_{MD,t-1}, u_{MS,t-1})$. Then, given these structural disturbance values for the previous time period and the known autocorrelation parameters, ρ_i, the "informed" expectation of the structural and reduced-form disturbances in period t would no longer necessarily be equal to zero. In particular, for the reduced-form disturbance ε_{Yt}, which is crucial to the monetary policy decision for time period t, the "informed" expectation is[15]

$$E_t(\varepsilon_{Yt}) = \rho_Y \cdot u_{Y,t-1}, \tag{22}$$

where the notation E_t makes explicit that the expectation in question is an "informed" expectation, conditional on all information known as of the beginning of time period t. The corresponding informed optimal policy for time period t would then be

$$r_t^{**} = \gamma_{11}^{-1}(Y_t^* - \gamma'_1 z_t - E_t(\varepsilon_{Yt})), \tag{23}$$

in contrast to the "uninformed" policy in equation (18) based on the "uninformed" zero expectation of ε_{Yt}. In summary, the informed optimal policy r_t^{**} differs from the uninformed optimal policy r_t^* by an adjustment factor involving the informed expectation $E_t(\varepsilon_{Yt})$,

$$r_t^{**} = r_t^* - \gamma_{11}^{-1} E_t(\varepsilon_{Yt}). \tag{24}$$

4.2 The Intermediate Target Variable Procedure

A simplified version of the assumption of an information lag, as is familiar in the literature of intermediate target variables, is to assume that, as of the beginning of time period t, the actual values M_{t-1} and R_{t-1} are known but the actual value Y_{t-1} remains unobserved. This lack of data for Y_{t-1} renders the simple approach of equations (22) to (24) infeasible. Under either the rate alternative or the reserves alternative, lack of knowledge about $\varepsilon_{Y,t-1}$ or $e_{Y,t-1}$ renders knowledge of the structural disturbance terms $(u_{Y,t-1}, u_{MD,t-1}, u_{MS,t-1})$ via equations (6') or (8') impossible.[16]

15. Note that $u_Y = \varepsilon_Y$, from eqq. (6'), is particular to the rate alternative. Eqq. (8') show that this simplifying property, which is not important for the analysis of this section except for reducing the amount of algebra to be done, does not hold for the reserves alternative.

16. Because variable Y does not appear in eq. (4'), knowledge of M_{t-1}, R_{t-1}, r_{t-1}, and z_{t-1} is sufficient to yield the structural disturbance $u_{MS,t-1}$; nevertheless, the structure of eqq. (6') or (8') prevents solving for $u_{Y,t-1}$ and $u_{MD,t-1}$, despite the knowledge of $u_{MS,t-1}$.

Hence any informed nonzero expectation $E_t(\varepsilon_{Yt})$ must follow from the known reduced-form disturbances $(\varepsilon_{M,t-1}, \varepsilon_{R,t-1})$. As the following analysis shows, use of the money stock as an intermediate target variable is equivalent to deriving the informed expectation $E_t(\varepsilon_{Yt})$ in a particular way from the single known reduced-form disturbance $\varepsilon_{M,t-1}$.[17]

The analytic role of an intermediate target variable, therefore, is to provide an effective rule for revising the a priori expectation $E(\varepsilon_{Yt}) = 0$ into the (in general) nonzero informed expectation $E_t(\varepsilon_{Yt})$. The autocorrelation ρ_Y is of no direct use for this purpose if data describing the recent history of Y are not available. In the presence of such data lags, the central bank may choose to act as if its target is some other variable for which recent data are in fact available.

The uninformed policy for time period t, based on the a priori expectation $E(\varepsilon_{Yt}) = 0$, is r^*_t in equation (18), and the resulting expectation of the money stock in that period is

$$M^*_t = \gamma_{21} r^*_t + \gamma'_2 \; t. \tag{25}$$

In other words, M^*_t is the value of M_t that is consistent with the target value of Y^*_t, based on the uninformed expectation $E(\varepsilon_{Mt}) = 0$. The essence of the use of the money stock as an intermediate target variable is that, with $\varepsilon_{M,t-1}$ known, it is possible to derive an (in general nonzero) informed expectation $E_t(\varepsilon_{Mt})$. If the central bank then acted as if its goal were to minimize the expected variance of M_t about M^*_t from equation (25), its informed optimal policy in the context of the intermediate target approach would be

$$r^{**}_t = \gamma_{21}^{-1} (M^*_t - \gamma'_2 \; t - \; t(\varepsilon_{Mt})). \tag{26}$$

---

17. The problem is in some ways analogous to the familiar errors-in-variables problem; the central bank cannot observe $\varepsilon_{Y,t-1}$ but must infer its value from the observable $\varepsilon_{M,t-1}$, which includes $\varepsilon_{Y,t-1}$ and another component. At first glance the conclusion of Kareken, Muench, and Wallace (1973), that the central bank's optimal solution to its information problem is to use all of the information variables available to it, seems to suggest using both $\varepsilon_{M,t-1}$ and $\varepsilon_{R,t-1}$ for this purpose. A closer look at eqq. (6'), however, shows that the known sum $c_1 \varepsilon_{R,t-1} + u_{MS,t-1}$ simply equals $\varepsilon_{M,t-1}$ and provides no new information; an analogous, though algebraically more complicated, proposition holds for eqq. (8').

Here the informed optimal policy differs from the uninformed optimal policy by an adjustment involving the informed expectation $E_t(\varepsilon_{Mt})$:

$$r_t^{**} = r_t^{*} - \gamma_{21}^{-1} E_t(\varepsilon_{Mt}). \tag{27}$$

How can the central bank derive this informed expectation $E_t(\varepsilon_{Mt})$? It is clear from equations (6') and (20) that, with full information available about Y_{t-1}, M_{t-1}, and R_{t-1},

$$E_t(\varepsilon_{Mt}) = \rho_{MD} \cdot u_{MD,t-1} + b_1 \rho_Y \cdot u_{Y,t-1}; \tag{28}$$

but the lack of information about Y_{t-1} prevents using this approach, just as it prevents using the direct approach of equations (22) to (24). Instead, the central bank must rely upon the limited information that is available—in particular, the reduced-form disturbance $\varepsilon_{M,t-1}$. Again from equations (6') and (20), it is possible to write the variance and first-period autocovariance of the ε_{Mt} series, respectively, as

$$E(\varepsilon_{Mt})^2 = s_{MD}^2 \left(\frac{1}{1 - \rho_{MD}^2} \right) + s_Y^2 \left(\frac{b_1^2}{1 - \rho_Y^2} \right) + s_{Y,MD} \left(\frac{b_1}{1 - \rho_Y \rho_{MD}} \right), \tag{29}$$

$$E(\varepsilon_{Mt} \cdot \varepsilon_{M,t-1}) = s_{MD}^2 \left(\frac{\rho_{MD}}{1 - \rho_{MD}^2} \right) + s_Y^2 \left(\frac{b_1^2 \rho_Y}{1 - \rho_Y^2} \right) + s_{Y,MD} \left(\frac{b_1(\rho_Y + \rho_{MD})}{1 - \rho_Y \rho_{MD}} \right).$$

Hence variance $E(\varepsilon_{Mt})^2$ and autocovariance $E(\varepsilon_{Mt} \cdot \varepsilon_{M,t-1})$ are simply weighted avarages of the variances s_{MD}^2 and s_Y^2 and covariance $s_{Y,MD}$, with the weights determined by the autocorrelation coefficients ρ_{MD} and ρ_Y and the coefficient b_1 from the underlying structural economic model. Following a "linear regression" procedure, the ratio of this variance and autocovariance permits deriving the informed expectation $E_t(\varepsilon_{Mt})$, given the observed $\varepsilon_{M,t-1}$, as

$$E_t(\varepsilon_{Mt}) = m \cdot \varepsilon_{M,t-1} \tag{30}$$

and setting the informed optimal policy from equation (27) as

$$r_t^{**} = r_t^{*} - \gamma_{21}^{-1} m \cdot \varepsilon_{M,t-1}, \tag{31}$$

where $m = E(\varepsilon_{Mt} \cdot \varepsilon_{M,t-1}) / E(\varepsilon_{Mt})^2$. (32)

A comparison of equations (24) and (31) indicates that using the money stock as an intermediate target variable, in the absence of recent data on income, is equivalent to using the assumption

$$E_t(\varepsilon_{Yt}) = \gamma_{21}^{-1} \gamma_{11} m \cdot \varepsilon_{M,t-1} \tag{33}$$

to supply the informed expectation required for the application of equation (24). The final two right-hand-side elements in equation (33) simply state the informed expectation $E_t(\varepsilon_{Mt})$; the first two use the reduced-form model of equation (5') to rotate this expectation from the M dimension to the Y dimension by way of the r dimension.

Using the money stock as an intermediate target variable in this way is therefore equivalent to the covariance assumption

$$E(\varepsilon_{Yt} \cdot \varepsilon_{M,t-1}) = \gamma_{21}^{-1} \gamma_{11} \left[s_{MD}^2 \left(\frac{\rho_{MD}}{1 - \rho_{MD}^2} \right) + s_Y^2 \left(\frac{b_1^2 \rho_Y}{1 - \rho_Y^2} \right) + s_{Y,MD} \left(\frac{b_1(\rho_Y + \rho_{MD})}{1 - \rho_Y \rho_{MD}} \right) \right]. \tag{34}$$

The true expression for this covariance, however, is easily derivable from equations (6') and (20) as

$$E(\varepsilon_{Yt} \cdot \varepsilon_{M,t-1}) = s_{Y,MD} \left(\frac{\rho_Y}{1 - \rho_Y \rho_{MD}} \right) + s_Y^2 \left(\frac{b_1 \rho_Y}{1 - \rho_Y^2} \right). \tag{35}$$

The assumption stated in equation (34) clearly differs from the true covariance, as stated in equation (35). Rewriting the assumed covariance and the true covariance in terms of the parameters of the underlying structural system makes it even more convenient to consider the relevant differences between the two. The *covariance assumption implied by use of the money stock as an intermediate target variable* is

$$E(\varepsilon_{Yt} \cdot \varepsilon_{M,t-1}) = (b_2 + b_1 a_1)^{-1} a_1 [\rho_{MD} \cdot \sigma_{MD}^2 + b_1^2 \rho_Y \cdot \sigma_Y^2 + b_1(\rho_{MD} + \rho_Y) \cdot \sigma_{Y,MD}], \tag{36}$$

and the *true covariance* is

$$E(\varepsilon_{Yt} \cdot \varepsilon_{M,t-1}) = b_1\rho_Y \cdot \sigma_Y^2 + \rho_Y \cdot \sigma_{Y,MD}. \tag{37}$$

Comparison of the alternative covariance expressions in equations (36) and (37) shows clearly the importance of the assumption of a stable, interest-insensitive money demand function typically associated with proponents of the use of the money stock as an intermediate target variable. In the limit, stability of the money demand function implies $\sigma^2_{MD} = \sigma_{Y,MD} = 0$. In the limit, interest insensitivity of the money demand function implies $b_2 = 0$. If the money-demand function satisfies these two conditions, then both equations (36) and (37) identically reduce to a value of $b_1\rho_Y\sigma_Y^2$ for the covariance $E(\varepsilon_{Yt}, \varepsilon_{M,t-1})$. In the absence of these two conditions, the use of the money stock in the role of an intermediate target variable implies the assumption of a covariance $E(\varepsilon_{Yt}, \varepsilon_{M,t-1})$ that differs from the true covariance.

4.3 Optimal Procedure with Information Lags

How, then, should the central bank set monetary policy under these conditions of information lags and serially correlated structural errors? Two distinct alternative procedures are apparent for determining the informed expectation $E_t(\varepsilon_{Yt})$ required in equation (23).

First, using the information contained in $\varepsilon_{M,t-1}$, the central bank can apply the linear regression method of equations (30) to (32), which relies on the true covariance $E(\varepsilon_{Yt}, \varepsilon_{M,t-1})$ from equation (35).[18] As is clear from equations (6') and (20), however, the relationship between ε_{Yt} and $\varepsilon_{M,t-1}$ is not in fact linear, and so this method will be misleading when $u_{MD,t-1}$ has dominated $\varepsilon_{M,t-1}$.

18. This procedure is equivalent to using M as an "information variable" in the sense of Kareken, Muench, and Wallace (1973), since eq. (32) simply states the least-squares estimator of β in the regression equation $\varepsilon_{Yt} = \alpha + \beta\varepsilon_{M,t-1}$ + disturbance.

Second, the central bank can ignore the potential information contained in $\varepsilon_{M,t-1}$ and use equation (20) directly to formulate the necessary informed expectation as

$$E_t(\varepsilon_{Yt}) = \rho_Y^{T+1} \cdot u_{Y,\, t-T-1}, \tag{38}$$

where T is the length of the lag in the receipt of information about Y.

One way to evaluate these two alternative procedures is to compare the respective conditional variances of ε_{Yt} implied by each. This criterion is useful since, once the central bank uses any given expectation $E_t(\varepsilon_{Yt})$ to set its policy instrument by equation (23), the associated variance enters in a straightforward manner into the resulting variance of income $E_t(Y_t - Y_t^*)^2 | r_t^{**}$. If the central bank uses the procedure of equations (30) to (32) to derive $E_t(\varepsilon_{Yt})$, then, under conditions appropriate to the multivariate normal distribution,[19] the conditional variance of ε_{Yt} given $\varepsilon_{M,t-1}$ is

$$E_t[\varepsilon_{Yt} - E_t(\varepsilon_{Yt})]^2 |_{\varepsilon_{M,t-1}} = \sigma_Y^2 - \frac{(b_1 \rho_Y \cdot \sigma_Y^2 + \rho_Y \cdot \sigma_{Y,MD})^2}{\sigma_{MD}^2 + b_1^2 \sigma_Y^2 + 2 b_1 \sigma_{Y,MD}} . \tag{39}$$

If the central bank uses the procedure of equation (38) to derive $E_t(\varepsilon_{Yt})$, then the conditional variance of ε_{Yt} given $u_{Y,t-T-1}$ is

$$E_t[\varepsilon_{Yt} - E_t(\varepsilon_{Yt})]^2 |_{\varepsilon_{Y,t-T-1}} = \sigma_Y^2 (1 - \rho_Y^2) \left(1 + \sum_{\tau=1}^{T-1} \rho_Y^{2\tau} \right). \tag{40}$$

As equations (39) and (40) show, both procedures yield conditional variances no larger than σ_Y^2, the variance associated with the uninformed expectation $E(\varepsilon_{Yt}) = 0$. (In other words, the value of information, whether contained in $\varepsilon_{M,t-1}$ or in $u_{Y,t-T-1}$, is never negative.) The conditional variance in equation (39) is a fixed function of the parameters of the structural model and its disturbances, while the conditional variance in equation (40) is positively related to the information lag T. Furthermore, the conditional variance in equation (40) equals $\sigma_Y^2(1 - \rho_Y^2)$, or s_Y^2, if $T = 0$ (i.e., there is no information lag) and equals σ_Y^2 if $T = \infty$ (i.e., data on Y never

19. For reference, see e.g., Rao (1965, chap. 8).

become available). Given values of the relevant fixed parameters, therefore, there is some length of information lag, say T^*, such that the conditional variance in equation (40) is greater or less than the conditional variance in equation (39) as $T \gtrless T^*$. The length of the information lag on Y therefore determines whether the central bank should apply the procedure of equations (30) to (32) and (35), using the information in the previous period's value of the money stock, or the procedure of equation (38), using the information in the most recent available observation on income itself.[20]

4.4 Concluding Remarks

In summary, even in the context of the simple model employed above for illustrative purposes, the use of a particular irrelevant (in Tinbergen's sense) variable in the role of an intermediate target variable does not constitute optimal central bank operating procedure. In the example given here, use of the money stock as an information variable in the general linear regression form is superior to use of the money stock as an intermediate target variable, except under very restrictive conditions that render the two procedures identical; and use of the most recent available income data may itself be superior even to the former procedure.

Before leaving this subject, it is useful to consider several specific differences between reality and the restrictive assumptions made in the course of considering the simple four-variable model above. The central bank does indeed face questions such as those posed above, but it does so in a vastly more complex environment.

First, the actual world confronting the central bank contains many more than two irrelevant variables, and the appearance of unanticipated movements in any of them may provide useful information. Except for special cases either of zero covariance or of variables that are linear

---

20. A mixed procedure, incorporating both pieces of information, would lead to a conditional variance

$$E_t[\varepsilon_{Yt} - E_t(\varepsilon_{Yt})]^2 | \varepsilon_{M,t-1}, u_{Y,t-T-1},$$

which would be no greater than the minimum of the alternative conditional variances in eqq. (40) and (41) and would therefore be the true optimum procedure.

substitutes (as with ε_R and ε_M in the model above),[21] the central bank's optimal operating procedure would include the monitoring of all monetary and reserve aggregates and all interest rates, not to mention nonfinancial variables. The approach that Guttentag (1966) has described, in which the central bank "looks at everything," is a least partly optimal. To operate optimally, the central bank not only should "look at everything" but should do so in the context of the information-generating procedures illustrated by equations (30) to (32) above.

Second, the simple model used above is explicitly nondynamic except for the autocorrelated error terms. Redefining vector z to include lagged values of the model's exogenous and jointly determined variables, and substituting higher-order autocorrelation processes in equation (20), would render the model a more accurate description of actual fact. It is not the purpose of this paper to discuss specific problems involved in policymaking in a dynamic system; as is well known, future impacts of current policy actions render the decision problem significantly more complex. Nevertheless, it is important to be aware that more of past history is relevant to this problem than simply the most recent single set of observations.[22]

Third, the use of income as the single policy target variable in the analysis above is clearly unrealistic. The familiar goals of monetary policy include macroeconomic objectives such as employment, economic growth, price stability, and balance-of-payments equilibrium, as well as specifically financial objectives such as market stability. Given a set of preferences to facilitate evaluation of one such goal against another, generalizing the single variable Y in the analysis above to a vector of target variables is a straightforward extension of this analysis. Such a focus of monetary policy on a number of distinct target variables,however, would make the use of any single irrelevant variable as an intermediate target even less likely to be optimal than indicated by the analysis above.

---

21. See note 17.

22. A related problem is that the available data themselves often merit only limited confidence; see B. Friedman (1971), Axilrod and Beck (Federal Reserve Bank of Boston 1972, pp. 81-102), and Poole and Lieberman (1972) for an explicit treatment of the implications of inadequacies in data on monetary and reserve aggregates.

5. INFORMATION PROBLEMS: DATA LAGS AND STRUCTURAL LAGS

The intermediate target variable problem, as discussed in section 4, is most familiar in the targets-and-indicators literature (e.g., Brunner and Meltzer 1967; Holbrook and Shapiro 1970; Saving 1967) in the context of lags in the receipt of data on the ultimate targets of monetary policy. National Income Accounts data, for example, which describe various key income and spending totals, become available only once per quarter; and, until almost two months have elapsed in the subsequent quarter, those data which are available are only preliminary estimates based on severely limited sampling procedures. In contrast, the inherent cohesiveness of financial markets and the active supervision of a number of federal regulatory agencies render financial variables much more readily observable. Data on interest rates are typically available immediately on a daily basis, with little problem of sampling error, and reasonably reliable weekly estimates of reserve and monetary aggregates are available with a lag of only several days.[23] As a result, the central bank may use observations of financial variables to gain information about its policy targets, as section 4 describes.

Nevertheless, the presence of data lags as such is not a necessary condition for the use of an intermediate target variable or the other information-oriented procedures described in section 4. The presence of structural lags, because of which the values of monetary policy instruments in one time period influence the values of monetary policy targets in subsequent periods, can lead to formally equivalent information problems that policy operating procedures must confront. The documentation of such structural lags has constituted a separate literature unto itself (e.g., Ando et al. 1965; Cagan and Gandolphi 1969; de Leeuw and Gramlich 1968, 1969; M. Friedman 1961; M. Friedman and Schwartz 1963; Hamburger 1971; Modigliani, Rasche, and Cooper 1970; Rasche 1973), and several writers have followed M. Friedman (1959, 1961, 1968) in stressing the significance of these lags for monetary policy.[24]

---

23. See the references cited in note 22.

24. See Holt (1962), Theil (1964), and B. Friedman (1975) for a more general treatment of the implications of structural lags for policy decision making.

In the data lag case, the central bank needs an informed expectation of the reduced-form income disturbance in the current time period, $E_t(\varepsilon_{Yt})$, to use in setting the value of its instrument variable in that period. In the structural lag case, the value of the instrument variable in the current period will influence income (or other targets) several periods in the future, say Y_{t+T}, and so the central bank needs an informed expectation $E_t(\varepsilon_{Y,t+T})$ to use in determining policy for the current period.[25] Even if the value of Y_{t-1} is known, therefore, given a structural lag the best that the central bank can do without relying on observations of irrelevant variables is to follow the analogue of equation (38), that is,

$$E_t(\varepsilon_{Y,t+T}) = \rho_Y^{T+1} \cdot u_{Y,t-1}. \tag{41}$$

The right-hand-side of equation (40) then gives the conditional variance of $\varepsilon_{Y,t+T}$ given $u_{Y,t-1}$.

As in the data lag case, the central bank may be able to do better—i.e., to achieve a smaller conditional variance of $\varepsilon_{Y,t+T}$—by taking account of the information in the most recent values of the appropriate irrelevant variables. The parameters of the dynamic structural model, together with the autocorrelation structure of that model's disturbances, will imply an information procedure analogous to that of equations (30) to (32). Just as the length of the data lag determines which of the conditional variances in equations (39) and (40) is smaller given values of the other parameters involved, the length of the structural lag will similarly determine which of the two analogous procedures is superior.

6. THE INDICATOR PROBLEM

The concept of an indicator of monetary policy—defined so as not to be identical with targets or instruments or intermediate targets, all in the senses applied above—is one of the more elusive ideas of recent monetary economics.[26] This confusion remains, despite the voluminous literature devoted to the indicator question during the past decade.

---

25. In dynamic policy problems it is typical also to employ an additional parameter, a time-preference discounting factor, to evaluate the importance for current policy decisions of expected effects in future time periods.

26. See Saving (1967) for a clear explanation of the rationale for requiring that the indicator and the target be distinct. Sargent (1970) denied that the indicator problem as such even exists; his statement is in the spirit of the argument developed in this section.

Brunner and Meltzer (Brunner 1969, p. 2) defined the *indicator problem* as "the problem of constructing a scale that is invariant up to a monotone transformation and that provides a logical foundation for statements comparing the thrust of monetary policy." Elsewhere Brunner and Meltzer (1967, p. 187) they said that the monetary policy indicator, in their sense of the term, "summarizes in an index the relative degree of monetary ease or restraint." The clearest application of this indicator variable concept is the case in which the central bank seeks to control one target variable (say Y, as above) and has several instrument variables at its disposal for doing so. As in the analysis above, a reduced-form equation relates variable Y to the monetary policy instrument variables, as well as to all other exogenous and lagged endogenous variables in the system. The Brunner-Meltzer monetary policy indicator is then a weighted index of all the monetary policy instrument variables, with each variable's weight equal (or proportional) to its coefficient in the reduced-form equation for variable Y.

Several problems emerge immediately, however, upon any attempt to apply this indicator index concept to a generalized monetary policy framework.

First, such an index ignores any exogenous factors, other than monetary policy, that may influence the target variable. At some levels this direct focus of the indicator index is useful; if the central bank shifts policy in an expansionary way so as to offset the expected effects of a new contractionary fiscal policy, it is useful to be able to say that monetary policy has become expansionary, even if the expected final outcome for target variable Y remains unchanged. At other levels, however, this direct focus becomes misleading. If the central bank uses only one instrument variable, as in the analysis of sections 2-4, the Brunner-Meltzer indicator index is simply a linear transformation of the instrument variable itself. It may be argued that, in a realistic view of the monetary policy process, the true instrument variable involved in open market operations is the stock of securities in the portfolio of the System Open Market Account; yet it is not very useful to have an indicator index that records monetary policy as being expansionary if the central bank sells securities because of some movement of float, Treasury deposits in Federal Reserve Banks, or the gold stock. Indeed, the basic principle underlying Roosa's (1956) delineation of "dynamic" and "defensive" open-market operations is that it is useful to be able to talk about monetary policy in a way that abstracts from—that is, makes allowance for—certain nonpolicy exogenous influences.

While it is probably clear that a good indicator of the "thrust" of monetary policy should abstract from offsetting float but should not abstract from offsetting fiscal policy, these two examples represent the extremes of the category of exogenous influences. The actual list of such exogenous influences, equivalent to vector z in the model used in sections 1-4, includes a number of factors, such as financial market events, that lie between these two extremes. Drawing the line between those exogenous factors from which the indicator should abstract and those from which it should not is a necessary step in deriving a Brunner-Meltzer indicator index; and any such index depends fundamentally upon the particular line drawn. The problem is that the actual "thrust" of a monetary policy instrument variable typically proceeds toward the target variable by a transmission process that successively incorporates a number of exogenous and endogenous influences, and the choice of indicator variable is in part a choice of the particular point of that process at which the thrust is to be measured.

Second, nonlinear economic relationships lead to particular difficulties in defining a Brunner-Meltzer indicator index.[27] If the structure of the system is nonlinear, the system has no reduced form comparable to equations (5') or (7') above. In particular, in a nonlinear system the derivatives of Y with respect to the monetary policy instrument variables, which would be the coefficients of these variables in the reduced-form equation for Y if it did exist, are not constant but instead depend on the values of all the variables in the system. Since these derivatives are the

27. The analysis of sections 2-4 relies exclusively on linear models. Generalizing that analysis to a nonlinear system would preclude the convenience of the reduced form and would therefore render the algebra more complex, but it would not significantly change the key conclusions derived. By contrast, the problem here is of a different order, since a consistently defined Brunner-Meltzer indicator index becomes a logical contradiction in the context of a nonlinear system.

weights of the monetary policy instrument variables in the Brunner-Meltzer indicator index, the composition of the index itself is not invariant but depends on the values of all variables in the system.[28]

Third, as Chase (1967) has noted, the Brunner-Meltzer indicator index, constructed as described above, has the intended meaning only in the context of a policy framework with a unique target variable.[29] If, in the context of an expanded model, the central bank sought, for example, to maximize income Y while minimizing price inflation ΔP, then there would be two relevant reduced-form equations—one for Y and one for ΔP. Any given monetary policy instrument variable would enter both of these reduced-form equations, but with different coefficients in each. What would be the weights of the instrument variables in the indicator index in this case? Brunner and Meltzer suggested solving this problem by, first, computing two individual subindicator indices by the usual procedure of weighting each instrument variable by its derivative (coefficient) in the respective reduced-form equations for Y and ΔP and, second, computing the overall indicator index by weighting each such subindicator by the respective derivatives of Y and ΔP in the central bank's preference function.

Wholly apart from any difficulties that may be involved in identifying the cental bank's preference function, this overall indicator index for the two-variable case fails to meet its intended purpose for several related reasons. Even if the economic relationships in the system are linear, use of a nonlinear preference function would render the weighting of the overall indicator index dependent on the values of variables Y and ΔP. Perhaps

---

28. Note that a similar logical problem arises, even in a linear model, if the coefficients of the monetary policy instrument variables in the structural model are uncertain. See Goldberger, Nagar, and Odeh (1961) for the derivation of the variance-covariance matrix of the coefficients of a derived reduced form.

29. Again, the analysis of sections 2-4 proceeds in the context of the unique target variable Y, but extension to multiple target variables is straightforward. By contrast, the problem here is of a different order, involving a logical inconsistency.

more importantly, such an overall indicator index, weighted by the preference function derivatives with respect to variables Y and ΔP, could not support even ordinal inferences about monetary policy associated with concepts such as "easy-tight," "expansionary-contractionary," or "inflationary-deflationary."[30] Given its construction as suggested by Brunner and Meltzer, this overall indicator index could only support inferences associated with concepts such as "good-bad" or "appropriate-inappropriate."

Especially since all of these problems plague an attempted identification of a monetary policy indicator, it is appropriate to confront the basic question of whether having such an indicator is necessary or useful at all. The answer probably depends upon whom the indicator is presumed to serve.

The central bank itself is unlikely to find a monetary policy indicator useful. Sections 1-4 outline a targets-and-instruments conceptual framework for monetary policy decision making in the presence of additive uncertainty.[31] Use of such a framework by the central bank would require no specific indicator of monetary policy in the sense used here. The central bank must work through the various steps of the decision-making procedure, including the selection of instrument variables and the potential use of irrelevant variables for information purposes. Once having done so, the central bank has no need of a specific monetary policy indicator index.[32]

---

30. As the analysis above indicates, there is some ambiguity involved in associating cardinal inferences with the Brunner-Meltzer indicator index for a one-target case, but ordinal inferences may be unambiguous with only one target. In fairness to Brunner and Meltzer, it is appropriate to note that the context in which they originally suggested the indicator index was the question of accurancy of statements involving ordinal inferences.

31. See, e.g., Brainard (1967) and Zellner (1971, chap. 11) for a general treatment of the problems introduced by multiplicative uncertainty. B. Friedman (Federal Reserve Bank of Boston 1972, pp. 178-84) specifically illustrated the use of the targets-and-instruments framework for monetary policymaking in the presence of multiplicative uncertainty.

32. Saving (1967, p. 450) argued that the central bank would need such an indicator variable if it operated on the basis of an intermediate target

Market participants typically have their own reasons for wanting to know what actions the central bank is taking and what effects these actions are likely to have. These reasons are usually quite specific, however, and they therefore make the identification of the appropriate indicator a less ambiguous undertaking. In particular, a market participant's reasons for wanting an indicator of the "thrust" of monetary policy typically define the point at which that thrust should be measured. A market-maker in six-month Treasury bills, for example, is interested less directly in the likely implications of open market operations for income and price inflation than in the likely implications of these operations for the path of the six-month Treasury bill yield. His optimal monetary policy indicator, therefore, is the set of dynamic expected values of this yield which emerge as irrelevant variables in application of the targets-and-instruments framework outlined above. As is the case for the central bank, no simple shortcut can take the place of working through the steps of the analysis.

Finally, a broad range of observers want to monitor monetary policy for less specific reasons, ranging from political concern to intellectual curiosity. Many persons in this category lack the necessary time or tools for examining the several conceptual steps of the policymaking framework outlined above. Some indicator index of the thrust of monetary policy would probably be a useful summary tool for this group. The purpose of this paper is not to derive such a convenient index for popular usage but rather to point out that, should such a device be constructed, it has no significant role to play in the central bank's formulation of monetary policy.

---

variable: "Essentially, the policy-maker requires a separation of the change in his [intermediate] target variable into a policy effect and an exogenous effect. Since observation of the changes in the [intermediate] target variable yields only the total effect, some other variable or combination of variables is required to reflect the policy effect." In the context of the targets-and-instruments framework, however, the central bank's best estimate of the "policy effect" on any endogenous variable--including irrelevant variables used as intermediate target variables--is simply the movement in the instrument variable multiplied by the appropriate reduced-form coefficient.

7. CONCLUSIONS

Relying on a targets-and-instruments formulation of the monetary policy problem, this paper first clarifies certain confusions and inconsistencies that have plagued several attempts to apply control methodologies to monetary policy. Again using the targets-and-instruments structure, it then analyzes the basic issues involved in previous discussions of monetary policy in terms of a targets-and-indicators conception; much of the targets-and-indicators literature has itself been somewhat confused, if not at times positively opaque. In both efforts the targets-and-instruments analytical device makes it possible to identify the key issues involved and to understand the source of previous problems.

In particular, the results of the analysis of this paper support the following five specific conclusions.

(1) As Poole and others have shown, the instrument problem is nontrivial in the presence of uncertainty and merits the serious attention of monetary policymakers.

(2) The two-stage conception of the monetary policy process, which is familiar both in the recent monetary economics literature and in the Federal Reserve System's own descriptions of its operating procedures, contains several internal inconsistencies. Furthermore, given a targets-and-instruments policy planning framework as outlined here, this two-stage conception does not contribute to the efficiency of monetary policymaking. In its planning, therefore, the central bank would do better to abandon this two-stage conception and simply apply the targets-and-instruments framework directly to the monetary policy problem as a whole.

(3) Use of a specific noninstrument variable (such as the money stock) as an intermediate target variable does not in general constitute optimal central bank operating procedure. An alternative procedure for using irrelevant (in Tinbergen's sense) variables to gain information is always superior to the intermediate target variable procedure, except under very restrictive conditions that render the two procedures identical. In its operations, therefore, the central bank should "look at everything" in a particular way that yields the maximum useful information and should avoid relying on a particular intermediate target variable.

(4) Contrary to the impression given by some of the previous literature, this problem of information may arise not only in the context of lags in the receipt of data but also in the context of a structural lag by which monetary policy actions affect the ultimate targets of policy. Improvements in facilities for reporting data on policy targets will be useful for monetary policy but will not eliminate the need to use other variables for information purposes.

(5) The concept of an indicator of monetary policy is beset with ambiguities, but this intellectually unfortunate situation presents no problem for monetary policymakers. While some observers outside the central bank might find such an indicator useful if the conceptual ambiguities were resolved, the indicator would not contribute to the efficiency of monetary policymaking.

REFERENCES

Andersen, L. C., and Carlson, K. M. 1970. "A Monetarist Model for Economic Stabilization." Federal Reserve Bank of St. Louis REVIEW 52 (Apr.): 7-25.

Andersen, L. C., and Jordan, J. L. 1968. "Monetary and Fiscal Actions: A Test of Their Relative Importance in Economic Stabilization." Federal Reserve Bank of St. Louis REVIEW 50 (Nov.): 11-24.

Ando, A.; Brown, E. C.; Kareken, J.; and Solow, R. M. 1963. "Lags in Fiscal and Monetary Policy." In STABILIZATION POLICIES. Commission on Money and Credit. Englewood Cliffs, N.J.: Prentice Hall.

Ando, A. and Modigliani, F. 1965. "Velocity and the Investment Multiplier." AMERICAN ECONOMIC REVIEW 55 (Sept.): 693-728.

Axilrod, S. H. 1971. "Monetary Aggregates and Money Market Conditions in Open Market Policy." Federal Reserve BULLETIN 57 (Feb.): 79-104.

Brainard, W. C. 1967. "Uncertainty and the Effectiveness of Policy." AMERICAN ECONOMIC REVIEW 57 (May): 411-25.

Brunner, K., ed. 1969. TARGETS AND INDICATORS OF MONETARY POLICY. San Francisco: Chandler.

Brunner, K., and Meltzer, A. H. 1967. "The Meaning of Monetary Indicators." In MONETARY PROCESS AND POLICY, edited by G. Horwich. Homewood, Ill.: Richard D. Irwin.

Cagan, P., and Gandolphi, A. 1969. "The Lag in Monetary Policy as Implied by the Time Pattern of Monetary Effects on Interest Rates." AMERICAN ECONOMIC REVIEW 59 (May): 277-84.

Chase, S. B., Jr. 1967. "Comments." In MONETARY PROCESS AND POLICY, edited by G. Horwich. Homewood, Ill.: Richard D. Irwin.

Davis, R. G. 1969. "How Much Does Money Matter? A Look at Some Recent Evidence." Federal Reserve Bank of New York MONTHLY REVIEW 51 (June): 119-31.

_____. 1971. "Short-run Targets for Open Market Operations." In OPEN MARKET POLICIES AND OPERATING PROCEDURES. Staff Studies. Washington, D.C.: Board of Governors of the Federal Reserve System.

_____. 1972. "Estimating Changes in Deposits with Reduced-form Equations." Mimeographed. New York: Federal Reserve Bank of New York.
_____. 1973. "Implementing Open Market Policy with Monetary Aggregate Objectives." Federal Reserve Bank of New York MONTHLY REVIEW 55 (July): 170-82.
de Leeuw, F. 1965. "A Model of Financial Behavior." In THE BROOKINGS QUARTERLY ECONOMETRIC MODEL OF THE UNITED STATES, edited by J. Duesenberry et al. Chicago: Rand McNally.
de Leeuw, F., and Gramlich, E. 1968. "The Federal Reserve-MIT Econometric Model." Federal Reserve BULLETIN 54 (Jan.): 11-40.
_____. 1969. "The Channels of Monetary Policy." Federal Reserve BULLETIN 55 (June): 472-91.
de Leeuw, F., and Kalchbrenner, J. 1969. "Monetary and Fiscal Actions: A Test of Their Relative Importance in Economic Stabilization—Comment." Federal Reserve Bank of St. Louis REVIEW 51 (Apr.): 6-11.
De Prano, M., and Mayer, T. 1965. "Tests of the Relative Importance of Autonomous Expenditures and Money." AMERICAN ECONOMIC REVIEW 55 (Sept.): 729-52.
Dewald, W. G. 1963. "Free Reserves, Total Reserves, and Monetary Control." JOURNAL OF POLITICAL ECONOMY 71 (Apr.): 141-53.
Evans, M. K., and Klein, L. R. 1968. THE WHARTON ECONOMETRIC FORECASTING MODEL. 2d ed. Philadelphia: University of Pennsylvania.
Farr, H. T.; Roberts, S. M.; and Thomson, T. D. 1972. "A Weekly Money Market Model." Mimeographed. Washington, D.C.: Board of Governors of the Federal Reserve System.
Federal Reserve Bank of Boston. 1969. CONTROLLING MONETARY AGGREGATES. Boston: Federal Reserve Bank of Boston.
_____. 1972. CONTROLLING MONETARY AGGREGATES II: THE IMPLEMENTATION. Boston: Federal Reserve Bank of Boston.
Friedman, B. M. 1971. "Tactics and Strategy in Monetary Policy." In OPEN MARKET POLICIES AND OPERATING PROCEDURES. Staff Studies. Washington, D.C.: Board of Governors of the Federal Reserve System.
_____. 1975. ECONOMIC STABILIZATION POLICY: METHODS IN OPTIMIZATION. Amsterdam: North-Holland.
Friedman, M. 1959. A PROGRAM FOR MONETARY STABILITY. New York: Fordham University Press.
_____. 1961. "The Lag in the Effect of Monetary Policy." JOURNAL OF POLITICAL ECONOMY 69 (Oct.): 447-66.
_____. 1968. "The Role of Monetary Policy." AMERICAN ECONOMIC REVIEW 58 (Mar.): 1-17.
Friedman, M., and Meiselman, D. 1963. "The Relative Stability of Monetary Velocity and the Investment Multiplier in the United States, 1897-1958." In STABILIZATION POLICIES. Commission on Money and Credit. Englewood Cliffs, N.J.: Prentice-Hall.
_____. 1965. "Reply to Ando and Modigliani and to De Prano and Mayer." AMERICAN ECONOMIC REVIEW 55 (Sept.): 753-85.
Friedman, M., and Schwartz, A. J. 1963. A MONETARY HISTORY OF THE UNITED STATES, 1869-1960. Princeton: Princeton University Press.

Goldberger, A. S.; Nagar, A. L.; and Odeh, H. S. 1961. "The Covariance Matrices of Reduced-form Coefficients and of Forecasts for a Structural Econometric Model." ECONOMETRICA 29 (Oct.): 556-73.

Guttentag, J. M. 1966. "The Strategy of Open Market Operations." QUARTERLY JOURNAL OF ECONOMICS 80 (Feb.): 1-30.

Hamburger, M. J. 1970. "Indicators of Monetary Policy: The Arguments and the Evidence." AMERICAN ECONOMIC REVIEW 60 (May): 32-39.

_____. 1971. "The Lag in the Effect of Monetary Policy: A Survey of Recent Literature." Federal Reserve Bank of New York MONTHLY REVIEW 53 (Dec.): 289-98.

Hendershott, P. H. 1968. THE NEUTRALIZED MONEY STOCK. Homewood, Ill.: Richard D. Irwin.

Hendershott, P. H., and Horwich, G. 1969. "Money, Interest, and Policy." In SAVINGS AND RESIDENTIAL FINANCING, edited by D. P. Jacobs and R. T. Pratt. Chicago: United Savings and Loan Association.

Hicks, J. R. 1937. "Mr. Keynes and the Classics: A Suggested Interpretation." ECONOMETRICA 5 (Apr.): 147-59.

Holbrook, R. S. 1972. "Optimal Economic Policy and the Problem of Instrument Instability." AMERICAN ECONOMIC REVIEW 62 (Mar.): 57-65.

Holbrook, R. S., and Shapiro, H. 1970. "The Choice of Optimal Intermediate Economic Targets." AMERICAN ECONOMIC REVIEW 60 (May): 40-46.

Holt, C. C. 1962. "Linear Decision Rules for Economic Stabilization and Growth." QUARTERLY JOURNAL OF ECONOMICS 76 (Feb.): 20-45.

Kareken, J. 1970. "The Optimal Monetary Instrument Variable." JOURNAL OF MONEY, CREDIT AND BANKING 2 (Aug.): 385-90.

Kareken, J.; Muench, T.; Supel, T.; and Wallace, N. 1971. "Determining the Optimum Monetary Instrument Variable." In OPEN MARKET POLICIES AND OPERATING PROCEDURES. Staff Studies. Washington, D.C.: Board of Governors of the Federal Reserve System.

Kareken, J.; Muench, T.; and Wallace, N. 1973. "Optimal Open Market Strategy: The Use of Information Variables." AMERICAN ECONOMIC REVIEW 63 (Mar.): 156-72.

Kaufman, G. G. 1967. "Indicators of Monetary Policy: Theory and Evidence." NATIONAL BANKING REVIEW 4 (June): 1-11.

Modigliani, F.; Rasche, R.; and Cooper, J. P. 1970. "Central Bank Policy, the Money Supply and the Short-term Rate of Interest." JOURNAL OF MONEY, CREDIT AND BANKING 2 (May): 166-218.

Parkin, M. 1973. "Optimal Monetary and Fiscal Policy Rules in a Static Stochastic Economy." Paper presented at the Fourth Konstanz Seminar on Monetary Theory and Policy, Konstanz, West Germany, June.

Pindyck, R. S., and Roberts, S. M. 1974. "Optimal Policies for Monetary Control." ANNALS OF ECONOMIC AND SOCIAL MEASUREMENT 3 (Jan.): 207-37.

Poole, W. 1970. "Optimal Choice of Monetary Policy Instruments in a Simple Stochastic Macro Model." QUARTERLY JOURNAL OF ECONOMICS 84 (May): 197-216.

_____. 1971. "Rules-of-Thumb for Guiding Monetary Policy." In OPEN MARKET POLICIES AND OPERATING PROCEDURES. Staff Studies. Washington, D.C.: Board of Governors of the Federal Reserve System.

Poole, W., and Lieberman, C. 1972. "Improving Monetary Control." Brookings Papers on Economic Activity 4, no. 2, pp. 293-335.
Rao, C. R. 1965. LINEAR STATISTICAL INFERENCE AND ITS APPLICATIONS. New York: John Wiley.
Rasche, R. H. 1973. "Simulations of Stabilization Policies for 1966-1970." JOURNAL OF MONEY, CREDIT AND BANKING 5 (Feb.): 1-25.
Roosa, R.V. 1956. FEDERAL RESERVE OPERATIONS IN THE MONEY AND GOVERNMENT SECURITIES MARKETS. New York: Federal Reserve Bank of New York.
Sargent, T. J. 1970. "Discussion." AMERICAN ECONOMIC REVIEW 60 (May): 57-58.
Saving, T. R. 1967. "Monetary-Policy Targets and Indicators." JOURNAL OF POLITICAL ECONOMY 75 (Aug.): 446-56.
Shupp, F. R. 1972. "Uncertainty and Stabilization for a Nonlinear Model." QUARTERLY JOURNAL OF ECONOMICS 86 (Feb.): 94-110.
Simon, H. A. 1956. "Dynamic Programming under Uncertainty with a Quadratic Criterion Function." ECONOMETRICA 24 (Jan.): 74-81.
Starleaf, D. R., and Stephenson, J. A. 1969. "A Suggested Solution to the Monetary-Policy Indicator Problem: The Monetary Full Employment Interest Rate." JOURNAL OF FINANCE 24 (Sept.): 623-41.
Theil, H. 1957. "A Note on Certainty Equivalence in Dynamic Planning." ECONOMETRICA 25 (Apr.): 346-49.
_____. 1964. OPTIMAL DECISION RULES FOR GOVERNMENT AND INDUSTRY. Amsterdam: North-Holland.
Thomson, T. D.; Pierce, J. L.; and Parry, R. T. 1975. "A Monthly Money Market Model." JOURNAL OF MONEY, CREDIT AND BANKING 7 (Nov.): 411-31.
Tinbergen, J. 1956. THE THEORY OF ECONOMIC POLICY. Amsterdam: North-Holland.
Zecher, R. 1970. "Implications of Four Econometric Models for the Indicators Issue." AMERICAN ECONOMIC REVIEW 60 (May): 47-54.
Zellner, A. 1971. AN INTRODUCTION TO BAYESIAN INFERENCE IN ECONOMETRICS. New York: John Wiley.

OPTIMAL CONTROL AND SHORT-TERM MONETARY POLICY DECISIONS*

Robert H. Rasche

Michigan State University

In recent years monetary policy in the United States has been increasingly concerned with the behavior of monetary aggregates and their role in aggregate economic stabilization. This represents a transition from the more traditional concern about "money market conditions," that is, short-term interest rates, free reserves, and the like. The transition has been a slow and rather groping process. First, for the 1970-71 period, the emphasis was on obtaining a target value for the money stock by conducting open-market operations to attain federal-funds-rates values that were believed consistent with the money-stock target.[1] This policy was revised in January-February 1972, and currently directives are given to the Federal Reserve System manager in terms of a value of reserves available to support private deposits (RPD's), which value is believed to be consistent with the target path of the money stock.[2]

During 1972, the Federal Open Market Committee (FOMC) kept its target growth path for the money stock virtually unchanged, emphasizing more or less moderate growth in response to recent past growth paths (Jordan 1973, p. 14). At the same time, as illustrated by figure 1, the observed deviations of the money stock from a trend growth appear to have generated sizeable fluctuations in the directives given the System manager for reserve growth.

---

* An earlier version of the paper was presented at the 1973 Konstanz Seminar.

1. The first public indication of this shift of emphasis is reported in "Record of Policy Actions of the FOMC" for the meeting of February 10, 1970 (Federal Reserve *Bulletin*, May 1970, pp. 441-42).

2. See "Record of Policy Actions of the FOMC" for the meetings of January 11 and February 15, 1972 (Federal Reserve *Bulletin* , Apr. 1972, p. 394; May 1972, pp. 459-60).

Figure 1

Reserves Available to Support Private Nonbank Deposits

Operating Target and Actual Growth 1

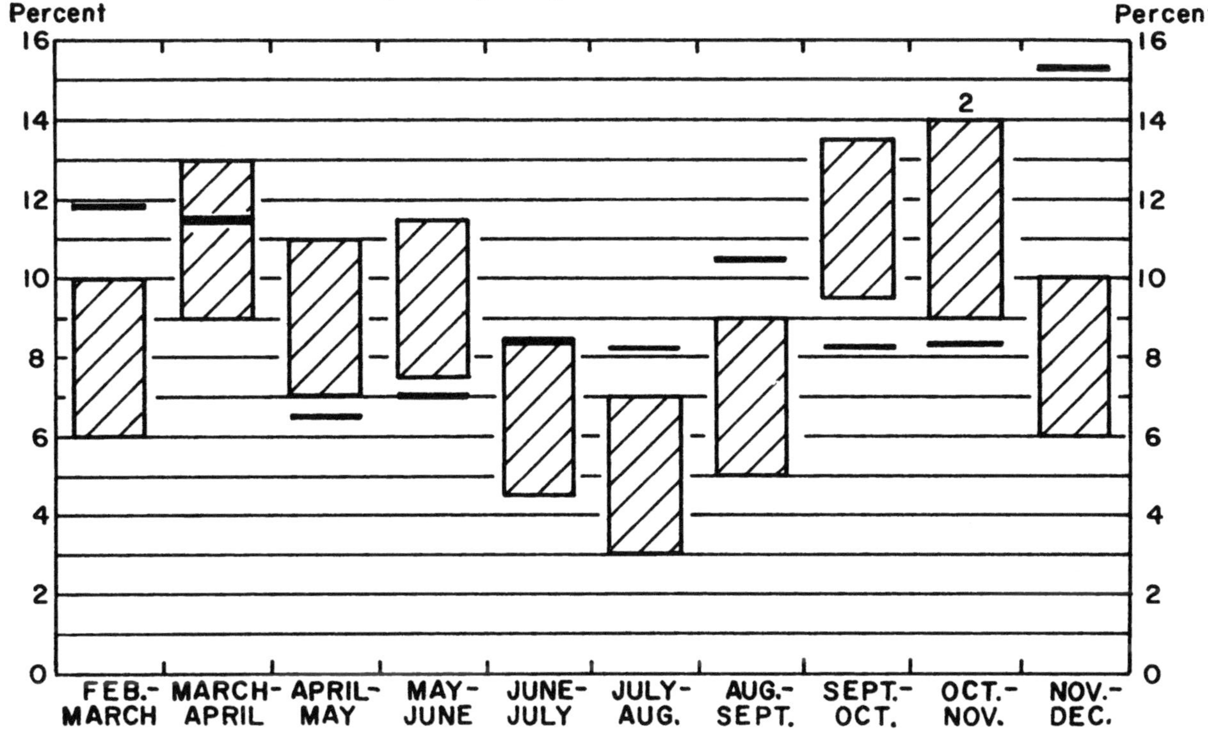

The purpose of this paper is to develop some implications of an optimal control model for the appropriate response of monetary policy in terms of desired reserve growth in short-run situations where the underlying policy goals are not revised but when deviations, either of a stochastic nature, or because of short-run forecasting errors, are observed. Section 1 discusses the use of optimal control models in the recent literature on the conduct of monetary policy and relates this to the established discussion on intermediate policy targets. Section 2 discusses the nature of the decision problem facing monetary policymakers in the short run. Finally, section 3 indicates a model for dealing with the decision problem and develops a reaction strategy for policymakers.

1. OPTIMAL CONTROL MODELS FOR ANALYSIS OF MONETARY POLICY

Recent research into the conduct of monetary policy has attempted to apply some elementary principles of optimal control theory to the problems confronting monetary policymakers in a world of uncertainty. The analysis typically has posed the problem of an expected-loss function, usually restricted to one argument such as real income that reflects the "ultimate goal" of macroeconomic stabilization policy. The expected loss to be minimized is subject to a static system of linear stochastic constraints. This framework has been used, for example, by Poole (1970, 1972) in two pioneering pieces in which he discusses the choice of a monetary aggregate versus an interest rate as the instrument of policy control. In a more recent piece (Poole and Lieberman 1972), he has extended the analysis to consider the monetary base as the alternative instrument to an interest rate. Pierce and Thomson (1973) have used a similar framework in their empirical discussion of the issue of reserve instruments versus interest-rate instruments, though not without some significant oversights (Rasche 1972).

These developments have tended to eclipse or ignore the long-standing controversy known as the targets-and-indicators issue (Brunner and Meltzer 1967; Saving 1967). In particular, the control theory approach seems to imply that the issue of intermediate target variables is irrelevant to the whole question of the optimal setting of the control variables.

The approach taken in the present analysis is to attempt to reinstate the intermediary target for policymakers within the optimal control discussion. Monetary policy decisions, at least as presently formulated in the United States, are reconsidered at very frequent intervals, generally once every four weeks. Within the span of time between FOMC meetings, it is possible that little if any information will become available on the "ultimate goal" variable of macroeconomic stabilization policy. For example, GNP data are generated only once every quarter, so approximately three FOMC meetings will pass before any new information becomes available. Data on prices, unemployment, and industrial production are compiled on a monthly basis in the United States, but the earliest release figures are frequently subject to extensive revisions and thus do not provide much reliable information over short time horizons. This observational lag on the variables that policymakers desire to control is one of the chief justifications for the use of intermediate target variables (Saving 1967).

Another limitation of the control theory analyses cited above is that they are framed in the context of static models. Thus the time horizon over which the planning period extends is not defined, and no provision can be made for feedback from policy decisions in one period to the environment in which decisions will be made in the later part of the planning period.

The dynamic analysis with which we shall be concerned will be confined to periods of sufficiently short duration that the policymakers will not observe, or should not think that they are observing, independent information that would cause them to revise their policy objective, that is, their intermediate target setting. On the other hand, within this period of time they will observe deviations of the actual target values from their desired settings because of short-term events that are represented by the stochastic component of the decision model. The question remains how to revise the instrument settings in response to these observed deviations.

2. THE LOSS (OBJECTIVE) FUNCTION

The above discussion indicates that the goal of the policymakers should be to minimize the expected loss generated by deviations of the intermediate target variables from some predefined optimal values over a finite number of decision periods (T). Within this time span, T periods, it is assumed that insufficient information will be available to warrant a change in the desired setting of the intermediate target variables.

What is the intermedite target? For purposes of this analysis, we shall choose the narrowly defined money stock, M_1. This appears to be consistent with present short-run objectives of monetary policy in the United States (Federal Reserve *Bulletin*, Apr. 1972). Following Poole (1972, p. 173), we find it preferable to state the target in terms of changes of the money stock over the planning periods.

One other element has to be introduced into the decision process. In modern control theory literature it is common to consider a penalty associated with changing the settings of the control variable. In terms of the monetary policy discussion, this means that it is not costless in terms of the policymakers' objectives to alter the policy instrument settings. In the policy literature, this issue has, unfortunately, been neglected. In the United States at least, policy is currently made within the historical context of attempts to stabilize, or damp out, very short-run fluctuations in short-term interest rates (or more generally, money-market conditions). To my knowledge, the rationale for the historical concern in relation to aggregate stabilization has never been clearly exposited, with the exception, perhaps, of the now-discredited free-reserves doctrine. On the other hand, this concern could be justified on microeconomic grounds; namely, aggregate stabilization policies must be conducted subject to the constraint that the policymakers do not "disrupt" the markets in which they intervene. The legitimacy of this concern depends on the empirical questions of how well financial markets could absorb short-run variation—that is, how large an increase in risk premiums would be necessary to compensate for the increased short-term variance—and of the stabilizing or destabilizing nature of speculative activity. Pitifully little attention has been given to either of these issues in domestic financial markets, and little more in foreign exchange markets, where the same questions are also crucially important for current policy discussions.

Therefore, the loss function that U.S. policymakers are visualized as seeking to minimize can be stated as

$$W = -E \sum_{t=1}^{T} \omega_1(\Delta \ln M_t - \gamma)^2 + \omega_2(\Delta \ln r_t)^2, \tag{1}$$

where M_t = money stock at end of period t,

r_t = short-term interest rates during period t, and

ω_1, ω_2 are the relative weights attached, respectively, to deviations of the change in the money stock from its desired change period (γ) and to the change in interest rates.

First, note that both of the arguments, M and r, enter in log form, so that the first differences are effectively percentage changes. For the money stock, this has the important property of making the expected loss independent of the size of the economy. In addition, as we shall see below, it allows us to state the constraints on the minimization process in linear form and use in straightforward fashion some recently developed control results.

Second, note that we have not assigned any explicit values to the weights ω_1 and ω_2. Since the interest-rate term is included because of a short-run constraint on policymakers, we can consider the differential reaction of weak versus strong constraints by examining the behavior of the optimal policy in response to variations in the size of the ratio ω_1/ω_2.

Third, it should be noted that we have restricted ourselves to considering loss functions without interaction terms (i.e., terms involving the product of $\Delta \ln r_t$ and $\Delta \ln M_t$). This implies that we do not allow any indirect cost of or compensation from a large deviation of one of the variables that is associated with a large deviation of the other variable.

3. A MULTIPERIOD MODEL OF THE CONTROL PROBLEM

The model that we shall assume as the framework within which monetary policymakers plan their decisions consists of two equations:

$$\ln M_t = \alpha_0 + \alpha_1 \ln Y_t + \alpha_2 \ln r_t + \alpha_3 \ln r_{t-1} + \varepsilon_t, \tag{2}$$

$$\ln M_t = \beta_0 + \beta_1 \ln R_t + \beta_2 \ln r_t + \nu_t, \tag{3}$$

where $\alpha_1, \beta_1, \beta_2 > 0$, and

$$\alpha_2, \alpha_3 < 0.$$

This model can be taken as a representation of the "money market" models that have become common in recent econometric representations of the determination of short-term interest rates and the money stock. The first equation is representative of the demand for cash balances by the nonbank public. The demand is specified as a function of some measure of economic activity, Y_t, such as GNP, household wealth, or industrial production, all of which have been used in at least one econometric study. At this point, the appropriate activity argument is not controversial for the conclusions of our analysis. Y_t can be considered as a vector representation with both income and wealth elements. Second, demand is represented as a function of both current and lagged interest rates. It is through the r_{t-1} term that control decisions of one period impinge upon the environment for future control decisions. This specific dynamic representation was chosen because it commonly appears in econometric results, and the presence of lagged-interest-rate effects has allegedly given the Federal Reserve System difficulties in monetary control in the recent past (Federal Reserve *Bulletin* , Aug. 1971).

The second equation specifies the money-supply process and represents the money stock as a function of some reserve aggregate, R_t, and current interest rates. Again, for the purpose of our discussion, it is irrelevant just which reserve magnitude is to be represented by R_t. In the current U.S. policy context, R_t can be thought of as representing reserves available to support private deposits. Note that if the reserve elasticity, β_1, were assumed equal to unity, then the money-supply process would represent the reserve-multiplier approach with the provision that the multiplier could be interest-elastic. Also note that the analysis could be expanded to introduce into equation (3) an impact of the discount rate, but this has been omittted in the interest of simplicity.

Finally, we must recognize that Y_t is not known with certainty, either for the time contemporaneous to the policy decision or for any of the future periods of the planning horizon. Rather, we assume that policymakers generate forecasts of $\ln Y_t$, denoted as $\ln Y^f_t$, and we assume that the forecasts are unbiased and that the forecast errors $(\ln Y_t - \ln Y^f_t)$ are homoskedastic and not serially correlated.[3] Thus equation (2) can be rewritten as

$$\ln M_t = \alpha_0 + \alpha_1 \ln Y^f_t + \alpha_2 \ln r_t + \alpha_3 \ln r_{t-1} \tag{4}$$
$$+ [\varepsilon_t + \alpha_1(\ln Y_t - \ln Y^f_t)]$$
$$= \alpha_0 + \alpha_1 \ln Y^f_t + \alpha_2 \ln r_t + \alpha_3 \ln r_{t-1} + u_t.$$

Finally, equations (3) and (4) can be transformed by taking first differences, yielding:

$$\Delta \ln M_t = \alpha_1 \Delta \ln Y^f_t + \alpha_2 \Delta \ln r_t + \alpha_3 \Delta \ln r_{t-1} + \Delta u_t, \tag{5}$$

and

$$\Delta \ln M_t = \beta_1 \Delta \ln R_t + \beta_2 \Delta \ln r_t + \Delta v_t. \tag{6}$$

The control problem facing the monetary policymakers is to minimize equation (1), subject to the linear restrictions imposed by equations (5) and (6), conditional upon the forecasts of economic activity over the planning horizon, $\Delta \ln Y^f_1, \ldots \Delta \ln Y^f_t$. The solution to this type of problem and its application to economic models has been the subject of a number of recent studies by Chow (1970; 1972*a*, *b*). He has shown that optimal control is provided by a linear feedback rule and has developed a scheme for computing the coefficients of the control rule for each period. The computations for the above model are developed in the mathematical appendix available from the author.

---

3. These restrictions postulate quite enlightened forecasters. All could be relaxed, but only at the cost of making the mathematics more tedious.

Originally it was planned that this paper would consider a three-period planning horizon that arises naturally in the context of monthly open-market committee meetings when many economic indicators are available only on a quarterly basis. The problem proved so messy that the fundamental results were being obscured by the algebra. Hence the results presented below deal with only a two-period planning horizon, but the general form of the results extends to a longer planning horizon.

The Chow result on optimal control in a model such as that of equations (1), (5), and (6) states that

$$X_t = G_t Y_{t-1} + g_t, \tag{7}$$

where X_t is a vector of the control settings, in our case the single element $\Delta \ln R_t$; and Y_{t-1} is a vector of the controlled (state) variables, in our case

$$\begin{bmatrix} \ln M_{t-1} \\ \ln r_{t-1} \end{bmatrix}.$$

The G_t matrix and g_t vector are computed according to the formula in Chow (1972*b*) as:

$$G_1 = \left[0, \left(\frac{\alpha_3}{\beta_1}\right)\left(1 - \frac{R'}{1 + \frac{\omega_2}{\omega_1} T^2}\right)\right], \tag{8}$$

$$g_1 = \left(\frac{\alpha_1}{\beta_1}\right)\left(1 - \frac{R'}{1 + \frac{\omega_2}{\omega_1} T^2}\right)\Delta \ln Y_1^f - \left(\frac{\alpha_1}{\beta_1}\right)\left(\frac{\frac{1}{\alpha_2}\frac{\omega_2}{\omega_1} TR'}{1 + \frac{\omega_2}{\omega_1} T^2}\right)\Delta \ln Y_2^f \tag{9}$$
$$+ \left(\frac{\gamma_1}{\beta_1}\right)\left(\frac{R'}{1 + \frac{\omega_2}{\omega_1} T^2}\right)\left(1 + \frac{1}{\alpha_2}\frac{\omega_2}{\omega_1} T\right),$$

$$G_2 = \left[0, \left(\frac{\alpha_3}{\beta_1}\right)(1 - R')\right], \tag{10}$$

$$g_2 = \left(\frac{\alpha_1}{\beta_1}\right)(1 - R')\Delta \ln Y_2^f + \frac{\gamma_1}{\beta_1} R', \tag{11}$$

where $R' = \dfrac{\alpha_2\omega_1(\alpha_2 - \beta_2)}{\omega_1\alpha_2^2 + \omega_2} \geq 0$, and

$$T = \frac{\omega_1\alpha_3}{\omega_1\alpha_2^2 + \omega_2} \leq 0 .$$

For convenience define R'' as $\dfrac{R'}{1 + \dfrac{\omega_2}{\omega_1} T^2}$, $\quad 0 \leq R'' \leq R'$.

Now, substituting (8) and (9) into (7) gives the optimal control rule for the first period, conditional upon the observed lagged change in interest rates:

$$\Delta \ln R_1^* = \left(\frac{\alpha_3}{\beta_1}\right)(1 - R'')\Delta \ln r_0 + \left(\frac{\alpha_1}{\beta_1}\right)(1 - R'')\Delta \ln Y_1^f \tag{12}$$

$$- \left(\frac{\alpha_1}{\beta_1}\right)\left(\frac{1}{\alpha_2}\right)\left(\frac{\omega_2}{\omega_1}\right) TR'' \Delta \ln Y_2^f$$

$$+ \left(\frac{\gamma_1}{\beta_1}\right) R''\left(1 + \frac{1}{\alpha_2}\frac{\omega_2}{\omega_1} T^2\right).$$

Substitution of (10) and (11) into (7) gives the optimal control rule for the second period, conditional upon the projected interest-rate change, $\Delta \ln \hat{r}_1$, under the optimal control policy during the first period:

$$\Delta \ln R_2^* = \left(\frac{\alpha_3}{\beta_1}\right)(1 - R')\Delta \ln \hat{r}_1 + \left(\frac{\alpha_1}{\beta_1}\right)(1 - R')\Delta \ln Y_2^f + \frac{\gamma_1}{\beta_1} R'. \tag{13}$$

Several things are immediately apparent from equations (12) and (13). The first is that the only initial condition that enters into the control settings is that on the interest rate. Since the lagged money stock does not enter into either the demand equation or the money-supply mechanism, its initial value is irrelevant in setting the control for the future changes.

Second, in addition to depending on the various elasticities, the nature of the control response will depend crucially on the synthetic variables R' and T. It is important to give some kind of interpretation of these variables. Suppose that $\omega_2 = 0$, so the loss function weights only deviations of the changes in the money stock from the desired change and is unconcerned with changes in interest rates. Under these assumptions $R' = (1 - \alpha_2/\beta_2) > 1$; α_2/β_2 measures the feedback effect on the money stock of a shock to the money-demand function that occurs through changes in current interest rates. The direction of this feedback effect is opposite that of the original shock. The interpretation of, say, equation (13) under these assumptions is clear. For given expected shocks through the money-demand function, $\alpha_3 \Delta \ln \hat{r}_1$ and $\alpha_1 \Delta \ln Y^f_2$, the larger the internally generalized feedback on changes in the money stock (represented by a larger R'), the smaller will be the required adjustment of the reserve setting, $\Delta \ln R^*_2$, from the setting that would be made in the absence of any projected shocks from the money-demand side, $\gamma_1/\beta_1 R'$. Note that, in the absence of any projected shocks from the money-demand side, changes in the reserve control variable would have to be larger as the negative feedback through the interaction of the money-demand and -supply equations is larger. At the other extreme, assume $\omega_1 = 0$ and $R' = R'' = 0$. Under this assumption—that all that matters in the loss function is interest rates—equations (12) and (13) become:

$$\Delta \ln R^*_1 = \left(\frac{\alpha_3}{\beta_1}\right) \Delta \ln r_0 + \left(\frac{\alpha_1}{\beta_1}\right) \Delta \ln Y^f_1, \tag{14}$$

and

$$\Delta \ln R^*_2 = \left(\frac{\alpha_3}{\beta_1}\right) \Delta \ln r_1 + \left(\frac{\alpha_1}{\beta_1}\right) \Delta \ln Y^f_2. \tag{15}$$

The coefficients in these two equations are just the negative of the ratios of the coefficients of $\Delta \ln r_{t-1}$, $\Delta \ln R$, $\Delta \ln Y_t$, and $\Delta \ln R$ in the reduced-form interest-rate equation. Hence the reserve control policy under these circumstances is to offset any influence on interest rates through projected shocks to the money-demand function.

In the general case, we have allowed for both interest-rates changes and money-stock deviations to enter the policymakers' loss function, and so the actual R' formula represents a weighting of the interest-rate stabilization effect and the money-change target in such a way as to equate the marginal loss of interest-rate changes and money-stock deviations for the specified weighting matrix.

The nature of the optimal reserve control formula for the first period of the planning span, $\Delta\ln R_1^*$, is of course considerably more involved in all but the interest-rate stabilization case. Consider the polar case where only money-stock deviations enter the loss function. In this case R' is greater than unity, and the larger the forecasted change in the activity variable in the second period, $\Delta\ln Y_2^f$, the lower the change in the reserve control in that period, $\Delta\ln R_2^*$. The control mechanism would withhold reserves and drive up interest rates to offset positive shocks to the money stock from projected increases in economic activity. The response of $\Delta\ln R_1^*$ to an equal projected change in activity in the first period would be smaller. Changes in interest rates caused by the withholding of reserves in that period would drive up interest rates, which would have to be offset by changes in the control setting in the second period. Thus, in the presence of the lagged-interest-rate effect, the response of the control setting to given projected shocks would be smaller the earlier these shocks occur in the planning period.

The forecast at the beginning of the planning horizon of shocks to the money-demand function in future periods suggests an unambiguous response in terms of the control setting. The larger the forecasted shock, $\alpha_1\,\Delta\ln Y_2^f$, the smaller should be the change in the control setting, $\Delta\ln R_1^*$. In this case we are involved with an intertemporal trade-off. All else equal, the smaller injection of reserves will produce higher current interest rates and is likely to increase the expected loss in the first period both because of interest-rate changes and because of money-stock deviations. On the other hand, higher interest rates today (first period) will produce a larger offsetting shock to the forecasted activity stimulus and thus will lower the expected change in interest-rate and money-stock deviation in the second period. If either ω_2 or ω_1 is zero, so that one or the other source of expected loss is of no concern, then this intertemporal trade-off goes to zero, since either the interest-rate change or the money-stock change in the second period can be allowed to accommodate whichever variable enters the loss function. The moral of this story is that, in the framework in which we have chosen to investigate the policymaking problem, intertemporal trade-offs are important only if the policymakers are concerned with both interest-rate and money-stock changes. In the case in which interest-rate changes don't matter, $\omega_2 = 0$, the control rule for the first period, as expressed in equation (12) reduces to

$$\Delta \ln R_1^* = \left(\frac{\alpha_3}{\beta_1}\right)(1 - R')\Delta \ln r_0 + \left(\frac{\alpha_1}{\beta_1}\right)(1 - R')\Delta \ln Y_1^f + \left(\frac{\gamma_1}{\beta_1}\right)R', \qquad (16)$$

which is exactly the same form as the control rule for the second period, equation (13). The symmetry result for the opposite extreme, $\omega_1 = 0$, has already been shown in equations (15) and (16).

The question that remains unanswered is in which direction the control setting responds at each point in time as different shocks to the system are assumed. The question cannot be answered without prior knowledge of the relative weights on changes in the interest rates and the money-stock changes in the loss function. This will determine the sign of $1 - R'$ and $1 - R''$. For a policymaker with relatively high aversion to deviations from the desired money-stock change, both $1 - R'$ and $1 - R''$ will be negative; thus, the more expansionary the environment, the smaller will be the reserves supplied to the system in all periods. At the other end of the spectrum, R' and R'' are both zero; so, the more expansionary the environment, the larger would be the reserves supplied to the system if a reserve control policy were maintained. It is likely that for this structure, as with the structure investigated in Rasche (1972), there is some point beyond which increasing aversion to interest-rate changes causes an interest-rate control policy to dominate a reserve control policy, almost regardless of the size of the elasticities of the various equations. It remains to be investigated whether the region where $1 - R'$ becomes positive is ever a feasible region, in the sense that reserve control would dominate an interest-rate control policy.

Even if $1 - R'$ is negative, so that the response of the control setting in the second period to changes in economic activity are offsetting in terms of the money stock, it is still possible that $1 - R''$ is positive, so that the reaction of the control setting in the first period would be the opposite. Again, this involves the trading of expected loss in the first period for expected loss in the second and is likely to occur only when the elasticity of the lagged-interest-rate term in the money-demand function is extremely high.

Finally, how should policymakers respond in adjusting the control setting in the second period when stochastic shocks or forecasting errors in the first period cause the observed changes in interest rates and the money stock to differ from their expected values? First, suppose that there is an observed deviation from the desired change in the money stock in the first period. From equation (13) it can be seen, given the particular specification of the model, that there should be no revision of the control setting, $\Delta \ln R_2^*$, for the second period. This contrasts sharply with the observed behavior of the U.S. monetary policymakers during 1972, of sharply changing the control setting from month to month. Could such sharp changes be consistent with an optimal control scheme if there were concern about interest-rate changes and deviations from the original projection of the first-period interest-rate change? In equation (13) it is difficult to evaluate the magnitude of $1 - R'$. At the money-stock-only extreme, $1 - R' = \beta_2/\alpha_2$, which is greater than unity if the interest elasticity of the money-supply relationship (reserve multiplier) is smaller in absolute value than the impact interest elasticity of the money-demand function. My own prejudice is that this is true, but some empirical results suggest the opposite. Even if $1 - R'$ could range from around -1.0 all the way to +1.0 (the value in a loss function in which only the interest rate matters), it appears in equation (13) multiplied by the ratio α_3/β_1. This is the ratio of the lagged-interest elasticity of the money-demand function to the reserve elasticity of the money-supply relationship, and I know of no studies that suggest that this ratio is very large. Hence it seems safe to conclude that the adjustment elasticity of the reserve control setting to observed deviations from the previous period's targetted interest-rate change should be relatively small.

The above is an attempt to analyze some of the characteristics of an optimal control rule for short-run monetary policy decisions under structures that are commonly postulated in empirical analysis. So far we have only been able to analyze the control rule under the assumption that a reserve control policy is optimal. Other work with static models (Rasche 1972) suggests that such control procedures will be dominated by interest-rate control procedures if the relative weight on interest-rate changes in the policymaker's loss function, ω_2/ω_1, is sufficiently high. The limits to dominant range for reserve control remain to be investigated for the dynamic model. Once this analysis is completed, more precise results should be achievable on the nature of the optimal control response.

REFERENCES

Brunner, K., and Meltzer, A. H. 1967. "The Meaning of Monetary Indicators." In MONETARY PROCESS AND POLICY, edited by G. Harwick. Homewood, Ill.: Richard D. Irwin.

Chow, G. C. 1970. "Optimal Stochastic Control of Linear Economic Systems." JOURNAL OF MONEY, CREDIT AND BANKING 2 (Aug.): 291-302.

_____. 1972 a. "Optimal Control of Linear Econometric Systems with Finite Time Horizon." INTERNATIONAL ECONOMIC REVIEW 13 (Feb.): 16-25.

_____. 1972 b. "How Much Could Be Gained by Optimal Stochastic Control Policies?" ANNALS OF ECONOMIC AND SOCIAL MEASUREMENT 1: 391-405.

Jordan, J. L. 1973. "FOMC Policy Actions in 1972." St. Louis Federal Reserve Bank REVIEW, March, pp. 10-23.

Pierce, J. L., and Thomson, T. D. 1973. "Some Issues in Controlling the Stock of Money." In CONTROLLING MONETARY AGGREGATES 11. Boston: Federal Reserve Bank of Boston, pp. 115-36.

Poole, W. 1970. "Optimal Choice of Monetary Policy Instruments in A Simple Stochastic Macro Model." QUARTERLY JOURNAL OF ECONOMICS 84 (May): 197-216.

_____. 1972. "Rules of Thumb for Guiding Monetary Policy." In OPEN MARKET POLICIES AND OPERATING PROCEDURES. Staff Studies. Washington, D.C.: Board of Governors of the Federal Reserve System, pp. 137-89.

Poole, W., and Lieberman, C. 1972. "Improving Monetary Control." BROOKINGS PAPERS ON ECONOMIC ACTIVITY 4, no. 2, pp. 293-342.

Rasche, R. H. 1972. "Criteria for the Choice of Operating Instruments for Open Market Policy." Michigan State Econometrics Workshop Paper 7206. Mimeographed.

Saving, T. R. 1967. "Monetary Policy Targets and Indicators." JOURNAL OF POLITICAL ECONOMY 75 (Aug.): 446-65.

RECENT EXPERIENCES WITH MONETARY POLICY IN THE FEDERAL REPUBLIC OF GERMANY*

Helmut Schlesinger

Member of the Directorate of the Deutsche Bundesbank

In recent years monetary policy has become a focus of interest in the economic policy field. This is partly because of the renaissance of monetary theory but mainly due to the worldwide acceleration of inflationary trends. In all Western countries it has become more and more urgent to resist these trends for the sake of maintaining our free economic and social systems. At the same time, other instruments of economic policy (fiscal policy, prices-and-incomes policy) have seemed less and less able to cope with the outstanding problems. In the Federal Republic of Germany there has been the additional feature that the Bundesbank, from the spring of 1973 onward, was given new, enlarged room for maneuver by the transition to floating. In this connection, commentators have often spoken of a "new monetary policy." Personally, I regard this as an overstatement. The final goals and policy instruments are, after all, just the same as ever. What we have done is formulate an interim goal for and pay more attention to the movement of central-bank money.

The special role of monetary policy in the fight against inflation, but also its responsibility for inflationary trends, is attributable to the fact that its starting point is a necessary, though not in itself a sufficient, condition of inflation—namely, an over-large expansion of the money stock in relation to the real scope for production. No matter what it is that triggers price rises, inflation cannot continue in the medium run without a corresponding expansion of the money stock, because the range of money substitutes available to the economy is limited and variations in the velocity of circulation of money are small in the medium term.

---

* An earlier version of the paper was presented at the 1976 Konstanz Seminar. A version in German was published in KREDIT UND KAPITAL 9 (1976): 433-54.

In modern times money is a liability of banks—the central bank as well as the commercial banks—and thus is created by a credit transaction. Yet the two sources of money are not of equal importance from the point of view of economic policy: the commercial banks cannot create money unless central-bank money is supplied, since such money creation is normally accompanied by an increase in currency in circulation and, in countries like Germany with minimum reserve requirements, by an increase in compulsory deposits with the central bank. The dominating role of the central bank in the money-creation process depends on its monopoly of the creation of central-bank money. This role can only be played effectively, however, if the central bank has its own money creation under control, that is, if it is not obliged to create central-bank money against its will—for example, by having to finance government deficits, intervene in the exchange market, or maintain a particular level of interest rates in the credit markets (to mention only a few of these subordinate functions, which, unfortunately, have become principal functions for many central banks around the world).

BASIC CONDITIONS FOR MONETARY POLICY

Lending to the government—the classical instance of the involuntary creation of central-bank money—has not so far been of any great significance in the Federal Republic. Our monetary system contains major safeguards against this abuse of the power to create money, as is readily understandable, considering the historical background of two government-financed inflations. The Bundesbank is permitted to grant direct loans to the Federal and Länder Governments only in limited amounts and only for short periods. Purchases of government securities might be regarded as indirect lending, but this is allowed only for monetary reasons (i.e., for the purpose of regulating bank liquidity) and not for financing deficits, although a sharp distinction is not always possible in this case.

For a long time the main obstacle to effective monetary policy was the Bundesbank's obligation to intervene in favor of the U.S. dollar. This was tantamount to an obligation to create any amount of actual or potential central-bank money as soon as the dollar had reached its lower intervention point. At times, the foreign exchange inflows assumed proportions large enough to undermine any systematic restrictive credit policy such as would have been appropriate to the cyclical situation, with an accelerating rate of price rises. Numerous attempts were made to neutralize the expansion of bank liquidity, but it was virtually impossible to offset the simultaneous increase in money in the hands of the general public.

Not until the transition to floating in March 1973 was the Bundesbank able to control the money stock in accordance with domestic needs. It is therefore not surprising that this transition coincided with the above-mentioned turning point in monetary policy. True, the obligation to intervene in favor of the U.S. dollar did not disappear without a trace but was succeeded by compulsory intervention under the European narrower-margins arrangement. Hence our autonomy in this respect is far from complete even today. In general, however, the inflows of foreign exchange resulting from the joint float have not been so large as to be unmanageable by compensatory control of the money stock. On the other hand, the monetary unrest of February and March 1976, when the Bundesbank had to take in "snake" currencies amounting to almost DM9 billion, showed that this intervention system also may easily become an obstacle to effective monetary policy.

THE BASIC INSTITUTIONAL CONDITIONS FOR MONETARY POLICY IN THE FEDERAL REPUBLIC OF GERMANY

As part of its restrictive policy in 1973-74, the Bundesbank thought it necessary almost to eliminate the banks' free liquid reserves, that is, their liquid assets that can be converted into central-bank money at any time, such as money-market paper and unused rediscount quotas. Free liquid reserves give the banks a kind of "autonomous expansion potential," a quasi-automatic right to draw on central-bank money. The size of the free liquid reserves is thus in a sense indicative of the length of the reins by which the Bundesbank is leading the banks. During the period of restriction, the reins had to be kept very tight in order for the Bundesbank's policy to be effective, for the Bank had found that since the beginning of the '70s the banks were no longer responding to a reduction in their free liquid reserves by changing their lending policies, in contrast to their previous behavior. In particular, it could no longer be certain that the banks regarded the holding of a certain minimum amount of free liquid reserves as indispensable.

A bank's decision to grant additional credit depends, after all, not on its stock of "free liquid reserves"—that is, on its holdings of rediscountable bills and other assets assignable to the Bundesbank at any time--but primarily on its assessment of its internal liquidity. This covers a much wider range of liquid assets, including short-term claims on other banks at home and abroad—that is, assets that banks are able to create autonomously and that can expand without being restricted by reserve requirements applying to the debtor. Significantly, such internal liquidity grew much more than the "free liquid reserves" between 1970 and 1972, and particularly between 1973 and 1975. The banks' assessment of their liquidity, however—like that of any economic agent—is governed not only by the size of their liquid assets relative to their liabilities but also by the extent to which liquidity can be obtained by borrowing, in addition to the utilization of liquid assets. The expansion of the domestic and foreign interbank money market—the Euro-currency market alone increased in volume by 2 1/2 times between the end of 1970 and the end of 1973 (Bank for International Settlements, 1975, p. 81)--was bound to reinforce the view that liquidity problems hardly existed. Hence it was essential to make clear to domestic banks the only limit to their expansion that they cannot determine themselves, namely, the shortage of central-bank money. The Bundesbank realized that it would not be able to do so simply by reducing the "free liquid reserves" to near zero but that it would be necessary to set a signal that all banks, irrespective of their liquidity assessment, understand--namely, a steep increase in the cost of central-bank credit. Even then the Bank was prepared to supply funds through the instruments of "special lombard loans" and short-term open-market operations in bills under repurchase agreements, though only at rates that reached 16 percent at the peak. Such a policy was conditional on the reduction of the free liquid reserves to near zero; this was virtually accomplished in March 1973.

When later on the Bundesbank tried to stimulate the money-creation process, it permitted--indeed, deliberately encouraged--the accumulation of free liquid reserves in order to enhance monetary growth. This policy, which lasted until the spring of 1976, gave rise, however, to some theoretical misunderstandings. The policy of accumulating liquid reserves is not incompatible with the "near zero liquidity ratio." Free liquid reserves are not essential to the smooth working of the credit system; their very existence in Germany is in large part due to basic institutional conditions of historical origin and characteristic of the German monetary system. There are, of course, countries that show that the banks' money creation can be controlled relatively well without free liquid reserves (the United States, Switzerland). But there are even more countries that prove that free rein can be given to inflationary monetary expansion without free liquid reserves; in these cases the central bank meets directly any demand that may arise for central-bank money.

It is, of course, understandable that some of those who have studied monetary theory with main reference to the U.S. literature do not do full justice to the German concept of free liquid reserves. It is overlooked, for instance, that even today in Germany the central bank's foreign exchange transactions are a much more important determinant of the banks' central-bank balances than they are in the United States. If intervention is compulsory, such transactions may result in central-bank balances' increasing far more than can be corrected by the instruments of fine tuning in Germany—that is, by open-market operations with nonbanks and, in the case of long-term securities, also with banks. Hence we continue to need instruments of coarse tuning--above all, changes in minimum reserve requirements and rediscount quotas—to neutralize sharp rises in banks' central-bank balances where necessary or, conversely, to provide banks with additional resources in the event of massive foreign exchange outflows. But some time elapses before such coarse instruments can be used. During this period the free liquid reserves act as a buffer: they rise or fall temporarily, but without these short-term movements necessarily being very significant. The longer-term size of the free liquid reserves is, however, a matter of strategic importance. One might characterize the Bundesbank's policy in this field since 1972 by saying that it now considers the margin for the acceptable size of the free liquid reserves in the somewhat longer run to be much smaller than it used to.

A TARGET FOR MONETARY GROWTH

The Bundesbank first set and publicly announced a quantitative target for monetary policy--an increase of about 8 percent in central-bank money in the course of 1975--in December 1974. Considering the situation at the time this target was fixed, this decision meant that the Bank was aiming at a certain acceleration of monetary expansion, for the growth of central-bank money up to then had been smaller. On the other hand, this figure was intended to make it clear that the Bank was envisaging further progress in the fight against inflation. The target was based on the recognition that in the medium term there is a close correlation between monetary expansion and the movement of national expenditure and that monetary policy is in a position, or must do its utmost to be in a position, to achieve the target set. We pointed out that the setting of a target for the growth of central-bank money was an experiment. We mentioned that the money stock cannot be guided precisely along a predetermined path, particularly not in the short run. Nevertheless, the formulation of a quantitative target for monetary policy appeared to us to be an important step toward putting economic policy decisions on a more rational basis, by bringing to the attention of all those involved in economic activity the limited scope for central-bank money creation compatible with stability. The overriding aim is, after all, to coordinate the decisions of the economic groups more effectively, to work more efficiently toward steady economic growth, and to reduce the necessity for correcting undesirable trends by massive countermeasures that may involve the danger of going too far. Needless to say, monetary policy has no influence on whether and to what extent the monetary framework it has marked out is used to expand production or to raise prices and costs. Whether the expansion takes the form of a growth in production at relatively stable prices or a price boom or a mixture of both depends in large part on the stance adopted by the government and on the social groups. But as the monetary growth target tends to act as a signpost, the pressure to exercise cost and price discipline is likely to grow. Indeed, experience even permits the conclusion that the formulation of this target helped to bring about a "social consensus" among all groups, even though other factors may have contributed more to this consensus.

The setting and announcement of the monetary growth target—and, indeed, the general aims of monetary policy as reflected in the decision of December 1974—met with widespread approval. By and large the decision was understood, and accepted, as we had hoped it would be. This approval, together with experiences in 1975, encouraged the Bundesbank to fix a growth target for central-bank money for 1976 as well. This target, unlike that for 1975, was formulated in terms of the average increase over the year. The change in central-bank money from month to month is subject to chance fluctuations; hence, if a target for year-on-year growth is chosen, temporary influences that in themselves are of little significance may affect the result more strongly than is likely if a target for average growth over a year is selected. For example, the fact that central-bank money rose by 10 percent between the end of 1974 and the end of 1975, and not by 8 percent as envisaged, was largely due to heavy government borrowing from banks towards the end of the year—excessively heavy, in fact, as it subsequently transpired, in relation to the government's financial needs. Since this borrowing, and thus the monetary expansion, distinctly slackened later on, a December-to-December comparison overstates the underlying trend of monetary expansion for 1975. In 1976 the Bundesbank's aim is that the average level of central-bank money over the year shall be 8 percent higher than the average for 1975; since in December 1975 it was already 5.4 percent above the latter level, its growth in the course of 1976 must be within narrow limits if it is not to overstep the mark again, as it did in the previous year. So far growth has been on the envisaged path.

QUANTIFICATION OF THE MONEY-STOCK TARGET

A question that often arises in the debate on money-stock targets is: Which economic facts should be used as a basis when fixing the monetary growth rate? Our answer to this question is pragmatic; that is, it depends on economic conditions at the time the target is formulated and those expected for the year ahead and on the associated general objectives of economic policy. In other words, we--unlike some purists in this field—do not consider it possible to disregard the position of the economy in the cycle and to release monetary policy from its anticyclical function.[1] On the other hand, monetary policy must no longer see itself exclusively as an instrument of anticyclical action; it must attach more importance than it used to to medium-term aspects, in order to exploit the opportunity to reduce cyclical swings.

When calculating the quantitative target, the Bundesbank took the following four primary factors into account: the expected growth of production potential, the expected change in the utilization of this potential, the rate of unavoidable price rises, and the expected change in the velocity of circulation.

The target does not necessarily become wrong if the growth possibilities are not fully utilized in the short run. Conversely, monetary growth does not have to be regarded as too rapid simply because the economy is using all the available capacity sooner than anticipated. In both cases the crucial question is: To what extent is this deviation of capacity utilization from the expected figure being offset by a corresponding deviation of the velocity of circulation? To clarify this point, the cyclical behavior of the velocity of circulation may be recalled.

There can be no doubt that the velocity of circulation fluctuates with the movement of the cycle, declining in a recession and increasing again in an upswing. Judging from past experience, its growth in periods of upswing is slower than its decrease in recession phases. It would be premature to regard this observation as a law, but there is reason to believe that the velocity of circulation will not increase in 1976 as much as it diminished in 1975. This, like the velocity of circulation as a whole, is not an autonomous phenomenon but to a large extent reflects the movement of the cycle. In

---

1. Claus Köhler (1976, p. 10) is of the same opinion: "The task of economic policy is not only to keep economic developments at the growth rate predetermined by the increase in production potential but also to remedy any undesirable trends. This means that deviations of the degree of utilization from normal utilization and unavoidable price rises are to be taken into account."

many respects it forms a parallel to the change in the utilization of the production potential, which is considered a yardstick of the movement of the cycle.

As a result of this common, albeit not quite identical, dependence on the business cycle of the utilization of the money supply and the utilization of production potential, the correct forecasting of the movement of the cycle is not so very important for determining the money-stock target. Wrong forecasts of the degree of utilization and the velocity of circulation may have the same cause, and the consequences of these wrong forecasts will cancel each other out, as it were. If there is an unforeseen setback (and a decline in the utilization of production potential), as in 1975, the available money stock is used less and the velocity of circulation falls; and the money stock target is correct after all. Conversely, if in 1976 the real national product grows more than initially expected, this need not be a reason for expanding the money stock more than originally planned, since the velocity of circulation can also be expected to increase more than anticipated. (In the event of such deviations it will, however, be necessary after some time to check whether they do largely cancel each other out, as assumed, and what the implications are for the future.)

Hence, in the last analysis only two variables are decisive for determining the target: the growth of production potential and the rate of unavoidable price rises. While production potential can be extrapolated "objectively" without much difficulty, the "rate of unavoidable price rises" naturally contains a "voluntaristic" element. The latter variable indicates that, on the one hand, price rises cannot be checked completely within twelve months (particularly as an annual average) after a high rate of increase in the previous year and that, on the other hand, great effort must be made to slow the growth rate. The other two variables—changes in the degree of utilization of production potential and changes in the velocity of circulation—also have to be taken into account, but with the qualification that,while these factors are difficult to forecast, the impact of mistakes in such forecasts is, as mentioned, limited.

Another question that had to be answered when setting the money-stock target was whether just one figure or a range between two figures should be chosen. An argument against choosing a single figure as the monetary growth target is that this gives monetary policy an appearance of precision that it can hardly live up to in practice. A range between two figures might prevent illusions in this respect. But considering that the purpose of the target, as explained before, is to make monetary intentions clear to all those involved in economic activity, the announcement of a range of figures would blur these intentions. If the target is expressed in the form of an annual average, which leaves a certain leeway in the course of the year, it is particularly advisable to select one figure instead of a range. If, however, the target is formulated in terms of the growth during a certain period, a range may be preferable.

CENTRAL-BANK MONEY AS THE TARGET

The Bundesbank is often asked why it selected central-bank money as the target and not one of the conventional definitions of the money stock such as M_1 (currency in circulation and sight deposits) or M_2 (M_1 plus time deposits for up to four years) or M_3 (M_2 plus savings deposits at statutory notice). Central-bank money in the Bundesbank's definition comprises currency in circulation and the minimum reserves maintained by the banks on their domestic liabilities. The fact that it does not include monetary assets in accordance with their purchasing power--this is true only of currency in circulation—but merely contains certain percentages of the banks' liabilities probably contributed to the misunderstandings to which the choice of this target was initially subject.

The Bundesbank thought it advisable for a number of reasons to base the formulation of its monetary growth target on central-bank money. It was strengthened in this resolve both by recent experience with monetary policy and by considerations of principle. Our recent experience with monetary policy may be outlined as follows.

If we could assume that the relationship between the various concepts of the money stock was fairly constant, that is, that all of these concepts supplied similiar information on monetary developments, the choice of a particular "definition" would be a matter of secondary importance. But this is not the case, as the last few years have shown. As a result of shifts in deposits due to differences in interest rates, the movements of M_1 and M_2 have diverged almost continuously since the middle of 1973. In 1975, for example, M_1 went up by over 13 percent, whereas M_2 declined slightly on balance. Judging from M_2, the policy of monetary expansion was far too weak, while M_1 tended to exaggerate the impact of monetary policy. In the case of M_1 the link with the expansionary measures of the Bundesbank was also apparent, but at best the direction (not, however, the size) of the interest-induced shifts was predictable; there could, accordingly, be no question of using M_1 or M_2 as the monetary growth target.

With a broad definition of the money stock, such as M_3, it would be possible to eliminate interest-induced shifts between sight deposits and time deposits or between savings deposits and time deposits. But the more broadly the money stock is defined, the further away one moves from the assumed relationship between the expansion of the money stock and the incease in demand for goods and services. On the other hand, the shifts cannot be ignored altogether. It has to be acknowledged that there is no clear-cut dividing line between money and other financial assets but only areas of declining "degrees of moneyness." This fact seemed to us to be adequately taken into account by the concept of central-bank money, in which the relative "weights" of sight, time, and savings deposits are 4:3:2. This weighting results from the differing sizes of the minimum reserve ratios, which are graduated in the manner stated, in accordance with the degree of liquidity of the deposits. This presumably makes better allowance for the "moneyness" of the deposits—at least in trend—than would a simple addition, as in M_3, where the weighting is 1:1:1 (although here, savings deposits for fixed periods are not included at all). In the end, admittedly, the movement of central-bank money does not differ very greatly from that of M_3: in 1975 a growth of 10 percent in central-bank money compared with a rise of 8.5 percent in M_3.

Finally, central-bank money is also superior to the other definitions of the money stock in terms of its statistical basis, since it is calculated from average figures during a month and is available more quickly. Of course, central-bank money is not a satisfactory monetary indicator in every respect. For instance, the great weight attached to currency in circulation may lead to distortions if this component is subject to special influences. Up to now, however, such swings have mostly corrected themselves after a few months. To sum up, it can be said that the decision as to the "right" money-stock concept was taken, not in the light of a formal or legal criterion, but only in the light of analytical and empirical expediency. Thus, in this case we are following the advice of authorities like Milton Friedman and Anna Schwartz (1970, p. 91), who said on the definition of money: "the selection . . . seems to us to be a matter of convenience for a particular purpose, not a matter of principle."

THE INDICATOR PROBLEM

The choice of central-bank money as a monetary target commends itself to a central bank for another reason, too: it brings out its monetary responsibility particularly clearly. The money creation of the banks and that of the central bank are, as already mentioned, inextricably linked through currency in circulation and the banks' obligation to keep a certain percentage of their deposits on account at the central bank as minimum reserves. Thus, central-bank money in the Bundesbank's definition shows, on the one hand, how large the banks' money creation was and, on the other hand, the extent to which the central bank supported this money creation. That the concept of central-bank money is in this respect Janus-faced—serving both as target and as indicator of monetary policy—is partly to blame for a misunderstanding that has apparently not yet been cleared up. The Bundesbank interprets central-bank money as an indicator of the monetary expansion that has already taken place, that is, as a money-stock concept sui generis. But many economists see central-bank money as the monetary base and use it as a supply-oriented indicator, that is, as an indicator of the stimuli generated by monetary policy: "Monetary *policy* is adequately described by the expansion of the quantity of central-bank money that the central bank makes available as the basis for monetary expansion" (German Council of Economic Experts, Annual Report 1974/75, para. 173; italics added). I shall revert to this supply-theory approach later on. But it is surely beyond dispute that, if the definition is based on the uses of central-bank money, criticism that central-bank money is not suitable for supply-theory approach is beside the point.[2]

The different indicator functions assigned to central-bank money/monetary base by these contrasting theoretical schools of thought have implications for the assessment of the success of monetary policy and for the question of the controllability of this monetary aggregate. Success is by definition directly visible in the Bundesbank's aggregate; this is, as noted, a money-stock concept, namely, the reflection in the central bank's balance sheet of the money held by the public. In the policy indicator monetary base, on the other hand, an attempt is made to show the stimulus imparted by monetary policy. But the success of the policy must be assessed by reference to other aggregates— M_1, M_2, or M_3. Thus, the problem of the multiplier arises as an additional difficulty.

In my view, the matter of primary interest is the measurement of the success of the policy, as revealed by the monetary aggregates and thus, also, by central-bank money. It is therefore only logical to use one of these aggregates for the formulation of the monetary policy target. The scope left to the banks for autonomous expansion is, of course, also of interest, as is the question of the stimulus that this may have on the monetary expansion process.

In the Federal Republic of Germany, as already indicated, a part is played in this connection by a particular category of assets, namely, "potential" central bank money, or the sum total of bank assets that can be

---

2. Needless to say, a different theory may—indeed, is bound to—arrive at a different definition of central-bank money or the monetary base. The inclusion or noninclusion of excess reserves in the definition is therefore not merely a question of expediency but a reflection of different basic theoretical positions. See Council of Economic Experts, Annual Report 1974/75, para. 382.

sold direct to the Bundesbank at any time and without major loss. These free liquid reserves mainly consist of the banks' portfolios of commercial bills readily discountable at the Bundesbank within the unutilized rediscount quotas, and eligible money-market paper. The free liquid reserves also include the excess reserves—that is, central-bank balances in excess of the required reserves—which to this extent constitute "actual" central-bank money. The "free liquid reserves" delimit the banks' autonomous for creating money, in contrast to the stock of central-bank money as defined by us, which has already been "absorbed" in a completed money-creation process.[3]

Another reason why this distinction has proved very useful is that it brings out the fact that transactions by the Bundesbank do not affect the central-bank money stock directly but—to take foreign exchange purchases as an example—initially only augment the banks' central-bank *balances*. Unless these balances are required to meet the cash needs of the public or to comply with reserve requirements on new domestic liabilities incurred by the banks, this does not result in a rise in central-bank money. Instead, the banks, which are traditionally in debt to the Bundesbank, reduce this debt, thus enlarging their rediscounting facilities, or acquire assets that they can resell to the Bundesbank if necessary, thereby increasing the "free liquid reserves."

THEORY AND PRACTICE OF MONEY-STOCK CONTROL

Just as central-bank money in our definition differs from the "monetary base"—the uses of central-bank money versus its supply—views on the control of the monetary base are not necessarily applicable to the control of central-bank money. The proponents of monetary-base theory teach that the money base, being part of the central bank's balance sheet, can obviously be controlled directly by the central bank. Should the central bank be under constraints with regard to particular transactions, this can, they claim, be offset by compensatory changes in other balance sheet items--above all, through open-market operations.

---

3. Lombard credit constitutes a special problem. If lombard credit is limited neither in quantity nor via the interest rate (e.g., by the interest rate rising with use of the credit), this opens up an additional means of ready access to central-bank money—a means that cannot, however, be delimited in quantitative terms.

Implicit in this claim is the assumption that the central bank ban be free from external constraints in controlling the monetary base. In a theory for a central bank, however, one must not disregard the fact that it is, after all, the central bank and bears a special responsibility for the monetary and banking system of the country—a responsibility that it has to meet even if it has to fight inflation at the same time. The argument that the central bank is on balance able to achieve the desired result with the monetary base at virtually any time thus does not come to grips with the real problem, which is that the central bank cannot do so at absolutely any time becasue this may disrupt the financial markets. On the basis of German conditions, a sharp distinction must be drawn between short-term and longer-term relationships. In the short run, the banks' demand for central-bank money, once it has arisen, is inelastic, and the banks must be able to satisfy it. The central bank may have no alternative to temporarily creating more monetary base than is consistent with its objectives. The central bank must not overstrain the capacity of the economy to adjust, particularly as long as it adheres strictly to one hundred percent compliance with the minimum reserve requirements; and it must respect the fact that the banks themselves are merely intermediaries, so that not only they but also their customers have to adjust. In the very short run, therefore, the central bank is obliged to meet the deficit of central-bank money. But the way it does so and, particularly, the price it charges—these, of course, are questions of monetary policy par excellence.

Short-term control of the monetary base also comes up against limits when an expansionary policy is being pursued. If domestic money creation is to be stimulated because monetary expansion appears to be too weak, more monetary base than currently required can be made available. Under the German system, this normally means the creation of free liquid reserves; it does not mean the creation of non-interest-bearing excess reserves in the banking system, as is sometimes recommended to us by those who fail to appreciate the institutional differences from the U.S. system. In my view, there is no reason to take a particularly negative view of this. Excess reserves create a permanent glut in the money market; the marginal cost of funds to banks goes down toward zero percent. There is no denying that this exerts a strong monetary stimulus—indeed, a stronger one is hardly conceivable; and it may well be that this stimulus proves too strong, so that a correction in the other direction soon takes place. Sharper fluctuations in short-term interest rates than really necessary, and perhaps also greater variations in the size of the monetary base, seem to me possible and are observable in countries without free liquid reserves. Under the German system, the free liquid reserves act as a cushion. On the other hand, the thicker the cushion, the more a contractionary measure is absorbed and the longer a stimulus and particularly a curb takes to make an impact; hence the authorities try from the outset to keep the cushion thin. Both *without* free liquid reserves, as in the United States, and *with* reserves, as in Germany, it has been found that in the very short run the monetary base cannot be controlled at will, that in the very short run the above-described constraints are operative. Saying this does not mean, however, that there is any reason to disparage the monetary policymakers' chances of correcting undesirable developments in the economy and thus steadying economic growth.

Although there is no prospect of controlling the money stock in the very short term, the chances of doing so over a somewhat longer period are quite good. The crucial point is the demand of banks and the general public for central-bank money; this demand is influenced, not by tuning off or on a flow of liquidity at very short notice, but by influencing the money-creation process itself. In concrete terms this means that nonbanks' demand for credit and monetary assets is strengthened or weakened through the interest-rate mechanism and that the supply of credit is controlled through changes in potential central-bank money and through the cost of procuring actual central-bank money. However, the feedback from the change in this condition to the stock of central-bank money and the eventual impact on the real economic process both take time. The reduction of time lags is therefore a permanent task of monetary policy, but this objective need not be pursued with abrupt changes of course. I should like to confine myself to the above remarks on the concept of money supply or money demand and its practical application. From the standpoint of the Bundesbank, and considering the institutional conditions in Germany, I can see only one possibility: to fix and change, as the central bank, the conditions on which the banks' demand for central-bank money can be met in the short run while monetary expansion can be kept on a medium-term planned growth path.

These conditions determine interest rates in the money market and then affect the banks' deposit and lending rates and other financial markets as well. Interest rates, and measures of liquidity policy to make them effective, are the variables through which the central bank acts upon banks and nonbanks to keep the money-creation process in harmony with ideas on the "right" expansion of the money stock—ideas that were formulated in advance but need constant reappraisal.

These qualifications may come as a disappointment to some monetary theorists who advocate stricter control of the money stock. But even so, they should not feel discouraged. Recent monetary theory has given a strong new impetus to practical monetary policy. The theories about the role of money in an inflation and the part played by the central bank in the money-creation process must be interpreted as a challenge to the monetary authorities, and in a number of countries they have been accepted as such. The challenge lies primarily in the fact that the monetary authorities should be willing to assume their share of the responsibility for unwelcome developments in the economy, both nationally and internationally. In the present state of knowledge it is, in my view, no longer possible in good faith to seek the causes of inflation only elsewhere--in the government, among management and labor, or in foreign countries.

Monetary policy is not practiced in the sterilized atmosphere of theoretical models. Even if it is based on generally valid theoretical findings, its design and practical implementation are heavily dependent on the institutional conditions confronting the central bank in its country—that is, in an environment that may be swarming with bacteria of every kind: political pledges without real basis, national and international struggles over the distribution of income, concentrations of economic power, competitive restrictions, wrong exchange rates, evasion of the national control of money creation by recourse to the uncontrolled international money market, etc. Hence the Bundesbank's transition from a more liquidity-oriented approach to the control of central-bank money should be seen not only against the background of the debate on monetary theory, which began years earlier, but as a reaction to changes in the institutional setup—in particular, to the end of the system of fixed exchange rates. The decisive factor in the success of monetary policy is, after all, that the central bank gets the political backing to translate theoretical findings into practical policies, in other words, that a certain consensus is arrived at among the political groups in a country. This includes, in particular, a critical public sensibility that gradually makes it impossible to seek to solve economic problems mainly by creating money, in accordance with the much-used method of John Law.

REFERENCES

Bank for International Settlements. 1975. 46th ANNUAL REPORT. Basle, Switzerland.

Friedman, M., and Schwartz, A. J. 1970. MONETARY STATISTICS OF THE UNITED STATES. New York: Columbia University Press.

German Council of Economic Experts (Sachverständigenrat zur Begutachtung der gesamtwirtschaftlichen Entwicklung). 1974/75. ANNUAL REPORT.

Köhler, C. 1976. PROBLEME DER ZENTRALBANKGELDMENGEN-STEUERUNG [Problems of controlling the central-bank money stock]. Arbeitspapier des Instituts für empirische Wirtschaftsforschung, Heft 4. Berlin.

MONETARY POLICY UNDER FLEXIBLE EXCHANGE RATES: THE SWISS CASE*

Kurt Schiltknecht**
Schweizerische Nationalbank

The introduction of a system of flexible exchange rates made it possible for central banks to pursue a monetary policy of their own, inasmuch as domestic monetary policy became less dependent on monetary policy abroad. The following describes how the Swiss National Bank has taken advantage of this possibility. My remarks on monetary policy will be preceded—so as to facilitate comprehension of the subsequent explanations—by a few particulars relating to economic trends in Switzerland in the postwar period. My comments on monetary policy under flexible exchange rates are subdivided into four parts. First, a few considerations are offered concerning the choice of the monetary policy target. Subsequently, the method adopted to accomplish the target is dealt with. In the third section, monetary policy from 1973 to the present time is explained by means of the growth rates of the monetary base and the money supply (M_1). In the last part, the effects of monetary policy on economic activity and exchange rate movements are described, insofar as these are already ascertainable.

Thus, my paper presents, above all, past history and not a theoretical foundation for Swiss monetary policy. Nor would a theoretical model do full justice to the actions of a central bank, considering that the theories of persons participating in monetary decision making are seldom identical.

---

* An earlier version of the paper was presented at the 1976 Konstanz Seminar. A version in German was published in the SCHWEIZERISCHE ZEITSCHRIFT FÜR VOLKSWIRTSCHAFT UND STATISTIK 113 (1977): 1-26.

** The author wishes to acknowledge the valuable suggestions given by members of the Economics and Statistics Department of the Swiss National Bank, in particular by J. R. Lademann and M. Thomann. Thanks are also due to W. Obi for translating the paper.

Ultimately, actual monetary policy always originates in a compromise of various theoretical ideas. If—this fact notwithstanding—I am describing the considerations that have led to the monetary decisions of the past three years, my remarks have to a certain degree a subjective touch. In this sense, responsibility for the paper, which should not be looked upon as an official document of the Swiss National Bank, lies with the author.

1. THE SWISS ECONOMY IN THE POSTWAR PERIOD

In the postwar period, Switzerland registered five more or less distinct business cycles (1946-49, 1950-53, 1954-58, 1959-67, and 1968-75). In none of these cycles was recession of such a pronounced nature as to show official unemployment rates clearly above one percent. The fluctuations in the participation rate that occur within the business cycle reflect, above all, immigration and migration movements of foreign workers. Only in 1975 was the "remigration" of foreign workers decisive in making the unemployment rate appear in too favorable a light. In each of the remaining recession years, the number of foreign workers merely stabilized without declining. What bearing the foreign labor force has on the Swiss economy may best be appreciated by noting that the share of foreign workers in the overall labor force rose from a very low level in the postwar years to almost 30 percent in the '70s.

Just as much as by the strong movement of workers across the frontier, the Swiss economy has been characterized by international capital movements. The importance of the latter may be illustrated by means of the monetary base and balance-of-payments identity:

$$B_t \equiv RES_t + CBC_t + OTH_t,$$

$$RES_t \equiv RES_{t-1} + FK_t - NKEB_t - NKEP_t,$$

where B = monetary base,

RES = net foreign assets, including gold, held by the Swiss National Bank,

CBC = central-bank credit to financial institutions,

OTH = others than RES and CBC,

FK = current account balance,

$NKEB$ = net capital exports of domestic banks, and

NKEP = net capital exports to nonbanks, including errors and omissions.

Owing to the lack of statistical data, it is not possible to go much further in subdividing the balance of payments. Some of the stock variables and some aggregated flow variables of these two identities are shown in table 1.

Table 1

Variables	1949	1953	1958	1967	1972	1974
B^*	6.1	6.6	8.9	15.3	21.1	25.5
RES^*	6.5	6.6	8.9	15.5	23.6	24.7
		i=50,..53	i=54,..58	i=59,..67	i=68,..72	i=73,74
ΣFK_i		2.0	2.3	-4.0	6.5	1.8
$\Sigma NKEB_i$		-0.5	-0.2	-0.7	22.1	-3.1
$\Sigma NKEP_i$		2.4	0.2	-9.9	-23.7	3.8

NOTE: All data in billion Swiss francs.
* Excluding swaps.

The figures show that the increase in the monetary base is almost exclusively accounted for by transactions relating to foreign trade and international capital movements. In the period 1950-74, somewhat more than half of the increase in the monetary base originated in current account surpluses. Roughly half of the increase was the result of surpluses in the balance of capital transactions. The compilation in table 1 also makes clear why, under the system of fixed exchange rates, the monetary policy of the Swiss National Bank was above all directed toward warding off the inflow of funds from abroad. The foreign business of the banks increased by leaps and bounds, in particular after 1966. While the banks' foreign assets were still at a level of SFr20 billion at the end of 1966, by the time of the changeover to flexible exchange rates they had reached a figure of roughly SFr97 billion. The rise in the liabilities of the banks vis-a-vis foreign countries turned out to be somewhat smaller during that period. Foreign liabilities increased "only" from SFr19 billion to SFr81 billion. At the present time, foreign assets account for roughly one-third of the overall balance sheet total of the banks. Together with the increase in the banks' foreign business, there was a rise in the net capital import by nonbanks. Considering these enormous capital movements, it is not surprising that in the course of time the Swiss National Bank lost control of the supply of money. The only possible solution to the problem in the end was the transition to flexible exchange rates.

Just how unfavorable the effect of the balance-of-payments development was, from the point of view of money supply, can be inferred from table 2. This table shows the average growth rates of the gross national product, the consumer price index, and the money stock. It can easily be seen how the growth rates of the money stock and inflation increased from cycle to cycle. The growth rate of real GNP, on the other hand, registered no actual increase. The jump of the average growth rate to 4.9 percent in the third cycle is not the result of productivity progress but is solely attributable to the heavy inflow of foreign workers.

Table 2

	Average Percentage Change			
	1950-53	1954-58	1959-67	1968-74
GNP, current prices	4.9	5.5	9.0	9.3
GNP, real	3.4	3.6	4.9	3.2
Consumer prices	0.8	1.2	2.9	5.9
Money stock $(t-1)$	*	3.4	7.4	7.4**

* Not available.

** Average Percent change, 1967-72: 9.5; 1973-74: 1.2.

The price stability of the '50s and the relatively small price increase of the '60s make clear why the control of inflation ranks high in Swiss economic policy and why the monetary policy described in the following was politically practicable.

2. THE CHOICE OF A MONETARY POLICY TARGET

For a closed economy, the proposal to use the stock of money as a target for monetary policy has been made on many occasions, though not always explicitly. Thus, in his essay "The Role of Monetary Policy," Milton Friedman writes:

> Of the various alternative magnitudes that it [the monetary authority] can control, the most appealing guides for policy are exchange rates, the price level as defined by some index, and the quantity of a monetary total .... For the United States in particular, exchange rates are an undesirable guide. Far better to let the market, through floating exchange rates, adjust to world conditions the 5 per cent or so of our resources devoted to international trade while reserving monetary policy to promote the effective use of the 95 per cent. [1968, p. 15]

As far as Switzerland is concerned, there is no such clear solution to the problem of balancing domestic objectives against external targets. The share of foreign trade in the Gross National Product being large, the exchange rate in Switzerland is to be weighted more heavily than in the United States. This, however, does not necessarily imply that, in the place of the quantity of money, the exchange rate is to serve as the major monetary policy target. On the contrary, we are of the opinion that, if monetary policy were determined by exchange rate considerations only, this would adversely affect the stability of the economy in the long run. Constant intervention in the foreign exchange market for the purpose of maintaining the stability of the exchange rate leads to an inflationary growth of the money supply—as we have seen time and again in the past fifteen years. It is an established fact that inflation not only leads to a misallocation of resources but also has a sustained effect on the exchange rate. This means that a monetary policy determined by exchange rate considerations may itself be the ultimate cause of exchange rate disturbances. We are not in a position today to make reliable statements on the long-term consequences of a monetary policy determined by exchange rate considerations. The danger that such a policy will have a destabilizing effect in the longer run cannot be ruled out. This is why a monetary policy determined primarily by exchange rate considerations is out of the question, as far as we are concerned.

Also doubtful, it appears to us—at least for an open economy—is a monetary policy using only constant monetary growth as the relevant guideline. It is true that by adopting such a guideline it may prove relatively easy to solve the inflation problem, but in that event the determination of the exchange rate is left entirely to market forces. If, for example, monetary policy abroad is attuned to a stable price level to a lesser degree than is the Swiss, this necessarily entails a rise in the exchange rate. The speed of adjustment in the monetary sector being greater than that in the real sector of the economy, competitive disadvantages are incurred by the export industry during the period of nonmonetary adjustment to changes in the exchange rate. Such distortions in international trade may in turn occasion internal economic fluctuations. Due regard is to be paid to this factor by influencing, to some extent, exchange rate fluctuations. This means that, as far as possible, the adjustment of exchange rates is to be delayed and stabilized, but it is not to be prevented. In part, this may be achieved by a flexible money-stock policy.

Another problem of money-supply policy in an open economy is connected with the price movement of imported goods. If, as was the case in 1973 and 1974, oil prices or the prices of other major import goods rise substantially, a country like Switzerland is faced with the question whether or not these price increases (expressed in domestic currency) are to be financed by a corresponding rise in the money supply. In favor of partial financing is the argument that the effects on economic activity that would result from nonfinancing are thereby spaced; that is, the economy would be given somewhat more time to adapt itself to changed conditions. This advantage has to be paid for by a domestic price increase. We are of the opinion that, from the economic point of view, partial financing of price increases for imports is more advantageous than complete renunciation of financing.

These are a few considerations explaining why, for an open economy, we advocate a flexible money-supply policy. Based on present-day conditions, we have come to the conclusion that in the next few years the growth of the narrowly defined money stock (M_1) ought to be kept within 3 and 7 percent in Switzerland. The choice of this range is supported by experience in the '50s with growth rates of that order. Moreover, a relatively wide margin seems to us to be essential for the absorption of disturbances relating to foreign trade. The size of this range forces us regularly to reexamine our short-term, (year-to-year) money-supply target. The margin of 3 to 7 percent does not mean that over a prolonged period of time (two to three years, for instance) we consider a money-supply growth of 7 percent appropriate. All we mean to imply by this 7 percent limit is that, currently, situations are conceivable in which a temporary money-supply growth of 7 percent might be justified.

It is not traditional for Switzerland to choose and to make known a specific target for money-supply growth. The pursuit of a specific money-supply policy was made possible only by the introduciton of flexible exchange rates. Prior to that, Switzerland's monetary policy had largely been confined to curbing the inflow of undesirable foreign funds with a view to preventing an inflationary growth of the money stock. The pursuit of a specific monetary policy had been additionally impeded by an inadequate number of instruments at the disposal of the central bank. With the transition to flexible exchange rates in January 1973, new prospects appeared for Switzerland's monetary policy. Already at the end of 1974, a money-supply target—for 1975—was fixed and made known for the first time. Based on subsequent experience, this procedure has been maintained up to the present. So far, the fixing of a money-supply target for one year has always been made at the end of a calendar year, its main determinants being the expected and the desired economic development for the year to come. To a certain extent, the monetary objectives of the major trading partners are also taken into account. The quantitative fixing of the money-supply target is based neither on an econometric model nor on a concept associated with a specific monetary theory.

Ultimately, the choice of the money-supply target must be described as a compromise among theoretical ideas, political considerations, and knowledge gained from empirical research. Some of the considerations that have been put forward in connection with the fixing of the money-supply growth rates for 1975 and 1976 will be dealt with in some detail in the section on the actual shaping of monetary policy since the introduction of flexible exchange rates (section 5).

3. THE CONTROL OF MONEY-STOCK GROWTH

The pursuit of a target-oriented money-supply policy requires precise ideas as to the extent and timing of adjustments of the monetary base. At the same time, it must also be clarified by what ways and means the base is to be changed. These questions were new to us, for, as already mentioned, Switzerland's monetary policy had previously been confined largely to warding off the inflow of foreign funds. It is therefore hardly surprising that in the field of money-supply control we have not yet settled on a concept. Based on our experience so far, however, the following schematic procedure has proved to be quite expedient:

1. Targetting of the money-supply growth for the year ahead
2. Targetting the monetary-base growth rate that is necessary to reach the planned growth of the money stock, M_1 (Today, the monetary base constitutes the operational target of Switzerland's monetary policy.)
3. Drawing up guidelines for the volume and the kind of increase of the monetary base in the first quarter
4. Testing results monthly, and if necessary revising the figure originally fixed for the increase in the monetary base
5. Targetting the increase in the monetary base for the second quarter, and so forth

So as to determine the increase in the monetary base required for a specific money-supply growth, we forecast the money multiplier. Up to the present time, this forecast has been made without an econometric model.[1] The longer-term (one-year) forecast is largely based on a comparison of the

1. Note of 1977: In the meantime a model to predict the money multiplier has been developed. See Büttler et al. (1977).

pattern of the money multiplier and its components (currency ratio, reserve ratio, excess-reserve ratio, and time-deposit ratio) with that of previous cyclical trends of a similar nature. The short-term forecast of the money multiplier, on the other hand, is based on a very simple, mechanistic procedure. The starting point is the following naive forecast model: take last month's multiplier and add the change in the multiplier that occurred at this time last year; or, defined mathematically:

$$m_t = m_{t-1} + m_{t-12} - m_{t-13} + \varepsilon_t,$$

where $m_t = M_t/B_t$,

m_t = the money multiplier,

M_t = the money stock (narrow definition),

B_t = the monetary base, and

ε_t = disturbances.

E. J. Bomhoff (1977, p. 334) has shown that in the United States this "naive model" predicts the money multiplier more accurately than, for instance, the model of the St. Louis scholars.[2] In Switzerland we have established that ε_t is not a random variable but shows a quite specific pattern. From figure 1 it can be seen that ε_t is negatively correlated to the difference between the change in the monetary base compared to the previous month and the change compared to the corresponding period of the previous year. Based on this relationship it is possible, in our experience, to establish fairly accurate short-term forecasts of the money multiplier. It is intended to improve the forecast method in the near future, however. An improvement is called for since in Switzerland the money multiplier has to be forecast in each case, not only for the next month, but at least for the next three months, considering that there is a time lag of roughly 1½ months before the money-supply figures become available. Control of the money supply is rendered even more difficult by the fact that the money stock can be calculated for the last day of the month only. This entails the risk of a change in the money-supply growth rate being effected merely on the

2. Contrary to the procedure described in the following, Bomhoff used in his work a Box-Jenkins model to forecast the money multiplier.

Figure 1

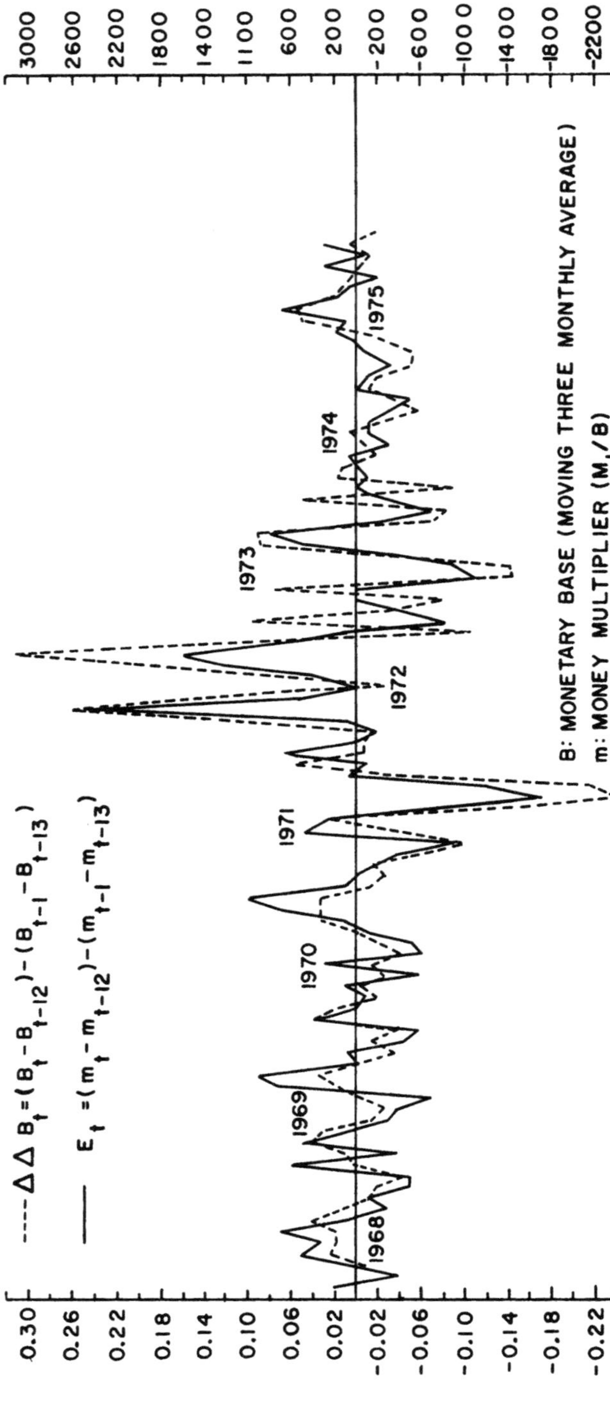

$\Delta\Delta B_t = (B_t - B_{t-12}) - (B_{t-1} - B_{t-13})$
$E_t = (m_t - m_{t-12}) - (m_{t-1} - m_{t-13})$
B: MONETARY BASE (MOVING THREE MONTHLY AVERAGE)
m: MONEY MULTIPLIER (M_1/B)
1968
1969
1970
1971
1972
1973
1974
1975
0.30
0.26
0.22
0.18
0.14
0.10
0.06
0.02
-0.02
-0.06
-0.10
-0.14
-0.18
-0.22
3000
2600
2200
1800
1400
1100
600
200
-200
-600
-1000
-1400
-1800
-2200

strength of a random error. For that reason, any alteration in the once-established target of the monetary base is decided upon only at a time when it may be assumed that a systematic deviation from the envisaged money-supply growth has taken place.

4. CONTROL OF THE MONETARY BASE

The net monetary base (monetary base less central-bank credits to domestic banks)[3] is under the control of the Swiss National Bank. At first sight it appears that there should be no difficulties in reaching the planned monetary-base target. In practice, however, difficulties arise due to the attempt to avoid erratic short-run fluctuations of the exchange rate. The experience of the last year has shown that purchases of foreign exchange to the extent of several hundred million Swiss francs are required to stop or to reduce heavy fluctuations in times of severe shocks in the international monetary system. For instance, since for 1976 a maximum increase in the net monetary base of SFr1.5 billion (a 6 percent increase) has been envisaged, it will take no more than two or three monetary disturbances of minor importance for the operational target to be exceeded.

The control of the monetary base is complicated, additionally, by the fact that in Switzerland the traditional central-bank instruments, for institutional reasons, play a relatively insignificant role. Consequently, other instruments have been chosen to influence the monetary base. In particular, monetary policy has made use of the fact that the Swiss banks transact voluminous capital exports. Some of these capital exports require the approval of the Swiss National Bank.[4] Since the end of 1974, conversion of more of the capital exports subject to license and denominated in Swiss francs has to be effected at the Bank.[5] In 1975, for instance, roughly SFr9

---

3. For the definition of the money base, see Swiss National Bank (1975*a*).

4. For regulatory details, see Federal Law on Banks and Savings Banks, Art. 8.

5. This procedure had been adopted before, for the first time in 1971. Its motivation lies, inter alia, in the fact that more and more multinational companies keep their funds raised in Switzerland as cash in Swiss francs. It is true that, despite the conversion obligation, this possibility still exists; however, costs for cash holdings are adversely affected by the conversion obligation.

billion had to be changed into foreign currencies at the Swiss National Bank. Thanks to these enormous capital conversions, it has largely been possible both to keep the monetary base under control and to smoothen the demand for foreign exchange. In practice, the procedure looks roughly like this: if the monetary base is above the envisaged target, the Swiss National Bank sells foreign exchange to the banks out of its own holdings. If, on the other hand, the monetary base is at or below the desired level, foreign exchange is acquired by means of intervention purchases in the market. The decision as to the time of intervention depends on the appraisal of the situation on the foreign exchange market. For a limited time, that is, over a period of roughly one month, the trend of the monetary base may thus be dominated by exchange rate considerations. If, however, there is a marked deviation from the envisaged growth of the monetary base, a corresponding adjustment of that base is called for. If the situation in the foreign exchange market permits, the adjustment is brought about by means of interventions therein. In general, an attempt is made to attune the activity of the Foreign Exchange Department to the requirements of monetary policy. Achieving this coordination is particularly easy because the number of staff members at the Swiss National Bank is small, which greatly facilitates an efficient exchange of information. Operations of some magnitude in the foreign exchange market that lead to an expansion of the monetary base in excess of the envisaged limit are only transacted after consultation with the Managing Board. On the following day, at the latest, information is available on all transactions that have influenced the monetary base. Adjustments to the course of the monetary base can therefore be planned—and, if necessary, effected—very quickly.

The 1975 volume of banks' capital exports was exceptionally large. Based on previous experience, a decline in capital exports must be expected, once a cyclical upswing gathers momentum. In that event, the other instruments that have already been used to control the monetary base will increasingly be employed. In the first place, sterilization rescriptions of the Confederation will be sold to or taken over from the banks, or the minimum reserve requirements on domestic and foreign deposits will be varied. (In this connection, it should be mentioned that the Swiss National Banks' power to call in minimum reserves is based on an emergency law that is timed to expire at the end of 1978. By that time, however, it is hoped that a revision of the National Bank Law will have been concluded. In the new law, the possibility, among others, of calling in minimum reserves is to be legally sanctioned.

Since the beginning of 1976 an additional possibility for controlling the monetary base has been utilized. The federal government is currently raising funds in expectation of a large budget deficit for 1976, in the form of bonded loan issues and bank credits in excess of what is required to cover its deficit of the current year. The funds that are not required are being neutralized—credited to the account held with the Swiss National Bank. In this way, it has been possible to adjust the excessive expansion of the monetary base that came about in January 1976 as a result of monetary disturbances. The monetary base will be increased in 1977 by a gradual release of the government's neutralized funds. In order to prevent monetary policy from being crossed by the federal government's behavior (e.g., by an unexpectedly rapid running down of the balance of neutralized funds), information sharing between the federal administration and the Swiss National Bank has been strengthened.

The tight monetary policy pursued in the initial phase of flexible exchange rates has been rather unorthodox. In a simplified way, the procedure might be described as the calling in of minimum reserves on those domestic credits that exceed a specific level previously fixed by the Swiss National Bank. In practice, things worked like this (Swiss National Bank 1973, pp. 41-43; 1974, pp. 50-51; 1975*b*, p. 42): the Swiss National Bank determined for a certain period of time (generally for one year) the permissible credit growth rate, expressed as a percentage of the level of domestic credits reached on July 31, 1972. From the beginning of 1973 until April 1974, the permissible growth rate was set at 6 percent. Subsequently, it was raised to 7 percent, at which level it remained until the expiry of credit limitation in the first quarter of 1975. If a bank exceeded the fixed credit growth rate, the excess amount involved had to be paid by that bank into a National Bank account that remained blocked until such time as credits were reduced to the permissible ceiling (but at least for three months). Already on the first key date, it became apparent that the calling in of all excess amounts would have led to serious disturbances in the money market. Therefore, only part of the excess amount was called in. This flexible attitude toward the calling-in policy was maintained until the lifting of credit limitation. The decision as to the amount to be called in was based on the money-market situation. The aim was to prevent an over-abrupt transition to tight monetary policy.

Also somewhat unorthodox has been the manner of remedying seasonal liquidity problems or liquidity problems started off by a temporary undercutting of the envisaged growth in the monetary base. Such liquidity problems are solved by means of swaps; that is, the Swiss National Bank takes over from the banks for a few days or for up to three months, foreign currencies in exchange for Swiss francs. On expiry of the time limit agreed upon, the counteroperations are effected. The swap cost is governed by the interest rates prevailing in the money market on each relevant occasion. The volume of swaps concluded is considerable, particularly at quarter-ends, but even more so at year-ends. The extent to which the swap facility is used depends, on the one hand, on the immediate liquidity position of the banks and, on the other hand, on their ideas of the degree of liquidity desired for publicity purposes. So far, the significance of the swaps for the money-supply process has not been systematically investigated. From a few simple analyses it may be assumed that the swaps' function is similar to that of the traditional central-bank credit, that is, the advance and discount facility offered by the central bank to the banks.

5. FLEXIBLE EXCHANGE RATES: 1973-1976

The monetary policy pursued under the regime of the flexible exchange rates may be subdivided into three periods. In the first, which lasted from the point of introduction of flexible exchange rates until the middle of 1974, a tight monetary policy was pursued to absorb the liquidity surplus that had accrued during 1971 and 1972. In mid-1974, an expansionary monetary policy was pursued, ending at the beginning of 1976. The current monetary policy may best be defined as the policy of transition toward continuous money-supply growth. The monetary policy of these three periods will now be described and explained with the aid of the growth rates of the monetary base and the money supply, M_1.

The Period from 1973 to Mid-1974

The transition to flexible exchange rates was preceded by enormous capital flows to Switzerland. It was in the second half of 1971, above all, that the huge capital inflow in connection with the abolition of the gold convertibility of the dollar started off an increase in the monetary base (see figure 2) that had hardly been thought possible. Within a few months, the base expanded by more than 50 percent; and this, as it had to, led to an inflationary money-stock growth. In a period of just under one year (August 1971-May 1972), the growth rates of M_1 fluctuated between 20 percent and 26.1 percent. This enormous growth in the supply of money was not without consequences. Among other things, the 3.6 average increase in the consumer price index in 1970 was up to 6.6 percent at the end of 1971. This sharp rise created, at last, a favorable political climate for effective inflation fighting. Prior to the introduction of flexible exchange rates, measures had already been taken to combat inflationary money-supply growth. As can be seen from figure 2, it was possible to reduce the monetary base as of mid-1972. The reduction was brought about, above all, by calling in minimum reserves on domestic and foreign liabilities as well as by compulsory conversion at the Swiss National Bank of banks' capital exports. In the second half of June 1972, the contraction of the monetary base was temporarily interrupted owing to the outbreak of a sterling crisis and the resulting capital inflow. When on January 23, 1973, fixed exchange rates were abolished, conditions were set for resuming a tight monetary policy. Almost simultaneously, the statutory base (Credit Decree) for an effective monetary policy was created.[6] In Switzerland, the main reason given for the change to flexible exchange rates was that further intervention

6. Federal Decree on Measures in the Field of Financing, December 20, 1972 (see Swiss National Bank 1973).

Figure 2

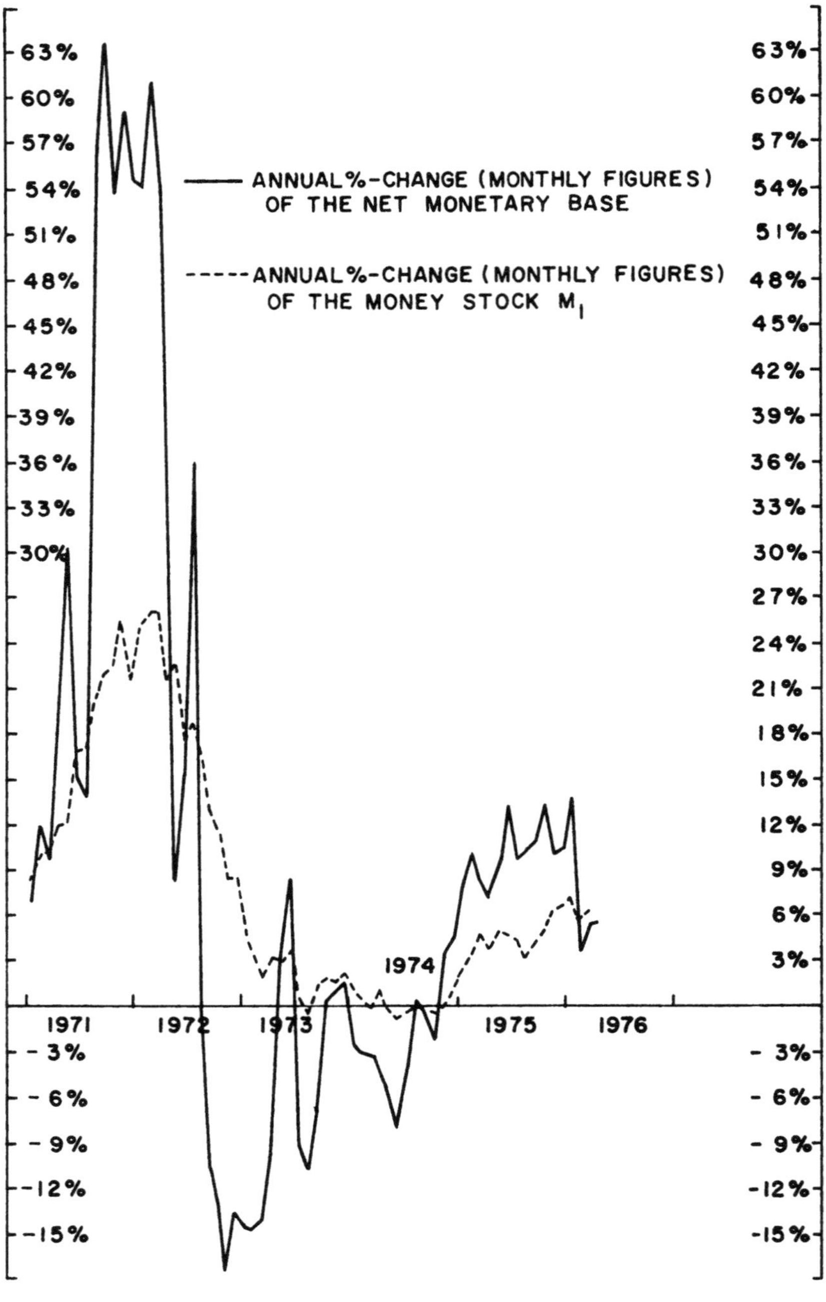

63%
60%
57%
54%
51%
48%
45%
42%
39%
36%
33%
30%
27%
24%
21%
18%
15%
12%
9%
6%
3%
- 3%
- 6%
- 9%
-12%
-15%
ANNUAL%-CHANGE (MONTHLY FIGURES) OF THE NET MONETARY BASE
ANNUAL%-CHANGE (MONTHLY FIGURES) OF THE MONEY STOCK M_1
1971
1972
1973
1974
1975
1976

in the foreign exchange market for the purpose of maintaining the system of fixed exchange rates would have rendered antiinflationary efforts suspect on account of the inherent increase in the monetary base.

Shortly after the change to flexible exchange rates, there was a heavy revaluation of the Swiss franc. In February 1973 an attempt was made to stop revaluation by interventions in the exchange market. The effect was trifling; on the other hand, the risk of an inflationary money-supply expansion arose again. Faced with the alternative of stable exchange rates versus stable prices, the Swiss National Bank and the federal government chose the latter. From February 1973 to January 1975, no further intervention purchases were transacted. Although intervention operations were abstained from, the net monetary base increased considerably in the course of time (see figure 3). When the exchange rate situation later improved somewhat, tight monetary policy was again effected. By sterilizing the funds that the banks had to pay in for their credit grants in excess of the permissible ceiling, the expansion in the net monetary base registered during the first six months was more than offset in the second half of the year. From November 1973 to June 1974, the net monetary base was stabilized at the level of SFr21 billion. At the beginning of 1972, its figure, by way of comparison, had still been as high as SFr25 billion. Until mid-1974, an increase in the net monetary base was abstained from, with the intention of reducing first the inflation potential that had been created by capital inflows in 1971 and 1972. Thanks to the considerable reduction in the monetary base and its subsequent stabilization, money-supply growth was quickly brought under control. Within a period of nine months, the yearly growth rate of M_1 dropped from 22.6 percent (May 1972) to 3.5 percent (February 1973). Subsequently, over a period of more than two years, the rates were below 3.5 percent, except in June 1973 (+3.7 percent). In the course of time, the Swiss National Bank's pursuit of a tight monetary policy forced the banks to resort to central-bank credits not only at month-ends but permanently (see movement of central-bank credits, figure 4). Special mention is made of this because normally—leaving month-end periods aside—no particular significance is attached to central-bank credits in Switzerland.

Figure 3

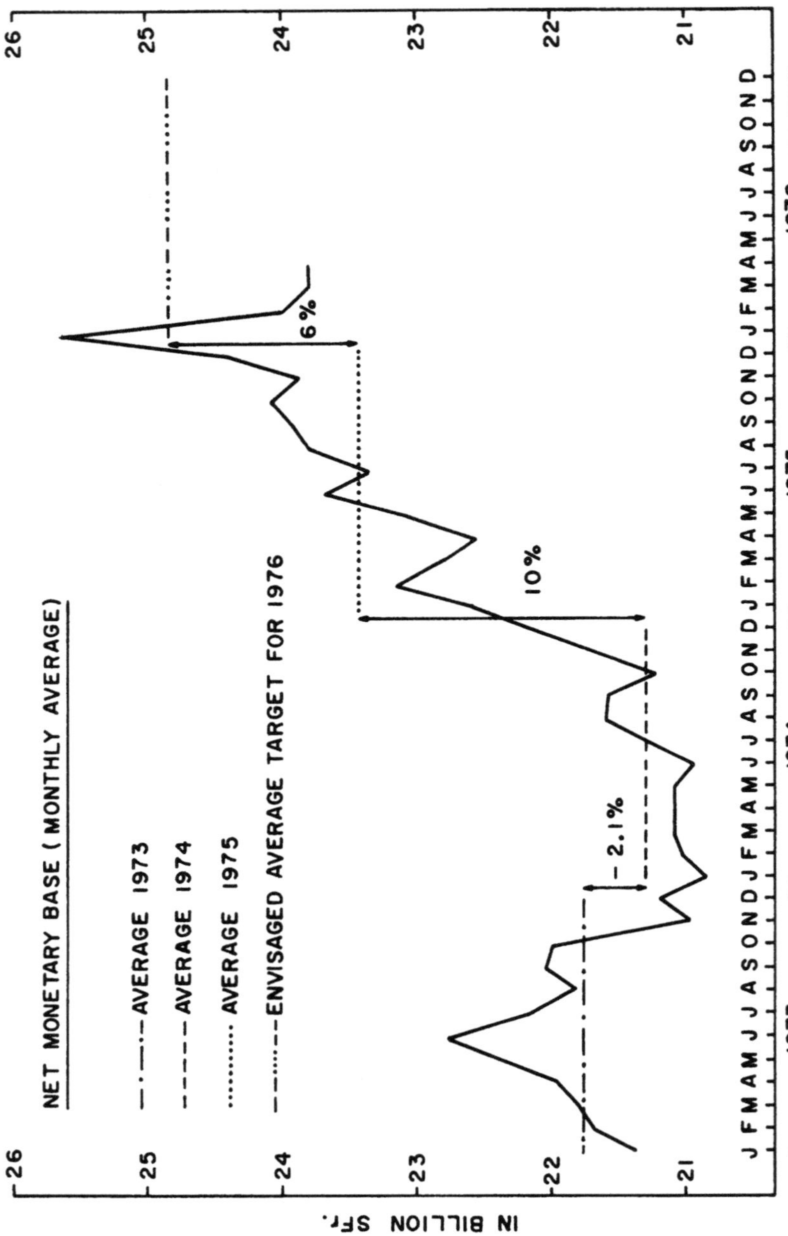
NET MONETARY BASE (MONTHLY AVERAGE)
AVERAGE 1973
AVERAGE 1974
AVERAGE 1975
ENVISAGED AVERAGE TARGET FOR 1976
- 2.1%
10%
6%
26
25
24
23
22
21
IN BILLION SFr.
J F M A M J J A S O N D J F M A M J J A S O N D J F M A M J J A S O N D J F M A M J J A S O N D
1973
1974
1975
1976

Figure 4

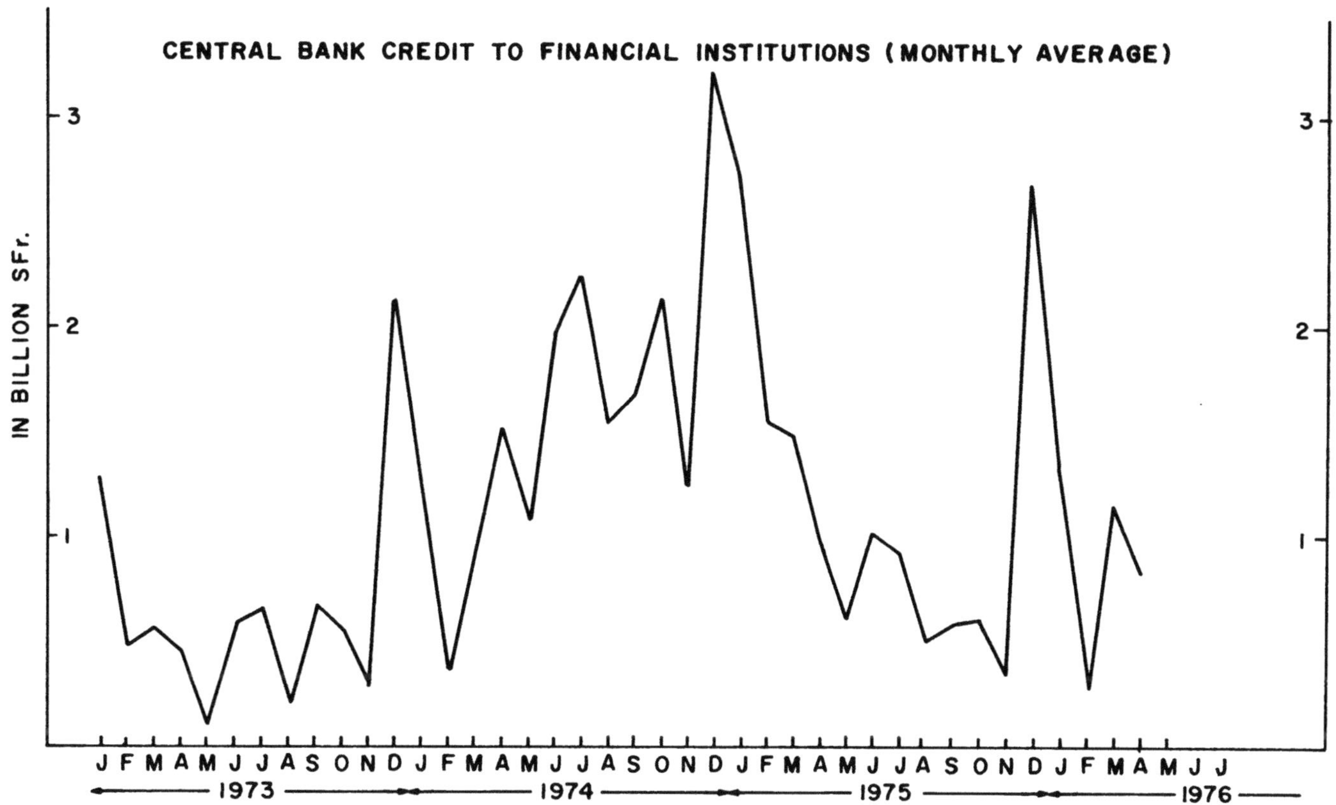

CENTRAL BANK CREDIT TO FINANCIAL INSTITUTIONS (MONTHLY AVERAGE)
IN BILLION SFr.
3
2
1
J F M A M J J A S O N D J F M A M J J A S O N D J F M A M J J A S O N D J F M A M J J
1973
1974
1975
1976

The Period from Mid-1974 through 1975

In mid-1974, the Swiss National Bank reached the view that "excess liquidity" had been absorbed and that, within limits, it would be appropriate for the monetary base to be increased again. To begin with, no explicit monetary policy target was made known. Money-supply targets for 1975 were worked out in the autumn of 1974 but not published until the first few days of 1975. Not only for the money supply, M_1, but also for the net monetary base, the envisaged yearly growth rate was 6 percent. The primary target was that for M_1, whereas that for the monetary base constituted an operational target only. The targets were based on the national income figures of the Working Group for Economic Forecasts. In these forecasts it was assumed that inflation would decline (see table 3). By choosing for M_1 a growth rate of 6 percent, it was intended to create the conditions for an undisturbed medium-term reduction of inflation. What was aimed at in particular was to avoid, by means of a gradual return to stable prices, those disturbances in the economy that are inherent in too rapid a change in inflation expectations. Very soon, the economic forecasts for 1975 proved to be too optimistic (compare forecast figures with those of the first provisional results for 1975 in table 3). The money multiplier dropped, and a 6 percent increase in the net monetary base was therefore insufficient for the money-supply target to be reached.

Table 3

	1975 Percentage Change	
	Forecasts*	Observed
GNP, current prices	+5.9	-1.1
GNP-deflator	+5.9	+6.3
GNP, real	0.0	-7.0

* By the Working Group for Economic Forecasts; figures issued autumn 1974.

By the spring of 1975, an average rise in the monetary base of roughly 10 percent was regarded as the new operational target. The money-supply target was not changed; on the contrary, in view of increasingly apparent recessionary signs, an expansionist increase of 6 percent in the money stock was called for in order not to risk a new inflation. At first, the growth rates of M_1 remained below the 6 percent target, but because they were showing an upward tendency, the operational target was left unchanged. As can be seen from figure 3, it was possible to bring about the increase in the net monetary base at a fairly steady pace. The absence of any great international monetary disturbances made a continuous monetary policy possible. Whereas the revised operational target of 10 percent could be met, the planned money-supply growth was not fully reached--the average increase in the money supply was 4.4 percent.

The increase in the net monetary base was largely brought about via the purchase of foreign exchange. An appreciably smaller contribution was made by the easing of minimum reserve requirements on foreign liabilities. The release of funds that had temporarily been neutralized as excess amounts in connection with the credit-growth limitation caused a further increase in the net monetary base. In consideration of the envisaged target, part of the increase was then reduced by another issue of sterilization rescriptions. Part of the additional monetary base was utilized by the banks to repay central-bank credits. In the course of 1975, central-bank credits again diminished in importance and dropped to the level they had shown prior to the initiation of a tight monetary policy in 1973.

The 1976 Period

Analogous to the 1975 target, a 6 percent growth of the money supply, M_1, is planned for 1976, too. A higher growth rate would endanger, in the long run, the success registered so far in the fight against inflation. Although a lower growth rate would be justifiable from the domestic point of view, this would lead to an even more pronounced revaluation of the Swiss franc, considering that in comparison to Switzerland most of the remaining industrialized countries have adopted a more expansive monetary policy.

Putting it in somewhat simplified terms, the money-supply target for 1976 may be considered a compromise between domestic and external money-supply requirements. Besides, in view of the recession, psychopolitical considerations also played a role.

A rough estimate has shown that, with the predicted growth of 3.5—4.5 percent in the Gross National Product at current prices, an increase of the net monetary based by 4-6 percent should be sufficient to reach the money-supply target. The expansion thus envisaged is smaller than the 10 percent registered in 1975.

Instead of showing a flatter growth line, the net monetary base, as a result of voluminous intervention purchases in the foreign exchange market, registered in January 1976 the biggest increase since the introduction of flexible exchange rates (+13.8 percent from January 1975). Connected with this was a distinct overshooting of the end-of-January money-supply target (annual growth rate: 7.2 percent). In February, however, the trend of the monetary base had already been adjusted. With the aid of the federal government, those funds that had flowed to the banks in January to calm down the foreign exchange market were again withdrawn from the market by the issue of government bonds. Thus it was possible to bring back to the envisaged growth line, not only the increase in the monetary base, but also the increase in the money supply. So far, a revision of the targets fixed for 1976 is not called for.

6. EFFECTS OF THE 1973-76 MONETARY POLICY

In the following, the effects of the monetary policy pursued under flexible exchange rates will be discussed. First, the effects on economic activity are dealt with; then the effects on the exchange rate of the Swiss franc are discussed. The arbitrary separation is made because of the central importance of the exchange rate question in an open economy.

Effects on Economic Activity

The money-supply policy of the past three years aimed, in the first place, for a return to stable prices. The reduction of the inflation rate was to be brought about without causing any serious disturbances in economic growth. A look at the movement of consumer prices in recent years shows that the objective of a stable price level has almost been reached (see figure 5). The pace at which the inflation rate declined was more rapid than expected. What also occurred unexpectedly last year was the deepest recession of the postwar period. Table 4 shows a few growth rates of the major components of national income for the years 1972-75, as well as the forecasts for 1976. This compilation shows the depth of the recession very clearly.

Table 4

	Percentage Change				
	1972	1973	1974	1975*	1976**
GNP, current prices	+13.2	+11.4	+ 8.3	- 1.1	+ 4.4
GNP, real	+ 3.2	+ 3.2	+ 2.0	- 7.0	+ 1.3
Consumption, real	+ 5.5	+ 2.3	- 0.5	- 2.5	+ 0.0
Construction, real	+10.6	+ 0.6	- 9.5	-25.0	-10.0
Fixed investment, real	+ 2.2	- 0.4	- 0.2	-13.0	- 3.0
Exports, real	+ 6.3	+ 7.5	+ 1.2	- 6.9	+ 2.4
Imports, real	+ 7.5	+ 6.5	- 1.4	-15.5	+ 1.0
GNP-deflator	+ 9.6	+ 8.1	+ 6.6	+ 6.3	+ 3.0
Consumption-price-deflator	+ 7.5	+ 9.1	+ 9.5	+ 6.5	+ 3.5
Investment-price-deflator	+ 9.2	+ 6.7	+ 5.4	- 1.1	+ 0.2
Export-price-deflator	+ 4.9	+ 4.6	+12.8	+ 3.2	+ 2.9
Import-price-deflator	+ 2.0	+ 6.3	+17.9	- 2.9	+ 2.1

* Provisional data.
** Forecasts (Sept. 1975).

It is not possible at the moment to indicate to what extent tight monetary policy in 1973 and 1974 was responsible for the economic recession. On the one hand, the national account figures for the years 1969-75 have only been available since February 1976. Because the national income account was being revised, national income statistics were not

Figure 5

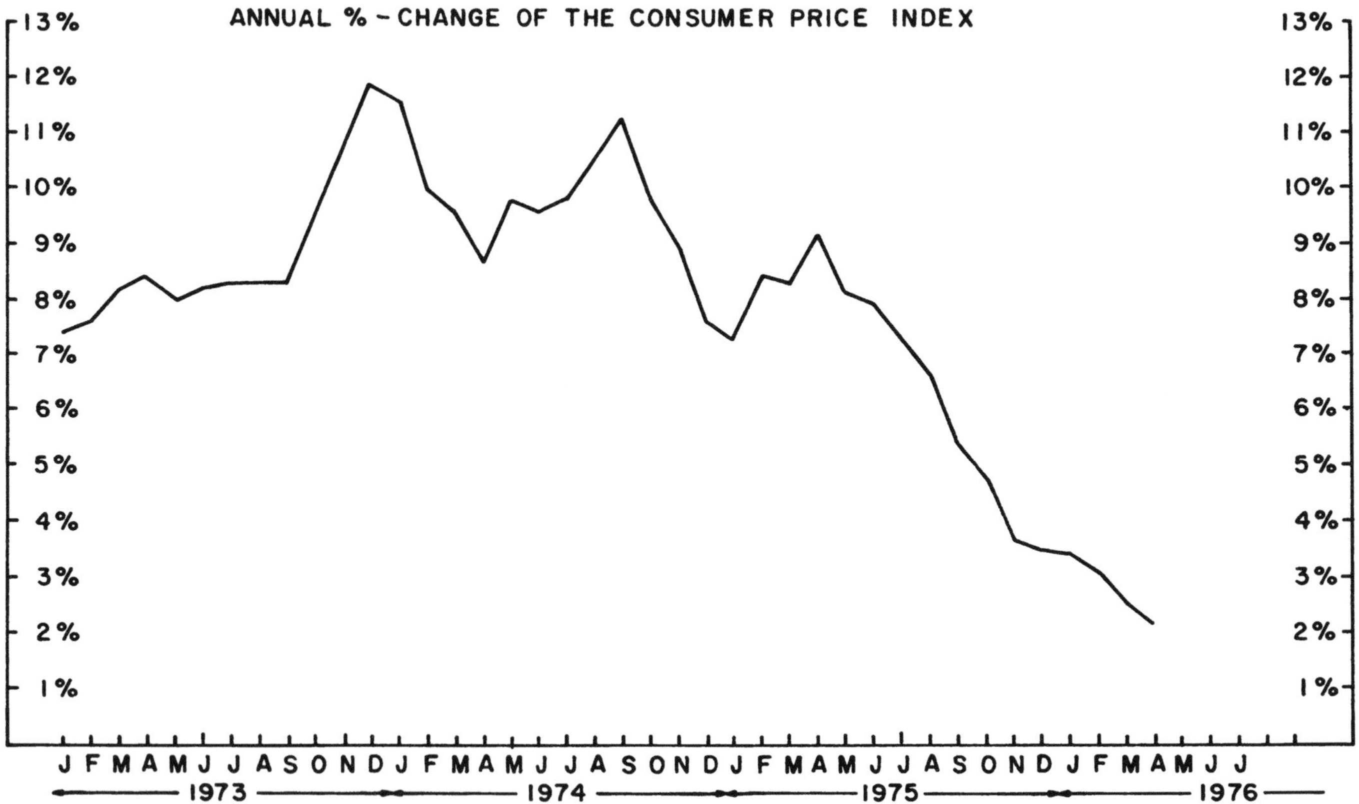

ANNUAL % - CHANGE OF THE CONSUMER PRICE INDEX
13%
12%
11%
10%
9%
8%
7%
6%
5%
4%
3%
2%
1%
J F M A M J J A S O N D J F M A M J J A S O N D J F M A M J J A S O N D J F M A M J J
1973
1974
1975
1976

published during the past six years. In the short time since the new statistics were made available, it has not been possible to analyze the years after 1969 in detail. Apart from this, in an economy as open as Switzerland's, it is very difficult to ascertain how much of economic activity is determined by domestic factors and how much by external factors. To be added to these difficulties is the oil crisis, with its effects on the economic process and on the exchange rates. What cannot yet be gauged, either, is the extent to which economic activity has been and will yet be influenced by the enormous revaluation of the Swiss franc. Another part of present-day difficulties is attributable to the large number of vacant dwellings, a result of the inflation-induced overproduction of dwellings in the early '70s. Ultimately, it is the coinciding of tight monetary policy with the oil crisis, the transition to flexible exchange rates, and recession abroad that prevents making a final appraisal of the money-supply policy of the past three years.

Effects on the Exchange Rate

When it was decided to give up fixed exchange rates and to direct our monetary policy toward controlling the supply of money, this also constituted a resolution, in principle, to leave the determination of the exchange rate to market forces. This decision is still valid, despite intervention purchases. Considering the fact that in the past three years Switzerland, in international comparison, showed a very low money-supply growth rate, a revaluation of the Swiss franc corresponds to theoretical expectations. In 1974, in particular, when short-term interest rates climbed to a level (see figure 6) never thought possible in Switzerland, the Swiss National Bank—not surprisingly—was charged with forcing the exchange rate up in an irresponsible way by means of its tight monetary policy. The call for a loose policy and for massive interventions in the foreign exchange market became more and more frequent. No heed was paid to these demands, although the revaluation of the Swiss franc assumed proportions (see figure 7) that, in our view, could no longer be explained solely by the fact that both our money-supply policy and Switzerland's economic growth rate were different from those of foreign countries. There are various

Figure 6

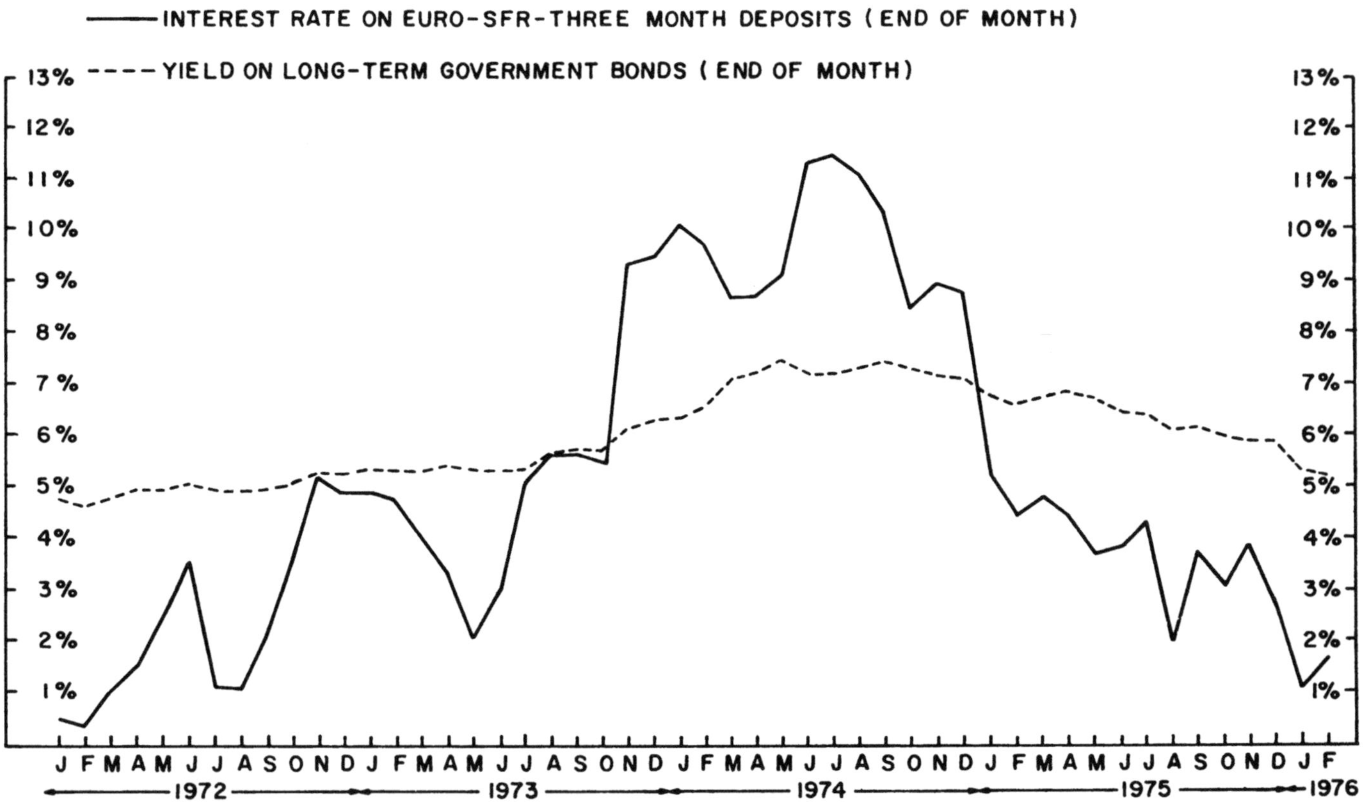

INTEREST RATE ON EURO-SFR-THREE MONTH DEPOSITS (END OF MONTH)
YIELD ON LONG-TERM GOVERNMENT BONDS (END OF MONTH)
13%
12%
11%
10%
9%
8%
7%
6%
5%
4%
3%
2%
1%
J F M A M J J A S O N D J F M A M J J A S O N D J F M A M J J A S O N D J F M A M J J A S O N D J F
1972
1973
1974
1975
1976

Figure 7

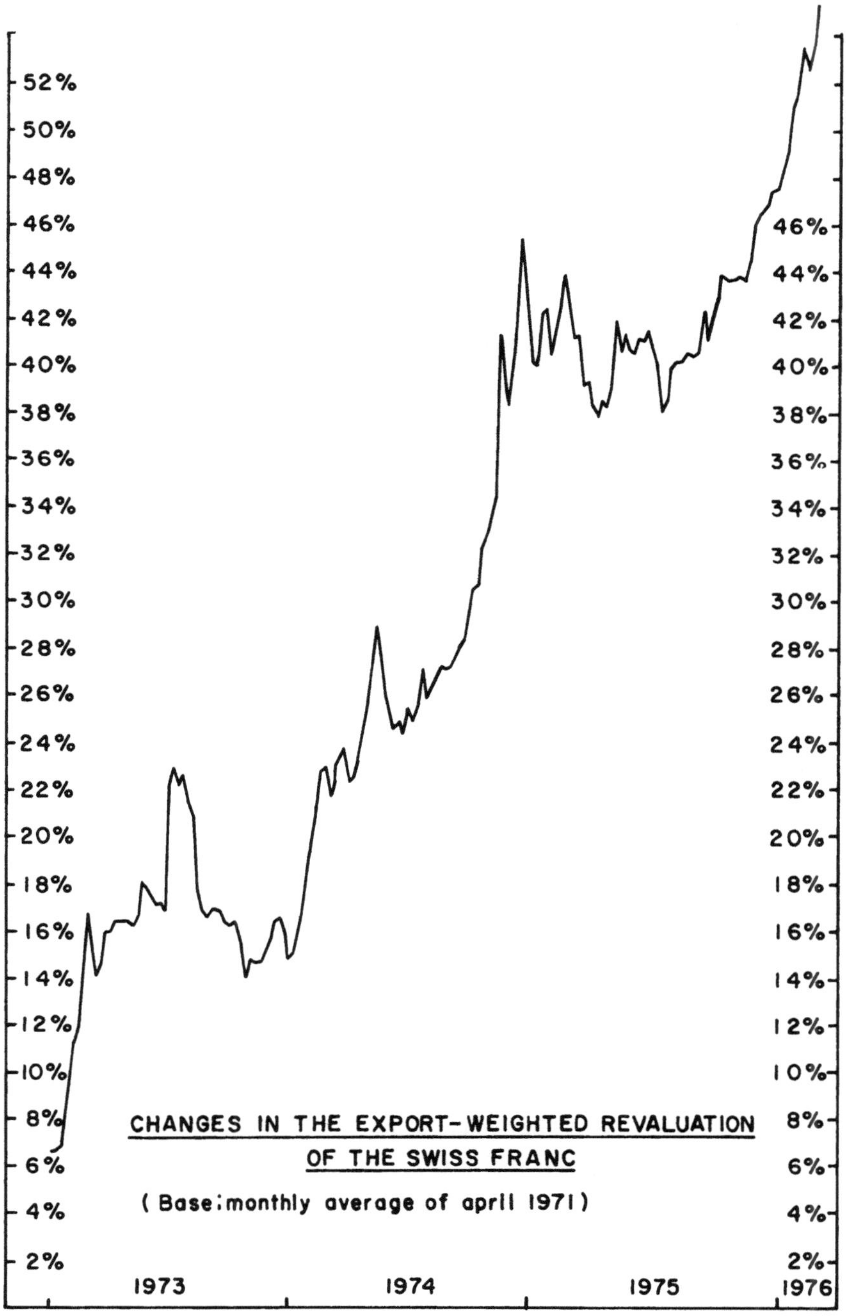

52%
50%
48%
46%
44%
42%
40%
38%
36%
34%
32%
30%
28%
26%
24%
22%
20%
18%
16%
14%
12%
10%
8%
6%
4%
2%
CHANGES IN THE EXPORT-WEIGHTED REVALUATION OF THE SWISS FRANC
(Base: monthly average of april 1971)
1973
1974
1975
1976

indications that the exchange rate of the Swiss franc is also influenced by the fact that it is looked upon abroad as a kind of risk-free store of value. Until recently, the Swiss franc shared this function with gold. This is revealed, inter alia, by the fact that up to the time of the "gold decisions" of Jamaica, for instance, the exchange rate between the Swiss franc and the German mark was in numerous phases parallel to the gold price per ounce in dollars. It was particularly in times of international monetary unrest or political crises that the Swiss franc was under heavy upward pressure.

Considering the fundamental revaluation factors (tight monetary policy, low inflation rate, etc.), and in order to prevent the exchange rate of the Swiss franc from being pushed up still further by speculative and risk-motivated capital inflows, various measures were taken to ward off the inflow of undesirable funds. Designing the measures was rendered difficult by a lack of adequate information on capital transactions. This is why, besides the actual measures designed to ward off foreign funds, additional regulations were decreed that tended to enable the establishment of improved capital-transaction statistics and to provide more information about foreign exchange dealings. Central to the measures taken is the so-called ban on interest payments and the provision for negative interest. To begin with, the banks were prohibited from paying interest on new foreign deposits in Swiss francs. In the course of time, the measures were tightened—with the interest ban extended to all foreign deposits in Swiss francs—and the commission charge was increased to 10 percent per quarter. It is possible to evade these regulations by forward transactions in the foreign exchange market. This is why the Swiss National Bank has directed the banks to reduce the volume of forward sales of Swiss francs to foreigners. Moreover, the banks are obliged to offset, at least daily, foreign currency liabilities by foreign currency assets and to notify the Swiss National Bank of sizeable foreign exchange contracts.

Our measures are surely not perfect, there being numerous possibilities for evasion. Provided that they make some contribution toward preventing an excessive increase in the Swiss franc rate, they serve their purpose.

Until there is some clarification, however, of the determinants of the Swiss franc's exchange rate development, a final appraisal of the protective measures will not be possible.

OUTLOOK

Faced with the alternatives of "stable prices or stable exchange rates," the Swiss National Bank opted for stable prices. This decision was initially criticized by large groups of the business community. The more the inflation rate declines, however, the more our money-supply policy meets with approval. Nevertheless, it will be possible only in two or three years to determine whether it was appropriate to opt for stable prices in an open economy and whether it will be politically and economically possible to continue this policy. Due to the experience gained so far in connection with making monetary policy consistent with a money-supply target, no change in monetary policy is called for just now. In all likelihood, a money-supply target will therefore be fixed for 1977 also.

REFERENCES

Bomhoff, E. J. 1977. "Predicting the Money Multiplier." JOURNAL OF MONETARY ECONOMICS 3, no. 3 (July).

Büttler, H. J., et al. 1977. "A Multiplier Model for Controlling the Money Stock." Mimeographed. Zurich: Swiss National Bank.

Friedman, M. 1968. "The Role of Monetary Policy." AMERICAN ECONOMIC REVIEW 58, no. 1 (March).

Swiss National Bank. 1973. 66th ANNUAL REPORT.

_____. 1974. 67th ANNUAL REPORT.

_____. 1975*a*. "Revision der Geldmengenstatistik" [Revision of the money-stock statistics]. MONTHLY REPORT, suppl. no. 8, Aug.

_____. 1975*b*. 68th ANNUAL REPORT.

INFLATION AND UNEMPLOYMENT WITH INDEXED WAGES: SOME ANALYTICAL ISSUES*

Michael Parkin
University of Western Ontario

The recent wave of two-digit inflation has brought a revival of interest in the idea of indexation--the adoption of price-level escalator (or deescalator) clauses in loan and employment contracts. The idea is at least 150 years old (Lowe 1822) and has been embraced by such great names in the history of economics as Jevons (1875), Marshall (1886, 1887, 1911), and Keynes (1927). The traditional debate focused on the contribution that such arrangements could make to the reduction of risk and to the avoidance of distortions in the allocation of resources and the distribution of income and wealth that would otherwise result from imperfectly anticipated inflation or deflation. A rather inconclusive paper by Robson (1960/61) began the small modern literature on these aspects of indexation, the most recent and important addition to which is Fischer (1975).

In the current revival of the debate at a more popular level, Friedman (1974) and Giersch (1974) have suggested that, in addition to having desirable effects on allocative efficiency and equity, indexation of wages would also have beneficial effects on the level of economic activity and of unemployment during a period of antiinflationary tight monetary policies. A related, but contrary, popular view is that wage indexation would act as a "flywheel" of inflation, having the capacity to perpetuate an explosive wage-price spiral into the indefinite future. It is this class of questions that this paper addresses, with an attempt to develop a rigorous analysis of the issues implicit in the above. Are Friedman and Giersch correct in predicting that an economy with indexed wages would be able to lower the rate of inflation (with an appropriate monetary policy) at lower cost in terms of

---

* An earlier version of the paper was written as part of the Manchester-SSRC Research Programme, "Inflation: Its Causes, Consequences, and Cures," and was presented at the 1975 Konstanz Seminar.

unemployment and reduced output? Or is the sharply contradictory popular view correct in holding that wage indexation would lead to price-level instability? Further, what difference, if any, does indexation make to the appropriate conduct of monetary policy? Most "monetarists" are "gradualists," but some favor a "big-bang" reduction in the rate of monetary growth. Does an indexed economy need an even more gradual reduction in the rate of monetary expansion than does a nonindexed economy, or does it lend itself better to the "big-bang" approach?

These, then, are the questions addressed. Their importance is clear. In every major country of the Western world, prices have risen each and every year since 1934, and, despite periodic cyclical reductions in the rate of inflation, its trend has been strongly upward. It may confidently be predicted that the next wave of elections in 1976 will be preceded by further monetary expansion and a further inflation burst in 1977. Attempts to control inflation by direct price and wage controls—predictably enough, in view of their long and undistinguished history--have demonstrably failed to make anything other than minor changes in the timing of inflation and have done nothing to modify its broad course. Clearly, if inflation is to be squeezed out, a sustained period of monetary tightness is required. Equally clearly, such a monetary policy is not going to be pursued by elected governments with four-to-five-year terms of office unless the social costs in terms of unemployment and output and the private costs in terms of lost elections can be reduced. If Friedman and Giersch are correct, then, the payoff from adopting indexation, especially of wages, could be enormous, making it possible for and even attractive to governments to pursue anti-inflationary monetary policies. If they are wrong, however, and if the opposing view is correct, the consequences of indexation could be catastrophic. Thus, it is of immense importance to try to sort out which view is correct.

Considering the importance of the questions posed here, there is surprisingly little serious economic analysis of them. This paper aims to make a start at such an analysis. It cannot, and does not, claim to provide a full and final, definitive set of answers. It does, however, attempt to set out a basic analysis that is capable of providing qualitative answers to the questions posed and also of setting out a framework that can be extended to analyze other monetary-macroeconomic aspects of indexation as well as used for empirical and quantitative analysis. In contrast to the study of the risk and allocative aspects of indexation, where there is a well-defined and widely accepted framework for analysis, the study of its monetary-stability and macroeconomic effects has to proceed on less fully worked out and universally accepted foundations. There are many alternative models of price and output dynamics that could be used as a starting point. In view of this, a combination of empirical relevance and analytical simplicity seems to be the relevant criterion for choosing among the alternatives. The model selected for present purposes is one that places major emphasis on the price- and wage-setting process and that makes extremely simple, though not wildly unreasonable, assumptions about money and asset markets.

The paper proceeds in the following order. First, the abstractions and the basic scenario or "story" within the framework of analysis are set out (section 1). Second, the basic building blocks of a complete model are set out (section 2). These are behavior propositions about the demand for and supply of money, goods, and labor and about the process whereby interest rates, wages, and prices are determined. The effects of indexation on this behavior are also analyzed. Third, the building blocks are brought together, and the behavior of the economy under nonindexed and indexed regimes is analyzed (section 3). The conclusions are brought together in section 4.

1. THE ABSTRACTIONS AND THE "STORY"

The economy has three types of agent: (1) a monetary authority, (2) firms, and (3) households. The monetary authority determines the supply of money. Firms demand labor and money and supply goods; they also *set* wages and prices. Households supply labor and demand goods and money. There is a bond (the market for which is not explicitly analyzed), the interest rate on which is market-determined and achieves continuous equilibrium in that market.

The *timing* structure of the story is its crucial feature, and a brief remark may be helpful in understanding why we need to be careful here. Suppose an economy without inflation reviews all contracts—on the average, say, once a year. In an economy *with* inflation, the faster its rate, the more frequently will contracts be reviewed. In the former (no-inflation) case, the purpose of a contract review is purely to adjust relative prices. In the latter case, the purpose is to adjust both absolute and relative prices. Now, if an indexation clause is to be introduced and if it is to make any difference to actual economic behavior, the indexed adjustments must clearly occur at more frequent intervals than those at which the contract review would otherwise have taken place. For if they do not, and if at the time of the index adjustment there also takes place a real or relative price adjustment, then clearly the price (wage) emerging as a combination of the index adjustment and relative-price adjustment will be the same as that which would have emerged in the absence of an indexation clause. The only difference would be in what the contracting parties say to each other. In order to build a model in which it is *possible* for indexation to have an effect, it is necessary, therefore, to have a timing structure that enables the index to apply with greater frequency than that with which contracts are reviewed.

The timing structure adopted is an extremely simple one. First, supply and demand choices in money, labor, and output markets are made *continuously* by *all* agents. The market determines the interest rate continuously. Second, prices of goods are set by firms at discrete intervals. The justification for this is that prices are costly to change and therefore only changed when the expected gain is sufficient to cover the cost. Over a fixed interval, t, all firms review their prices for a future period of length t. At each instant, τ, the number of firms setting their prices for the next t is constant. The time interval t is the one that will be adopted for formal analysis. All variables determined at each τ will be measured as ***averages*** centered at t; that is,

$$x_t \equiv \int_{t-1/2}^{t+1/2} x(\tau)d\tau \, .$$

First differences (and higher differences) will be defined as

$$\Delta x_t = x_t - x_{t-1}.$$

Wages will be reviewed *less* frequently than prices. Each firm will negotiate a new wage contract, at an interval $T > t$, to cover the next future period T; so that, over the price-review interval, $1/t$ firms will have reviewed their wages.

Index linking will be considered as taking place more frequently than once per T for the reasons given above, but the effect of varying its frequency will be analyzed.

With these remarks about the basic scenario and timing, let us now develop the building blocks of a model that will enable us to compare indexed and nonindexed economies.

2. THE BUILDING BLOCKS

In this section, the proximate determinants of the variables set out above are analyzed under both nonindexed and indexed regimes in both financial-asset and labor markets.

The Demand for and Supply of Money and the Demand for Goods

We assume a money-demand function of the form

$$m_t^d = p_t + \alpha y_t - \beta R_t, \qquad \alpha, \beta > 0, \tag{1}$$

where lower-case letters are logarithms (throughout),
upper-case letters are variables measured in natural units,
m^d = nominal balances demanded,
p = price level,
y = real output, and
R = nominal rate of interest.

The money supply is exogenous:

$$m_t^s = m_t; \tag{2}$$

and equilibrium prevails in the money market:

$$m_t^d = m_t^s. \tag{3}$$

These three equations together determine the demand for goods, y_t, as

$$y_t = \frac{1}{\alpha} (m_t - p_t + \beta R_t). \tag{4}$$

The assumptions made about the rate of interest are extremely strong (and probably ought to be relaxed). They are that the real rate, R^*, is constant and that the nominal rate is

$$R_t = R^* + \Delta p_t^e, \tag{5}$$

where Δp_t^e = average rate of inflation expected during t for a one-period horizon.

Under these assumptions the demand for goods, y_t, is

$$y_t = \frac{1}{\alpha}(m_t - p_t + \beta R^* + \beta \Delta p_t^e). \tag{6}$$

Price Setting

Price setting is assumed to be done by firms that behave in the manner described by Phelps (1966). They change their prices by the amount that they expect, on the average, other firms will change prices, and they adjust that change upward if they would like to supply less and downward if they would like to supply more. On aggregating over all firms (and all firms set prices once in the time unit t), we have

$$\Delta p_t = \phi(y_t - y^*) + \Delta p_t^e, \quad \phi > 0, \tag{7}$$

where y^* = equilibrium real output (assumed constant; i.e., we are abstracting from growth).

It is assumed that no prices are indexed and that the price level, p_t, and its rate of inflation, Δp_t, constitute the index for indexation purposes. The unindexed and the indexed economies are assumed to be identical in their price-setting behavior. It may be interesting to relax this assumption, allowing the frequency of price review to depend both on the rate of inflation and on the frequency of the application of the index to wages.

Wage Setting and the Excess Demand for Labor

The above discussion of price setting could be brief and straightforward because the price-review period and the period of analysis are the same. Wages require more care. We assume that firms face an excess-demand function for labor, of the form

$$x_{is} = \kappa(w_s - w_{is}) + \delta(p_s - w_s), \quad \kappa > \delta > 0, \tag{8}$$

where x_i = excess demand for labor by firm i,

w = average wage over all firms,

w_i = firm i's wage, and

s = $t, t+1, \ldots, T$.

From the first difference of equation (8) it is clear that

$$\Delta x_{is} = \kappa(\Delta w_x - \Delta w_{is}) + \delta(\Delta p_s - \Delta w_s) \qquad (9)$$
$$= (\kappa - \delta)\Delta w_s + \delta \Delta p_s - \kappa \Delta w_{is}.$$

Over the entire wage contract,

$$\sum_{s=t}^{T} \Delta x_{is} = (\kappa - \delta) \sum_{s=t}^{T} \Delta w_s + \delta \sum_{s=t}^{T} \Delta p_s - \kappa \sum_{s=t}^{T} \Delta w_{is}. \qquad (10)$$

Let us now consider the firm's wage choice in the absence of indexation. It sets a wage implying a nonzero Δw_{is} at $s = t$ and $w_{is} = 0$ for $s = t+1, \ldots, T$. Assume that the firm forms expectations about Δp_s and Δw_s for $s = t, \ldots, T$, such that

$$\Delta w_s^e = \Delta p_s^e. \qquad (11)$$

Also assume that the firm seeks to achieve a change in x_i over the period to T that just eliminates any x that had emerged in $t-1$; that is,

$$-x_{i_{t-1}} = \sum_{s=t}^{T} \Delta x_{is}. \qquad (12)$$

Then the firm will choose a Δw_{is} given by

$$-x_{i_{t-1}} = \kappa \sum_{s=t}^{T} \Delta p_s^e - \kappa \Delta w_{is} \qquad (13)$$

for $s = t$ and a $\Delta w_{is} = 0$ for $s = t+1, \ldots, T$. Therefore,

$$\Delta w_{is} \begin{cases} = \frac{1}{\kappa} x_{i_{t-1}} + \sum_{s=t}^{T} \Delta p_s^e & \text{for } s = t \\ = 0 & \text{otherwise.} \end{cases} \qquad (14)$$

Since the same fraction $(1/T)$ of firms is described by equation (14) at each t, the average movement of wages will be determined simply as

$$\Delta w_t = \gamma x_{t-1} + \frac{1}{T} \sum_{s=t}^{T} \Delta p_s^e, \quad \gamma = 1/\kappa T > 0. \qquad (15)$$

Now consider the behavior of indexed wages. The starting point is still equation (10), with the assumptions given in equations (11) and (12); that is,

$$-x_{i_{t-1}} = \kappa \sum_{s=t}^{T} \Delta p_s^e - \kappa \sum_{s=t}^{T} \Delta w_{is}. \tag{16}$$

But now, the firm must choose an initial wage change but also commit itself to

$$\Delta w_{is} = \Delta p_s \tag{17}$$

for $s = t + 1, \ldots, T$. Whether it must also commit itself to

$$\Delta w_{it} = \Delta p_t$$

depends on the frequency of the application of the index.

In order to allow the frequency of the index adjustment to be a variable, let ν be the fraction of the wage-review period for which the wage set at the beginning of the wage-contract period will apply. Thereafter, let the index adjustment be undertaken. Thus, we have for the individual firm the problem to choose a Δw_i for fraction ν or T with $\Delta w_i = \Delta p$ for the balance, $1 - \nu$, of T. We have, therefore,

$$-x_{t-1} = \kappa \sum_{s=t}^{T} \Delta p_s^e - \kappa \, [\, \Delta \tilde{w}_{it} + (1 - \nu) \, \Delta p_t] \; - \; \kappa \sum_{s=t+n}^{T} \Delta p_s. \tag{18}$$

But, since the firm must now choose Δw_{it} while forming an expectation of Δp_s^e, $s = t, \ldots, T$, we have

$$\Delta \tilde{w}_{it} = \frac{1}{\kappa} x_{i_{t-1}} + \nu \Delta p_t^e. \tag{19}$$

Wages for the ith firm actually rise during t by the following:

$$\Delta w_{it} = \Delta \tilde{w}_{it} + (1 - \nu) \Delta p_t. \tag{20}$$

Therefore,

$$\Delta w_{it} = \frac{1}{\kappa} x_{i_{t-1}} + \nu \Delta p_t^e + (1 - \nu) \Delta p_t. \tag{21}$$

From $s = t + 1, \ldots, T$, firm i's wage change will be simply

$$\Delta w_{is} = \Delta p_s.$$

Since we have an equal fraction of firms reviewing their wage contracts each t, aggregating over all firms gives the behavior of wages on the average as

$$\Delta w_t = \gamma x_{t-1} + u\Delta p_t^e + (1-u)\Delta p_t, \tag{22}$$

where $u = v/T$.

The cases in which wages are perfectly indexed and wages are unindexed can be seen as special cases of equation (22) when $u = 0$ and $u = 1$, respectively, Note that $u = 1 \rightarrow v = T$; that is, wages are only linked when contracts are reviewed.

This completes our discussion of wage setting under indexed and nonindexed regimes.

The excess demand for labor is obtained by aggregating equation (8) over the economy and noting that

$$w_t = \sum_{i=1}^{n} w_{it},$$

that is,

$$x_t = \delta(p_t - w_t). \tag{23}$$

The unemployment rate of labor is not explicitly introduced into the analysis, and x may be regarded as an inverse proxy for that variable.

Expectation Formation

There are many alternative expectation-formation schemes that could be used. That adopted is one that has featured in most of the empirical work on the subject since Cagan (1958) first introduced it, namely,

$$\Delta p_t^e = \lambda\Delta p_t + (1-\lambda)\Delta p_{t-1}^e. \tag{24}$$

This implies that the T-period expectation for wage setting will be

$$\sum_{s=t}^{T} \Delta p_s^e = T\Delta p_t^e. \tag{25}$$

This completes our brief presentation of the building blocks. We now put them together in order to analyze the behavior of various indexed and nonindexed economies.

3. THE COMPLETE MODEL

Nonindexed Economy

Our nonindexed economy may be set out as:

$$y_t = \frac{1}{\alpha}(m_t - p_t + \beta R^* + \beta \Delta p_t^e), \tag{6}$$

$$\Delta p_t = \phi(y_t - y^*) + \Delta p_t^e, \tag{7}$$

$$\Delta w_t = \gamma x_{t-1} + \Delta p_t^e, \tag{26}$$

$$x_t = \delta(p_t - w_t), \tag{23}$$

$$\Delta p_t^e = \lambda \Delta p_t + (1 - \lambda) \Delta p_{t-1}^e, \tag{24}$$

where all except equation (26) are repeated for convenience, and equation (26) is equation (15) using equation (25). First, it will be noticed that the system contains a recursive structure, w_t and x_t being determined non-interactively with p_t and y_t. Taking advantage of this, consider first the behavior of p_t and y_t. These are given by

$$\left.\begin{aligned} \Delta p_t &= a \Delta p_{t-1} + b \Delta p_{t-2} + c \Delta m_t + d \Delta m_{t-1}, \\ &\text{and} \\ y_t &= a y_{t-1} + b y_{t-2} + e \Delta m_t - 2e \Delta m_{t-1} + e \Delta m_{t-2}, \end{aligned}\right\} \tag{27}$$

where $a = \dfrac{2(1 - \lambda) + \frac{\phi}{\alpha}[1 - \lambda(1 + \beta)]}{1 - \lambda + \frac{\phi}{\alpha}(1 - \beta\lambda)}$,

$$b = \frac{-(1 - \lambda)}{1 - \lambda + \frac{\phi}{\alpha}(1 - \beta\lambda)},$$

$$c = \frac{1}{1 - \lambda + \frac{\phi}{\alpha}(1 - \beta\lambda)},$$

$$d = \frac{-(1 - \lambda)}{1 - \lambda + \frac{\phi}{\alpha}(1 - \beta\lambda)},$$

$$e = \frac{1/\alpha}{1 - \lambda + \frac{\phi}{\alpha}(1 - \beta\lambda)},$$

Given the signs of the parameters (all positive), the system will be stable if and only if

$$\beta\lambda < 1 \tag{28}$$

and will approach its equilibrium cyclically. That equilibrium will, of course, be

$$\Delta p^* = \Delta m^*, \tag{29}$$

and

$$y = y^*,$$

where an asterisk denotes a steady-state value.

It is very easy to get a feel for how this economy behaves by considering the following experiment. Suppose the economy is initially in full equilibrium with the actual and expected rates of inflation equal to each other and to the rate of monetary expansion; that is,

$$\Delta p_o = \Delta p_o^e = \Delta m_o.$$

In this situation, excess demand will be zero. This state of affairs is depicted as the interval from t_o to t_1 in figure 1. At t_1, let the rate of monetary expansion fall but then maintain a new lower level forever as shown by the step-drop in the line labeled Δm^*. At that instant there will be a fall in excess demand (i.e., the creation of excess supply) of an amount given by $1/\alpha$ times the change in the rate of monetary expansion. Also, the inflation rate will fall by ϕ/α times the change in the rate of monetary expansion. This change in the inflation rate will, for the purpose of the intuitive diagrammatic analysis, be presumed to be less than the change in the rate of the monetary expansion. Immediately after the point t_1, the inflation rate exceeds the rate of monetary expansion, and real balances are falling. The falling real balances will be adding additional excess supply through equation (6), and by t_2 the inflation rate will have fallen via equation (7) to equal the rate of monetary expansion. Immediately after this, excess demand will begin to turn around. From t_2 to t_3, real balances are rising, since the rate of inflation is below the rate of monetary

Figure 1

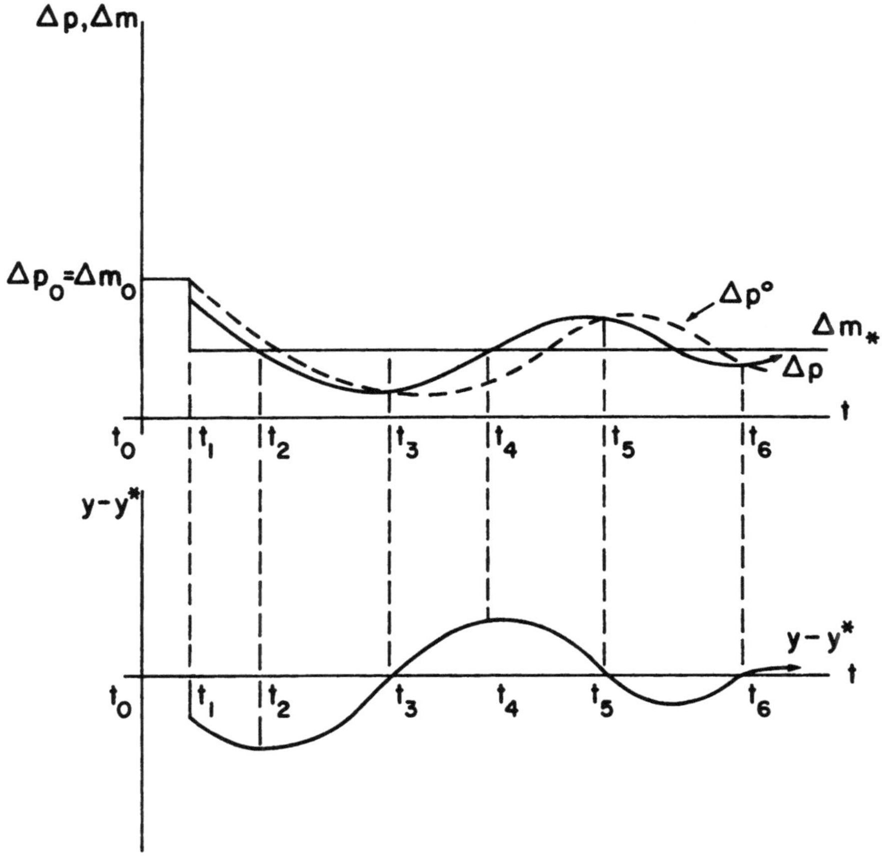

Δp,Δm
Δp₀=Δm₀
Δp°
Δm*
Δp
t
t0
t1
t2
t3
t4
t5
t6
y-y*
y-y*
t
t0
t1
t2
t3
t4
t5
t6

expansion. Inflationary expectations, however—which, by equation (24), lag behind the actual rate of inflation—will be above the actual rate; and excess demand will continue to be negative although falling toward zero. At t_3 actual and expected inflation become equal to each other, and excess demand reaches zero. There is however, at this point, a continued increase in the stock of real balances, since both the actual and the expected inflation rates are now below the rate of monetary expansion. This growth in real balances adds to excess demand as indicated in the bottom part of the picture; and, with excess demand increasing, the actual and expected inflation rates continue to increase. Again, with excess demand rising, the actual rate of inflation will eventually overtake the rate of monetary expansion, and real balances will begin to fall. Thus, excess demand will again turn down. It will reach zero next at t_4, when the expected rate has caught up with the actual rate. Both the actual and the expected inflation rates and excess demand will continue to cycle in a damped fashion until the full equilibrium is reached, at which excess demand will be zero and the actual and expected inflation rates will have settled down to equal the rate of monetary expansion.

Now consider the behavior of wages and the excess demand for labor. Because of its intrinsic interest, we focus only on the latter. Its behavior, given the behavior of prices, is described by

$$x_t = (2 - \lambda - \delta\gamma)x_{t-1} - (1 - \lambda)(1 - \delta\gamma)x_{t-2} + \delta(1 - \lambda)(\Delta p_t - \Delta p_{t-1}). \tag{30}$$

Notice that the nonhomogeneous part of equation (30) is proportional to the change in the rate of inflation; equation (30) therefore defines a dynamic trade-off which says that, if x_t was maintained at a constant value x^*, then the rate of inflation would be changed by the constant absolute amount

$$\Delta^2 p_t = \frac{1}{1 - \lambda} \cdot x^*. \tag{31}$$

The behavior of x_t would approach x^* if $\Delta^2 p$ was held constant; that is, the x_t path in equation (30) is stable, given the signs of the parameters, and will converge monotonically if and only if

$$\lambda = \delta\gamma. \tag{32}$$

Since this is a rather stringent condition, it seems best to regard the convergence of x to x^* for a given $\Delta^2 p$ as cyclical. Since, from equation (30), a constant growth rate of m, following a one-shot change in that growth rate, sets up a cycle in Δp and therefore in $\Delta^2 p$, the behavior of x in such a case will be a cycle around a cycle and will be of too high an order to inspect analytically.

This completes the discusison of the unindexed economy. Let us now turn to an indexed economy and compare its behavior with that described above.

An Indexed Economy

The behavior of an indexed economy can be analyzed by considering the behavior of the wage rate and the excess demand for labor independently of (recursive to) the rate of inflation and real output.

We use equation (22) as the behavior of wages in an indexed economy, together with equations (23) and (27):

$$\Delta w_t = \gamma x_{t-1} + u \Delta p_t^e + (1-u)\Delta p_t, \tag{22}$$

$$x_t = \delta(p_t - w_t), \tag{23}$$

$$\Delta p_t^e = \lambda \Delta p_t + (1-\lambda)\Delta p_{t-1}^e. \tag{27}$$

Then, given the behavior of Δp_t, we obtain the following expression for the behavior of x:

$$x_t = (2-\lambda-\delta\gamma)x_{t-1} - (1-\lambda)(1-\delta\gamma)x_{t-2} + u\delta(1-\lambda)(\Delta p_t - \Delta p_{t-1}). \tag{33}$$

It is immediately clear that equation (33) is identical to equation (30), the nonindexed case, with the important exception of the last term. It is this last term that measures the extent to which labor-market excess demand (and therefore the unemployment rate) is disturbed as the inflation rate changes. From equation (33) it is clear that this varies directly with u, the frequency of indexing. If wages are indexed continuously, so that $u = 0$, there is no labor-market disturbance arising from a change in the rate of inflation. If the index only applies at contract dates, $u = 1$, the economy behaves as if it were not indexed.

This simple and obvious result is easily interpreted. The dynamic trade-off between x and the rate of change of the rate of inflation is made more favorable as a result of index-linking wage rates. Wage indexation, far from imparting instability, makes the level of employment more stable. The rate of inflation and the movements in real output will be determined by monetary conditions as set out in equation (27) above. The case of complete and continuous indexation is, however, of special interest. If $u = 0$ and if money is the only source of disturbance, $x = 0$ and $y = y^*$ will be a continuous feature of the economy. In that case, using equation (6),

$$y_t = \frac{1}{\alpha} (m_t - p_t + \beta R^* + \beta \Delta p_t^e), \tag{6}$$

with

$$\Delta p_t^e = \lambda \Delta p_t + (1 - \lambda) \Delta p_t^e \tag{24}$$

and

$$y_t = y^*,$$

the rate of inflation becomes

$$\Delta p = \frac{1 - \lambda (1 + \beta)}{1 - \beta\lambda} \Delta p_{-1} + \frac{1}{1 - \beta\lambda} \Delta m_{-1} - \frac{1 - \lambda}{1 - \beta\lambda} \Delta m_{-2}. \tag{34}$$

This is, of course, the famous Cagan model. It is important to emphasize that in this case, a once-and-for-all change in the rate of monetary expansion (Δm) will produce an overshoot in the rate of inflation which will then (if the stability condition is satisfied) monotonically approach the rate of monetary expansion. The impact effect on Δp of changing Δm from a steady rate, Δm^*, to Δm_o is

$$d\Delta p = \frac{1}{1-\beta\lambda}(\Delta m_o - \Delta m^*), \tag{35}$$

which, since $\beta\lambda < 1$ for stability, guarantees an overshoot effect.

Subject to the limitations of the analysis, we are now able to draw implications for the appropriate conduct of monetary policy in a wage-indexed economy. First, a faster approach to the desired rate of inflation is possible than in the no-indexation case because a change in the inflation rate can be achieved with less disturbance of real output. A big-bang change in the rate of monetary expansion will lead, however, to an overshoot in the inflation rate; hence, a gradualist monetary policy still seems to be desirable even in the indexed economy.

4. CONCLUSIONS

Within the framework of the particular model employed, it has been shown that:

1. an indexed economy is no more prone to instability than is a nonindexed economy; indeed,
2. a continuously indexed economy is unambiguously stable and would behave in the most classical manner, with the real economy fully insulated from monetary shocks.

Many matters have been neglected in the analysis presented here, and generalizations are clearly needed. Some obvious ones are the introduction of (1) a variable real rate of interest, and (2) international factors.

Throughout, we have ignored real shocks and the response of an indexed economy to such shocks. The choice was deliberate. Real shocks require changes in relative prices. If contracts are required at certain intervals to adjust for real shocks, it is hard to see how the presence of index clauses can make it either more or less easy to put through any necessary relative-price adjustments required by changes in real factors.

Additionally, we have ignored any effects that indexation might have on the basic parameters of the models. Since indexation reduces risk, it may be expected to increase the responsiveness of asset demands and factor demands to changes in yields and changes in real wages. In terms of the model, indexed asset yields might raise the value of β, and indexed wages may raise the value of δ and lower the value of γ (= $1/\kappa$). Any rise in the value of β will only affect the indexed-bond case and will strengthen the qualitative result that such indexation on its own raises the real response to a monetary shock. With indexed money and financial assets, the value of β becomes irrelevant. Any change in δ seems unlikely to be dominant and would to some extent be offset by any change in γ. This certainly merits further investigation, however, both in theoretical and empirical terms.

The analysis presented here provides a ready basis for empirical work on economies that have introduced indexation. Variants on the models developed here could be estimated for such countries as Brazil and Finland for periods when various types of indexation were in operation and for nonindexed periods, and the quantitative contribution of indexation to the stabilization programs could thereby be assessed.

The agenda for future work in this area is clearly larger than the brief list of existing achievements. The analysis presented here does reach some conditional predictions, however, and provides one possible basis for further progress. Further, it is highly suggestive that indexation, especially of wages, should be taken seriously as a means whereby antiinflationary monetary policy can squeeze out inflation without leading to massive transitional unemployment. It also suggests that nonmoney-asset-yield indexation is unhelpful. Further work is urgently needed to check out the robustness of these conclusions.

REFERENCES

Cagan, P. 1958. "The Demand for Currency Relative to Total Money Supply." New York: National Bureau of Economic Research.

Fischer, S. 1975. "The Demand for Index Bonds." JOURNAL OF POLITICAL ECONOMY 83, no. 3 (June): 509-34.

Friedman, M. 1974. "Monetary Corrections." Institute of Economic Affairs, Occasional Paper 41. Reprinted in ESSAYS ON INFLATION AND INDEXATION, by H. Giersch et al., pp. 25-61. Washington, D.C.: American Enterprise Institute for Public Policy Research.

Giersch, H. 1974. "Index Clauses and the Fight against Inflation." In ESSAYS ON INFLATION AND INDEXATION, by H. Giersch et al., pp. 1-23. Washington, D.C.: American Enterprise Institute for Public Policy Research.

Jevons, W. S. 1898. MONEY AND THE MECHANISM OF EXCHANGE, chap. 25, "A Tabulor Standard of Value," pp. 318-26. New York.

Keynes, J. M. 1927. "Evidence Presented to the Committee on National Debt and Taxation." In MINUTES OF EVIDENCE (Colwyn Committee) 1: 278, 287. London: His Majesty's Stationery Office.

Lowe, J. 1822. THE PRESENT STATE OF ENGLAND IN REGARD TO AGRICULTURE, TRADE AND FINANCE, WITH A COMPARISON OF THE PROSPECTS OF ENGLAND AND FRANCE. London.

Marshall, A. 1886. "Reply to the Royal Commission on the Depression of Trade and Industry." Reprinted in OFFICIAL PAPERS BY ALFRED MARSHALL, pp. 9-12. London: Macmillan, 1926.

_____. 1887. "Remedies for Fluctuations of General Prices." Reprinted in MEMORIALS OF ALFRED MARSHALL, edited by A. C. Pigou, pp. 188-221. London: Macmillan, 1925.

_____. 1911. "Letter to Irving Fisher." In MEMORIALS OF ALFRED MARSHALL, edited by A. C. Pigou, p. 476. London: Macmillan, 1925.

Phelps, E. S. 1968. "Money-Wage Dynamics and Labor-Market Equilibrium." JOURNAL OF POLITICAL ECONOMY 76, no. 4 (July/Aug.): 678-711.

Robson, P. 1960/61. "Index-linked Bonds." REVIEW OF ECONOMIC STUDIES 28: 57-68.

MIX
Papier aus verantwortungsvollen Quellen
Paper from responsible sources
FSC® C105338

Printed by Libri Plureos GmbH
in Hamburg, Germany